WORK with ENGLISH

Englisch für berufliche Schulen

Isobel Williams
Steve Williams

Cornelsen

Work with English wurde geplant und entwickelt von der Redaktion Moderne Fremdsprachen des Cornelsen Verlags, Berlin.

Verfasser/innen:	Isobel Williams, Berlin Steve Williams, Corio Bay Media, Melbourne
Berater/innen:	Marilyn Clifford-Grein, Stuttgart; Dorothee Gräter, Essingen; Gabriele Holtermann, Ludwigsburg; Martina Jost, Darmstadt; Thomas Pache, Euskirchen; Elke Uthoff, Osnabrück
Projektleitung:	Jim Austin
Redaktion:	Andreas Goebel
Redaktionelle Mitarbeit:	Roderick Cox, Christine House, Laura Spratling Oliver Busch, Shanti Deutschmann, Fritz Preuß (Wörterverzeichnisse)
Bildredaktion:	Gertha Maly
Layout und technische Umsetzung:	Anna Bakalović und Annika Preyhs, Berlin
Umschlaggestaltung:	Ellen Meister
Illustrationen:	Oxford Designers & Illustrators Uli Österle (S. 122, 138)

Erhältlich sind auch:

Workbook	(ISBN-13: 978-3-464-06276-0; ISBN-10: 3-464-06276-7)
Workbook Lehrerfassung	(ISBN-13: 978-3-464-06277-7; ISBN-10: 3-464-06277-5)
Handreichungen zum Unterricht mit Audio-CDs und CD-ROM	(ISBN-13: 978-3-464-06278-4; ISBN-10: 3-464-06278-3)
2 Audio-CDs	(ISBN-13: 978-3-464-06279-1; ISBN-10: 3-464-06279-1)

www.cornelsen.de

1. Auflage, 1. Druck 2006

Alle Drucke dieser Auflage sind inhaltlich unverändert und können im Unterricht nebeneinander verwendet werden.

Druck: Stürtz GmbH, Würzburg

ISBN-13: 978-3-464-06275-3
ISBN-10: 3-464-06275-9

Inhalt gedruckt auf säurefreiem Papier aus nachhaltiger Forstwirtschaft.

Vorwort

Work with English ist die komplette Neubearbeitung des bewährten Lehrwerks für die Berufsfachschule. Der zweijährige Kurs baut auf den Englischkenntnissen eines Hauptschulabschlusses auf und führt zum mittleren Schulabschluss. Vorausgesetzt wird ein Wortschatz von ca. 600 Wörtern, der im Anhang aufgeführt ist.

Damit Niveauunterschiede in heterogenen Klassen ausgeglichen werden können, enthält die Neuausgabe von **Work with English** eine Vorabunit (*Let's work with English*), in der grammatische und lexikalische Grundlagen aufgefrischt werden. Die anschließenden 15 Units sind auf zwei Lernjahre aufgeteilt. Units 1–8, die jeweils 8 Seiten umfassen, sind für das erste Lernjahr konzipiert, Units 9–15 für das zweite Lernjahr. Sie umfassen jeweils 10 Seiten, darunter eine Doppelseite *Exam practice*. Die Schüler/innen werden hier zuverlässig auf die aktuellen Abschlussprüfungen vorbereitet.

Neben den abwechslungsreichen Geschichten und Schauplätzen – ein Workcamp, eine Londonreise, eine Abenteuertour durch Neuseeland, ein Austauschjahr in Australien, eine junge Familie in Irland oder Jugendliche in einer amerikanischen Kleinstadt – greift **Work with English** immer wieder Themen auf, die unmittelbar aus dem Lebensumfeld heutiger Jugendlicher gegriffen sind. So bekommen die Schüler/innen Gelegenheit, sich über Handys, Fernsehserien, Stars oder ihre Lebensgewohnheiten Gedanken zu machen. Unit 8, am Ende des ersten Lernjahres, bereitet gezielt auf die Stellenbewerbung auf Englisch vor, nachdem schon in den ersten Units die Themen Schule und Ausbildung besprochen wurden.

Ein besonderer Schwerpunkt von **Work with English** liegt auf der Entwicklung kommunikativer Kompetenzen im Sinne der Bildungsstandards und des Gemeinsamen Europäischen Referenzrahmens. Immer wieder werden Wendungen für das Alltagsgespräch aus dem Themenzusammenhang isoliert und gesondert trainiert.

Eine Doppelseite *World of work* pro Unit bietet Einblicke in den englischsprachigen Berufsalltag: im ersten Lernjahr (Units 1–8) anhand allgemein berufsbezogener Materialien, im zweiten Lernjahr (Units 9–14) anhand branchenspezifischer Texte und Aufgaben (9 und 12 kaufmännisch, 10 und 13 gewerblich-technisch und 11 und 14 gesundheitlich-sozialpädagogisch). Unit 15 rundet den Kurs wieder mit einem allgemein beruflichen Thema ab.

In jeder Unit weist ein *Intercultural corner*-Kasten auf kulturelle Unterschiede hin oder vermittelt landeskundliches Grundwissen. Ebenfalls in jeder Unit leiten *Learning to learn*-Kästen, integriert in die Texte und Übungen, zur Entwicklung methodischer Kompetenz an. Grammatik wird in solider und abwechslungsreicher Form geübt, wobei auch hier kommunikative und visuelle Anstöße eingearbeitet wurden.

Zum Nachschlagen steht im Anhang eine *Grammar summary* zur Verfügung. Für stärkere Klassen gibt es außerdem, angelehnt an Thema, Grammatik und Wortschatz der einzelnen Units, 15 *Further reading*-Texte mit Aufgabenapparat. Für manche Partnerübungen gibt es *Pairwork files*, die konkrete Gesprächssituationen vorstellen.

Work with English ist ein praxisnahes, inhaltlich und gestalterisch modernes Lehrwerk, das einen handlungsorientierten Unterricht ermöglicht und die Lernenden zur Arbeit mit der englischen Sprache motiviert.

Wir, die Autoren und der Verlag, wünschen viel Freude und Erfolg!

Inhalt

	Unit	Title	Grammar
	0	**Let's work with English**	*To be* · *There is / are* · Plurals · Possessive *-s* · Pronouns · *Much / many / a lot of* · *Can/can't* · Times and dates · Numbers · Countries and nationalities · *a/an*
YEAR 1	1	**Saying hello**	Simple present
	2	**Free time**	Present progressive
	3	**Other cultures**	Simple past
	4	**Keeping up to date**	The *going to* future · Comparatives and superlatives
	5	**Eating and drinking**	Adverbs · Quantifiers · *Some/any*
	6	**Jobs and training**	Present perfect
	7	**That's life (or is it?)**	Modal verbs
	8	**The right job**	Relative clauses 1
YEAR 2	9	**Destination NZ**	Future forms
	10	**Keep in touch**	Conditional sentences type 1
	11	**Fame and fortune**	*-ing* form and infinitive
	12	**How others live**	The passive
	13	**Modern love**	Past perfect · Indirect speech
	14	**Kicking the habit**	Conditional sentences types 2 + 3
	15	**Drive to arrive alive**	Past progressive · Relative clauses (2)

Pairwork files	148
Further reading	152
Grammar summary	180
Chronologisches Wörterverzeichnis	186
Alphabetisches Wörterverzeichnis	226
Grundwortschatz	238
Geographische Namen	241
Unregelmäßige Verben	242

Learning	World of work	Page
		6
Wie kann ich mein Englisch verbessern?	The first day at work	14
Wie man Vokabeln lernt	People at work	22
Wie man mit Unterschieden zwischen Deutsch und Englisch zurechtkommt	Volunteering at a hostel	30
Wie man seinen Standpunkt formuliert	What's important at work	38
Einen Text überfliegen	Talking to customers	46
Vorsicht Wörterbuch!	Job satisfaction	54
Wie kann ich mein Hörverständnis verbessern?	Talking about your job	62
Schriftliche Mediation: Den Inhalt eines englischen Textes im Deutschen wiedergeben	Job interviews	70
Wie man das freie Sprechen verbessern kann	Travel and tourism	78
Wie man das Internet zum Lernen nutzen kann	Keeping technology working	88
Tipps zum Schreiben von Texten	Looking after people	98
Eine Mind Map erstellen	Working in an office	108
Wie man mit schwierigen Texten zurechtkommt	Manufacturing jobs	118
Wie man aus seinen Fehlern lernt	Working with young people	128
Tipps für das Gruppengespräch auf Englisch	Vocational training in Germany and the UK	138

Erläuterung der Symbole
Partnerarbeit
Gruppenarbeit
Text auf der Audio-CD

Erläuterung der Farben
allgemein
kaufmännisch
gewerblich-technisch
hauswirtschaftlich-sozialpädagogisch

Let's work with

Sind Sie fit für den Einstieg in *Work with English?* Oder haben Sie das Gefühl, dass Ihr Englisch ein paar Aufwärmübungen gebrauchen könnte?
Bevor Sie mit Unit 1 loslegen, schauen Sie sich diese acht Seiten an, um die wichtigsten Grundlagen aufzufrischen und sich in Startposition für den Kurs zu bringen. Viel Erfolg – und natürlich: *Have fun!*

1 Parts of speech (Wortarten)
Sort these words into their grammar categories. Add more words you can think of.

~~happy~~ • ~~man~~ • ~~near~~ • ~~correctly~~ • ~~my~~ • ~~write~~ • quickly • run • cat • talk • your • plane • good • well • her • happily • dog • sadly • go • funny • sing • over • boy • school • swim • under • city

noun	adjective	adverb	preposition	pronoun	verb
man	*happy*	*correctly*	*near*	*my*	*write*

2 **The simple present of the verb to be (die einfache Gegenwart des Verbs to be)**
a **Look at the cards and make sentences about the people.**

Example: *1 I'm Sam Smith. I'm from England. I'm 36. I'm a teacher.*

① Surname: Smith
First name: Sam
From: England
Age: 36
Job: teacher

② Surname: Hall
First name: Randy
From: the United States
Age: 52
Job: doctor

③ Surname: MacDonald
First name: Chris
From: Scotland
Age: 22
Job: shop assistant

④ Surname: O'Brien
First name: Pat
From: Ireland
Age: 41
Job: nurse

English!

b **Now ask and answer questions with your partner.**

What's your name?

How old are you?

Where are you from?

C **Read the text about Helen Jones and her family.**

Helen is an English teacher. She's 38. She lives at 23 Highland Road, Oxford with her family. Her husband, Keith, is a dentist. He's at the surgery at the moment. His phone number is 80 76 52 93. Helen and Keith have three children, Paul, Donna and Lucy. They're at school today. Paul is 15, Donna is 13 and Lucy is 8.

Now ask questions about the Jones family. Use the answers which are given.

This is Helen.
1 What's *her job*?
She's a teacher.
2 How ... ?
She's 38.
3 What's ... ?
It's 23 Highland Road, Oxford.

REMEMBER

What's his job?
He's a / an ...
~~His job is ...~~
He's ~~dentist~~ *a dentist*.

This is Keith.
4 What's ... ?
He's a dentist.
5 Where ... at the moment?
He's at the surgery.
6 What's ... ?
It's 80 76 52 93.

Here are Paul and Donna.
7 How ... ?
Paul's 15 and Donna is 13.
8 Where ... today?
They're at school.

Paul has another sister.
9 What's ... ?
Her name is Lucy.
10 How ... ?
She's 8.

d **Make negative sentences. Choose the beginning of the sentence from column A and an ending from column C. Join them with the correct form of the verb from column B.**

Example: *1 Peter isn't at school today.*

A	B	C
1 Peter ✓	'm not 're not isn't aren't	sisters. They're cousins.
2 I		a warm country.
3 Fast food		in the computer class. We're in the English class.
4 The weather		interesting. I prefer football.
5 Rita and Sylvia Brown		good today.
6 We		good for you.
7 Rugby		a teacher, I'm a student.
8 Scotland		at school today. ✓

e **Work with a partner. Ask questions and give short answers.**

Example: Are you British? *No, I'm not.*

1 Is it raining?
2 Is it Tuesday today?
3 Are you tired?
4 Is English a lot of fun?
5 Is the teacher watching us?
6 Are the other students busy?
7 Is your neighbour asleep?
8 Are your parents at work?

Now ask and answer questions about yourself.

3 There is / There are

Translate the missing parts of these sentences.

Example: Es gibt kein Wasser im Badezimmer.
There is no water in the bathroom.

1 Es gibt viele Geschäfte in unserer Straße.
... a lot of shops in our street.
2 Gibt es am Bahnhof eine Bank?
... a bank at the station?
3 Wir müssen zu Fuß gehen, es gibt hier keine Bushaltestelle.
We have to walk, ... a bus stop here.
4 Ich wohne in Nr. 12, aber es gibt keine Hausnummer.
I live at No. 12 but ... no number on the door.
5 Gibt es einen Supermarkt in der Askew Road?
... a supermarket in Askew Road?
6 Es gibt keine Jobs hier, ich glaube ich gehe nach München.
... any jobs here, I think I'll go to Munich.
7 Hoffentlich gibt es in der Kantine noch etwas zu essen.
I hope ... still something to eat in the canteen.
8 Gibt es irgendwelche Probleme?
... any problems?

DANGER!
Es gibt = ~~It gives~~
There is / There are

4 Plurals (Pluralbildung)

a Make plurals then decide which one is the 'odd one out' (= which is different from the others).

Examples:	party – boy – family	animal – person – flower
	parties – boys – families	*animals – people – flowers*
	Odd one out: boys.	*Odd one out: people.*

1 bus – nose – house
2 banana – potato – apple
3 man – girl – woman
4 child – student – mother
5 ear – tooth – leg
6 foot – shoe – sock
7 party – lady – day
8 photo – disco – tomato

b Complete the text with the plurals of the words in brackets.

These ... [1] (person) are waiting for the 10 o'clock bus. They arrived at the bus stop ten ... [2] (minute) ago. It's five past ten now and the bus is late. The two ... [3] (woman) start to complain*. "Where's the bus?" one of them asks.
"My ... [4] (foot) are cold."
"It's a scandal," says the other woman. "The bus company doesn't care about us at all. My ... [5] (hand) are frozen."
"Oh, stop it," says the man. "Don't you have thick ... [6] (sock) and ... [7] (glove)?"
Just then two ... [8] (bus) arrive at the bus stop.
"Look," says the man. "I have an idea. You ... [9] (lady) get on the first bus and I'll get on the second one."
"Why? Is the first bus warmer?" one of the women asks.
"No," says the man, "but if we take different buses, I won't have to listen to your ... [10] (complaint*) any longer."

* complain = *sich beschweren*, complaint = *Beschwerde*

5 The possessive form (der s-Genitiv)

a Read the sentences and decide if 's is the short form of is or the possessive form.

Example:

This is Jill's pet snake.	It's very friendly.	It's called Fang.
Jill's = possessive 's	*It's = It is*	*It's = It is*

1 Toby's mum is from London.
2 This is Aly's favourite group.
3 Patsy's hobby is collecting old LPs. She's a Beatles fan.
4 Mike's girlfriend's from Scotland. She's from Glasgow.
5 The dog's plate's empty. Its food's in the cupboard in the kitchen.
6 Fly's a DJane. She's in the club right now.

b Put the words in brackets into the plural or add the possessive 's.

Example: These are not my *shoes* (shoe). They are *Peter's* (Peter).

1 ... (Frank) mobile phone is cool.
2 Only two ... (teacher) have ... (laptop).
3 Is that ... (Lucy) sister?
4 All the ... (name) are on the ... (English teacher) list.
5 How many ... (sweatshirt) do you have?
6 Simon and Les are ... (brother).
7 These are all ... (Mandy) ... (computer game).
8 Ivan and Ricky don't have ... (dictionary). They have to use ... (Patrick).

6 Pronouns (1): possessive determiners and subject pronouns (Possessivbegleiter und Subjektpronomen)

a Copy and complete the speech bubbles with the correct forms of the pronouns.

b Decide if 'Sie/sie' in sentences 1–4 is she, you or they, then translate the sentences.

1 <u>Sie</u> mag Rap. *She likes Rap.*
2 Sind <u>Sie</u> aus Deutschland?
3 <u>Sie</u> ist 17 Jahre alt.
4 <u>Sie</u> sind alle Fußballfans.

C Now decide if 'Ihr/ihr' in sentences 5–8 is her, your or their, then translate the sentences.

5 Meera ist 16. Ihr Bruder heißt Kashif.
6 Pete und Laura wohnen in England. Ihre Eltern kommen aus Amerika.
7 Das ist Rebecca. Ihr Freund lebt in Deutschland.
8 Ist das Ihre Tasche?

7 Pronouns (2): object pronouns (Objektpronomen)

Complete the sentences with the correct pronouns.

Example: Jane doesn't like dogs. She's afraid of *them*.

1 We're going to the club. Would you like to come with ... ?
2 Who is that girl? Why are you looking at ... ?
3 It's cold. Can you give ... that pullover, please?
4 Natalia needs some money. Can you lend ... some?
5 Theresa and Phil are late. Please tell ... to hurry up.
6 Phil darling, I love ... .
7 We're tourists. Can you help ..., please?
8 Excuse me, can you tell ... the time, please?

8 Much / Many / A lot of

Choose much, many or a lot of.

Example: How *much* time do you spend on homework?

1 There aren't ... good clubs in this city.
2 How ... pocket money do you get every week?
3 Joe doesn't read ... . He doesn't have ... books.
4 Our team has no chance. ... our players are ill.
5 Paula doesn't have ... money.
6 I wasn't hungry at lunchtime, so I didn't eat ... .
7 How ... people are coming to the party?
8 I know ... people in my street.

REMEMBER

much = viel (unzählbar)
many = viele (zählbar)

Much und many stehen in Fragen und verneinten Sätzen:
How much homework do we have to do? – Not much.
How many tests do we have this week? – Not many. Only two.

A lot of steht in Aussagesätzen:
There are a lot of good films on TV this week.

9 Can / Can't

What can Mark, Sophie, Paul and Louise do? What can't they do?

Example: Mark *can* ride a motorbike, but he *can't* drive.

can/can't	speak English	speak French	ride a motorbike	drive	swim	ski	program a computer
Mark	✓	✗	✓	✗	✓	✗	✓
Sophie	✓	✓	✗	✗	✓	✗	✗
Paul	✗	✓	✗	✗	✓	✓	✗
Louise	✗	✓	✓	✗	✓	✗	✗

1 Mark ... speak English, but he ... speak French.
2 Sophie ... speak English, but Paul and Louise ... .
3 Sophie, Paul and Louise ... speak French.
4 Only Paul ... ski.
5 Everybody ... .
6 Only Louise and Mark ... .
7 Nobody ... .
8 Only Mark ... .

10 Times

Write out the times in full.

Example: 

ten o'clock in the morning / ten a.m.

REMEMBER

Mit o'clock drückt man die volle Stunde aus.

Die 24-Stunden-Uhr (z.B. sixteen thirty statt half past four) wird vor allem bei genauen Zeitangaben wie Fahrplänen verwendet. Sagen Sie in the morning/afternoon/evening oder a.m. (morgens, vormittags) / p.m. (nachmittags, abends), wenn die Tageszeit nicht eindeutig ist.

11 Dates

a Write out the dates in full.

Example: 

2 March 1997

REMEMBER

Man schreibt 4 June, aber man spricht the fourth of June.

Vorsicht bei den Jahreszahlen:
Man braucht nur and, wenn es eine 0 in der Jahreszahl gibt.
2005 = twothousand and five
Hundred wird meistens weggelassen.
1996 = nineteen ~~hundred~~ ninety-six
aber: 1800 = eighteen hundred

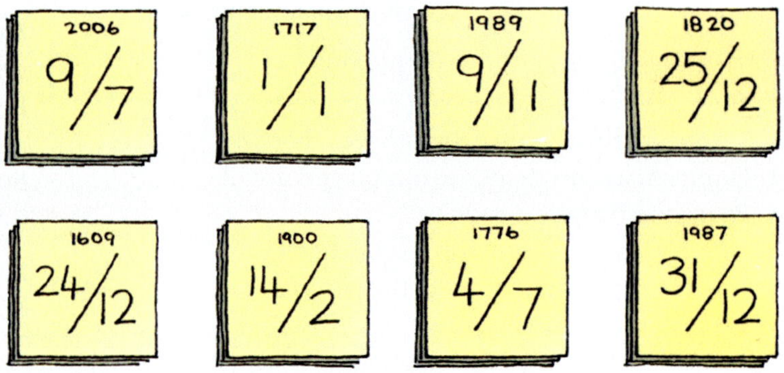

b Match the dates above with these special days.

New Year's Eve • Valentine's Day • New Year's Day • Final of the World Cup • Christmas Eve • Fall of the Berlin Wall • Christmas Day • Independence Day

c Write and say the following dates.

1 Your date of birth.
2 Your mother's/father's/friend's birthday.
3 Today's date.
4 Next Sunday's date.
5 The first day of the school holidays.
6 The last day of the school holidays.

12 Countries and nationalities

a Work in small groups. Find the names of the countries 1–8 in the box. Which group can finish first?

Australia • Austria • China • Germany • Italy • Russia • Switzerland • USA

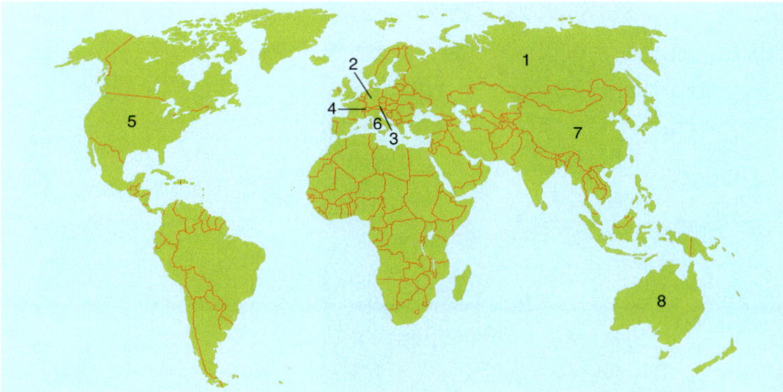

b Now match the countries with the nationalities a–h.

a German
b Austrian
c Swiss
d Australian
e American
f Italian
g Chinese
h Russian

c Make sentences by combining things from this table.

Example: *The Rhine is a German river.*

The Rhine			Swiss	river.
Ferrari			Australian	chocolate bar.
The waltz			German	fast-food chain.
McDonald's	is	a	Chinese	singer.
Toblerone		an	Austrian	car company.
Kylie Minogue			American	dance.
Vodka			Russian	drink.
Shanghai			Italian	city.

REMEMBER

a/an

Vor einem Vokal (a, e, i, o, u) wird **a** zu **an**:

a German car, an English film

13 Numbers

a Match the numbers in the box to the words a–h.

95 • 17 • 23 • 50 • 15 • 59 • 32 • 70

a seventeen
b seventy
c fifty
d fifteen
e thirty-two
f twenty-three
g ninety-five
h fifty-nine

b Work with a partner. First Partner A reads out a number and Partner B finds this number in the box. Then swap roles.

14 • 39 • 93 • 44 • 33 • 41 • 13 • 43

1 Saying Hello

At a workcamp

We're at a workcamp in Chicago.
On the first day at camp we always play a game called, 'In the hot seat'.
One person answers questions about home, family and hobbies.

1 **It's Nina's turn to answer questions. Read or listen to her and the others and check your list from 'Before you start'. How many of your ideas do you hear?**

2

PHILIP You're next, Nina. What's your full name?
NINA Nina Weber.
MARIA Where are you from?
NINA I'm from Germany. I live in Nonnenhorn. It's a village on Lake Constance.
SABINE Do you live with your mum and dad?
NINA My parents are divorced. I live with my mum and my stepfather.
RONNIE Oh. You're part of a patchwork family. Me too.
NINA Sorry? I don't understand. What does 'patchwork family' mean?
MARIA I think it means that a mum and dad don't live together any more. They live with new partners and their kids. It's two families in one house.
NINA Right. With stepbrothers and stepsisters.
RONNIE That's it. Do you have any stepbrothers or stepsisters?
NINA No, I don't. I have a real brother, Florian. He's married. And I have a half-brother – erm, is that right? My mum and my stepfather have a child.
PHILIP Yes, that's right. That's your half-brother.
NINA Good. – His name's Andreas. He's only 8. I don't have any sisters.
RONNIE You're lucky. I have three sisters and two stepsisters. It's horrible.
SABINE Why do you say it's horrible? I'm an only child. I don't have any brothers or sisters. I sometimes think ...

BEFORE YOU START

Discuss in small groups and make a list of questions.
What do you want to know when you meet a new person?

What's your name?
Where are you from?
Do you have any hobbies?
Do you like ...?

MARIA Hey. It's Nina's turn. Do you have any pets, Nina?
NINA Yes, I have a cat. Her name's Tinka.
BIROL What's your job?
NINA I don't have a job yet. I go to vocational college all week.
PHILIP Do you like it?
NINA Yes, I do. It's great. I do office administration, marketing, computer studies. I don't always understand the ...
RONNIE School. Who's interested in school? Do you have any hobbies? What kind of music do you like? I play lead guitar in a reggae band. Our group plays gigs all over the place. We usually play ...
MARIA Ronnie, please. Nina's in the hot seat. We don't want to hear about you and your group at the moment. You can tell us later.
RONNIE OK. But what about my question? What's your favourite type of music?
NINA Well, actually, I like reggae too, Ronnie.
RONNIE Yes!

(321 words)

2 **Now Nina has to fill in a card with her personal details. Copy her card into your exercise book, read the text or listen again and complete the card.**

I'm from	...
I live in	*Nonnenhorn*
My family	*My parents are divorced. I have ...*
My pet	...
My favourite type of music is	...

3 **Answer the questions.**

1 Where does Nina live?
2 Who does she live with?
3 Who are Florian and Andreas?
4 How many sisters and step sisters does Ronnie have?
5 What is the name of Nina's pet?
6 What does Nina learn at school?
7 What is Ronnie's hobby?

REMEMBER

Wenn Sie eine Vokabel vergessen haben oder sich nicht sicher sind, fragen Sie:

What's ... in English?
What does ... mean?
Is ... right?

4 Match these descriptions to words from the text.

1 The son of your mum and dad is your ... .
2 Mum and Dad.
3 When two people aren't married any more, they are ... .
4 A slang word for a child.
5 The daughter of a mum or dad's new partner is your ...sister.
6 An animal friend.
7 The new man a mum marries is your ... .
8 The son of your mum and her new partner is your ... -brother.
9 Parents and children from different families live together in a ... family.
10 This person has no brothers and sisters.

Now use the ten words to complete this chatroom conversation. Use each word once.

ziggy I'm an ... [1]. I live with my ... [2] and my ... [3] dog, Joey. We're a boring little family.

weird You're lucky that your mum and dad are together. My mum and dad are ... [4]. I live with my mum and her new partner, Dave. I don't like him. He's a typical ... [5]. He always bosses me around.

gillie You poor ... [6] :-(I have a super family. I have a ... [7]. His name's Ralf, and I have a ... [8]sister, Penny. We aren't real sisters, but we're really close. My mum has a new baby, Johnny. He's my ... [9]-brother. He's great. We're a really happy ... [10] family.

5 Read the chatroom conversation again. Who would say each of the following sentences?

1 I really like my half-brother.
2 I am sad that my parents aren't together anymore.
3 At home we have a pet.
4 I can never do what I want when my stepfather is at home.

6 Write sentences about Nina, e.g. where she lives and what she does at vocational college. Then write about where you live, what you do at college, etc.

Nina lives in Nonnenhorn, a village on Lake Constance.
Her parents ...
I live in ... I go to vocational college ...

Language

SIMPLE PRESENT (einfache Gegenwart)

Aussagen	Verneinungen	Fragen	Kurzantworten
I live in Nonnenhorn. Ronnie plays gigs all over the place. We usually play ...	I don't have (do not have) any brothers and sisters. Sabine doesn't have (does not have) any brothers and sisters. I don't always understand.	Do you like it? Does Ronnie like school? What kind of music do you like?	Yes, I do. / No, I don't. Yes, he does. / No, he doesn't.

- Die einfache Gegenwart (simple present) wird verwendet für gleich bleibende Zustände und regelmäßige, wiederholte Handlungen.
- In der 3. Person Singular (he/she/it und Substantive) wird in der Regel (wie z. B. bei play) ein -s an die Grundform angehängt.
- Außer bei dem Verb to be werden Verneinungen und Fragen in der einfachen Gegenwart mit dem Hilfsverb do (in der 3. Person Singular mit der Form does) gebildet.
- Außer bei dem Verb to be werden do bzw. does, don't oder doesn't in Kurzantworten wiederholt.
- Die einfache Gegenwart wird häufig mit folgenden Signalwörtern gebraucht: always, never, often, sometimes, usually. Sie stehen meist vor dem Hauptverb.

QUESTION WORDS (Fragewörter)

What ...?	Was ...?	Why ...?	Warum ...?
When ...?	Wann ...?	How ...?	Wie ...?
Where ...?	Wo ...?	How many ...?	Wie viele ...?
Who ...?	Wer ...?	How often ...?	Wie oft ...?

DANGER!

In Sätzen, in denen does oder doesn't steht, fällt das -s in der dritten Person des Verbs weg!

Heike doesn't work~~s~~.

Practice

7 Complete sentences with the correct form of the verbs in brackets.

Example: John ... (like) beer. He ... (not drink) vodka.
John likes beer. He doesn't drink vodka.

1 Sophie ... (work) in an office. She ... (not go) to school.
2 I ... (speak) English and German but I ... (not speak) Russian.
3 Carole ... (put on) her make-up carefully. She ... (not do) her homework carefully.
4 Tony and Bob ... (talk) too much. They ... (not pay attention) in class.
5 Harun ... (wear) nice clothes but he ... (not spend) too much money.
6 Linda ... (sing) gospel. She ... (not like) rap.
7 You ... (not have) any friends. You ... (play) with your computer all the time.
8 They ... (not live) at home with their parents, they ... (live) in a flat.

8 **Talk to a partner. Ask questions with a form of do and give short answers.**

Example: ... you play football?
A: *Do* you play football?
B: *No, I don't.*

1 ... you have a pet?
2 ... our teacher look happy?
3 ... we have to do a lot of homework?
4 ... you work in a supermarket?
5 ... you like sport?
6 ... you sometimes visit a chatroom?
7 ... the school have a good canteen?
8 ... the others look busy?

INTERCULTURAL CORNER

Kurzantworten

Im Englischen werden Fragen selten nur mit Yes oder No beantwortet. Für die Ohren eines Muttersprachlers kann ein einfaches Yes oder No sogar unhöflich klingen. Stattdessen gibt man Kurzantworten, die in der Regel aus drei Wörtern bestehen:

Is he German? – Yes, he is.
Do they live in America? – No, they don't.

9 **Make sentences from these words. Put the verb in the right form and add a form of do when necessary.**

Examples: always / enjoy / Martin / parties → *Martin always enjoys parties.*
not go out / in the evening / Lucy / usually → *Lucy doesn't usually go out in the evening.*

1 he / dance / never
2 often / TV / watch / you / ?
3 in a band / drums / in / play / she / sometimes
4 always / look / tired / why / you / ?
5 eat / I / meat / never
6 early / not get up / Linda / usually
7 not go / often / they / to the disco
8 football / play / sometimes / you / ?

10 **Write five sentences about yourself. Use always / never / often / sometimes / usually.**

11 **Here are some questions and answers about Birol and the workcamp. Complete the questions with words from the box. Use each word once.**

How • How many • How often • What • When • Where • Who • Why

1 ... do Maria and the others ask Birol questions? – To get to know him.
2 ... is he from? – He's from Germany.
3 ... does he go to vocational college? – Once a week.
4 ... does he do there? – He's a trainee mechanic.
5 ... does the game 'In the hot seat' work? – The person in the hot seat answers questions.
6 ... does Birol leave the house each morning? – At 8.00.
7 ... answers Birol's question? – Nina answers the question.
8 ... sisters does Birol have? – He has three sisters.

12 Find a way through the table so that the questions and answers form a short conversation.

START

Do you live in London?	No, we don't. Do ...	you live with your mother?	No, I don't. I ...
No, I don't. I live in Glasgow. And does ...	you and your friends like Glasgow?	you have any brothers or sisters?	live with my father and my stepmother. Do ...
Pete still live in London?	Yes, he does. Do ...	Yes, I do. I ...	have one sister. And do ...
your sister like music?	have two sisters and a half-brother. Does ...	Yes, I do. I ...	you have any brothers or sisters?
Yes, she does. And do ...	you still play the drums in your band?	Yes, I do. Tell ...	your sister to come to our concert!

END

13 Everyone who goes to a workcamp fills in an application form. Copy Ronnie's form into your exercise book. Then listen as he fills it in, and complete.

3

1 Name
2 Address
3 Date of birth
4 Do you have an email address?
5 Do you have a passport?
6 Do you have a driver's license?

14 Ask and answer questions with a partner.

PARTNER A: Look at File 1 on page 148.
PARTNER B: Look at File 6 on page 150.

LEARNING TO LEARN

Wie kann ich mein Englisch verbessern?

Englisch kann man auf viele unterschiedliche Weisen lernen.
Hier sind ein paar Tipps – aber bestimmt fallen Ihnen noch mehr Möglichkeiten ein!

- Filme in Originalfassung sind mit Untertitel leichter zu verstehen – und vielleicht klappt es beim zweiten Mal schon ohne Untertitel!
- Ein Magazin für Ihr Hobby gibt es ganz bestimmt auch in englischer Sprache.
- Warum nicht mal eine SMS oder E-Mail auf Englisch schreiben?
- CDs haben meist Booklets mit Texten – wer mitliest, versteht mehr.

The world of work

1 **It's Susanne's first morning at work. Read the text and complete the statements. Only one option is correct.**

The first day at work

The first morning

Susanne is nervous. She starts today as a trainee at a British firm called *Your Gift*.
The firm produces wooden toys and souvenirs for gift shops.
Susanne arrives at the factory at 8.30. Mr Young, the personnel manager, is friendly. He welcomes Susanne, then he introduces Chris Binns. Chris works in the Sales Department. He also looks after the trainees. "Welcome to *Your Gift*," he says.
Chris shows Susanne the office. It's bright and friendly with posters on the walls and lots of plants. Susanne and Chris work together on a spreadsheet. Susanne does computer studies at college, so it isn't difficult to use the program. At 10.30 it's time for coffee and a chat. Susanne tells Chris about college. After coffee, Chris takes Susanne round the factory to meet other colleagues. Susanne isn't nervous any more and starts to enjoy the day.

1 *Your Gift* is a ...
- a toy shop.
- b place where nervous people go.
- c firm where people produce nice things.

2 The personnel manager is ...
- a young.
- b nervous.
- c nice.

3 Chris ...
- a works with plants.
- b helps the trainees.
- c teaches at college.

4 After coffee, Susanne ...
- a works in the factory.
- b gets to know people at work.
- c goes back to college.

Now choose a new title for the text. Give reasons.

Ⓐ ***Drink coffee, be happy***

Ⓑ ***Getting started***

Ⓒ ***Chris and Susanne at work***

Ⓓ ***Toy story***

2 Listen to people saying hello at *Your Gift*. Which phrases from the box do you hear?

4

Good morning. • Hi there! • Hello! • How are you? • I'm ... • My name's ... • How are you doing? • Nice to meet you. • How's it going?

3 Listen again and match the dialogues with the pictures.

4

A

B

C

4 Work with a partner. It's Partner B's first day at *Your Gift*. Use phrases from the box to make up the dialogue in English. When you have finished, swap roles.

Fine thanks. And you? • Good morning/afternoon. (2 x) • How are you? • I'm ... • I'm fine, too, thanks. • I'm from ... • My name is ... • This is your desk/office/computer. • Where are you from? • Thank you.

A	B
Begrüßen Sie B und stellen Sie sich vor.	
	Begrüßen Sie A und stellen Sie sich auch vor.
Fragen Sie B, wie es ihm geht.	
	Beantworten Sie die Frage. Fragen Sie A ebenfalls.
Antworten Sie. Fragen Sie B, woher er/sie kommt.	
	Beantworten Sie die Frage.
Zeigen Sie B seinen neuen Arbeitstisch/ Arbeitsplatz/Computer.	
	Bedanken Sie sich.

Now introduce your partner to the rest of the class.

2 Free time

5 Getting a date

1 Chuck is trying to get a date with Alison.
Listen, or read the text, then do the exercise on the opposite page.

CHUCK Hi. Is anyone sitting here?

ALISON No. Not at the moment.

CHUCK Wrong. You are. And now I am too. I'm Chuck, by the way. I usually look brighter than this but I'm a bit tired today. I was out clubbing last night. I always go clubbing at the weekend: every Friday and Saturday night actually. Do you know Prince's? It's one of the best clubs in Soho.

ALISON Is that right? I hardly ever go to Soho.

CHUCK Really? Soho's great. It's got clubs, bars, discos – everything. How about going to Prince's together sometime? What are you doing on Friday?

ALISON I always go to a jazz dance class on Friday evenings.

CHUCK Jazz dance. Nice. What time does it finish? I could pick you up after your class. I have a scooter.

ALISON No, thanks. I go to the pub afterwards with the other girls.

CHUCK Oh, right. Girls' night out. Cool. What about Saturday, then? Shall we go to the cinema? Let's go and see an action film. Or would you like to see a comedy instead?

ALISON Look, sorry. I'm waiting for my friends, OK?

CHUCK No problem. I'm not doing anything else today. I can wait with you. So, Saturday. We can have a drink before the film starts.

ALISON No, thanks. I can't go out on Saturday. I do sport in the mornings then I go shopping in the afternoon. Saturday evenings I usually make a few phone calls and meet my mates.

CHUCK Busy life! Sunday, then? What about Sunday? You could come round to my place. What do you think?

ALISON Look, don't you understand? I'm not interested in clubbing in Soho, I don't like action films and I don't want to go to the cinema with you, and I most definitely don't want to go round to your place.

CHUCK What am I doing wrong? Oh. Sorry. Am I annoying you?

ALISON Yes, you are.

CHUCK Would you like me to go and sit somewhere else, then?

ALISON That's a good idea.

CHUCK OK. Look, I'm going. But – before I go – can I have your telephone number, please?

(339 words)

BEFORE YOU START

You have three minutes to collect words and make a word spider showing what you do in your free time. Which group has most words?

Decide if the following statements are true or false. Correct the false statements.

1 Chuck is sitting in the café when Alison comes in.
2 Chuck is tired.
3 Alison always goes to Soho at the weekend.
4 On Friday she usually goes to the cinema.
5 Chuck has a car.
6 Alison is waiting for her friends.
7 Alison wants to go out with Chuck.
8 Chuck gives Alison his phone number.

Now write three statements about the text: two correct ones and one false one. Can your partner tell which is the false one?

LEARNING TO LEARN

Wie man Vokabeln lernt

Zum Vokabellernen ist es ganz wichtig, ein Vokabelheft zu führen. Dort sollten Sie alle neuen Wörter mit deutscher Übersetzung eintragen.

Oft ist es hilfreich, sich statt einzelner Wörter gleich feste Ausdrücke und Wendungen einzuprägen:

club – go clubbing	auf Parties / in Clubs gehen

So wissen Sie gleich, wie das Wort im Satzzusammenhang verwendet wird. Denn dort gibt es viele Unterschiede zwischen dem Englischen und Deutschen. Denken Sie an die verschiedenen Möglichkeiten, das deutsche Wort „machen" im Englischen auszudrücken:

photo – take photos	Foto – Fotos machen, fotografieren
sport – do sport	Sport – Sport machen/treiben
phone call – make a phone call	Anruf – einen Anruf machen, telefonieren

2 Finish the sentences with information from the text. Use your own words.

Example: Today Chuck doesn't look *bright because he went clubbing last night.*

1 At the weekend Chuck ...
2 On Fridays Alison ...
3 Chuck has a few ideas about Saturday. They could ...
4 When Chuck asks Alison about Saturday, she says that ...
5 At the end of the story Chuck asks for ...
6 All through the story Alison thinks Chuck is ...

3 How can you express these ideas in a different way? Find the words and phrases in the text.

1 now (lines 1–11)
2 a little (lines 1–11)
3 very seldom (lines 12–20)
4 Fine. (lines 21–30)
5 absolutely (lines 31–38)
6 getting on your nerves (lines 31–38)

4 Can you translate these sentences? (They are all in the text.)

1 Wie wär's, wenn wir mal zusammen zu Prince's gehen?
2 Was machst du am Freitag?
3 Wie sieht's denn mit Samstag aus?
4 Sollen wir ins Kino gehen?
5 Wir können noch was trinken gehen, bevor der Film anfängt.
6 Du könntest zu mir kommen.

Language

PRESENT PROGRESSIVE (Verlaufsform der Gegenwart)

Aussagen	Verneinungen	Fragen	Kurzantworten
I'm waiting for my friends. He's reading a book.	You're not / You aren't listening to me. She's not / isn't talking loud enough.	Is anyone sitting here? Are you waiting for a friend?	Yes, I am. – No, I'm not. Yes, you are. – No, you're not / you aren't.

- Die Verlaufsform der Gegenwart (present progressive) wird verwendet, wenn man ausdrücken will, dass jemand *jetzt* / *gerade* / *im Augenblick* etwas tut oder dass gerade etwas geschieht.
- Das present progressive steht auch für Handlungen und Vorgänge, die von vorübergehender Dauer und noch nicht abgeschlossen sind, aber nicht unbedingt zum Zeitpunkt des Sprechens geschehen: *I'm doing a course in computer studies.*
- Häufige Signalwörter in Verbindung mit dem present progressive sind: at the moment, now, just, still, today.
- Einige Verben, die Zustände oder Gefühle ausdrücken, werden nicht im present progressive gebraucht, z. B. *be, believe, forget, hate, have, know, like, love, need, remember, want.*

Practice

5 Complete the sentences in the present progressive.

Example: I ... (work) in a restaurant this week.
I'm working in a restaurant this week.

1 You ... (speak) too fast.
2 You ... (not work) very hard at the moment.
3 He ... (go) to school by bike today.
4 Listen! Someone ... (play) the piano.
5 I ... (help) my parents this week.
6 They ... (not fight) with each other any more.
7 Toby and Mary ... (wear) the same pullovers.
8 Iris ... (do) her homework at the moment.

'I'm working in a restaurant this week.'

REMEMBER

Who bedeutet nicht nur *wer*, sondern auch *wen* oder *wem*:

Who are you phoning?
Who does Sarah live with?

6 Make questions. Use the present progressive.

Example: What / you / study?
What are you studying?

1 What / Mary / do?
2 Who / John / phone?
3 he / watch TV / at the moment?
4 Why / you / look at me?
5 What / you / eat?
6 Why / she / look / out of the window?
7 What / we / do / here?
8 you / write / in your book?

7 In English it sounds rude to answer simply with Yes or No. Give polite short answers.

Example: Is your sister working today? *No, she's not.*

1 Is our teacher looking at us?
2 Are your classmates working hard?
3 Are you studying for the exam this week?
4 Is it raining?
5 Am I talking too loud?
6 Are we working too slowly?
7 Are a lot of students wearing jeans today?
8 Are you concentrating?

8 Choose the correct form of the verb. Say why you have chosen it.

Example: He usually *phones* / *is phoning* his dad on Sunday.
Simple present: phones (regelmäßige, wiederholte Handlung)

1 Kenny *plays* / *is playing* football every Saturday.
2 *I do* / *I'm doing* a course in marketing this year.
3 Who *does* / *is doing* gymnastics regularly?
4 I *don't like* / *am not liking* sport.
5 My cousins *stay* / *are staying* with us at the moment.
6 Rachel *doesn't work* / *isn't working* just now. She's on holiday.
7 They *sometimes wear* / *are sometimes wearing* very expensive sports clothes.
8 You *remember* / *are remembering* everything.

9 **Translate the missing parts of these sentences into English.**

1 *Lass mich bitte in Ruhe. Ich arbeite gerade.* – Leave me alone, please. I ... .
2 *Du hörst mir nie zu.* – You ... .
3 *Ivan sieht gerade fern.* – Ivan ... at the moment.
4 *Geht deine Schwester am Wochenende auf Parties?* – ... clubbing at the weekend?
5 *Was machst du gerade?* – What ... you ... ?
6 *Jetzt lernen wir Englisch.* – We ... at the moment.
7 *Frank fotografiert viel.* – Frank ... a lot of photos.
8 *Anne schaut aus dem Fenster.* – Anne ... .

10 **Write six sentences about yourself and your friends using the words in the box and the correct form of the verb.**

always • at the moment • now • sometimes • today • usually

Example:

Steffi always wears nice clothes.

I'm working hard today.

11 **Chuck always uses the same phrases to ask girls out. This time, he's chatting up Julie. Match her answers to Chuck's invitations from exercise 4, then listen and check.**

6

12 **Choose the best thing to say in these situations.**

1 You would like to invite someone to a party.
 a Do you want to come to my party?
 b Would you like to come to my party?

2 Someone asks you to go to the cinema with them.
 a Thanks. I'd like to.
 b OK. I'll go to the cinema with you.

3 You don't have any money to pay for your cola.
 a Can you pay for my cola, please?
 b Pay my cola for me, please.

4 Someone gives you a ticket for a concert.
 a Please.
 b Thanks a lot.

5 You have to pass a lot of people to get to your seat in the cinema.
 a I want to get to my seat.
 b Excuse me, please.

6 Someone asks you to go to the pub, but you can't go.
 a No, I can't.
 b Sorry, I can't.

INTERCULTURAL CORNER

Sich höflich ausdrücken

Im Englischen werden häufiger als im Deutschen „Höflichkeitsfloskeln" verwendet. Das mag Deutschen übertrieben erscheinen; für englische Muttersprachler kann es jedoch unhöflich klingen, wenn man sie weglässt.

Sagen Sie nicht **I want**, sondern **I'd like to**. Wenn Sie um etwas bitten, sagen Sie immer **Please** und **Thank you**.
Excuse me und **Sorry** werden weit häufiger als die entsprechenden Ausdrücke im Deutschen verwendet.

13 **Work in groups of three. Take turns to give and refuse invitations. Plan your weekend together. Tell the rest of the class.**

Tuesday 1

➢*ROCK AND POP*
Simply Red: Royal Albert Hall. 8pm. *Ends November 2*
Echo & The Bunnymen: Shepherd's Bush Empire. 8pm.
Nine Black Alps: Camden Electric Ballroom. 8pm. *Also December 14*
New Pornographers: Borderline. 8pm. *Also 93 Feet East. November 3*
Donavon Frankenreiter: Astoria. 8pm.
Athlete: Hammersmith Apollo. 8pm. *Also November 2*
Polysics: Barfly. 8pm.
Wir Sind Helden: Garage. 8pm. *Also November 2*

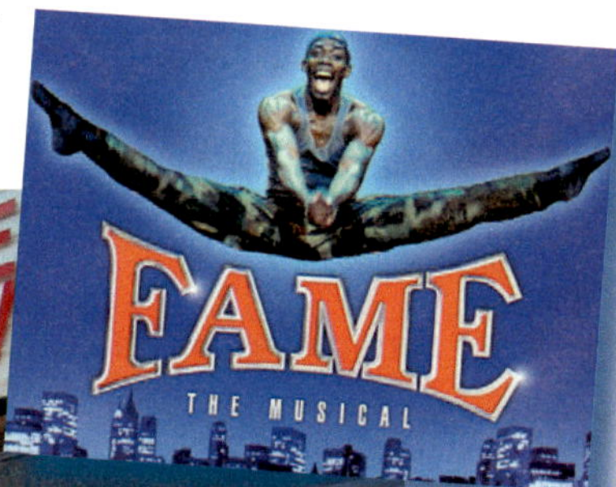

● Science Museum
☞ Exhibition Road, SW7.
☎ 0207 942 4454; South Kensington ⊖
Outstanding collections form an unparalleled record of mankind's greatest inventions and achievements. Exhibits of actual equipment, instruments and machinery tell the story of the history of science and industry, from the first steam locomotive and the beginnings of photography to man's first flight in space and computer technology. Open daily 10am-6pm. Free. Special events include:
Inside the Spitfire - the story of the legendary WW2 fighter plane and its designer R J Mitchell. Until **Jan 2006**.

Brick Lane: East End flea market along Cheshire Street, E1 and corner of Bethnal Green Road, where the real junk can be found. 7am-1pm. (Aldgate East ⊖).

The world of work

People at work

1 a **Match the jobs (1–4) to the places of work (a–d). Then listen and look at the photos. Who does what?**

7

1 nurse	3 programmer	a factory	c department store
2 trainee mechanic	4 shop assistant	b hospital	d office

Bob Graves

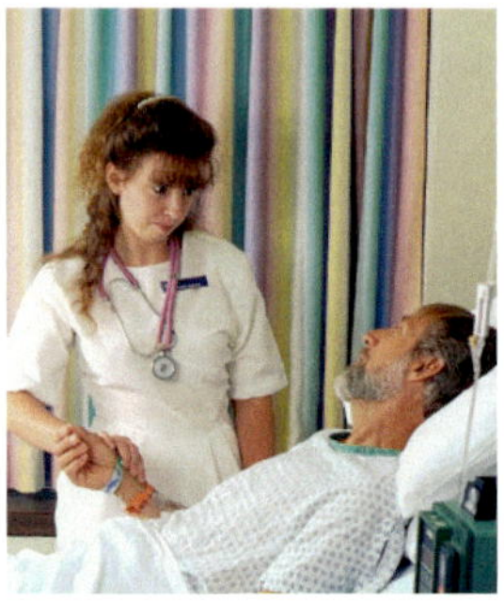

Susan Brown

Martin Smith

Gail Johnston

b **Listen again and make notes. Then write 35–40 words about two of the people.**

- Give the people's names.
- Say where they are from.
- Say where they work and what they do.

Gail Johnston is from ...

2 **Here are some jobs. Which would/wouldn't you like to do? Say why.**

electrician   baker   dental assistant   care assistant for the elderly

I enjoy helping people.

I think that's a boring job.

That's my dream job.

Working nights is no fun.

I don't like to work too hard.

It could be fun.

I wouldn't like to get up early.

I like to give people advice.

3 **Read the text then say if the sentences below are true or false. Correct the false sentences.**

Good manners at work

We all know that good manners are important and we know how to behave correctly in German-speaking countries. But do you work for a British company? Is it an American firm? Things that are polite in Germany are sometimes not polite enough in English-speaking countries. Here are some tips.

Saying 'Hello'

What do you do and what do you say when you meet someone in a British or an American company? Usually, people shake hands when they meet for the first time in a business situation. It's quite unusual to shake hands in informal situations.

German people often say only their last name when they introduce themselves. This sounds hard and unfriendly in English. Say your full name, 'My name's Lisa Müller' and don't be shocked by the reply, 'Hello, Lisa'. Colleagues usually use their first names in English-speaking countries. The boss is different, of course. Don't use his or her first name unless he or she says it's OK.

Being polite

Most days, the first thing you'll hear from a colleague is, 'How are you?' You answer, 'Fine, thanks. And you?' Then your colleague says, 'I'm fine, too, thanks.' After that you can talk about other things.

Making small talk

People often make small talk at work. They talk about the weather, pets or their hobbies. While German workers tend to concentrate on their work and only make small talk during breaks, in the English-speaking world small talk is integrated into the working day – when you meet someone at the photocopier or in the lift, for example.

1 It's important to be very polite at work in Britain and America.
2 People never shake hands in business situations in the UK or the USA.
3 In the UK or the USA always introduce yourself with your last name only.
4 English speakers will probably use your first name when they speak to you.
5 You can always call your boss by his/her first name.
6 British and American colleagues never ask each other how they are feeling.
7 British workers like to have a chat with colleagues.

4 **A colleague who doesn't speak good English asks you to help with the article above. Summarize the article in German. Write one sentence for each paragraph.**

'Hello, I'm Brian. Lovely weather, isn't it?'

3 Other Cultures

1 **Anne Diehl took a year out and travelled round the world. Read these pages from her weblog and find out who the people in the drawings are.**

http://www.bloggers-point.com/blog92

Anne's blogs

A trip round the world

17 June 20..

Last year I watched a TV programme about a group of bikers. They flew to the USA and rode Route 66. Brilliant! I started to dream about a trip to faraway places.
When I told Mum and Dad about the idea, they insisted on two things: I was not allowed to travel alone and I had to complete my training first.
Well, this year I finished. Mum and Dad helped me out with some money. I asked two of my mates – Alex and Sarah – to come with me and they said yes. Three weeks ago we planned our route, went to a travel agent's and bought a 'round the world' ticket. Look out, World! Here we come!

22 June 20..

First stop London
We arrived in a backpackers' hostel in Piccadilly. At Piccadilly Circus there are loads of pubs, bars and clubs, so the first night we ended up in a pub. At first we didn't know that you pay for your drinks when you get them, but the barman was used to Germans, so he told us how it works in British pubs. Later we sat with some Irish guys and they explained that British people usually buy a 'round'. That means that one person pays for everybody's drinks, then someone else pays for the drinks next time round. Drinks are expensive in London, though, so we didn't stay in the pub for long.

Next day we went up on the London Eye and looked out over London. When you're at the top you can see everything – the British Museum and Covent Garden in the north, the Houses of Parliament and Westminster Abbey in the south-west, and Buckingham Palace in the west. The Tower of London is in the east. In the afternoon we went to the British Museum. We finished up at Covent Garden and watched jugglers and fire-eaters.

London Eye

25 June 20..

Next stop Glastonbury.
We were lucky to get tickets. There are some wicked bands this year. Here's the line-up: (325 words)

BEFORE YOU START

Imagine you could travel round the world. Where would/would't you like to go? What would you like to see? Plan your route then report back to the class.

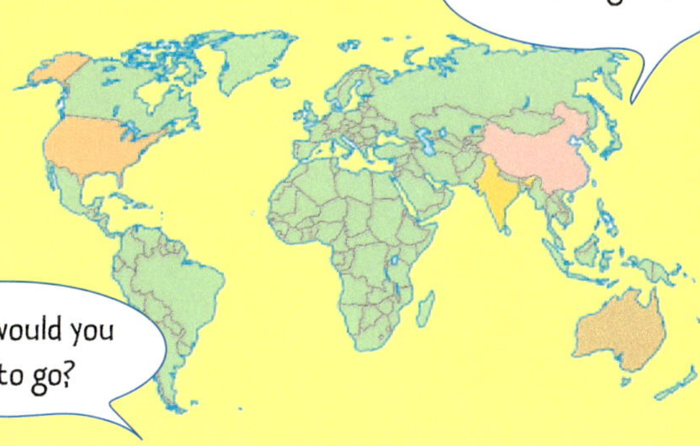

I'd like to go to ...

Then I'd like to see ...

First I'd like to go to ...

Where would you like to go?

2 Read these questions and statements and decide who said what.

1 What can I get for you?

2 I want to go round the world.

3 Here's some extra pocket money for you.

4 Anything else?

5 We think you should ask one or two friends to go with you.

6 Here are your tickets and your itinerary (Reiseplan).

7 Don't worry. Alex and Sarah want to see the world, too.

8 Where did you buy your rucksack, Anne? We need to buy one, too.

3 Choose the standard English form for these colloquialisms (*umgangssprachliche Ausdrücke*) from the text.

1 mates (line 6) — a friends — b neighbours
2 loads of (line 11) — a a lot of — b not many
3 guys (line 14) — a people — b tourists
4 wicked (line 26) — a really good — b really bad

4 Find the English words for the following. Check your answers in the text.

1 Reise (17 June)
2 reisen (17 June)
3 Ausbildung (17 June)
4 „landen“ (22 June)
5 Glück haben (25 June)
6 Eintrittskarte (25 June)

5 Without looking back at the text, put this summary in the correct order.

a On the first evening, they went to a pub.
b After her training, Anne planned her trip with two friends.
c After a few days, they went to Glastonbury.
d The following day, they saw some of London's most famous places.
e Anne saw an interesting TV programme about faraway places.
f Her parents said she could go on a trip, but she had to do some things they wanted first.
g Their first stop was London, where they found a cheap place to stay.

6 Work with a partner.
Compare the map of central London with the text and say what 1–4 are.

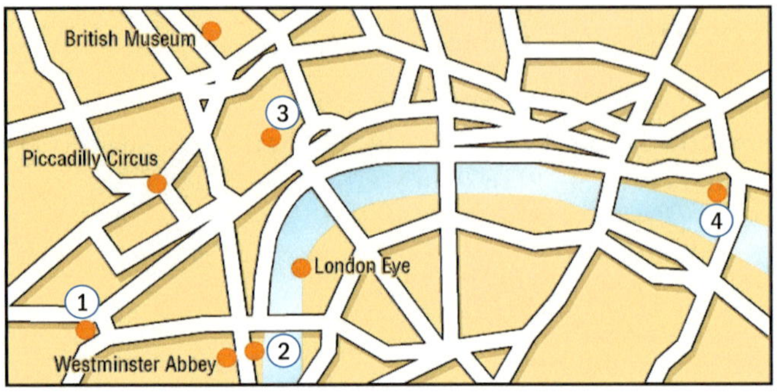

7 In groups use Anne's weblog to talk about differences between British and German pubs.
Which do you prefer? Why?

INTERCULTURAL CORNER

London

In London kann man an einem Tag eine Menge erleben, nur eines nicht: Langeweile. Morgens könnten Sie z.B. im Science Museum an Experimenten herumtüfteln. Zum Mittagessen gehen Sie einfach in einen Pub – anders als in deutschen Kneipen gibt es dort auch viele Gerichte, wie z.B. ein traditionelles „Roast Beef Dinner".

Ein Highlight für den Nachmittag ist Madame Tussauds. Dort stehen täuschend echte Wachsfiguren vieler berühmter Persönlichkeiten! Reservieren Sie Ihre Karten im Voraus im Internet, dann vermeiden Sie die lange Schlange.

Abends fällt die Wahl zwischen all den Clubs nicht leicht. In Camden, Liverpool Street oder Leicester Square pulsiert das Londoner Nachtleben – bunt, laut und multikulturell.

Language

SIMPLE PAST (einfache Vergangenheit)

Aussagen	Verneinungen	Fragen	Kurzantworten
I watched a TV programme. I told Alex about the idea.	My sister didn't (did not) come with me.	Did you book your rooms on the internet?	Yes, I did. / No, I didn't.
Anne was happy in London.	Anne's dad wasn't (was not) worried about her.	Was it easy to get tickets for Glastonbury?	Yes, it was. / No, it wasn't.
Things were great there.	Sarah's parents weren't (were not) happy.	Were you in the museum the whole afternoon?	Yes, we were. / No, we weren't.

- Die einfache Vergangenheit (simple past) beschreibt abgeschlossene Ereignisse und Zustände.
- Bei regelmäßigen Verben wird die einfache Vergangenheit gebildet, indem man -ed an die Grundform hängt. Unregelmäßige Verben bilden eine eigene Form (siehe die Übersicht auf Seite 242).
- Did + Grundform wird verwendet, um Fragen zu stellen.
  In Verneinungen steht did not (Kurzform: didn't) + Grundform.
- Die Vergangenheitsformen von be sind was und were. Verneinung: was not (wasn't) und were not (weren't).

- Die einfache Vergangenheit wird häufig mit folgenden Signalwörtern gebraucht: yesterday, last week/month/year, three days / two years ago, When ... ?
- Zeitangaben stehen am Satzanfang oder -ende. Ago steht immer am Ende der Zeitbestimmung.

DANGER!

In Fragen steht immer did mit der Grundform des Verbs!

Did you ~~saw~~ *see* ...?
What ~~did you~~ *did you do* yesterday?
When ~~went you~~ *did you go* to America?

Did steht nicht mit dem Verb to be!

I ~~didn't be~~ *wasn't* at school yesterday.

Practice

8 Complete another part of Anne's weblog with the verbs in brackets in the simple past.

http://www.bloggers-point.com/blog97

29 July 20..
Yesterday we ...[1] (visit) Yellowstone National Park. Yellowstone ...[2] (be) the first national park in America. We ...[3] (drive) to the hot springs and ...[4] (look at) Old Faithful – that's a famous geyser which shoots hot water and steam into the air. While we were there, it ...[5] (shoot up) to about 15 feet. Alex ...[6] (not read) the guide so he ...[7] (not know) what to expect. He ...[8] (get) a terrible fright.

9 Complete the answers to these questions.

Examples: Did Anne finish her training before her trip? – *Yes, she did.*
Did Anne and her friends stay in hotels? – No, *they didn't*. They *stayed* in hostels.

1 Did Anne go to Ireland? – No, ... She ... to England.
2 Did she finish her training first? – Yes, ...
3 Was Anne excited about her trip? – Yes, ...
4 Did Anne and her friends go to a restaurant on the first evening? – No, they ... . They ... to a pub.
5 Were the drinks in the pub cheap? – No, ... They ... expensive.
6 Was the barman German? – No, ... He ... English.
7 Did the three friends visit the British Museum? – Yes, ...
8 Did they see any musicians in Covent Garden? – No, ... They ... some jugglers and fire-eaters.

10 Make negative sentences.

Example: I travelled a lot last year. *I didn't travel a lot last year.*

1 Jim lived in India 20 years ago.
2 We were in America last Christmas.
3 They hired a car in Britain last month.
4 Tanja bought a new rucksack yesterday.
5 You told me about your last holiday.
6 Andy was in the sun too long yesterday.
7 We went swimming in the morning.
8 I stayed with my dad last summer.

11 Complete the questions.

Example: How much *did the trip cost?* – It cost €1,000.

1 When ... the USA? – I went there in July.
2 What about your friends? ... with you? – Yes, they went with me.
3 ... San Francisco? – Yes, we went to San Francisco.
4 How long ... there? – We stayed there for 10 days.
5 ... the Golden Gate Bridge? – Yes, we saw it.
6 ... on a cable car? – No, we didn't ride on a cable car.
7 ... Alcatraz? – No, we didn't visit Alcatraz.
8 ... the weather good? – Yes, it was great.

12 Complete the dialogue with had, did, was or were.

A We went to Canada on holiday in February.
B Really? That's great. Which places ... [1] you visit?
A We ... [2] in Toronto for two weeks, and then in Quebec for four days.
B ... [3] the weather very cold?
A Yes, it ... [4] freezing! But we still ... [5] a great time.
B ... [6] you explore the beautiful countryside outside the cities, too?
A Yes, we ... . [7]. It ... [8] amazing!

13 You and your partner went on one of these holidays together last year. Write a weblog describing your best day.

14 When she got back home, Anne told her English friend, Mark, about where she went and what she saw. Listen and choose Anne's route.

8

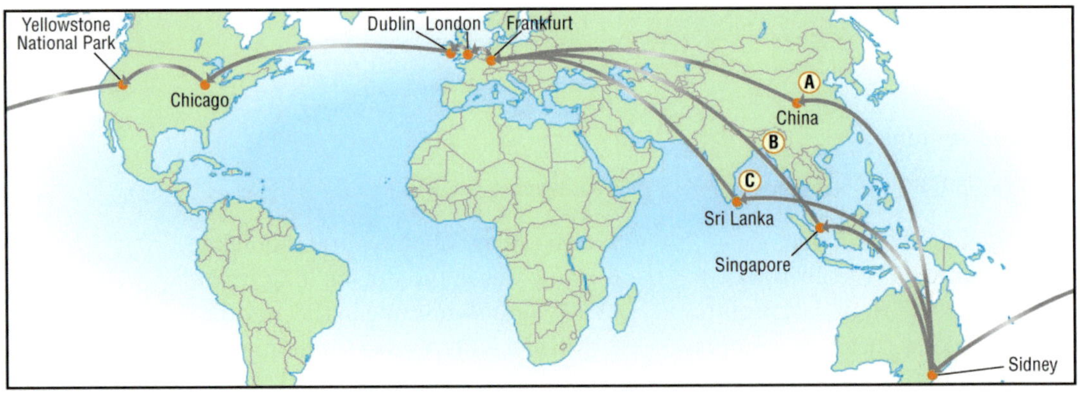

15 **First, sort these words and phrases into 'interested' / 'not interested'. After that, listen to Anne and Mark again. Which words and phrases does Mark use?**

8

interested	not interested
That sounds great!	

1. That sounds great!
2. I'm sure it is but ...
3. What about .... ?
4. Now that's my thing.
5. Tell me about ...
6. I'm not only interested in ...
7. Really?
8. That's not really my thing.

LEARNING TO LEARN

Wie man mit Unterschieden zwischen Deutsch und Englisch zurechtkommt

Wenn Sie sich die Wendungen aus Übung 15 ansehen, fällt Ihnen sicher auf, dass man das meiste im Deutschen etwas anders formulieren würde. Merken Sie sich daher immer die Formulierung als ganze, damit Ihnen das nächste Mal bei der Frage „Wie sage ich das jetzt auf Englisch?" nicht nur einzelne Wörter, sondern ganze Sätze einfallen. Folgende Tipps erleichtern Ihnen das Einprägen:

- Gehen Sie die Dialoge und Texte aus der Unit durch und notieren Sie sich Ausdrücke, die vom Deutschen abweichen, im Vokabelheft. Hier ein paar Beispiele aus Unit 3:

a couple of days/months ago	*vor ein paar Tagen/Monaten*
to pay for sth	*etwas bezahlen*
to buy a round (in a pub)	*(in der Kneipe) eine Runde geben*
That's not really my thing.	*Das ist eigentlich nichts für mich.*

- Lernen Sie die Wendungen, indem Sie sie laut nachsprechen.
- Halten Sie die englische Spalte bedeckt und versuchen Sie, die deutschen Wendungen aus dem Gedächtnis ins Englische zu übersetzen.
- Schauen Sie sich die Wendungen ab und zu wieder an und lesen Sie sie laut.

16 **You are going to tell each other about a trip.**

PARTNER A: Tell your partner where you went and what you did.
PARTNER B: Use words and phrases to show you are interested.

Now swap roles.

The world of work

Volunteering at a hostel

1 This notice is in the reception at a youth hostel in Edinburgh. Read it quickly. Does it give information about a) activities at the youth hostel, b) people who can help you if you have any problems, or c) places to go in Edinburgh?

Welcome!

Our youth hostel is famous for its great atmosphere!

Our aim is to make your stay as nice as possible but, just in case …

Are you sick?

Our doctor's name is Dr I. M. A. Killer. His telephone number is 332 1597.

Do you have toothache?
Our dentist is called Dr Will Pullit.
His telephone number is 667 8600.

The doctor and the dentist work together in Payne Street. The name of the surgery is 'The Payne Centre'.

Is the youth hostel on fire?
Call the Fire Brigade.
Their number is 999.

The caretakers' room is next to the reception. Our caretakers are Kevin and Pete.

Our receptionists this month are Monique and Martin.

Have fun and enjoy your stay!

Linda Ashley – Secretary

2 Now answer these questions.

Example: What's I. M. A. Killer's job? *He's a doctor.*

1 What does Dr Pullit do?
2 Where is their surgery?
3 What's the name of the surgery?
4 What does Kevin do?
5 Where is the caretakers' room?
6 What's Monique's job?

3 **Another guest at the hostel, who doesn't speak good English, asks you the following questions about the notice board. Answer them in German.**

1 Für wen ist diese Tafel?
2 Was mache ich, wenn ich zum Arzt muss?
3 Was mache ich, wenn es brennt?
4 Wer sind meine Ansprechpartner in der Herberge?

4 **Monique and Martin are working in the youth hostel as volunteers. Listen to them talking and choose the correct endings. (Only one option is correct.)**

9

1 Martin is
- a enjoying the work, even though it's not what he wanted to do.
- b happy because the job is just the way he thought it would be.
- c unhappy because there's too much work to do.

2 Monique is interested in
- a working with Martin.
- b getting a job in another country.
- c people from other countries.

3 Martin applied for the job so that he could
- a teach German to English people.
- b practise his English.
- c get away from other German-speakers.

4 The main reason Monique is working in the hostel is to
- a live cheaply in a foreign country.
- b speak English.
- c get to know people

5 **Use the internet to find a voluntary job you are interested in and write a short email applying for the job. Include the following:**

- your name and age
- why you are interested in doing the job
- appropriate skills you have
- when you are available for work

4 Keeping up to date

1 People have different opinions about body decorations. Read the chatroom thread. Who do you agree/disagree with? Why?

http://www.cool-teen-chat.com/

Home | Chat rooms | Contact | Log in | Links | Help | Search

COOL TEEN CHAT

Current users
- Lela
- spike
- MoJo
- TAP
- pothead

Lela	A lot of the kids at my school have tattoos and piercings. I think it's horrible. Why do people do it?
Spike	Tattoos and piercings are a statement. They show which group you belong to and they show how hard you are. I have a lot of piercings and I'm going to get more.
Tap	That's typical for someone covered in weird bits of metal and even weirder drawings. You people are even more stupid than you look.
Mojo	Now THAT'S typical. You don't have a tattoo or studs, so you think that people who do are stupid. These things are decoration. I have a silver belly button ring. It looks good. Nose jewellery looks even better, but my mum's totally against that so I'm not going to buy a nose ring ☹
Lela	Studs and rings and tattoos are a real turn-off. Do these people ever think about their future? How are they going to get a job? Do they want to shock people?
Spike	You can't shock anybody where I live. Almost everybody round here has some form of decoration. It's the people who don't have anything who look weird.
Mojo	You're lucky, Spike. My mum goes on at me all the time about what the neighbours think. But I've seen photos of her when she was my age. She wore the palest pink lipstick, black eyeliner and the biggest false eyelashes you've ever seen. How sad can you get?
Spike	That was the fashion for that generation. Your mum followed fashion then, so she doesn't have the right to go on at you for following our fashion today. Does your mum have pierced ears?
Mojo	Yes, she does.
Spike	OK. Then just point out to her that that's her form of decoration and you have yours.
Pothead	I got a tattoo of a rose on my shoulder last year. A few months later I went to India on holiday with my mum. When she saw my tattoo she went mad. We were at a market and she just started screaming at me. That was so embarrassing! Then suddenly she stopped. There were two old market ladies sitting at a stall. One of them had a cross tattooed on her forehead – it was as black as night – and the other one had red henna designs all over her hands. Mum and I both laughed. She's actually going to get a tattoo herself now. Cool, eh?

(406 words)

BEFORE YOU START

1 Would you ever go into a shop like this? Why? / Why not?

2 Which of these body decorations do you have / would you like to have?

earrings • lip rings • nose rings • piercings • studs • tattoos

3 Describe a tattoo you would like.

2 Match the beginnings of the sentences (1–8) to the endings (a–h) to make true sentences.

1 Lela doesn't understand
2 Spike believes that
3 Tap thinks that
4 Mojo's mother doesn't like
5 Lela thinks that
6 In the area where Spike lives,
7 Mojo thinks that
8 Pothead is

a people with body decorations will not get a job.
b certain kinds of jewellery.
c pleased that his mum is open to new ideas.
d people with piercings are not very intelligent.
e too much make-up looks really stupid.
f tattoos and piercings show how tough you are.
g why people have tattoos and piercings.
h almost everyone has tattoos and piercings.

3 a Copy this table and complete it with the correct words from the text.

noun	horror	stupidity	?	luck	?	embarrassment
adjective	?	?	decorated	?	fashionable	?

b Now use words from the table to complete this text.

Yesterday, Hannah's mum came home wearing a tattoo of a snake. Hannah screamed. "That's ...[1]!" she said.
"Why did you do that, Mum?" she asked. "I'm not going out with you like that. It's really ....[2]. People will laugh at you."
"I thought that was ...[3]," her mum said. "Lots of people have a body ...[4]. It's the ...[5]."
Hannah was really upset. "That's right, it is fashionable, but it's mostly young people that have tattoos. And that's cool. But these things look ...[6] on older people. You're 35, not 15, remember."
Hannah's mum laughed. "Don't worry," she said. "It's not a permanent tattoo. I'll wash it off before we go out." Hannah laughed, too. "I'm ...[7] to have such a crazy Mum," she said.

4 Talk in groups. What do you think about older people with tattoos?

I think it looks ...

In my opinion, ...

I think it's ...

5 You have five minutes to brainstorm English words to do with the topics on the right. Which group has most words?
Now use some of the words to describe a classmate. Write the descriptions on pieces of paper and give them to your teacher to read out. Can the class guess who the people are?

colours	accessories	clothes
black	earrings	jeans
green	scarf	
blue		

6 A friend in America is thinking about getting a tattoo. Write to him/her saying what you think. Write 80–100 words.

LEARNING TO LEARN

Wie man seinen Standpunkt formuliert

Bevor Sie anfangen zu schreiben, sollten Sie Ideen sammeln und stichwortartig festhalten. Auch Formulierungen, die Ihnen dazu einfallen oder die Sie aus dem Text einfließen lassen wollen, können Sie neben den einzelnen Stichwörtern notieren.

Ordnen Sie Ihre Ideen anschließend in drei Teile: Einleitung, Darlegung/Begründung Ihres Standpunktes und Zusammenfassung.

Einleitung *I think ... • In my opinion, ... • In my view, ...*
Begründung *This is because ... • In addition, ... • On the one hand ... but on the other hand ...*
Schluss *To conclude, ... • To finish with, ...*

7 With a partner, write the dialogue between Mojo and her mother. Role-play your dialogue for the class.

Language

THE *GOING TO* FUTURE (das Futur mit *going to*)

Das Futur mit going to wird für Pläne und Absichten verwendet, also z. B. um auszudrücken, was man gerade vorhat.
Mit going to kann man auch sagen, dass etwas höchstwahrscheinlich geschehen wird.
Das going to-Futur wird mit am/is/are going to + Infinitiv gebildet.

Aussagen	Verneinungen	Fragen mit Fragewörtern	Ja/Nein-Fragen und Kurzantworten
She's going to get a tattoo.	I'm not going to buy a nose ring.	How are they going to get a job?	Are you going to travel to India? Yes, I am. / No, I'm not..

COMPARATIVES AND SUPERLATIVES OF ADJECTIVES (die Steigerung von Adjektiven)

Im Englischen gibt es zwei Arten der Steigerung: eine mit -er/-est und eine mit more/most. Auf welche Art ein Adjektiv gesteigert wird, hängt vor allem von seiner Länge ab.

	Adjektiv	Komparativ	Superlativ
Einsilbige Adjektive	long big	longer bigger	(the) longest (the) biggest
Zweisilbige Adjektive, die auf -y enden	lucky	luckier	(the) luckiest
Adjektive mit zwei und mehr Silben	famous horrible	more famous more horrible	(the) most famous (the) most horrible
Unregelmäßige Adjektive	good bad	better worse	(the) best (the) worst

- Auf -er/-est werden gewöhnlich einsilbige Adjektive sowie zweisilbige, die auf -y enden, gesteigert. Achtung: Bei den zweisilbigen auf -y wird das -y zu -i.
- Wenn ein einsilbiges Adjektiv mit einem einfachen Konsonanten endet (big, thin usw.), wird dieser verdoppelt.
- Mit more/most werden zweisilbige Adjektive, die nicht auf -y enden, sowie alle Adjektive mit mehr als zwei Silben gesteigert.
- Vergleiche können mit -er / more ... than oder (not) as ... as gebildet werden:
  The blue T-shirt is nicer than the red one.
  Elke is as old as Patrick.
  Paris is not as big as Istanbul.

Practice

8 a Ask and answer questions using going to.

Example: You / listen to music / this evening? (No / watch TV)
Are you going to listen to music this evening? – No, I'm not. I'm going to watch TV.

1 You / eat / in the school canteen today? (No / eat in the café down the road)
2 You / visit / your dad at Christmas? (No / stay with my mum)
3 We / play / football this weekend? (No / play baseball)
4 Where / Gabi / book the tickets? (at the travel agency)
5 What / we / do / after school today? (homework)
7 Tony / watch / a DVD at the weekend? (No / play computer games)
8 How many people / you / invite / to the party? (100)

b Make up more questions and answers with a partner. Find another pair and ask/answer questions.

9 Look at the pictures. Use the verbs in the box to say what is going to happen.

Start like this: *The person in picture number 1 is going to … In picture number 2, …*

buy a pair of jeans • fall • get a tattoo • rain • turn right • do a test

10 Draw sketches like the ones above. Can your partner guess what is going to happen?

11 Complete the sentences with the comparative form of the words in brackets.

Example: Piercings look *worse* (bad) than tattoos in my opinion.

1 You look … (thin) than last month. Have you lost weight?
2 Tim doesn't pay attention in class. He's … (interested) in looking at the girls.
3 It's … (cold) today than it was yesterday.
4 In Australia, petrol is … (cheap) than in Germany.
5 Flying is … (fast) than going by train.
6 I like living in the city. It's … (exciting) than living in the countryside.

12 a Make your own comparisons. Use the correct forms of the words in the box.

bad • exciting • expensive • friendly • good • healthy • interesting • nice

Examples: *Coke is more expensive than milk.*
Milk is not as expensive as Coke.

boys / girls | cats / dogs | German food / American food | Coke / milk

b Use the superlative forms of the adjectives above to compare these things.

Example: *Techno is better than country, but rap is the best.*

techno / country / rap | motor bikes / scooters / mountain bikes | horror films / comedies / sci-fi

stamp collecting / watching DVDs / going shopping | the English / Scottish / German football team

INTERCULTURAL CORNER

The United Kingdom

The United Kingdom (das Vereinigte Königreich) besteht aus England, Northern Ireland, Scotland und Wales. The Republic of Ireland, der größte Teil Irlands, ist ein eigener Staat, der nicht zu Großbritannien gehört.

Im Alltag hört man meist die Bezeichnung Britain oder the UK. Vorsicht: Nicht alle Briten sind Engländer. Nur wer aus England kommt, ist English – die anderen sind Irish, Scottish oder Welsh. Wenn Sie nicht wissen, aus welchem Teil des Vereinigten Königreichs jemand kommt, fragen Sie einfach: *Where are you from?*

13 a **Hannah and Aidan are shopping. Listen. What does Hannah buy? Does Aidan buy anything? Why / Why not?**

10

b **Listen again and complete the sentences using the correct form of the adjectives in brackets and than or (not) as … as. The pictures will help you.**

1 The shop they are in at the moment is ... Billie's Boutique. (nice)
2 The blue jacket is ... the red one. (cheap)
3 The black jeans are ... the grey jeans. (expensive)
4 The grey jeans aren't ... the black ones. (tight)

DANGER!

Denken Sie daran: jeans steht immer im Plural.

~~This is~~ *These are* my jeans, not yours.

Vorsicht, wenn es um mehrere Jeans geht:

zwei (Paar) Jeans = two pairs of jeans

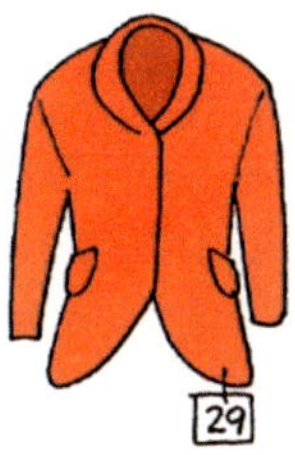

14 a **Listen again. Which of these expressions do Hannah and Aidan use?**

10

b **Use some of them to talk to your partner about what he/she is wearing.**

1. What do you think?
2. I don't like it much.
3. It's all right, I suppose.
4. Do you like ... ?
5. I prefer ...
6. What do you think of ... ?
7. That's great!
8. I like ...
9. That's really nice.

The world of work

What's important at work

1 **Read these extracts from articles about clothes at work and choose the two best headlines.**

A

First impressions count. Even though it's wrong, people usually look at our clothes and our hairstyle and decide what and who we are.
Does this mean that we can't wear interesting clothes at work? Of course not. But remember – some clothing and jewellery don't 'fit' with certain jobs. You can't wear jeans and sweatshirts if you work as an insurance agent. Some companies have a dress code that employees must follow. If you look around, you'll find that all the employees are dressed in a similar way. When you start work, look carefully at what your colleagues are wearing and copy their style. That way you can't go wrong.

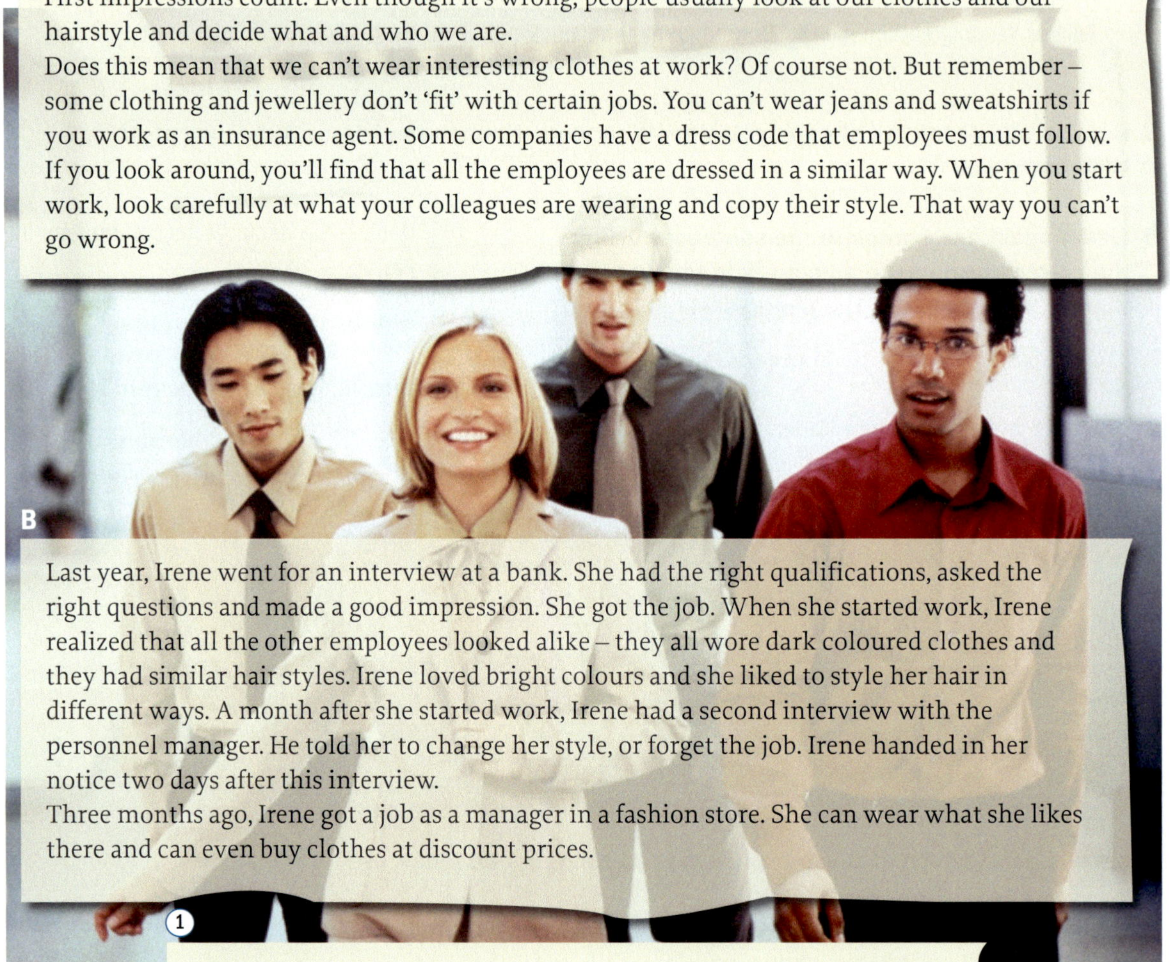

B

Last year, Irene went for an interview at a bank. She had the right qualifications, asked the right questions and made a good impression. She got the job. When she started work, Irene realized that all the other employees looked alike – they all wore dark coloured clothes and they had similar hair styles. Irene loved bright colours and she liked to style her hair in different ways. A month after she started work, Irene had a second interview with the personnel manager. He told her to change her style, or forget the job. Irene handed in her notice two days after this interview.
Three months ago, Irene got a job as a manager in a fashion store. She can wear what she likes there and can even buy clothes at discount prices.

(1) **Change your style to keep your job – is it worth it?**

(2) **What to wear for an interview**

(3) **Dress like the rest and you'll pass the test**

2 **Match the beginnings of the sentences (1–4) with the endings (a–d) to express important ideas in the texts.**

1 When you meet someone for the first time, remember that
2 If you dress like the other people at work,
3 When you go to an interview, it helps
4 In some workplaces employees have to fit in or

a they will lose their job.
b to show interest in the job.
c what we wear tells people something about us.
d you will fit in.

3 **Read text B again. Do you agree with what Irene did after her second interview? Why / Why not? What would you do in the same situation? Discuss in groups.**

4 **This questionnaire could help you decide what kind of job you should do. Choose a, b or c then check below.**

Your first step to the ideal job

1 What is your idea of an ideal workplace?
  a outside
  b inside
  c always on the move
2 What sort of clothes do you feel best in?
  a casual clothes
  b smart clothes
  c anything interesting
3 How do you like your hair?
  a as short as possible
  b neat and tidy
  c dyed
4 How important is it for you to work with people?
  a not important
  b important
  c as long as the people are fun, it's OK
5 How do you like to travel to work?
  a on foot or by bike
  b by bus or car
  c on a motorbike, a scooter or roller blades
6 What are your favourite colours?
  a greens, browns, dark reds
  b black, white, grey
  c all colours as long as they are bright

mostly a – agriculture, forestry, gardening
mostly b – office work, administration, insurance
mostly c – teaching, acting, anything creative

5 **Tom is going to start work soon. Listen. Which of these things are important for him?**

11

working with his hands • a big salary • nice colleagues • near to his home • not too much to do • responsibility • long holidays • short working hours • flexi-time • a nice office • travelling • working in a team • a company car • job satisfaction

6 **What is your dream job? Write about 80 words describing it.**

5 Eating and drinking

1 First skim the texts. Which of the photos in 'Before you start' do they refer to? Then read or listen to all the texts and do the exercises below.

12

Ⓐ

Adam was a healthy, 18-year-old US basketball player. Yesterday afternoon he collapsed and died of heart failure after a game. His teammates said that he sweated a lot during the second half of the game and he had problems breathing. He didn't talk to anybody at half-time but drank some cans of energy drink very quickly.

Somebody phoned Adam's parents and they drove to the stadium as quickly as they could. But Adam was already dead when they arrived.

Reports come in regularly about health problems which happen after people drink energy drinks and do sports. However, the team coach says he will continue giving his players energy drinks. 'I don't have any problems with that,' he said.

(119 words)

Ⓑ

Inbox - Outlook Express

File Edit View Tools Message Help

Inbox

Energy drinks – be careful!

Energy drinks contain caffeine – around 80mg per can. That's about the same as an average cup of coffee and twice as much as in a can of coke.

You can drink up to five cups of coffee a day without any problems. But if somebody drinks a lot of energy drinks in a short space of time, they might become ill: their heart could start beating very fast, they might feel dizzy and they could have circulation problems.

Of course you can enjoy a few energy drinks now and again and you won't notice anything – you'll just feel a bit fitter. But don't drink too many all at once. And remember:

energy drinks + alcohol = danger!

(113 words)

Ⓒ

LOOK IN

Energy drinks are not the only things we can take if we haven't had enough sleep.

Have you consumed any of the things in the box today?

Pat Gill, a doctor at the Institute for Heart Studies in London says, 'Everyone knows that cigarettes are dangerous. We also know that we should take less sugar and eat fewer sweets and chocolate bars. We should also try to cut down on fat and caffeine. It's really difficult to kick some habits, though.'

(88 words)

LEARNING TO LEARN

Einen Text überfliegen

Manchmal werden Sie aufgefordert, einen Text nur kurz zu überfliegen (Skim the text ...), um das Thema zu erfassen. Fangen Sie dann nicht an, Wort für Wort zu lesen - lesen Sie die Aufgabenstellung genau, schauen Sie sich die Abbildungen an, lesen Sie die Überschriften und halten Sie nach häufig wiederkehrenden Schlüsselwörtern Ausschau. Das genügt in der Regel für diese Art Aufgabe.

BEFORE YOU START

What do you do when you feel tired but you want to go to a party later on? Match the phrases a–e to the photos, then add your own ideas and rank them (1 = best).

a take a shower
b smoke
c make a cup of coffee
d have a rest
e drink an energy drink

1 
2 
3 
4 
5 

2 a Where is each text from?

email • newspaper • letter • website • magazine • advertising brochure

Example: *I think text A is from ... The second text could be from ...*

b What is the purpose of each text? Choose one or more of these phrases.

to persuade people to do something • to entertain • to give information • to shock people • to make people think • to make people laugh

Example: *I think the purpose of text A is to ...*

3 Read these statements and decide if they are true or false. Correct the false statements.

1 The basketball player had problems with his health before he died.
2 The doctors at the hospital couldn't save his life.
3 It can be dangerous to drink energy drinks and do sports.
4 Energy drinks always give people heart trouble.
5 Adding beer or whisky to an energy drink makes it work better.
6 Energy drinks are not the only things which are bad for you.
7 Doctors say smoking is OK.
8 It's easy to give up smoking or eating too many sweets if you really want to.

4 Complete the sentences with the opposites of the words in brackets. Then check in the texts.

1 When the girl arrived at the hospital, she was already ... (alive). The doctors couldn't do anything to save her. (*text A*)
2 Hurry up, please. Try to get the work done as ... (slowly) as possible. (*text A*)
3 Drinking too much alcohol can make you ... (well). (*text B*)
4 Do you ride your motorbike without a helmet? I think that's very ... (safe). (*text C*)
5 You should smoke ... (more). (*text C*)
6 Would you like to ... (increase) the number of cigarettes you smoke? Why don't you try a nicotine patch? (*text C*)

5 Match the words and phrases in columns A, B and C to make sentences about Adam's death. Don't forget to put the verbs in column B into the correct form.

A	B	C
In the US, a basketball player	consume	a lot during the second half of the game.
At half-time he	have	a lot of caffeine.
These drinks	continue	problems breathing.
Adam	collapse	to give his players energy drinks.
He also	contain	after a game.
After Adam's death, the coach	sweat	several cans of energy drink.

6 Work in groups. You have five minutes to collect as many words as possible under these headings. Which group has most words?

fast food	school meals	homemade meals
hamburger		

7 a You have found a forum about food on the internet. Complete this part with the words in the box. There are two words too many.

breakfast • drink • fast • healthy • kitchen • meals • ~~nutrition~~ • water

We get lessons about *nutrition*[1] and somebody in the … [2] decided to change the menus. They don't give us … [3] food like hamburgers and chips. We get really … [4] meals including salad, rice, fish and fruit. There are also … [5] fountains all through the school. That means when we are thirsty, we don't need to pay money for a sugary drink. We just take some water. I really enjoy my school … [6] now. What are things like at your school?

b Talk to somebody about your school canteen. Make notes about:

- the type of food you can buy there
- drinks you can get
- freshness
- variety
- healthiness

Our canteen only sells fresh food.

c Post your own message on the forum above, saying what things are like in your school canteen.

The drinks are too sugary.

Language

QUANTIFIERS (Mengenangaben)

zählbar	nicht zählbar
Yesterday I had **a few** energy drinks. You should eat **fewer** sweets and chocolate bars.	I've only eaten **a little** chocolate. I know I should take **less** sugar but it's so hard!

- **A few** wird mit zählbaren Substantiven verwendet, **a little** mit nicht zählbaren.
- Steigerungsformen: **a few** – **fewer** – **fewest**, **a little** – **less** – **least**.

SOME/ANY

Aussagen	Verneinungen	Fragen	Angebote/Bitten
You may have some problems. Somebody phoned Adam's parents. They bought something for lunch.	I don't have any problems with that. I don't know anybody who eats fish. He never eats anything at lunchtime.	Have you consumed any of these things? How can anybody eat snails? Have you got anything to drink?	Would you like some sugar in your coffee? Would you like somebody to help you? Would you like something to eat?

- Some und any bezeichnen oft eine unbestimmte Menge oder Zahl.
- Vor nicht zählbaren Substantiven wie *butter* oder *music* bedeutet some „etwas", vor zählbaren Substantiven im Plural „einige / ein paar". not ... any ist die Verneinung von some und bedeutet „kein/e". Oft gibt es für some und any jedoch keine direkte Entsprechung im Deutschen.
- Some wird vor allem in bejahten Aussagesätzen, Angeboten und Bitten verwendet.
- Any steht meist in verneinten Aussagesätzen und in Fragen.

ADVERBS OF MANNER (Adverbien der Art und Weise)

Mit Adverbien beschreibt man, wie etwas geschieht. In der Regel werden Adverbien durch Anhängen von -ly an das Adjektiv gebildet:
He drank four cans of energy drink very quickly.

Achtung: Bei Adverbien, die von Adjektiven auf -y abgeleitet sind, wird das -y zu -i:
My parents say I could easily stop smoking.

Das zu good gehörende Adverb ist well:
She's a good player. She plays well.

Einige Adverbien (fast, hard, early, late) haben die gleiche Form wie das Adjektiv:
On weekdays I have to get up early but at the weekend I get up late.
He works quite hard but sometimes he works too fast.

Practice

8 Transform these sentences by replacing the adjective with an adverb.

Example: She's a slow worker. *She works slowly.*

1 He's a dangerous driver. He drives ... .
2 They have regular meetings. They meet ... .
3 Your English is really good. You speak really ... .
4 Kathy is a fast talker. She talks ... .
5 The train came to a sudden stop. It stopped ... .
6 Ivan was late for work. He always comes ... .
7 It's very noisy in here. Tom is playing so ... .
8 I know you are careful. Please check this ... .

9 Decide which word to use to complete the sentences.

easy/easily

1 It was quite *easy* to win against them.
2 I don't like maths – it's not ...
3 You can solve that puzzle ... .

dangerous/dangerously

7 Kev drives really ... .
8 Look, Sam's got a knife – that's ... !
9 Surfing is a ... sport.

good/well

4 Jane speaks German ... .
5 He is a ... tennis player.
6 Our team played ... last season.

nice/nicely

10 That's Ken. He's very ... .
11 Looks great! You've done it very ... .
12 Behave ... and people will like you.

10 Choose the correct expression.

1 There were only *a few* / *a little* people in the canteen.
2 I tried to eat *fewer* / *less* chocolate today but I couldn't.
3 He has to save money so smokes *fewer* / *less* cigarettes now.
4 Only take *a few* / *a little* piece of cake.
5 My mum has cut down on fat. She eats *fewer* / *less* butter now.
6 Drinking *a few* / *a little* energy drinks is OK.
7 There are *a few* / *a little* bottles of beer in the fridge.
8 There are *fewer* / *less* nice cafés in our town now.

11 a Complete these sentences with some or any.

1 Would you like ... water?
2 Is there ... butter?
3 ... people don't like meat.
4 There's ... sugar in the cupboard.
5 I don't want ... coffee, thanks.
6 Are there ... shops around here?
7 There aren't ... pizzas left.
8 Add ... salt to the soup.
9 I never have ... breakfast.

b Now complete the following sentences with anybody, anything, somebody or something.

1 Does ... know where the ketchup is?
2 ... is cooking fish.
3 There's ... in my salad. I think it's alive!
4 I can't eat ... with nuts in it.
5 ... has eaten my yoghurt!
6 He always eats the same things. He never tries ... new.
7 Hm. ... smells good here. Are you making a pizza?
8 Has ... been to the Lucky Chinese Restaurant? Is it good?

12 a Listen and find out where Pete and Linda decide to eat.

13

1

2

3

4

5

6

INTERCULTURAL CORNER

Essen in Großbritannien

Wenn Sie in Großbritannien essen gehen, werden Sie manche Unterschiede zu Deutschland finden. Hier sind einige Beispiele:

- Eine Würstchenbude suchen Sie in Großbritannien umsonst. Statt Currywurst mit Pommes sind dort **Fish and chips** verbreitet. (Achtung: Pommes frites heißen in GB **chips**, in den USA (**French**) **fries**. Unsere Chips heißen in GB **crisps**.) Und natürlich gibt es auch den hierzulande üblichen **Kebab**, indische oder chinesische Schnellimbisse oder **burger takeaways.**
- Eine direkte Entsprechung für „Guten Appetit" gibt es im Englischen nicht. Man kann **Enjoy your meal** sagen, aber oft sagt man zu den Tischnachbarn nichts vor dem Essen.

b **Listen again. Which of the following phrases do you hear?**

a I'm starving.
b Shall we get a burger?
c No, I don't want a burger.
d I know you usually prefer takeaways.
e I fancy a sit-down meal today.
f We can go to McDonald's.
g Do you like McDonald's?
h I don't want to go to McDonald's.
i What about a pizza?
j I don't like pizza.
k Let's go back to the snack bar.
l I'd rather have a salad.

13 **Now Pete and Linda are ordering their meal at a snack bar. Complete the conversation by putting the sentences (a–k) in the correct order (1–11). Then listen and check.**

14

ASSISTANT Can I take your order?
PETE Yes, I'd like a salami pizza, please.
ASSISTANT Would you like any salad with it?
PETE ...

a I'll have a coke.
b Yes. I'll have a coke, too, please.
c I'll have two cheeseburgers and chips.
d What would you like to drink with your pizza?
e How much is the salad?
f £2.75.
g No, thanks. I won't have any salad.
h Single or double cheeseburgers?
i And would you like something to drink, too?
j Single, please.
k And you?

14 **a** **Make a list of snack bars, cafés and restaurants in your area. Talk to a partner about where you would like to eat. Use expressions from exercise 12.**

b **Work with a partner and order a meal in Snacky Snacks.**

PARTNER A: You are the customer.
PARTNER B: You are the assistant. Go to File 2 on page 148.

Now swap roles.

The world of work

Talking to customers

1 Read these notices about talking to customers. The people in the pictures below have not read the notices. What are they doing wrong? Tell them how to behave correctly.

FACE TO FACE

- GREET THE CUSTOMER IMMEDIATELY
- ASK HOW YOU CAN HELP
- BE POLITE
- SMILE
- SAY GOODBYE TO THE CUSTOMER AND WISH THEM A NICE DAY

ON THE PHONE

- ASK FOR THE CALLER'S NAME AND WRITE IT DOWN IMMEDIATELY
- USE THE CALLER'S NAME TWO OR THREE TIMES DURING THE PHONE CALL
- TAKE NOTES
- BE POLITE
- THANK THE CUSTOMER FOR THEIR CALL AND SAY GOODBYE

2 A friend whose English isn't very good asks you to explain the things on the notices above. Tell your friend in German about the points on the notices.

3 **Match 1–6 with a–f to form a short telephone conversation, then role-play the conversation with a partner.**

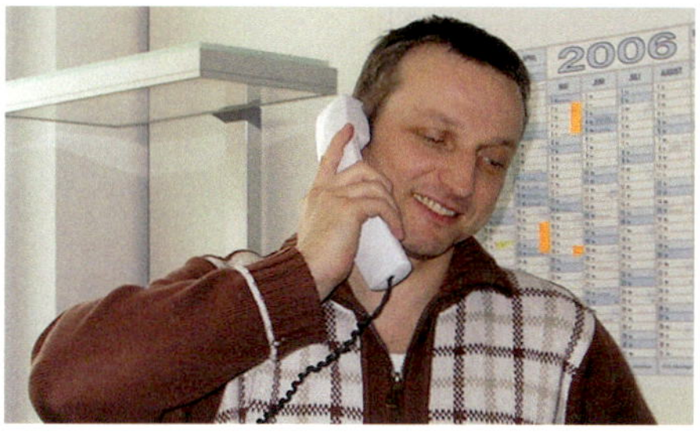

1 Garfield's Limited, Chris Downs speaking. How can I help you?
2 Sorry, Mr Timm isn't in the office just now.
3 Sorry, I don't know. Can I take a message?
4 Does Mr Timm have your number?
5 0985 295633. Fine, I'll ask Mr Timm to call you back.
6 You're welcome. Goodbye.

a Yes, please. Tell him I called and ask him to phone me back.
b Thanks.
c Oh. When will he be back?
d Goodbye.
e This is Sara Schmidt speaking. Can I speak to Mr Timm, please?
f I think so, but here it is just in case. It's 0985 295633.

4 15 **Gregor Mann is an office management trainee at ILPRO GmbH. Today he's working on the switchboard. Complete the phone call with the expressions from the box. Then listen and check.**

didn't understand • have your name, please? • ~~I help you~~? • I'll tell • in her office • put you through • repeat that, please? • spell that, please? • take a message? • the line, please

GREGOR ILPRO, Mann. Guten Tag.
CALLER Erm. Gu ... Gu ... . I'm sorry, do you speak English?
GREGOR Yes I do. How can *I help you*[1]?
CALLER I'd like to speak to Vanessa Bach, please.
GREGOR Can I ...[2]?
CALLER Of course. It's Jennie Hood.
GREGOR Hold ...[3], Ms Hood. I'll ...[4].

GREGOR I'm sorry, Ms Hood. I'm afraid Ms Bach isn't ...[5] at the moment. Can I ...[6]?
CALLER Oh, yes please. Could you ask Ms Bach to call me at Zarsky & Co. in Glasgow?
GREGOR Erm. Zarsky? Sorry, could you ...[7]?
CALLER Yes, of course. That's Z-A-R-S-K-Y. The number is 0141 976 8600.
GREGOR Sorry, I ...[8]. It's a bad line. Could you ...[9]?
CALLER 0141 976 8600.
GREGOR 0141 976 8600. Thanks. ...[10] Ms Bach that you called, Ms Hood. I'm sure she'll get back to you soon.
CALLER Thanks. Goodbye.
GREGOR Goodbye.

5 **Work with a partner. Role-play the telephone conversation using your own details.**

6 Jobs and training

1 **These people are talking about jobs and training. Scan the texts quickly and match the speakers to the photos. Then listen, or read what they say.**

Annie

Carol

Bella

16

A I enjoyed English and French so I wanted to do something with foreign languages when I left school. That's why I chose to train to be a foreign language correspondent. The course looked interesting because it includes commercial correspondence and translating, but up till now it's been mostly bookkeeping. I've done that already at school. I'm so disappointed. I've applied for jobs, but I can't get anything without a qualification. My mum says I'm lucky to have a place at college, but sometimes I wonder. How long have I been on the course? Six months – but it seems like six years. It's so boring.

B Primary school was OK but I hated secondary school. The older pupils there bullied me all the time. Do you know how that feels? You can't win. You just have to get out. I dropped out of school before my final exams and took a job in a bakery. I don't like it much. The conditions are bad – it's hot and dusty – and I have to get up really early. But I'm sticking it out because there's one good thing about it – day release classes. I go to college once a week and that's a lot of fun. And when I get my certificate I can get a better job.

C I had a lot of problems at school. I didn't pass any exams and I was frustrated. I caused a lot of trouble. Then, just before I left school they gave me some tests and found out that I have a learning difficulty. I've felt a lot better since they told me about that – I didn't feel stupid anymore. I went to special classes and that helped a lot. When I left school I got a place here and did three years training. I've finished my training now and they've taken me on permanently. I can't believe my luck. I love working with children.

(318 words)

BEFORE YOU START

1 **Which did you enjoy more – primary school or secondary school? Which subjects did you like/dislike? Tell your group.**

2 **What do you like/dislike about vocational college? Why?**

2 Who says what? Match these statements to Annie, Bella or Carol.

Example: "When I was a kid, I liked school." *Bella*

1 "Why did I start this course?"
2 "I don't like my job, but vocational college is good."
3 "You don't need to have great exam marks to get a job you like."
4 "Problems with other pupils forced me to leave school early."
5 "I was a trouble-maker at school."
6 "I've always liked learning languages."

3 Can you remember the words from the text which match these definitions? They all have to do with school.

1 where you are learning today (Carol)
2 place where young children learn (Bella)
3 place where older teenagers learn (Bella)
4 learners (Bella)
5 to leave school before taking examinations (Bella)
6 the last tests you do before you leave school (Bella)
7 problems at school, for example with reading and writing (Annie)
8 not intelligent (Annie)

4 Complete the sentences with the words in the box. They all have to do with training.

bookkeeping • commercial correspondence • course • day release classes • foreign languages • translating

1 We write a lot of business letters in our ... classes.
2 I don't go to the factory on a Friday. I go to my ... instead.
3 We always use dictionaries when we are ...
4 My ... takes two years.
5 The ... classes are difficult for me. I'm not very good at counting.
6 ... are great! I love Italian and French.

5 **Use a dictionary to find the corresponding …**

a) nouns:	disappointed (line 4)	lucky (line 5)
b) verbs:	test (line 15)	training (line 18)
c) adjectives:	qualification (line 5)	difficulty (line 16)
d) adverbs:	bad (line 11)	special (line 17)

LEARNING TO LEARN

Vorsicht Wörterbuch!

Wenn Sie ein Wort nachschlagen, denken Sie daran, dass Wörter mehr als eine Bedeutung haben können Nehmen Sie also nicht gleich die erste Übersetzung, die das Wörterbuch anbietet. Achten Sie auf die Hinweise in Klammern und die Abkürzungen – sie werden meist vorne im Wörterbuch erklärt. Wichtig sind vor allem:

- die Wortart: für Adjektiv steht oft **adj**, für Nomen **n** oder **noun**, für Verb **v** oder **vb**, für Relativpronomen **rel pron** usw.
- die Anzahl: für Einzahl steht oft **sg** (Singular), für Mehrzahl **pl** (Plural)
- das Sachgebiet: z.B. **mech** für Mechanik, **econ** für Wirtschaft
- ob ein Verb regelmäßige (**reg**) oder unregelmäßige (**irreg**) Vergangenheitsformen bildet
- nötige Ergänzungen wie **sth** (something) = etwas, oder **sb** (somebody) = jemand, jemanden

6 **Talk about Annie, Bella or Carol. Make notes and tell your partners.**

ANNIE
How did she feel when she was at school?
Why did she cause trouble at school?
Why is she so happy at work?
Was it really 'luck' that helped Annie get the job? Why?

BELLA
Why was she unhappy at secondary school?
Did she do the right thing when she dropped out?
Why is she so happy at college?
Should Bella stick it out in the bakery? Why?

CAROL
Why did she choose to become a foreign language correspondent?
Why is she bored?
Why does her mum say that she's lucky to have a place at college?
Should Carol continue with her course? Why?

7 **Your American pen pal has asked you about your experience at school. Write 80–100 words including the following points:**

- what you liked and didn't like
- any problems you had
- your favourite / least favourite subject (why)
- what you do with other students after school

Language

PRESENT PERFECT (vollendete Gegenwart)

Aussagen	Verneinungen	Fragen	Kurzantworten
I've (I have) done that already. It's (It has) been mostly bookkeeping.	Paul hasn't (has not) started his training yet.	How long have you been on the course?	Yes, I have. / No, I haven't (have not).

- Das present perfect wird für Vorgänge und Handlungen verwendet, die irgendwann einmal – oder noch nie – stattgefunden haben, ohne Angabe des Zeitpunkts. Erwähnt man den Zeitpunkt, steht das simple past:
  Have you been to America? *Warst du mal in Amerika?* (unbestimmter Zeitpunkt)
  Yes, I went there last year. *Ja, ich war letztes Jahr da.* (bestimmter Zeitpunkt)
- Man benutzt auch das present perfect, wenn man sagen will, dass etwas in der Vergangenheit begonnen hat und bis in die Gegenwart andauert, also noch nicht abgeschlossen ist.
- Das present perfect wird mit have / has + Partizip Perfekt (3. Form des Verbs) gebildet. (Die Formen unregelmäßiger Verben finden Sie in der Übersicht auf Seite 242.)
- Bei der Verneinung steht not oder never zwischen have / has und dem Verb.
- Bei Fragen ohne Fragewort steht have / has am Satzanfang.
- Das present perfect wird häufig mit folgenden Signalwörtern gebraucht: already, always, before, ever, How long ... ?, just, lately, never, recently, up till now, (not) yet.
- Since und for (= seit) stehen im Englischen mit dem present perfect.
  Achtung: Im Deutschen steht in diesem Fällen meist die Gegenwart.
  I've lived in Dublin for three years.
  Ich wohne seit drei Jahren in Dublin.

DANGER!

since/for

I've felt a lot better since last Sunday.
(since = „seit“ + konkreter Zeitpunkt: seit wann?)

I haven't been to the disco for three weeks.
(for = „seit“ + Zeitdauer: wie lange schon?)

Practice

8 Make complete sentences using the present perfect.

Example: you / do your homework / yet?
Have you done your homework yet?

1 I / already / finish it
2 Paul / just / start his training
3 you / do this kind of exercise before?
4 Annie / always / want to be a nursery nurse
5 she / never / be so happy
6 you / ever / think about the future?
7 he / be very busy recently
8 I / get good marks up till now

9 Give short answers.

Example: Have you spoken to the teacher about your exam results yet? – Yes, *I have.*

1 Have you seen Mary lately? – Yes, ...
2 Has John phoned his mum? – Yes, ...
3 Have Tony and Mary been shopping yet? – No, ...
4 Has the teacher looked at your exercise book recently? – No, ...
5 Has Lucy invited you to her birthday party? – Yes, ...
6 Have you ever been to France? – No, ...

10 Complete the questions for the answers.

Example: *Have you seen* Star Wars Episode 3? – No, I haven't seen it.

1 How many people ... ? – I've invited fifteen people.
2 How long ... ? – He's been here for six months.
3 ... to the disco recently? – No, I haven't been there for weeks.
4 How long ... ? – I've known Sarah for almost a year.
5 ... to London? – Yes, I went there last year. It's great.
6 ... any Stephen King books? – Yes, I've read all of them.
7 How many text messages ... ? – I've sent five text messages so far.
8 ... your holiday? – No, we haven't planned anything yet.

11 a Choose since or for. Say why.

Example: He hasn't phoned *since/for* a week.
He hasn't phoned for a week. (Zeitdauer → for)

1 I've lived in this town *since/for* Easter.
2 We've been at this college *since/for* six months.
3 John has been on a diet *since/for* a month.
4 Patty has only written once *since/for* Christmas.
5 Have you seen Mike *since/for* last week?
6 My grandma has been in hospital *since/for* two weeks.
7 They haven't spoken to us *since/for* a long time.
8 He hasn't been to school *since/for* ages.

b Translate the sentences into German.

12 Complete the sentences with the simple past or the present perfect form of the verbs in brackets.

1 The Berlin Wall ... (come down) in 1989.
2 How long ... (you / learn) English?
3 I ... (just / eat) in the new canteen. The food's great.
4 I ... (not have) time to do my homework yesterday.
5 My sister ... (visit) New York several times.
6 Brian ... (crash) his scooter two weeks ago.
7 Irene ... (not come) yet. She's always late.
8 (you / hear) ... the latest? Tracey and Ben ... (split up) last week.

13 **Chris is talking to a friend about college. Listen and choose the correct ending or endings for each sentence.**

17

1 Chris
   a was at the club with Babs last week.
   b hasn't been to the club for a long time.
   c has been too tired to go out recently.

2 Chris started at the hotel
   a at 5 o'clock this morning.
   b 5 weeks ago.
   c 5 months ago.

3 Chris goes to college
   a fulltime.
   b once a week.
   c only on Thursdays.

4 Chris and his mates
   a never go out together after college.
   b don't enjoy college.
   c are tired after college.

5 Chris works
   a from six a.m. till two p.m.
   b from two p.m. till ten p.m.
   c at different times.

6 Chris
   a has just had two weeks holiday.
   b gets one free day a week.
   c is going to have a great holiday soon.

INTERCULTURAL CORNER

Urlaub ist nicht gleich Urlaub

In Deutschland haben es Arbeitnehmer mit 28–30 bezahlten Urlaubstagen im Jahr vergleichsweise gut. In Großbritannien sind es ca. 20, in anderen EU-Ländern sind es zwischen 25 und 30.
In den USA hingegen fangen Arbeitnehmer mit ca. 10 Urlaubstagen an. Zwar bekommen sie nach einigen Jahren Beschäftigung längeren Urlaub, doch lange nicht so viel wie in der EU.

14 **Take turns to interview each other in English about your training. Make notes so that you can tell the class about your partner.**

College is a lot of fun.

It's fine / good / bad / awful.

Why did you choose ... ?

How long have you been on the course?

No, I'm not happy with ...

Are you pleased with / happy about ... ?

15 **A careers adviser visits your school and talks about the following jobs.**

a **Match the jobs to the pictures.**

① ② ③ ④ ⑤ ⑥ ⑦

a mechanic
b shop assistant
c social worker
d nurse
e nursery nurse
f baker
g programmer

b **Would you like to do any of these jobs in the future? Why?**

The world of work

Job satisfaction

1 a **You are going to read a short article about European employees' feelings about their work. Can you guess which of these things workers are satisfied or dissatisfied with?**

pay • holidays • workmates • working hours • sick leave • the job • the boss

b **Now read the article. Were your guesses correct? Does anything surprise you?**

More than 500,000 European employees took part in a survey asking how they feel about their job, their boss, their workmates, pay and benefits.
The survey found out that most employees enjoy their job. They are also satisfied with holidays, paid sick leave and their working hours. People only complained about their pay and the boss.
In the Netherlands 43% of the employees who took part in the survey said they were unhappy with their pay; in Switzerland the number rose to 56%. 65% of employees in Britain said that their wages were too low.
Though more than half of the workers said their boss was OK, almost 40% didn't like their boss. Most of the people who didn't like their boss worked in the UK and France.
Even though, most of Europe's workers are happy with the job they do and they identify with the company they work for. Most important, almost everyone gets on well with their workmates. For a lot of employees, going to the canteen at lunchtime or having a chat in the coffee break is what is most important at work.

2 **Copy and complete this bar chart in your exercise book.**

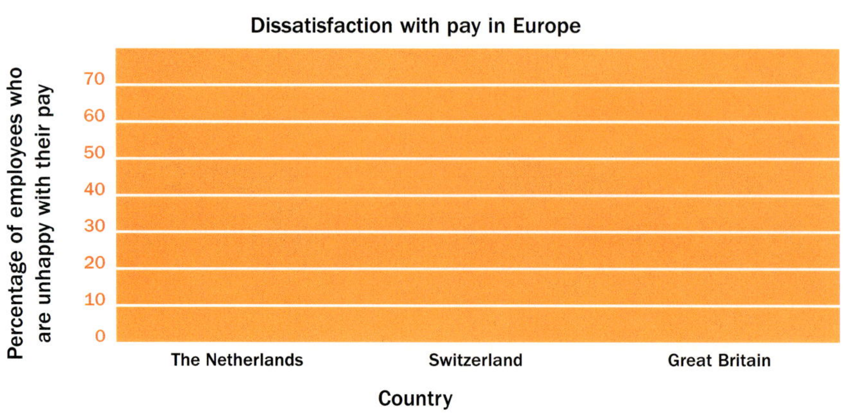

3 **Decide if these statements are true or false. Correct the false statements.**

1 People in the USA took part in a survey about their work.
2 More than half a million people answered the questions.
3 Most of the people who took part in the survey said they were happy at work.
4 More than half of the employees in Britain are satisfied with their pay.
5 Most of the workers do not like their boss.
6 Most people dislike the company they work for.
7 A lot of employees do not like their co-workers.
8 Employees think that breaks are a waste of time.

4 **In groups decide on a title for the text. Which group has the best title?**

5 a **Listen to three people talking about their day. Match the pictures to the speakers.**

18

b **Listen again. How do the people help each other?**

c **Listen for a third time. Which of these phrases do you hear?**

1 Have you got that?
2 How are you?
3 I just can't get the hang of it.
4 Never mind.
5 No idea.
6 Sure.
7 What about you?
8 You can say that again.

Now match the phrases above with the German in the box.

Alles klar? • Das kannst du laut sagen. • Ich krieg's einfach nicht hin. • Keine Ahnung. • Macht nichts. • Na klar. • Und du? • Wie geht's?

d **Together with a partner, choose one of the dialogues and write a continuation. Then role-play your dialogue for the class.**

7 That's life (or is it?)

1 *Twenty* magazine is running a series of articles about TV programmes. This one is about soap operas. Listen, or read the article. Does the author think watching soaps is good or bad?

19

IT'S ALL RIGHT, MUM, I'M NOT DESTROYING MY BRAIN CELLS – I'M ONLY RELAXING

by Janie Davidson

Most of us watch soap operas. The biggest teenage soap in Germany is *Gute Zeiten, schlechte Zeiten* (Good times, bad times). What makes it so popular? Well, just look at the title. Everybody has good times, everybody has bad times. A soap is just like real life.

One of the main topics is problems. We all share at least some of them with our favourite soap characters: our parents tell us what we must and mustn't do; we have disagreements with friends; trouble at school; no money .... If you're lucky, you'll be able to talk about a soap character's problems with another fan – and that might even help you work out your own problems.

It's great to talk about the latest episode of a soap. The characters are just like friends. Sometimes we might even like them more than we like certain people in the family. Because we like them, we may try to be like them. We identify with them; we copy their clothes and style; we adopt their ideas and attitudes.

Some people say there's a danger that soap fans might try to live the kind of life which is shown in soaps, for example, spending a lot of money on designer clothes or longing for a really expensive car. That's why some kids are not allowed to watch soaps. But their parents shouldn't worry: we can still tell the difference between TV and real life.

Or at least, we can tell the difference between soap and reality as the plots are sometimes totally unbelievable! Do you remember the girl who had a one-night stand with that Australian guy just before her wedding? Then the guy appeared at the church. He was the bridegroom's brother, just home from Australia for the wedding. I thought that was very unrealistic.

Could watching every day turn you into a soap junkie? A friend of mine got really annoyed if he missed his soap. He always had to get home in time for the start of the episode – until he met a really nice girl and started spending his evenings with her – just like in a soap.

(370 words)

BEFORE YOU START

What is your favourite soap opera or telenovela? How often do you watch it? Why do you like it? Make a list, ranking your top three favourites. Compare with the rest of the class.

2 **Match the beginnings and endings of these statements to make sentences about soap operas.**

1 We like soap operas
2 Soap opera characters sometimes
3 It may help us
4 Some fans prefer soap opera characters
5 Critics of soap operas say that fans
6 Most soap opera fans
7 Some of the soap stories
8 The author's friend doesn't have time

a to real people they know.
b are not like real life.
c know what is real and what is a story.
d when we talk about their problems with a friend.
e for soaps now because he has a girlfriend.
f might do stupid things to be like the characters.
g worry about the same things that we worry about.
h because they reflect reality.

3 a **Look at these words from the text. Use your dictionaries to find the opposites.**

a real (line 6)
b more (line 18)
c a lot of (line 25)
d expensive (line 27)
e remember (line 33)
f always (line 41)

b **Now use the words you have found to complete these sentences.**

1 This T-shirt is nice and it doesn't cost too much. It's really … .
2 I'm too fat. I've decided to eat … so that I can lose weight.
3 I had such a strange dream last night. It was so … .
4 Oh, you have got some milk left. Could you give me …, please?
5 Don't … to phone your mum!
6 I … watch soaps. I hate them.

4 **Match the types of TV programmes (a–f) to these programme titles.**

Example: *1 e,*

1 World Cup Special
2 The Million Dollar Question
3 Today
4 The Wonderful World of Elephants
5 Don Drake Investigates
6 Chart Review

a game show
b documentary
c music programme
d news broadcast
e sports programme
f detective story

5 a **Talk about TV programmes you watch, and agree on which is the best / the most interesting one. Make notes about:**

- how often it is on and how often you watch it,
- what it is about,
- why you like it.

b **Use your notes to write an email to an American friend. Tell him/her about your favourite TV programme. Write 80–100 words.**

Language

MODAL VERBS (Modalverben)

can / be able to (können)

- Can drückt eine Fähigkeit oder eine Möglichkeit aus.
- Can wird nur in der Gegenwart benutzt. Das simple past lautet could/couldn't. Andere Zeiten werden mit dem Ersatzverb to be able to gebildet.
  We can still tell the difference between TV and real life.
  If you're lucky, you'll be able to talk about your favourite soap with another fan.

must / have to (müssen)

- Must und have to drücken eine Verpflichtung oder Notwendigkeit aus.
- Must wird nur in der Gegenwart benutzt.
  You must do your homework before you watch TV.
- Have to kann in allen Zeiten verwendet werden.
  Do I have to wait till your soap opera is finished?
  He always had to get home in time.
- Die Verneinung von must ist not have to (nicht müssen).
  You don't have to pay for that. It's free.

DANGER!

Achtung:

must not / mustn't = nicht dürfen
Let's go home now. We mustn't be late.

be allowed to (dürfen)

- Erlaubnis und Verbot in zusammengesetzten Zeitformen wie present perfect oder will future werden mit dem Ersatzverb to be allowed to ausgedrückt:
  We won't be allowed to watch that film. It's too late.

could, may und might (könnte/n)

- Could, may und might drücken eine Möglichkeit aus.
  Could watching soap operas turn you into a soap junkie?
  We may try to be like them. We might even like them more than we like our friends.

should/shouldn't (sollen / nicht sollen, sollte/n)

- Should/Shouldn't werden benutzt, um Ratschläge zu erteilen bzw. um auf eine Pflicht hinzuweisen.
  What should I do now?
  You shouldn't watch too much TV.

Practice

6 **Complete the sentences with can/can't, could/couldn't or a form of be able to.**

Examples: I'm sorry. I ... (not come) to your party next weekend.
I'm sorry. I can't come to your party next weekend.
Jill spoke too fast. I ... (not understand) her at all.
Jill spoke too fast. I couldn't understand her at all.

1 I don't have any money so I ... (not go shopping) next weekend.
2 No, I ... (not speak Spanish) but I ... (speak Italian).
3 Tony was very young when he got his driving licence. He ... (drive a car) when he was 18.
4 ... (you/swim) when you were a child?
5 Paul ... (not come to the party) last weekend. He was really sad about that.
6 Even now Millie ... (not understand) why Andi left her.
7 We are locked out. We ... (not find) our keys.
8 ... (you/come) home early next time?

7 **Complete the sentences with must or a form of have to.**

Examples: I *must* get my hair cut soon.
Paul's mum was ill so he *had to* go home to look after her.

1 He ... ask his dad for money yesterday.
2 It's late. You ... go now.
3 Sally was nearly late for her meeting with Dave. She ... get a taxi.
4 I went to school by bus yesterday. The bus was full and I ... stand all the way.
5 You'll ... come a bit earlier tomorrow. There's a lot to do.
6 Tim forgot his keys again yesterday. He ... climb into the house through the window.
7 The cat was stuck up a tree. We ... call the fire brigade to get her down.
8 You ... go and see that film. It's really great.

8 **What should the people in the pictures do? Choose a suitable phrase and use should.**

Example: *The person in picture number 1 should ...*

buy flea powder • take those stupid shoes off • stop drinking • call the police • go to bed • tell him she doesn't want to see him any more

9 **Write sentences with might or might not.**

Example: Perhaps I'll go swimming this afternoon.
I might go swimming this afternoon.

1 I think Dave will come round this evening.
2 If we're lucky, it will snow at Christmas.
3 Maybe I'll be out late tonight.
4 Perhaps Gina won't come to the party.
5 I probably won't watch DVDs at the weekend.
6 I suppose my parents won't like the new show.

10 **Ask each other about your plans for the weekend. Choose from the list and answer with may, might or must.**

Example: A: *What are you doing at the weekend?*
B: *I'm not sure. I really must clean my room.*

- *clean my room*
- *visit my grandma*
- *go to the cinema*
- *watch TV*
- *try out my new computer game*
- *see my Dad*
- *look after my sister*
- *buy a guitar*

11 **Choose mustn't or don't have to and complete the sentences.**

1 Penny phoned to say she'll be late. We *mustn't / don't have to* wait for her.
2 My dad's mobile phone is working again so I *mustn't / don't have to* write him any more emails.
3 Tony will be at the party but you *mustn't / don't have to* talk to him if you don't want to.
4 It's a great film. You *mustn't / don't have to* miss it.
5 Look after your ID card. You *mustn't / don't have to* lose it.
6 You *mustn't / don't have to* do all the housework. I'll help you.
7 I *mustn't / don't have to* buy a present for Carol. My mum's going to buy something.
8 You *mustn't / don't have to* forget to turn off the lights.

12 **a** **You have five minutes to write questions using these modal verbs.**

have to • should • can • could • be allowed to

b **After your teacher has checked the questions, pass them to the group on your left. Listen to their answers together with the rest of the class.**

INTERCULTURAL CORNER

Fernsehgewohnheiten in den USA und Europa

Im Alter von 18 Jahren haben amerikanische Teenager durchschnittlich mehr Zeit vor dem Fernseher (25.000 Stunden) verbracht als im Klassenzimmer. 56% der amerikanischen Jugendlichen zwischen 13 und 17 haben einen Fernseher in ihrem Zimmer.

Während EU-Bürger im Durchschnitt 204 Minuten (drei Stunden und 24 Minuten) täglich fernsehen, sind es bei US-Amerikanern 260 Minuten.

Aber nicht nur in der Dauer, sondern auch in der Funktion des Fernsehens gibt es Unterschiede. In südlichen Ländern läuft der Fernseher z. B. oft nur im Hintergrund – beim Essen oder in geselliger Runde. In anderen Ländern, so in Deutschland, wird der Fernseher normalerweise wesentlich bewusster eingeschaltet.

LEARNING TO LEARN

Wie kann ich mein Hörverständnis verbessern?

- Je häufiger Sie Englisch hören, desto leichter wird es Ihnen fallen, Muttersprachler zu verstehen. Möglichkeiten zum Englischhören gibt es viele: Radio und Fernsehen (BBC World, CNN), DVDs in Originalfassung, Audiofiles aus dem Internet (auf www.bbc.co.uk kann man sich z. B. BBC-Radiosendungen als Livestream anhören).
- Überlegen Sie sich vor dem Hören, worum es in dem Text geht. (Welche Thematik? Worauf lässt der Titel schließen? Gibt es Fotos oder Illustrationen?)
- Versuchen Sie beim ersten Zuhören, den Text sinngemäß zu erfassen, und bleiben Sie nicht an Einzelwörtern hängen. Erst beim zweiten Mal sollten Sie auf Einzelheiten achten.

14 20 **Listen to Darren, Monica and Paul in the latest episode of *For Love or Money* and find the correct ending for each sentence.**

1 Darren and Monica are
- a enemies.
- b secret lovers.
- c colleagues.

2 Monica loves
- a Paul.
- b Paul and Darren.
- c Darren.

3 Paul was hurt in
- a a car crash.
- b a skiing accident.
- c an accident at work.

4 Paul will
- a be able to stop using his wheelchair soon.
- b have to use his wheelchair forever.
- c have an operation soon.

5 Darren thinks Monica should
- a look after Paul.
- b not look after Paul.
- c find someone else to look after Paul.

6 Paul tells Monica she should
- a stay with him.
- b go away with Darren.
- c give up Darren.

The world of work

Talking about your job

1 **Read the text and do the task which follows.**

Training for work can be very rewarding but it can also be tiring and depressing. Here are some personal stories.

Alan Watson is eighteen. He works in a home for the elderly.

"I'm training to be a care assistant for the elderly. I was brought up by my grandparents and I like old people. I enjoy the work but it's sometimes difficult. I have to lift some of the people into their wheelchairs and that's tiring. Apart from that, a lot of the old people are very forgetful so you need a lot of patience."

Janice Green is nineteen. She's training as an office management assistant in a company which imports food from all over the world.

"I chose this job because I wanted to use my foreign languages. My boss says I'll be allowed to write orders and letters later, but at the moment I'm checking parcels when they come in. It's not very interesting and I'm getting a bit bored. I hope I'll be able to do something more demanding soon."

Maggie Simmons is twenty-one. She is a trainee police officer.

"I knew quite early in my life that I wanted to work in the police force. It's OK working shifts but it's hard sometimes when we have difficult people like junkies and alcoholics. Some of the people we deal with are very nice, though. When we can help people, it's very satisfying."

Decide if these statements are true or false. Correct the false statements.

1 Alan likes his job.
2 He gets angry when the people he looks after can't remember things.
3 Janice is very happy with her job.
4 She has to write to customers abroad.
5 She is looking forward to doing more interesting work later.
6 Maggie works as an office manager at a police station.
7 She doesn't mind working at different times.
8 She doesn't like any of the people who come to the police station.

2 a Colleagues of Alan, Janice and Maggie call a radio show and talk about the trainees. Who is each person talking about?

21

Example: *I think the first speaker is talking about ...*

b Listen again. What do they say about the three trainees? Take notes.

c Now use your notes and the text on the opposite page to write a short profile of one of the trainees (ca. 50 words).

Example: *Maggie is in her early twenties. She always wanted to work in the police force. She ...*

3 Give your opinion on the following statements from the radio show.

1 Police work must be very difficult.
2 It's often difficult to work with the elderly.
3 Trainees often get boring, routine jobs to do.

4 Work in groups of three. Say things about Janice, Maggie and Alan. Your partner has to find out who you are talking about.

Example: A: *This person works with old people.*
B: *That must be Alan. Now this person ...*
C: *I think that's ...*

5 a What do Alan, Janice and Maggie have to do in their work? Match the drawings with their jobs.

1

2

3

4

5

6

b Which of these things would you enjoy doing? Which wouldn't you like to do? Say why.

8 The right job

1 **Scan the text quickly, then match each title a–g to the correct section 1–7.**

Example: *1 b*

a Arrive on time
b Do some research
c Dress smartly
d Be polite and friendly
e Ask questions
f Tell the truth
g Plan your answers

22

Get that job! Seven tips for your first job interview

Before the interview

1

Find out everything that you can about the company. The company website is the best place to start. How many employees work for the company? What are its main products or services? Is the company part of a larger group? Use this information in the interview to impress the interviewer. It could be the 'x-factor' which makes you the best candidate.

2

Choose suitable clothes for the interview. First impressions are very important: an untidy appearance says to the interviewer, 'I'm careless and lazy'. A suit might not be necessary, but your clothes should be clean and smart – even if the job is in a dirty workplace.

3

Think about questions the interviewer may ask, and plan some answers. Some typical interview questions are: 'What is your biggest strength?', 'What is your biggest weakness?' and of course 'Why do you want this job?' Good preparation always helps you to feel (and look) more confident. A practice interview with a friend is a good idea.

4

Think of some questions you can ask the interviewer. The questions should be intelligent ones about the job or the company. Don't just ask about salary and holidays: the interviewer might think that you aren't interested in the job itself.

At the interview

5

Make sure that you arrive on time. A candidate who arrives late won't get the job, unless he or she has a very, very good excuse. If something unexpected happens, and you really can't arrive on time, phone the company to let them know that you are going to be late.

6

Be friendly and polite. Smile when you meet the interviewer. Try to be confident, but also respectful – don't sit down until the interviewer asks you to. You should never try to tell jokes or make the interviewer laugh.

7

Never lie to the interviewer about your qualifications or work experience. Remember, the person you are speaking to may have interviewed hundreds of people, so he or she probably knows that you are lying. Don't take the risk.

(345 words)

BEFORE YOU START

You have a job / an apprenticeship interview tomorrow.
Make a list of six things you are going to do before the interview.
Now compare notes with a partner and agree on the six best ideas.
Example: *Check the address ...*

2 **Read or listen to the text. Are these statements true or false, according to the text? Correct the false ones.**

Example: You don't need to find out about the company before the interview.
False. You need to find out everything that you can about the company before the interview.

1 Company websites don't usually have much useful information for job candidates.
2 You don't always need to wear a suit for a job interview.
3 Before the interview, you should think about questions that the interviewer might ask.
4 The candidate shouldn't ask questions in a job interview.
5 It doesn't matter if you are a few minutes late for the interview.
6 You should smile at the interviewer when you meet him/her.
7 Telling jokes in the interview is a good idea.
8 Interviewers can usually recognize a lie.

3 **What are these people doing wrong? Explain what they should do instead.**

Example: *The person in picture number 1 hasn't prepared answers. She should ...*

4 **Find the words in the text.**

a **Find the word which has the opposite meaning.**

Example: worst (section 1) ↔ *best*

1 to finish (section 1)   2 dirty (section 2)   3 early (section 5)

b **Find the word which has the same or a similar meaning.**

4 firm (section 1)   5 workers (section 1)   6 appropriate (section 2)

c **Find the corresponding noun.**

7 to produce (section 1)   8 strong (section 3)   9 to prepare (section 3)

5 **Your friend has a job interview next week. What should he/she do? Summarize the text on page 70 in German. Write one sentence for each section.**

LEARNING TO LEARN

Schriftliche Mediation: Den Inhalt eines englischen Textes im Deutschen wiedergeben

Manchmal werden Sie aufgefordert, einen Text sinngemäß ins Deutsche zu übertragen. Sinn der Sache ist nicht, ihn Wort für Wort zu übersetzen, sondern die wesentlichen Informationen auf Deutsch wiederzugeben. Das nennt man Mediation, im Gegensatz zur Übersetzung. Mediation trainiert die Fähigkeit, fremdsprachliche Unterlagen zu verstehen und an jemanden, der die Fremdsprache nicht beherrscht, weiterzugeben.

Hier ein paar Tipps für eine gelungene Mediation:

1. Lesen Sie die Aufgabe genau durch – sollen Sie den ganzen Text oder nur Teile daraus wiedergeben?
2. Lesen Sie den Text und klären Sie Verständnislücken. Es kommt nicht auf jedes einzelne Wort an, aber Sie sollten verstehen, was der Verfasser sagen will. Konzentrieren Sie sich immer zuerst auf die Hauptsätze, besonders auf die Verben.
3. Fassen Sie die wesentlichen Informationen stichwortartig auf Deutsch zusammen.
4. Vergleichen Sie Ihre Notizen mit dem Text. Haben Sie alle wichtigen Aspekte erfasst?
5. Formulieren Sie aus den Stichpunkten einen zusammenhängenden Text.

6 **Dan and Sally have just had interviews.**
23 **Did they follow the advice from the text? Copy the table, then listen to the recording. Write ✓ for 'yes', ✗ for 'no' and ? for 'not clear'.**

	Dan	*Sally*
1 Research?	✗	
2 Practice interview?	✓	
3 Smart clothes?		
4 On time?		
5 Respectful?		
6 Asked questions?		

7 **Role-play: preparing a job interview.**

PARTNER A: You have an interview next week. Ask your partner for advice.
PARTNER B: You are a careers adviser. Help your partner.

Example: A *What should I wear?*
B *I think you should ...*

What should I ... ?

I think / don't think you should ...

You could ...

Don't forget to ...

Language

RELATIVE CLAUSES (Relativsätze)

Relativsätze sind Nebensätze, die ein Nomen näher definieren. Sie werden mit Relativpronomen eingeleitet. Relativsätze werden normalerweise nicht durch Kommas markiert.

Personen näher beschreiben: who **oder (seltener)** that
A candidate who/that arrives late won't get the job.

Dinge, Tiere oder Begriffe näher beschreiben: which **oder** that
This is the 'x-factor' which/that makes you stand out.

Kein Relativpronomen
Who, which und that können entfallen, wenn sie das Objekt vertreten:
Think about questions (which/that) the interviewer may ask.
The person (who/that) you are speaking to may have interviewed hundreds of people.

Practice

8 a Complete the sentences using who or which.

Example: The girl ... got the job was very happy.
The girl who got the job was very happy.

1 The questions ... they asked me were difficult.
2 This is the manager ... is going to be your boss.
3 This is the office ... we work in.
4 The person ... interviewed me was friendly.
5 Can I see the letter ... you wrote?
6 That is the factory ... I worked in last summer.
7 Ms Jones is the manager ... interviewed me.
8 Is this the job ... Sam applied for?

b Now decide whether the relative pronoun is necessary in each sentence.

Example: The girl who got the job was very happy. *necessary (who = Subjekt)*

9 Complete the sentences with relative clauses.

Example: I'm applying for the job .... (I found it on the internet.)
I'm applying for the job (which/that) I found on the internet.

1 The candidate ... didn't get the job. (He arrived late.)
2 The candidate ... impressed the interviewer. (She asked good questions.)
3 Dee applied for the job .... (She saw it in the newspaper.)
4 I wore the shirt .... (I bought it on Tuesday.)
5 I'm going to buy the suit .... (It costs 200 euros.)
6 Mike is looking for the webpage .... (It has job vacancies.)
7 Did you find the book ... ? (It gives career advice.)
8 Is that the company ... ? (You want to work for it.)

10 Pick a word from the box. (Don't tell your partner the word!) Use the grid to make a definition for the word, then read out your definition. Can your partner guess the word?

boss • candidate • clerk • colleague • dictionary • mechanic • photocopier • programmer • trainee

Example: A *It's someone who supervises your work.*
B *That's your boss.*

			applies	an office job.
			does	cars.
			learns	copies of documents.
			makes	for a job.
It's	someone something	who which	repairs	instructions for computers.
			supervises	to do a job.
			tells	with you.
			works	you the meanings of words.
			writes	your work.

11 Tara Bachmann wants to get a summer job in the UK. Read her letter on the opposite page, then find the English expressions for the following.

Example: Sehr geehrte Frau ... *Dear Ms ...*

1 Bewerbung
2 sich bewerben um
3 Anzeige
4 verantwortungsbewusst
5 Ich habe gute Englischkenntnisse
6 Lebenslauf
7 Ich freue mich darauf ...
8 Mit freundlichen Grüßen

12 Write your own letter of application for one of these summer jobs, using Tara's letter as a model.

We need polite and friendly
call centre operatives
who speak fluent German. No experience needed.
Apply to: Mr John O'Reilly, Celtic Marketing plc,
19 Duffy Street, Dublin 16, Republic of Ireland.

Hard-working and fit?
Earn £££ in the summer holidays as
a **factory worker**.
Apply to: Mr Brian Evans, Wiley & Sons plc,
19 Park Road, Cardiff CF10 1KH, UK.

INTERCULTURAL CORNER

Lebensläufe auf Englisch schreiben

Lebensläufe in englischsprachigen Ländern unterscheiden sich in manchen Punkten von deutschen:
- Es gibt kein Foto.
- Es werden keine Angaben zum Elternhaus gemacht.
- Zeugnisse werden nicht beigelegt.
- Statt Empfehlungsschreiben werden Ansprechpartner genannt, die Auskunft über den/die Bewerber/in geben können.

Achtung bei der Übersetzung deutscher Schultypen ins Englische:
- Grundschule = *primary school*
- Hauptschule/Realschule = *secondary school*
- Berufsfachschule = *vocational college*

26 April 20..

Dear Ms Todd

Job application: Summer Camp Assistant

I am writing to apply for work as a Summer Camp Assistant.
I found the advertisement on your website.
I am sixteen years old and finished secondary school last year. Now I am doing a two-year course in childcare at a vocational college in Freiburg.
I would make a good summer camp assistant because I am fit and energetic, I enjoy working with children of all ages and I am responsible and hard-working. I speak good English.
When I finish college I want to work with children, so this job would be very good experience for me.
I can work from 29 July to 7 September.
Please find enclosed my CV. I look forward to hearing from you.

Yours sincerely

Tara Bachmann
Tara Bachmann
Enc.

REMEMBER

Anrede:
Dear Sir or Madam
wenn Sie den Namen nicht kennen
Dear Mr ...
an einen Mann
Dear Mrs ...
an eine verheiratete Frau
Dear Ms ...
allgemein an eine Frau, verheiratet oder unverheiratet

Wenn es eine Betreffzeile gibt, kommt sie nach der Anrede.

Die erste Zeile nach der Anrede beginnt immer mit einem Großbuchstaben.

Schluss:
Yours faithfully
wenn der Brief mit *Dear Sir or Madam* begonnen wurde
Yours sincerely
wenn der Brief mit *Dear Mr/Mrs/Ms ...* begonnen wurde

Wenn Sie eine Anlage zu dem Brief hinzufügen, schreiben Sie *Enc.* (*= enclosure*) unten.

13 **Copy the Cyber-CV into your exercise book and complete it with your own details.**

http://www.cyber-cv.com

Apple .Mac Amazon eBay Yahoo! News

Create your own Cyber-CV!

It's quick and easy – just complete the form and click on 'Submit'.

First name: [ ] Family name: [ ] Age: [ ]
School/College subjects: [ ]
Schools (name, years): [ ]
Languages (state 'basic', 'fluent' or 'native speaker'): [ ]
Other skills (e.g. computer): [ ]
Hobbies and interests: [ ]
[Submit]

The world of work

Job interviews

1 **Match the jobs to the job groups 1–3.**

care assistant • car mechanic • carpenter • dental assistant • nurse • electrician • estate agent • sales assistant • telephone order clerk • travel agent • factory technician • youth worker

1 Caring for people
2 Selling goods or services
3 Making or repairing things

2 **For each of the job groups from exercise 1, list the THREE personal qualities you think are most important.**

Example: *1 A person who cares for people should / must be friendly …*

enthusiastic • fit • friendly • good at communicating • good at maths • good with their hands • patient • polite • self-confident • technically-minded • tolerant • well-organized

3 **Your friend has found this advertisement on a jobs website. He/She wants to know what the advertisement says. Explain to him/her in German what the job is and what the requirements are.**

Apprentice Joiner/Carpenter **GMC Construction, Banbury**
This is an excellent opportunity for a young person who wishes to train to become a qualified joiner and carpenter. Practical skill with your hands is essential and good maths is also an advantage – you will need to make accurate measurements and follow diagrams. You must be healthy and fit. No experience is necessary.
Salary £7.5k Apply now

4 GMC interviews three candidates for the job. Listen to the interviews and note the following information about each candidate:

24

- Work experience
- School subjects and grades
- Health and fitness
- Interest in the job

Example: *Gary: worked in a shop; maths grade C; ...*

Gary

Louise

Josh

5 Discuss: Which candidate should get the job, and why?

6 Listen again to the interviews. Which of the following phrases do you hear?

24

Gary's interview

1 a Do you have any work experience?
  b Have you had any work experience?
2 a How good are you at maths?
  b Are you good at maths?
3 a I want to earn really good money.
  b I really want to start earning good money.

Louise's interview

4 a I don't like maths that much.
  b I'm not very interested in maths.
5 a I'm really good at things like that.
  b I'm very good at that sort of thing.
6 a I'd like to learn a practical trade.
  b I want to learn a practical trade.

Josh's interview

7 a I worked at the local football club in the summer.
  b I have worked at the local football club.
8 a I like making things with my hands.
  b I like working with my hands.
9 a We'll let you know by the end of the week.
  b We'll be in touch at the end of the week.

7 Work in a group of three or more. Role-play an interview for the job in exercise 3. (Use expressions from exercise 6.)

STUDENT A: Turn to File 3 on page 148.
STUDENTS B, C ETC.: Turn to File 8 on page 151.

9 Destination NZ

1 a Match the captions to the photos.

bungy jumping • hang-gliding • whale watching • white-water rafting

A

B

C

D

b Scan the webpage on the opposite page to find out where you can do these activities.

Example: *You can go bungy jumping at Kawarau Gorge.*

2 Now read or listen to the text. Complete these sentences in your own words.

Example: At the welcome party you *can meet new people.*

1 Queenstown is great for people who ...
2 At Kawarau Gorge, tourists ...
3 If you haven't tried hang-gliding before,
4 Kaikoura is a good place to learn about Maori life because ...
5 Wildlife lovers will enjoy Kaikoura because ...
6 Carolyn and Claire have decided ...

3 Find the words or expressions in the text.

Example: a very large animal which lives in the sea (Introduction) – *whale*

1 you live in this when you go camping (Introduction)
2 a place where planes take off and land (Day 1)
3 to relax and do nothing (Day 2)
4 a person who is doing something for the first time (Day 4)
5 a person who shows other people how to do something (Day 4)
6 a meal which you cook outdoors (Day 5)

BEFORE YOU START

How much do you know about New Zealand? Do the quiz to find out.

1 When it's spring in New Zealand, it's ... in Germany.
   a spring   b autumn   c winter
2 New Zealand is nearest to:
   a India   b South America   c Australia
3 Which sport was invented in New Zealand?
   a bungy jumping   b tennis   c handball
4 The original inhabitants (*Ureinwohner*) of New Zealand are called:
   a Aborigines   b Kiwis   c Maori

25

Kiwi Challenge

Introduction

We run adventure holidays on New Zealand's beautiful South Island. South Island is a land of contrasts: snowy mountains and green forests; wild rivers and quiet lakes; whales and penguins! You will need good outdoor clothes and lots of energy. You won't need tents – we will provide all your camping equipment. (New Zealand is in the Southern Hemisphere, so it is summer here when it is winter in Europe.)

Day 1: Arrival

Our minibus will meet you at Christchurch airport and take you to Queenstown. With 300 different adventure activities, Queenstown will be your base for three exciting days. In the evening there will be a 'welcome' party and disco – a great chance to get to know everyone.

Day 2: Bungy jumping

On day 2 we will drive to Kawarau Gorge – the home of bungy jumping. You will do a 43-metre jump from the Kawarau Bridge. Don't worry – bungy jumping is very safe, and we have lots of experience! If you're scared of heights, you can chill out, have a beer and watch your friends jump instead!

Day 3: White-water rafting

Are you ready for a day of fun on the Shotover River? No experience is required, but you must be able to swim.

Day 4: Hang-gliding

Our hang-gliding school is in The Remarkables mountains above Queenstown. Beginners will fly with an instructor in a tandem hang-glider. If you aren't interested in hang-gliding, you can spend the day on the beach instead.

Day 5: Whale watching

In the morning of day 5, your minibus will take you to Kaikoura. This is the best place in New Zealand to watch sea life. At Kaikoura you will be the guests of the local Maori community. They will take you on a six-hour boat trip to see whales, dolphins and seals. In the evening there will be a traditional Maori barbecue to end your Kiwi experience.

This is what our clients say:

"Bungy jumping was scary – but lots of fun!" Fabian and Lena, Germany

"We're going to come back next year – thank you, Kiwi Challenge!" Carolyn and Claire, England

"Take the Kiwi Challenge! You'll love the people, the places and the activities!" Jed, Canada

(372 words)

4 **A friend wants to know about adventure sports in New Zealand, but she doesn't understand English very well. Summarize in German the relevant information from the text.**

5 **Tell your partner about your holiday.**

PARTNER A: Turn to File 4 on page 149.
PARTNER B: Turn to File 9 on page 151.

LEARNING TO LEARN

Wie man das freie Sprechen verbessern kann

Lassen Sie beim Sprechen immer mal wieder Ausdrücke einfließen, um Interesse, Überraschung, Anerkennung usw. zu äußern – so etwas macht eine Unterhaltung gleich viel lebendiger.

Cool!	Cool!	*Really?*	Echt?
Great!	Super!	*Right. / Oh, right.*	Ah ja. / Ach so.
I see.	Ach so.	*OK then.*	Alles klar.
Oh dear!	Oh je!	*Fine.*	Gut.
Oh no!	Oh nein!	*You're kidding!*	Das ist jetzt nicht dein Ernst!

Language

WILL FUTURE (Zukunft mit *will*)

Die Zukunft mit will wird für Vorhersagen sowie spontane Entscheidungen, Versprechen und Angebote benutzt. Oft wird will zu 'll abgekürzt. Die Verneinung von will heißt won't.

The weather will be good.	(Vorhersage)
It's cold. I'll close the window.	(spontane Entscheidung)
I'll show you how to do it.	(Versprechen, Angebot)

GOING TO FUTURE (Zukunft mit *going to*)

Be going to benutzt man, wenn man von Plänen und Absichten spricht.
We're going to come back next year.

PRESENT PROGRESSIVE WITH FUTURE MEANING (Verlaufsform der Gegenwart mit Zukunftsbezug)

Wenn für Pläne schon konkrete zeitliche Abmachungen getroffen worden sind, steht häufig die Verlaufsform der Gegenwart. Meist weist dann eine Zeitangabe auf den Zukunftsbezug hin.
I'm meeting a friend this evening.

SIMPLE PRESENT WITH FUTURE MEANING (einfache Gegenwart mit Zukunftsbezug)

Die einfache Gegenwart verwendet man für Fahrpläne, Programme usw.
The minibus leaves at 10 o'clock.

6 Put the verbs in brackets in the will future.

Example: This year a million tourists ... (visit) Christchurch.
This year a million tourists will visit Christchurch.

1 Next January it ... (be) warm and sunny in New Zealand.
2 You ... (not need) to take your own tent.
3 If Selim goes to New Zealand, he ... (have) a great time.
4 How long ... (the boat trip / last)?
5 ... (we / see) lots of whales at Kaikoura?
6 How much ... (the trip / cost)?
7 Leila is scared of heights, so she ... (not like) bungy jumping.
8 Hurry up! We ... (not get) to the airport on time.

7 Identify the tense and explain in German why it is used.

Example: There will be lots of tourists on the beach. – *will future: Vorhersage*

1 I'm doing my homework this evening.
2 The plane lands at 8.30 p.m.
3 She's going to visit her cousin in the USA.
4 The exam won't be difficult.
5 I'll answer the phone.
6 We're going to do a bungy jump.
7 We're doing a bungy jump on Sunday.
8 I won't forget your birthday again!

8 Complete the sentences, using the will or going to future.

Example: She likes dolphins so she ... (enjoy) the visit to Kaikoura today.
She likes dolphins so she will enjoy the visit to Kaikoura today.

1 She ... (see) the beautiful Kawarau Gorge next week.
2 I think they ... (find) hang-gliding very exciting.
3 If you find the game difficult, I ... (help) you.
4 We ... (explore) South Island tomorrow.
5 I promise I ... (not miss) the plane!
6 He ... (not come) to the beach with us as he doesn't feel very well.
7 They ... (learn) a lot about the Maori community, I'm sure.
8 ... (you / come back) to New Zealand next year?

9 Answer the questions with your own ideas.

Example: What are you doing at the weekend?
I'm playing football at the weekend.

1 What time does college finish today?
2 When are you going to take your driving test?
3 How many people will live in Germany in 2050?
4 What are you going to do when you finish college?
5 Where are you going to spend your next holiday?
6 How old will you be in 2035?
7 What are you having for dinner this evening?

REMEMBER

Ein Tipp zum Umgang mit Zeitformen:
Wenn Sie Fragen beantworten, benutzen Sie in der Antwort einfach die Zeitform aus der Frage.

10 Jack and Hollie live in Auckland, New Zealand. They are planning some activities for Hollie's German cousins, who are coming to visit them.
Listen to the recording and put these activities in the order in which they are mentioned.

26

Example: *E, ...*

11 Listen again and complete Hollie's email with expressions from the box. There are three expressions too many.

26

beer • chill out • friends • go bungy jumping • go mountain biking • go shopping • go to the beach • have a barbecue • ~~in two weeks~~ • invite • music • pubs • shops

Inbox - Outlook Express

File Edit View Tools Message Help

Inbox

From | Subject | Received

From: Hollie Jackson

To: Fabian Deutz; Lena Seidel

Subject: Your visit

Hi Fabian! Hi Lena!
You'll be here *in two weeks* [1] !! It will be so great to see you! We've planned lots of things to do:
On Saturday we're going to ... [2]. Then on Sunday we're going to ... [3].
You'll love it!
On Monday we're going to ... [4] . The ... [5] in Auckland are really good.
Then on Tuesday we're going to ... [6]. We're going to ... [7] all our ... [8].
There will be ... [9] and live ... [10].
It'll be GREAT!!
Lots of love
Hollie :-D

1 message(s), 0 unread | Working Online

12 An exchange group from a British vocational college is coming to your town.

a Brainstorm some activities that you can do with the exchange students in your local area.

b Copy this plan and write down a programme of activities.

Friday evening:	*Welcome party*
Saturday afternoon:	
Saturday evening:	
Sunday morning:	
Sunday evening:	

c Present your plan to the whole class. Use the going to future to tell them about your decisions.

Example: *On Friday evening we're going to have a welcome party for the exchange students …*

13 Write an email to the exchange class telling them about your plans. Add any extra details you can think of.

Example:

Hi!
We're looking forward to meeting you. We have planned some great things to do.
On Friday evening we're going to have a welcome party at our college. There's going to be a disco and a barbecue …

INTERCULTURAL CORNER

Englisch auf dem Flughafen

Wenn Sie mit dem Flugzeug unterwegs sind, werden Sie feststellen, dass Englisch auf Flughäfen die Sprache Nr. 1 ist. Die folgenden Formulierungen werden Sie immer wieder hören, wenn es um Abfertigung, Passkontrolle usw. geht. Welche von ihnen passen zu den Illustrationen?

May I see your passport / ID card, please?
Here's your boarding pass, sir/madam.
Did you pack these bags yourself?
Your flight leaves from gate 20.
Have a pleasant flight.
Flight BA 101 is now boarding at gate 20.
Boarding card, please.
Do you have anything in your pockets?
Come through, please.
The baggage reclaim is over there.

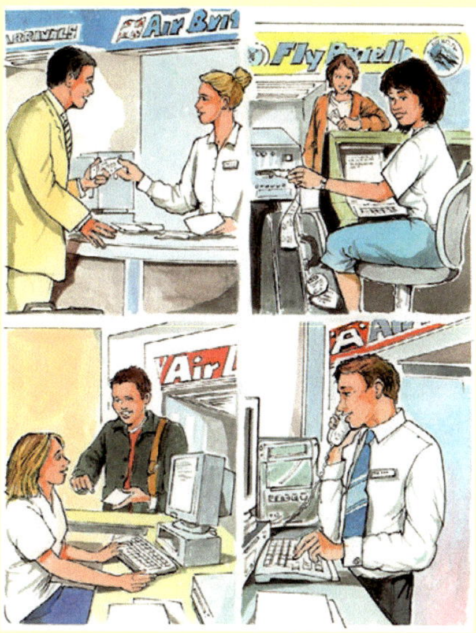

The world of work

Travel and tourism

1 Read the job descriptions, then match each job title to the correct description.

hotel receptionist

travel agency salesperson

airline customer service agent

A This person makes sure that passengers and their luggage get on the right planes. He or she works at a check-in desk and uses a computer terminal to check in passengers. He or she also weighs the passengers' luggage, gives them boarding passes and answers their questions about departures and arrivals.

B This person welcomes guests when they arrive. He or she makes room reservations for guests over the phone, by letter, fax or email and face to face. He or she also hands out keys to guests. He or she uses a computer, a fax machine and a telephone switchboard.

C This person sells holidays and tickets. He or she talks to the client to find out what kind of holiday the client wants. Then he or she uses a computer to book the holiday. He or she also helps clients to plan journeys and books their air, rail or ferry tickets and accommodation.

2 Decide which of the three jobs matches each description best.

Example: 'You'll need a good knowledge of geography in this job.'
travel agency salesperson

1 'You'll have to work shifts because guests can arrive at any time of the day or night.'
2 'You'll have to stay calm and friendly when flights are late and everybody thinks that it's your fault!'
3 'You'll be under pressure to sell enough holidays.'
4 'It's a nice, clean, quiet place to work, and when you're off duty, you may be able to use facilities like the pool, gym and restaurant for free.'
5 'It's an exciting place to work – all those aircraft flying off to distant places! You'll meet people from all over the world.'

3 Petra Buchheim works as a flight sales executive at British Airways. She receives a phone call from a passenger who needs to change his flight.
Listen to the conversation and write down the missing details.

27

Flight reservation alteration	
Booking reference:	923830
Surname:	Brownlow
First name:	Ralph
Current flight details	
Flight number:	BA 0965
Departure airport:	
Destination airport:	New York – JFK International
Departure date:	
Departure time:	
Arrival time:	
New flight details	
Flight number:	
Departure airport:	
Destination airport:	
Departure date:	
Departure time:	
Arrival time:	

4 Listen again. Which of these expressions do you hear?

27

1 May I have your booking reference, please?
2 Is that correct?
3 When would you like to travel?
4 I'll just see what's available.
5 One moment, please.
6 It won't take a moment.
7 Are those details correct?
8 I've done that for you, sir.
9 You're welcome.
10 Have a pleasant journey.

5 Role-play: booking a flight.

Partner A: Turn to File 5 on page 149.
Partner B: Turn to File 7 on page 150.

'You'll need a good knowledge of geography in this job.'

Exam practice

Young Germans abroad

Young Germans love a holiday. At least eighty per cent of us will go on holiday this year. That's nearly 13 million tourists between the ages of 14 and 30. We'll spend over 800 euros each on our holiday.

So why do we do it? The main reason is to enjoy warm, sunny weather – nearly 60 per cent of us give that as an important reason. We also want to have new experiences, and share them with our friends. Of course, another reason for going on holiday is to meet new people – maybe even a new boyfriend or girlfriend. A quarter of young Germans hope that they will find romance on holiday.

Most of us want to go abroad. Spain is our number-one holiday destination, but our neighbours Holland and Austria are also popular, and Italy is another favourite. When we choose a holiday, we look for good weather, a location by the sea or a lake, good value for money and friendly local people. Adventure or activity holidays are the most popular, closely followed by beach holidays.

Amongst young adults, car and plane are the favourite ways to get to our holiday destination. Only seven per cent of us want to go by train.

Have you planned your next holiday yet? (212 words)

Text comprehension

1 Finish the sentences using information from the text. Use your own words.

a Twenty per cent of young Germans ...
b When we go on holiday, it's important to ...
c Most young German tourists don't want to ...

2 Answer the questions about the text.

a How does the text define 'young Germans'?
b Which of these isn't mentioned as a reason for choosing a holiday destination: sunny weather; nice scenery; being close to water?
c Which type of transport is unpopular for young German tourists?

3 What do you think about the different kinds of holiday mentioned in the text? Give your opinion.

4 Ask the author of the text one question each about the first three paragraphs. Use three different question words or types of question.

Grammar

5 Fill in the gaps with the correct forms of the verbs in brackets.

a At the moment I ... (sit) by the lake and ... (write) a postcard.
b How many British tourists ... (fly) to Spain next year?
c Alex and Lisa ... (visit) Austria twice so far.
d The train for Frankfurt ... (leave) at 9.30 tomorrow morning.

6 **Make comparisons using the comparatives of the adjectives in brackets.**

a Spain ↔ Holland (sunny)
b activity holidays ↔ beach holidays (good)

Vocabulary

7 **Complete the sentences with the corresponding adjective for the word in brackets.**

a I don't want to sit on the beach – I want to be ... . (activity)
b The film was very ... . (romance)

8 **Complete the sentences with a word or phrase which means the same as the word in brackets.**

a ... we can go to Portugal in the summer. (maybe)
b We spent ... five hundred euros in Italy. (over)

9 **Complete the sentences with the opposite of the word in brackets.**

a How was your ... holiday? (next)
b Be careful not to ... your plane ticket! (find)

10 **Use a dictionary to translate the <u>underlined</u> expressions.**

a Are you <u>looking for</u> adventure or relaxation?
b We're <u>looking at</u> a website about South Africa.
c Jugendlichen <u>unter</u> 18 Jahren ist der Zutritt verboten.
d <u>Unter</u> anderem suche ich ein gutes Wörterbuch.

Writing

11 **Write an email to your British penfriend. Tell him/her about your summer or winter holiday plans (where you want to go, how much money you need, what you're going to do, etc). Write 80–100 words.**

Mediation

12 **Übertragen Sie den Inhalt des Textes 'Young Germans abroad' ins Deutsche. Übersetzen Sie nicht Wort für Wort. Schreiben Sie ganze Sätze.**

13 **What would you say in these situations?**

a Sie haben sich am Telefon verwählt.
b Sie fragen Ihren Freund, was er heute Abend im Fernsehen sehen wird.
c Sie laden jemand zu einer Party ein.
d Sie wollen einen Termin beim Zahnarzt.
e Sie erkundigen sich nach der Ankunftszeit des Zuges nach Manchester.
f Sie haben etwas akustisch nicht verstanden.

10 Keep in touch

1 **Rosie keeps a weblog about things that make her angry. This week she's writing about mobile phones. Scan the text on the opposite page, then match the cartoons to Rosie's points 1–6.**

Example: *1b*

(a)

(b)

(c)

(d)

(e)

(f)

INTERCULTURAL CORNER

Ein Handy ist kein *handy*

Das Wort „Handy“ sieht zwar englisch aus, aber kein Brite würde auf die Idee kommen, dass damit ein mobile phone (kurz: mobile) gemeint ist. Mobiltelefone heißen im amerikanischen Englisch cell(ular) phones.

Englisch ist bestens geeignet für text messages (SMS), weil man mit Buchstaben und Ziffern viele allgemein verständliche Abkürzungen wie c u l8r (see you later) schreiben kann, um seine SMS schneller zu tippen und kürzer zu fassen. Natürlich gibt es wie im Deutschen auch Abkürzungen, die nur für Eingeweihte verständlich sind, wie GALL (Get a life, loser!) oder SYS (See you soon).

Geben Sie SMS shortcuts in eine Suchmaschine ein, um weitere geläufige Abkürzungen zu finden.

BEFORE YOU START

1 Think of ten things you can do with a mobile phone.

2 How useful are these functions, in your opinion? Put them in order from 1 (most useful) to 10 (least useful). Compare your list with a partner.

http://www.rosies-blogspot.co.uk/rant114 Google

Apple .Mac Amazon eBay Yahoo! News

Rosie's rants

Rant 114: Phone rage

Yesterday I was on the bus, on my way home from college. A girl sat down opposite me. She was about 19, I suppose. After a few minutes she took out her mobile phone and began a very personal phone conversation with her boyfriend. It was really embarrassing. And then she turned to me and said 'Do you mind? This is a private conversation.' Can you believe that? I was so surprised, I actually said 'Oh, sorry.'

This experience made me think about mobile phones. Now, don't get me wrong, I couldn't live without my mobile, but some mobile users drive me crazy. So here are some tips for all you 'phone idiots' out there:

1 **Keep it to yourself.**
(This one's for you, Girl On The Bus.) People will be embarrassed if they hear your private conversations. What is worse, complete strangers will find out the names of your friends, parents and lovers. So, don't have private conversations in public places.

2 **Don't phone and drive.***
If you phone while you are driving a car or riding a bike, you won't be able to concentrate on the road. If you don't concentrate, you'll probably have an accident. That serves you right. What is worse, you might kill someone less stupid than you.

3 **Speak quietly.**
If you have loud phone conversations in quiet places, people will hate you. Don't shout – you're using a phone for goodness' sake!

4 **Switch to 'vibrate'.**
You probably think your new ring tone is incredibly cool, but the rest of us on the bus / in McDonald's / in the pub don't want to hear it every five minutes. Please switch your phone to 'vibrate' mode when you are in public.

5 **Face-to-face comes first.**
Some people answer the phone wherever they are, whatever they are doing. If you constantly interrupt face-to-face conversations to answer your phone, people will get angry. You are saying to them 'You are less important than this phone call.'

6 **Turn it off.**
If your phone rings in the cinema, it will spoil the film for other people. You can avoid this problem:
Step 1: Find the 'off' switch.
Step 2: Use it!

(364 words)

* This is illegal in many countries.

2 Read the text. Decide whether these statements are true or false. Correct the false statements.

Example: Rosie overheard a phone conversation at college.
False. Rosie overheard a phone conversation on the bus.

1 Rosie found the girl's phone conversation interesting.
2 The girl was angry because Rosie listened to her conversation.
3 Rosie doesn't have a mobile phone.
4 You should make personal phone calls where there are lots of people.
5 When you are using a mobile phone, you need to speak loudly.
6 You should use 'vibrate' mode in public places.
7 It's OK to interrupt an important conversation if your phone rings.
8 When you are in the cinema, you should turn off your phone.

3 Find the opposites of these words. Then check in the text.

Example: easy (Intro) ↔ *difficult*

1 public (Intro)
2 better (Tip 1)
3 intelligent (Tip 2)
4 loudly (Tip 3)
5 whisper (Tip 3)
6 old (Tip 4)
7 last (Tip 5)
8 on (Tip 6)

4 How would you say it in German?

1 Do you mind? (Intro)
2 Can you believe that? (Intro)
3 Don't get me wrong. (Intro)
4 (They) drive me crazy. (Intro)
5 Keep it to yourself. (Tip 1)
6 What is worse, ... (Tip 1)
7 That serves you right. (Tip 2)
8 For goodness' sake! (Tip 3)
9 ... wherever they are ... (Tip 5)

5 Discuss the following in a group.

1 Do you follow all of Rosie's tips? (Be honest!)
2 What annoys you about other mobile phone users?

6 Write your own opinion (approx. 80 words) about Rosie's rants.

LEARNING TO LEARN

Wie man das Internet zum Lernen nutzen kann

Im Internet findet man englischsprachige Texte, Audio- und sogar Videodokumente zu allen erdenklichen Themen. Hier ein paar Tipps, wie Sie mit Hilfe des Internets Ihre Sprachkenntnisse verbessern können:

- Suchen Sie interessante Texte (z.B. über Ihr Hobby) und drucken Sie sie aus, damit Sie sie gründlicher lesen, schwierige Wörter unterstreichen und Übersetzungen daneben schreiben können.
- Laden Sie sich Audiodateien herunter und hören Sie sich mehrmals an.
- Chatrooms und Foren geben zwar Alltagssprache wieder, sind aber oft schnell und nachlässig geschrieben. Hier gewöhnt man sich leicht Fehler an – zum Beispiel von Nutzern, deren Muttersprache gar nicht Englisch ist.
- Finger weg von Übersetzungsprogrammen! Sie sind nicht zuverlässig und produzieren meistens nur kompletten Unsinn.

Language

CONDITIONAL SENTENCES TYPE 1 (Bedingungssätze Typ 1)

Bedingungssätze des Typs 1 bestehen aus zwei Teilen: if-Satz und Hauptsatz. Der Nebensatz mit if nennt die Bedingung und steht im simple present, der Hauptsatz nennt die Folge und steht im will future.

1 *People will be embarrassed if they hear your private conversations.*
2 *If you forget your PIN number, you won't be able to phone.*
3 *If you don't concentrate, you'll probably have an accident.*

- Statt will kann man auch ein Modalverb (z. B. can, could, may, might, must) verwenden, um Folgen zu nennen, die nicht zwangsläufig, aber trotzdem möglich sind:
  If you talk loudly, you could/may/might annoy someone.
- Steht die Bedingung zuerst, setzt man danach ein Komma (Satz 2, 3). Steht die Folge zuerst, braucht man kein Komma (Satz 1).

DANGER!

1 Verwechseln Sie nicht if mit when:

If she phones me, ... (if = „wenn“ als Bedingung, im Sinne von „falls“)
When she phones me, ... (when = „wenn“ als Zeit- oder Häufigkeitsangabe, im Sinne von „dann, wenn“ oder „immer, wenn“)

2 If und will kommen nie im selben Teilsatz vor:

If I ~~will~~ phone you, ...

Practice

7 Complete these sentences with the correct form of the verbs in brackets.

Example: If Zack ... (drink) too much beer, he ... (feel) sick.
If Zack drinks too much beer, he will feel sick.

1 I ... (phone) him if I have time.
2 If we go by bus, it ... (take) half an hour.
3 If you ... (send) me a text message, I will call you later.
4 The computer ... (not work) if you forget your password.
5 If Sara ... (smoke) in here, she ... (get) into trouble.
6 I ... (take) that phone away from you if you ... (not turn) it off!
7 If they ... (send) texts in class, the teacher ... (know).
8 What ... we ... (do) if she ... (be) late?

8 Complete these conditional sentences. Add commas where necessary.

Examples: If it rains (we / get wet) — *If it rains, we will get wet.*
We will be late (miss the bus) — *We will be late if we miss the bus.*

1 If you don't answer the phone (miss the call)
2 If you leave a message (I / return your call)
3 Lea won't lose her job (work harder)
4 If Sam doesn't answer (we / leave a message)
5 We will delete the email (it / contain a virus)
6 You will lose your file (click on 'Quit')
7 If you click on 'OK' (the computer / shut down)
8 Pete won't be happy (you / lose his phone)

9 **Complete the sentences with if or when.**

Example: *If* you don't answer the phone, I'll call back later.

1 ... you chat on your mobile and drive at the same time, you'll probably have an accident.
2 ... I leave college, I'll look for a job.
3 The teacher will get angry ... I don't do my homework.
4 ... my phone rings in the cinema, people usually get angry.
5 ... my phone is switched of, you'll have to leave me a message.
6 She might give me her phone number ... I ask her.
7 ... you get home, send me a text message.
8 We always chat for an hour ... she rings me.

10 **Discuss these questions with your partner, then write answers.**

What will happen if ...

- you use your phone in class?
- you ride your moped too fast?
- you leave your phone on the bus?
- you forget your best friend's birthday?

11 **Match the definitions (a–f) to the mobile phone expressions (1–6).**

Example: *1 c*

a You can use as much as you like.
b This is how long you can speak for.
c You make a legal agreement.
d You use your phone to send a written message.
e You pay before you use it.
f You need this to browse web pages, download files, etc.

12 **Jake goes into a mobile phone shop to find out what tariffs are available.**
28 **Listen to the recording, then complete the information about the different mobile phone tariffs on the following page.**

At mobilET we have the right tariff for every mobile phone user:

Business

___ [1] minutes' talk time a month
Unlimited ___ [2] messages a month
Unlimited ___ [3] access

Power

___ [4] minutes' talk time a month
___ [5] text messages a month
10 free ___ [6] a month

Budget

___ [7] talk time a month
60 ___ [8] a month

Pay as you go

no ___ [9]
no monthly fee
Only pay for the ___ [10] you make!

13 Listen again and complete the phrases below.

28

Example: Can I *help you*, sir?

1 I'd like to change ... .
2 Do you have ... ?
3 I don't want to ... music.
4 I just want to make ... and send ... .
5 I don't ... 120 minutes' talk time.
6 Well, in that case pay as you go ... .

14 Role-play the dialogue in English.

PARTNER A: You work in a mobile phone shop.
PARTNER B: You want a new mobile phone tariff.

A	B
Begrüßen Sie den Kunden / die Kundin und fragen Sie, ob Sie helfen können.	
	Grüßen Sie zurück und sagen Sie, dass Sie einen neuen Handytarif haben möchten.
Fragen Sie, ob er/sie bereits ein Handy hat.	
	Bejahen Sie.
Fragen Sie, wie viel Geprächszeit er/sie benötigt.	
	Antworten Sie.
Fragen Sie, wie viele SMS er/sie ungefähr pro Monat sendet.	
	Antworten Sie.
Fragen Sie, ob er/sie Internetzugang braucht und Musik herunterladen möchte.	
	Antworten Sie.
Schlagen Sie einen passenden Tarif von Aufgabe 12 vor.	

The world of work

Keeping technology working

1 Find these people's professions in the text.

a

b

c

Service technician – a job with a future

We all depend on technology, but what happens when it doesn't work? We need someone to fix the problem – fast. The need for good technicians is greater than ever, and will continue to increase. If you are technically-minded, with good IT skills, and are also friendly, polite and a good communicator, you will probably do well in one of these jobs:

1 **Telecommunications technician**
Telecommunications technicians install, test and repair telephone, fax, internet and satellite systems. They may work in a factory, in customers' homes or offices or outdoors at a site.

2 **Help-desk professional**
Help-desk professionals help people who have problems with their IT hardware and software. They communicate with the user to identify the problem and suggest how to solve it. They do this over the phone, by email or in internet chatrooms.

3 **Computer service technician**
Computer service technicians install new computer systems, upgrade software and repair computers and peripherals (e.g. printers and scanners). They may work for a small computer repair shop, be part of the after-sales team for a big computer store or work in the IT department of a bank, hospital or other large organization.

2 Read the text again. What jobs do these people do?

Lisa

Taksim

Ann

3 Complete the sentences with verbs from the text. Change the form of the verbs if necessary.

Example: We *depend* on this computer system: we really need it. (Intro)

1 The number of calls to the helpdesk has ... by 200 per cent. (Intro)
2 Our company needs to ... a new internet connection – the old one is too slow. (Section 1)
3 The technician ... the system to find out what the fault was. (Section 1)
4 We haven't ... the problem yet: it could be a software fault or a hardware fault.' (Section 2)
5 They ... their email software – they needed a new version. (Section 3)
6 Sorry, we can't ... your computer – you'll have to buy a new one. (Section 3)

4 Listen to the four help-desk calls. Find the correct options in the diagram.

29

Example: *1 a, f, ...*

Problems
- a The screen is blank.
- b *Gunfighter 2* doesn't run.
- c *Photoshop* is running slowly.
- d The printer doesn't work.

Questions
- e How much memory does the computer have?
- f Is the cable in place?
- g Is the paper stuck?
- h Which PC do you have?

Answers
- i A Macintosh.
- j No.
- k 1 gigabyte.
- l Yes.

Solutions
- m You need a Windows PC.
- n Push the 'eject' button.
- o Connect the cable.
- p Install more memory.

5 Role-play a help-desk call with a partner.

PARTNER A: You are the customer. Choose a problem from exercise 4, then phone the help desk.
PARTNER B: You are the help-desk professional. Help the customer to solve the problem.

Exam practice

The internet generation

Today's young adults have grown up with computers, the internet and mobile phones. For older people, the internet is a place to find information, to shop and to read newspapers online. Teenagers and young adults, on the other hand, mostly use it to communicate with each other.

On average, people between 14 and 21 spend almost eight hours a week online. For about five hours they chat to friends online in chatrooms and forums and by email. Only one in ten young adults uses the internet to keep up with news – six in ten say that they watch the news on TV or read a newspaper.

Many young people (about 20 per cent) have set up their own website or weblog (blog). 'My blog is my personal space on the internet,' says one blogger. 'I can write anything I like there. Then other people can write comments. When I started, it was just my friends, but now people all over the world read my blog. Last night there was a comment from a girl in India.'

(179 words)

Text comprehension

1 **Finish the sentences using information from the text. Use your own words.**

a Older people don't usually use ...
b When they want news, most young people ...
c A weblog is a website where ...

2 **Answer questions about the text.**

a In what ways do younger and older people use the internet differently?
b On average, how much time do young adults spend online?
c Why does the blogger in the last paragraph like weblogs?

3 **Do you think that young people spend too much time on the internet? Give your opinion.**

4 **Ask the blogger in the third paragraph (lines 8–11) three questions about his/her blog. Use three different question words or types of question.**

Grammar

5 **Fill in the gaps with the correct form of the verbs in brackets.**

a A boy from Australia ... (write) a comment on my blog yesterday.
b I ... (not use) the internet to keep up with news – I buy a newspaper.
c Fifteen people ... (read) this forum at the moment.
d If people write stupid comments in your blog, you ... (be) angry.

Vocabulary

6 **Complete the sentences with the corresponding adjectives for the words in brackets.**

a The best thing about Chloe is that she's always ... . (friend)
b I didn't think that the website was very ... – it didn't answer my questions. (use)

7 **Complete the sentences with words or phrases which mean the same as the words in brackets.**

a ... I'm going to write a few emails. (This evening)
b When Tim ... to write his blog, nobody was interested in it. (start)

8 **Complete the sentences with the opposites of the words in brackets.**

a The problem is, not many blogs are ... to read. (boring)
b I'm going to ... spending so much time on the internet. (start)

9 **Use a dictionary to translate the underlined expressions.**

a How much money did you spend on your new mobile phone?
b How much time did you spend online today?
c Ich sehe fast jeden Tag fern.
d Hast du gestern Ralf gesehen?

Writing

10 **How important is the internet in your life? What have you used it for this week? Write an email to a friend. (80–100 words)**

Mediation

11 **Übertragen Sie den Inhalt des Textes 'The internet generation' ins Deutsche. Übersetzen Sie nicht Wort für Wort. Schreiben Sie ganze Sätze.**

12 **What would you say in these situations?**

11 Fame and fortune …

1 **Can you match the descriptions (a–d) to the films? Guess the answers, then scan the text on the opposite page to check.**

a a romantic blockbuster
b a story about young travellers in Thailand
c the true story of America's most successful con man
d the true story of American millionaire Howard Hughes

1 The Beach

2 Catch Me If You Can

3 Titanic

4 The Aviator

2 **Read the text and complete the 'Celebrity Snapshot'.**

Celebrity Snapshot

Name: *Leonardo Wilhelm DiCaprio*
Date and place of birth: …
Parents' names: …
Appearance: …
Profession: …
Other interests: …

Important career achievements:

	Year	*Achievement*
1	*1991*	*first role in a film*
2	…	…
3	…	…

3 **Match these reviews to the three films described in 'Critics' Choice' in the text on page 99. There is one review too many: can you find the fourth film in the text?**

(A) 'The film was nice to look at, but confusing. There were lots of good-looking young backpackers. Unfortunately, none of it made any sense.'

(B) 'It's really two films in one: a thrilling disaster movie with great special effects and a silly romantic drama.'

(C) 'The film has funny moments, but it isn't really a comedy. It is touching, but it isn't really a drama. Instead, it is an amazing true story – amazing because he was able to fool so many people for so long.'

(D) 'He was a selfish businessman, and completely crazy. This boring, very long film makes him into some kind of all-American hero.'

BEFORE YOU START

1 Look at the photos. Can you identify these famous people?
2 What are/were they famous for?
3 Which of them do you admire most/least?
4 Would you like to be famous? Why (not)?

A

B

C

30

In the Movies: Leonardo DiCaprio

Biography

Leonardo Wilhelm DiCaprio was born on November 11, 1974 in Los Angeles, California. His mother, Irmelin, is a German immigrant and his father, George, is Italian. Leonardo's parents divorced when he was young, but they both continued to help Leonardo in his career: Irmelin managed Leonardo's finances and George read his new scripts.

Leonardo ('Leo' to his friends and fans) likes partying and he loves dating beautiful women. He once admitted being 'obsessed with girls'.

On the other hand, he has shown his serious side in his environmental campaigns. His work for Global Green USA and Natural Resources Defense Council has involved making speeches and environmental films.

Career

As a teenager, Leonardo auditioned unsuccessfully for hundreds of roles, but he never gave up his dream of becoming an actor. Finally he got his first big-screen role in the horror film **Critters 3** (1991). His first leading role was in **This Boy's Life** (1993). In the same year he got an Oscar nomination for his role in **What's Eating Gilbert Grape?**

Leonardo's role in **Titanic** (1997) was his big break – this romantic blockbuster made him an international film star. In the following year he starred in the action-packed historical adventure **The Man in the Iron Mask** (1998).

Leonardo's blond hair and blue eyes made him a teen idol. That wasn't always a good thing: some critics thought that he was 'just a pretty face'. Leonardo later proved them wrong by playing difficult roles such as mad businessman Howard Hughes in **The Aviator** (2004).

Critics' Choice

In our opinion, these are Leonardo's three best films so far:

The Aviator (2004)

This is the true story of American millionaire Howard Hughes. Hughes wanted to produce the best films and design the fastest aeroplanes in the world. He risked his money and his life, and eventually went mad.

The Beach (2000)

In Thailand a young tourist, Richard, discovers a beautiful island and a secret community of young travellers. It seems like paradise, but there are hidden problems ...

Catch Me If You Can (2002)

Like **The Aviator**, this film is based on a true story. Frank Abagnale was the most successful con man in the history of the USA. Abagnale worked as a doctor, an airline pilot and a lawyer – all before he was 18!

(392 words)

INTERCULTURAL CORNER

Englisch rund ums Kino

Briten gehen **to the cinema** (ins Kino), um **films** zu sehen, während Amerikaner **to the movie theater** gehen, um sich **movies** anzuschauen.
Der **director** (Regisseur) hofft, dass sein Film ein **box office hit** (Kassenschlager) und kein **flop** (Reinfall) wird. Die unbekannte **extra** (Statistin) will **film star** / **movie star** werden. Vielleicht wird sie eines Tages sogar einen **Oscar** gewinnen. Wenn sie in **Tinsel Town** (Hollywood) keinen Erfolg hat, wird sie ihr Glück möglicherweise **on Broadway** in einem **musical** versuchen.
Fremdsprachige Filme werden selten in den großen **multiplex cinemas** gezeigt. Sie laufen eher in den kleinen **arthouse cinemas** (Programmkinos). Sie werden nicht **dubbed** (synchronisiert), sondern mit **subtitles** (Untertiteln) versehen.

4 **Copy and complete the following mind map of the text.**

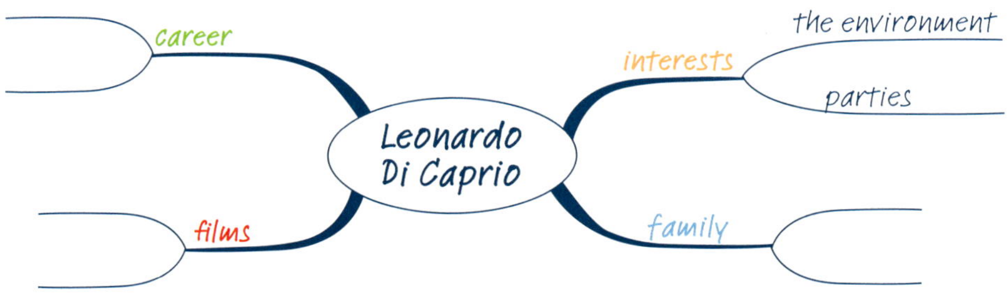

5 **Write a short text (80–100 words) for a website about your favourite musician, film star, sportsperson or other celebrity.**
Give details of the person's life (date and place of birth, family, etc.) and career. Say why you admire him/her.

LEARNING TO LEARN

Tipps zum Schreiben von Texten

1 Machen Sie sich eine Übersicht über das, was Sie schreiben wollen. Sie können z. B. Überschriften machen und dazu alle Punkte auflisten, die Ihnen einfallen. Meist eignet sich eine Mind Map am besten, um alles anschaulich um das Thema herum zu ordnen.

2 Gliedern Sie Ihre Ideen in eine Einleitung (worum es in dem Text geht), einen Hauptteil und einen Schluss (kurze Zusammenfassung oder Fazit).

3 Schreiben Sie einen ersten Entwurf. Jetzt können Sie auch Vokabeln nachschlagen, die Ihnen fehlen.

4 Gehen Sie Ihren Text noch einmal durch und prüfen Sie, ob die Länge stimmt und ob alles logisch und sprachlich korrekt ist.

5 Fertigen Sie nun die Reinschrift in Ihrem Heft an. Achten Sie dabei auf Rechtschreibfehler.

Language

-ING FORM AND INFINITIVE

Verb + -ing-Form
Auf einige Verben wie admit, avoid, dislike, don't mind, enjoy, involve, stop, suggest folgt die -ing-Form:
Leonardo enjoys going to parties. He has stopped playing romantic roles.

Verb + Infinitiv
Auf andere Verben wie agree, choose, decide, expect, hope, learn, manage, prefer, want, would like folgt der Infinitiv:
Hughes wanted to make the best films in the world.

Verb + -ing-Form oder Infinitiv
Auf die Verben begin, continue, hate, like, love und start kann sowohl die -ing-Form als auch der Infinitiv folgen:
He loves dating beautiful women.
He loves to date beautiful women.

DANGER!

Bei remember gibt es einen Bedeutungsunterschied, je nachdem, ob darauf eine -ing-Form oder ein Infinitiv folgt:

I remember seeing that film.
Ich erinnere mich daran, den Film gesehen zu haben.
I'll remember to see that film.
Ich werde daran denken, den Film zu sehen.

Präposition + -ing-Form
Wenn auf eine Präposition ein Verb folgt, muss man die -ing-Form des Verbs verwenden:

Verb + Präposition: *She's thinking of becoming a singer.*

Adjektiv + Präposition: *I'm not interested in becoming a film star.*

Substantiv + Präposition: *I haven't given up my dream of becoming a footballer.*

Practice

6 Decide which of the alternatives is correct. (Both may be correct.) Write out the correct sentences.

Example: Would you like watching / to watch a DVD?
Would you like to watch a DVD?

1 Did you enjoy *watching* / *to watch* her latest film?
2 He expected *getting* / *to get* an Oscar for that performance.
3 I don't mind *watching* / *to watch* American sitcoms.
4 I love *going* / *to go* to the cinema at the weekends.
5 Will Leonardo continue *making* / *to make* successful films?
6 He hates *going* / *to go* to Hollywood parties.
7 We like *reading* / *to read* gossip about Hollywood stars.
8 She had to learn *speaking* / *to speak* Italian for that role.

7 Write out each sentence using the correct form of the verbs in brackets.

Example: You can't avoid ... (do) your homework.
You can't avoid doing your homework.

1 I don't enjoy ... (surf) the internet.
2 She has decided ... (learn) Spanish.
3 I'm thinking of ... (get) a new mobile phone.
4 Sven is interested in ... (learn) to play the guitar.
5 You must learn ... (control) your temper.
6 He doesn't expect ... (pass) his exams.
7 Tom is afraid of ... (look) stupid.
8 Anja agreed ... (help) her brother with his homework.

8 Write five sentences which are true for you, using expressions from the box.

Example: *I love watching DVDs.*

be famous • go to the cinema • go to work • learn English • listen to music • play computer games • play football • travel round the world • watch DVDs • watch talkshows

I love ...
I would like ...
I don't mind ...
I hate ...
I'm interested in ...

9 Go round the class. Ask questions to find a person who has the same sentence as you.

Example: You: *Hamid, what do you love doing?*
Hamid: *I love playing computer games.*

Write the person's name next to the sentence.
When you have names next to all five sentences, you can sit down.

10 Radio station ROXX FM is interviewing rock musician Casey Ellis.

31 **Listen to the interview, then choose the correct option or options to complete the sentences.**

1 Casey became famous ...
- a two years ago.
- b when she was nine.
- c because of a talent competition on TV.

2 As a child, Casey ...
- a became a professional musician.
- b learned to play the guitar.
- c enjoyed singing.

3 Casey loves playing live because ...
- a it's fun.
- b it's easy.
- c she gets a lot of money.

4 Casey hates ...
- a giving interviews.
- b reading about herself in the newspaper.
- c reading newspapers.

REMEMBER
to play **the** guitar – Gitarre spielen

5 Casey enjoys ...
- a going to showbiz parties.
- b meeting well-known musicians.
- c dating celebrities.

6 In the future, Casey hopes to ...
- a keep on making music.
- b make a lot of money.
- c make a new CD.

11 Can you remember what Mike and Casey said – a or b? Listen again to check your answers.

31

1
- a With me in the studio today is rock musician Casey Ellis.
- b My guest today is rock musician Casey Ellis.

2
- a Hi, Casey! How are you?
- b Hi, Casey, and welcome to ROXX FM.

3
- a When did you become a musician?
- b When did you decide to become a musician?

4
- a What do you love about your work?
- b Do you love your work?

5
- a It's such a great feeling.
- b It feels so great.

6
- a I'd like to have a normal life.
- b I just want to have a normal life.

7
- a What do you hope to do in the future?
- b What are your plans for the future?

8
- a You're welcome, Mike. Don't mention it.
- b You're welcome, Mike. It's been a pleasure.

12 Now role-play an interview with a famous person. You can use the language from exercise 11.

PARTNER A: You are the ROXX FM reporter.
PARTNER B: You are a famous person. (Tell your partner who you are.)

A	B
Begrüßen Sie den Gast.	
	Grüßen Sie zurück.
Fragen Sie ihn/sie, wann seine/ihre Karriere als Musiker, Filmstar usw. begonnen hat.	
	Beantworten Sie die Frage.
Fragen Sie, was er/sie an der Arbeit mag.	
	Beantworten Sie die Frage.
Fragen Sie, was er/sie an der Arbeit absolut nicht mag.	
	Beantworten Sie die Frage.
Fragen Sie, was er/sie in der Zukunft vorhat.	
	Beantworten Sie die Frage.
Bedanken Sie sich für das Interview.	

The world of work

Looking after people

1 Read the webpage and match each photo to the correct job.

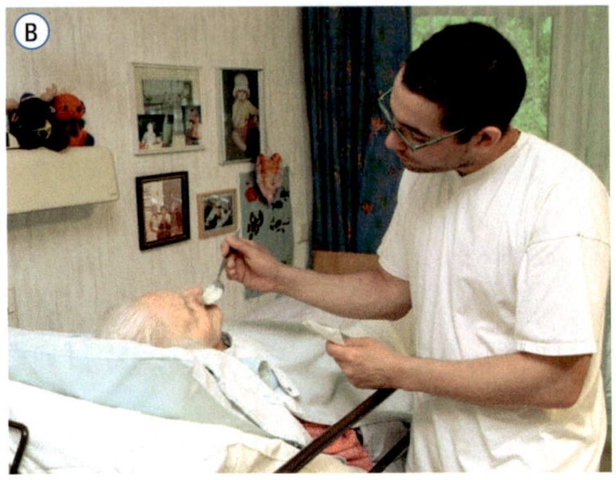

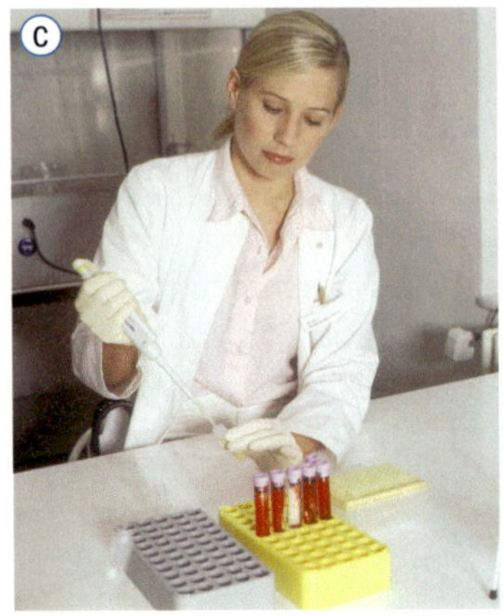

A CAREER IN CARING

Do you enjoy working with people? Are you friendly, caring and responsible? If so, one of these jobs could be the right one for you.

Nurse

Many nurses work in hospitals. Their work can include checking patients' temperature and blood pressure, giving drugs and injections, cleaning and dressing wounds and giving blood transfusions. They may help surgeons during operations.

Other nurses work in doctors' surgeries. Their work can include treating small injuries, taking blood samples and helping patients to lose weight or give up smoking.

Nursery nurse

Nursery nurses work with younger children, usually up to seven years old. They often work in nurseries and in infant schools.

Making sure that the children are safe, happy and well is an important part of the work, but nursery nurses also plan and supervise activities like reading, painting and drawing, music and cooking. Their work may also involve bathing, changing and feeding younger children.

Care assistant for the elderly

Aged care assistants help elderly people in their daily life. They may work in day centres or nursing homes or they may visit clients in their own homes.

Aged care assistants may help their clients to get dressed and to get around the home. They may also organize social activities. Less able clients may need help with intimate tasks such as using the toilet and washing themselves. For people who are still able to live in their own homes, home care assistants often do general household chores such as cleaning, shopping and laundry.

2 Join the sentence halves together. Then decide which job it is.

1 You have to know how to dress
2 The job involves feeding
3 I've checked the patient's
4 When you visit Mr Jones, you'll need to do
5 Mrs Smith needs some help
6 Every week we organize

a with getting dressed.
b temperature and blood pressure.
c some household chores.
d minor wounds. – *Nurse*
e social activities for our clients.
f and changing babies.

3 Jade doesn't know what she wants to do when she leaves school, so she talks to a careers adviser.

32

Listen to the conversation. Which of these questions does the careers adviser ask?

1 What sort of things are you interested in?
2 What are your best subjects at school?
3 Can you be more specific?
4 Would you like to work in a hospital?
5 Are you good at looking after children?
6 Would you enjoy working in an office?
7 What do you enjoy doing in your spare time?
8 What do you think about becoming a nursery nurse?

4 Listen again and make notes about Jade's answer to each question.

32

5 Role-play a conversation with a careers adviser.

PARTNER A: You are a careers adviser. Interview your partner, using questions from exercise 3. You can change some words.

PARTNER B: You are the interviewee. Answer your partner's questions.

6 Copy and complete this 'Jobseeker Profile'.

JOBSEEKER PROFILE

Name:

Answer these questions. Write full sentences.

What type of work are you interested in doing?

What things are you good at doing?

What things are you not so good at doing?

What do you enjoy doing in your free time?

Submit

REMEMBER

She's good ~~in~~ *at* maths.
I'm good ~~in~~ *at* working with people.

Exam practice

Starting out in music

When you close your eyes and imagine your ideal career, does it involve rapping with Eminem or touring with U2?

Many young people dream of becoming a pop star, but very few turn the dream into reality. You'll need talent, hard work and luck to succeed.

Performing live is a great way to get your music to an audience. It's also a good way of discovering what improvements you need to make. If you aren't good enough, the audience will tell you!

When you have some experience, the next step is to make a 'demo' CD. If you (or a friend) are good at using a computer, you can do this at home, but using a professional recording studio isn't as expensive as you think. You don't have to record a whole album of music, just three or four tracks.

You should make lots of copies of your demo CD and send them to suitable music companies. Don't forget to include a short autobiography and a photo.

Another way of letting people hear your music is to put it on a website. These days, many bands have enthusiastic online fans before a radio station has played one of their songs. (200 words)

Text comprehension

1 Finish the sentences using information from the text. Use your own words.

a To be successful in the music business, you must ...
b You should perform live if you can, because ...
c After you have made your demo CD, ...

2 Answer the questions about the text.

a How can a new band make a demo CD? (2 ways)
b What should the band put on its demo CD?
c How can the band find fans? (3 ways)

3 Give your opinion on the following statement from the text.

'Many young people dream of becoming a pop star.'

4 Ask the author of the text three questions about becoming a pop star. Use three different question words or types of question.

Grammar

5 Fill in the gaps with the correct forms of the verbs in brackets.

a We ... (record) our demo CD on Saturday.
b If you ... (not work) hard enough, you won't succeed.
c Georgie ... (play) in a band since 2005.
d She ... (learn) to play the guitar in 2004.

6 **Answer the questions using short answers.**

a Have you ever been to a football match?
b Are you going to go to the cinema this weekend?

7 **Make these sentences negative.**

a Matt likes listening to rap music.
b He has downloaded Eminem's latest video.

Vocabulary

8 **Complete the sentences with the corresponding adverb for the word in brackets.**

a Although they worked hard, they weren't ... good musicians. (reality)
b Ben can play the piano quite ... . (good)

9 **Complete the sentences with a word or phrase which means the same as the word in brackets.**

a Alice ... that her boyfriend was going out with another girl. (discovered)
b ... fans downloaded the song from the band's website. (lots of)

10 **Complete the sentences with the opposite of the word in brackets.**

a Blank CDs are very ... . (expensive)
b Do you ... the first album by Oasis? (forget)

11 **Use a dictionary to translate the underlined expressions.**

a Touring with the Rolling Stones was a great experience.
b She has fifteen years' experience in the music industry.
c Hast du auf deinem Zimmer Musik gehört?
d Der Kopfhörer muss wohl kaputt sein: Ich höre nichts.

Writing

12 **Write a short review for a music or cinema forum about a concert or film that you saw recently (80–100 words).**

Mediation

13 **Übertragen Sie den Inhalt des Textes 'Starting out in music' ins Deutsche. Übersetzen Sie nicht Wort für Wort. Schreiben Sie ganze Sätze.**

14 **What would you say in these situations?**

a Sie fragen nach dem Weg zum Bahnhof.
b Sie haben jemanden angerempelt und entschuldigen sich.
c Sie möchten eine Packung Kaugummi kaufen.
d Jemand lädt Sie ins Kino ein. Sie sagen zu.
e Sie essen im Restaurant. Das Essen ist kalt und Sie beschweren sich.
f Sie möchten eine Zeitung kaufen.

12 How others live

1 a **Scan the text on the opposite page. Which of these options did Daniela choose for her working holiday in Australia?**

b **Now say which of them you would be interested in.**

2 **Now read or listen to the text and complete these sentences in your own words.**

Example: WWOOFers are not given money, they *get food and a place to stay.*

1 Daniela wanted to go to Australia because ...
2 She was surprised to find that Australia is ...
3 The Hoskins think that it is important to ...
4 Daniela finds the Hoskins' life lonely because ...
5 Australia's nickname is 'The Lucky Country' because ...
6 Although Australia doesn't have much water, ...

INTERCULTURAL CORNER

Wissenswertes über Australien

Australien ist mit seinen 8 Millionen km² kaum kleiner als Europa, doch leben dort nur 20 Millionen Menschen – weniger als in Bayern und Baden-Württemberg zusammen. Der größte Teil der Bevölkerung lebt in den großen Städten Melbourne, Sydney, Brisbane und Perth.

Das australische Englisch unterscheidet sich in mancher Hinsicht vom britischen oder amerikanischen. Australier benutzen gerne Kurzformen: So werden **sunglasses** zu **sunnies**, ein **barbecue** ist ein **barbie**, **Australia** ist **Aussie** (Aussprache: 'Ozzy') und aus **Australians** werden **Aussies**. Dafür richtet sich die Schreibweise nach den britischen Regeln (**metre**, **programme**), nicht nach den amerikanischen (**meter**, **program**).

Australier gehen eher locker miteinander um. Meistens redet man sich mit Vornamen an. Zur Begrüßung hört man oft **G'day!** (= **Good day!**) oder **How are you going?**, wobei **Hi!** und **Hello!** ebenfalls gebräuchlich sind. Auf **How are you going?** antwortet man mit **Good, thanks!** – selbst wenn es nicht wahr ist.

BEFORE YOU START

Here are some reasons why young Germans go to Australia. Choose three reasons that would be important for you. Now compare ideas in small groups.

- do watersports
- learn work skills
- get a suntan
- take great photos
- speak better English
- make new friends
- see strange animals
- visit the Outback

33

WWOOFing in Australia

WWOOF stands for 'Willing Workers on Organic Farms'. (It is pronounced 'woof'.) WWOOFers aren't paid for their work; instead, they are given free board and lodging by their host families. Because WWOOFing is seen as voluntary work, WWOOFers don't normally need a working visa.

Daniela Kieser from Kassel is a WWOOFer in Australia. She is working for three months on an organic farm in western Victoria. We interviewed her about her experiences.

Why Australia?

I always wanted to visit Australia: it seemed so exotic, with its Aborigines, the Outback and strange animals like kangaroos and koalas. Now I realize that it is also quite European in some ways. Everyone speaks English, so you don't feel like an outsider. There are even quite a lot of German-speaking immigrants here.

What's your host family like?

My host family – John and Barbara Hoskins and their sons Lachlan and Alex – are really friendly. I was given my own bedroom and I have been treated like one of the family since day one.

What about the work?

The Hoskins run a small organic farm, and they are very 'green': their house is powered by solar energy, all the water is taken from rainwater tanks and chemicals are not used on the farm. I water the vegetable garden, repair fences, plant trees and feed the animals, including chickens, sheep and goats. It's fun, but it's hard work, and it's hot and dusty.

Is there a 'downside'?

Yes. I couldn't live here for ever: it's too isolated. We are about 40 km from Balmoral, and that's just a small country town: a shop, a church and a pub – that's it! The only big city in Victoria is Melbourne, and that's 400 km away. When I leave here, I'm going to Melbourne and Sydney for some nightlife!

What do you think of Australia now?

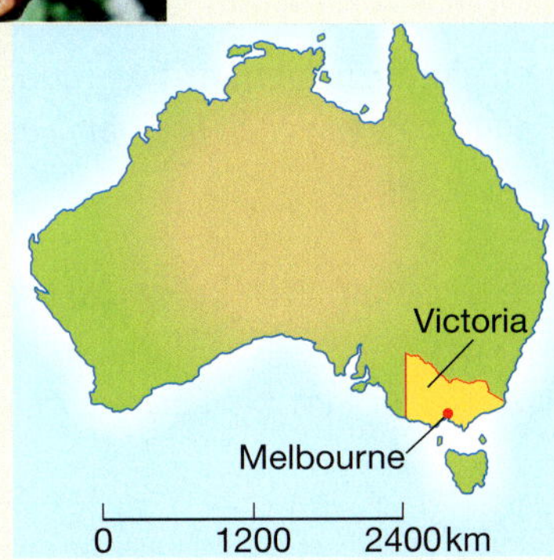

Australia is awesome! Its nickname is 'The Lucky Country', and Australians really are lucky: they have gorgeous beaches, beautiful cities and lots of unspoilt nature. No wonder most of them are so laid-back and friendly! On the other hand, Australians aren't doing enough to protect their beautiful environment. Australia is the driest continent, but a huge amount of water is used for agriculture. That's bad for the environment, and the problem will be made worse by global warming.

(388 words)

3 **Choose the correct answer or answers.**

Example: *1b, c*

1 According to Daniela, Australia is ...
- a dangerous and exciting.
- b strange and interesting.
- c similar to Europe in some ways.

2 When you work for WWOOF, you get ...
- a free accommodation.
- b free food.
- c money.

3 The Hoskins ...
- a don't like strangers.
- b care about the environment.
- c live in a small town.

4 Daniela ...
- a finds farmwork hard.
- b enjoys working on the farm.
- c is looking forward to visiting Australian cities.

5 Balmoral ...
- a is a large town in Victoria.
- b doesn't have a cinema.
- c is near Melbourne.

6 Daniela thinks that Australians ...
- a should use less water.
- b should use more water.
- c should look after their environment better.

4 **You are writing an article for a college magazine about working holidays in Australia. Summarize relevant information from the text in German. Write one or two sentences per section.**

Language

THE PASSIVE (Passiv)

Das Passiv wird verwendet, wenn man auf eine unpersönliche Art und Weise über Fakten, Vorgänge usw. berichten will. Man hebt dann nicht den Verursacher (also z. B. die handelnde Person), sondern den Vorgang hervor. Oft wird der Verursacher nicht genannt.
WWOOFers aren't paid for their work.

Soll der Verursacher einer Handlung genannt werden, steht im Passivsatz by (= von, durch).
They are given free board and lodging by their host families.
Their house is powered by solar energy.

Simple present: am/are/is + Partizip Perfekt → *No chemicals are used on the farm.*

Present perfect: have/has + been + Partizip Perfekt → *I have been treated like one of the family.*

Simple past: was/were + Partizip Perfekt → *I was given my own bedroom.*

Will future: will + be + Partizip Perfekt → *The problem will be made worse by global warming.*

Practice

5 **Complete these passive sentences with the verb forms in the box.**

are • be • been • been • has • is • was • ~~were~~ • will

Example: The animals *were* fed two hours ago.

1 When will the fence ... repaired?
2 Have you ... paid yet?
3 You ... be treated like one of the family.
4 Women and men ... treated equally.
5 My mobile phone ... stolen last week.
6 ... your moped been repaired yet?
7 The housework hasn't ... done for weeks.
8 The garden ... watered every week.

6 **Complete the answers to these FAQs by using the passive forms of the verbs. Use the same tense as in the question.**

Example: How do you pronounce WWOOF? It *is pronounced* 'woof'.

WWOOFing in Australia – FAQs

1 Do all WWOOF farms use organic farming methods?
Yes. Organic farming methods … on all WWOOF farms.

2 Do I need a working visa?
No. A working visa … , because WWOOFing is voluntary work.

3 Do WWOOF hosts pay WWOOFers for their work?
No. WWOOFers … for their work.

4 Will my host give me free accommodation?
Yes. You … free accommodation – usually a spare bedroom, sometimes a tent or a caravan.

5 Do the host families provide food?
Yes, usually all meals … by the host.

6 How do I make a booking?
Bookings … by phone, mail or email – just contact the host farmer directly.

7 What work do WWOOFers do?
The work that … depends on your skills and what the farmer needs, e.g. general farmwork, repairs, even computer work.

8 Do WWOOF hosts accept WWOOFers with children?
Children … on some farms – check with the host.

7 **Make the following sentences negative. Then give the right information.**

Example: WWOOFers are given ~~money~~. (food and accommodation)
WWOOFers aren't given money. They're given food and accommodation.

1 Most English-language films are made in ~~England~~. (the USA)
2 Bungy jumping was invented in ~~Australia~~. (New Zealand)
3 The Harry Potter books were written by ~~William Shakespeare~~. (J. K. Rowling)
4 In the future, Australian houses will be powered by ~~oil~~. (solar energy)
5 Cricket is played a lot in ~~Germany~~. (Australia)
6 Daniela has been treated like ~~an employee~~ by the Hoskins. (a member of the family)
7 The party will be organized by the ~~teachers~~. (students)
8 The WWOOFers' accommodation is provided by ~~hotels~~. (the host farmers)

8 Lachlan Hoskins has come to Germany to stay in Munich. The local radio station interviews Lachlan about the differences between Germany and Australia.

34

Read the speech bubbles. Do you think they are about Australia, Germany or both? Listen to check your answers.

Australia	Germany	both
	... *it rains so much* ...	

... all that traffic ...

It's all right, I suppose.

... it rains so much ...

... soccer isn't played much ...

... dry and brown ...

... eat a lot of meat ...

... a lot more formal ...

... there isn't enough room ...

... castles, churches and so on ...

Football or soccer?

GB 'Soccer' is the official name for *Fußball*, but in everyday speech it is called 'football'.

USA 'Football' only means American football; 'soccer' means *Fußball*.

Aus 'Football' is a general term for soccer, rugby and Australian-rules football (a game which is very popular in Australia but which isn't played anywhere else); 'soccer' means *Fußball*.

9 Listen again and make notes. Answer these questions about the interview.

34

Example: How is the weather in Germany different from the weather in Australia?
It rains more in Germany.

1 What does Lachlan notice about the buildings in Germany?
2 How is the traffic in Germany different from the traffic in Australia?
3 What similarity is there between German and Australian food?
4 What difference does Lachlan find between German and Australian beer?
5 What surprised Lachlan most about Germany?
6 How do neighbours address each other in Australia?

10 **In groups of three, role-play an interview with a foreign student.**

PARTNER A: You are the radio reporter. You only speak German. Ask about:
- the host family
- the weather
- the place where the student is staying
- traffic, German cars
- German food and drink
- the student's best/worst experience

PARTNER B: You are the interpreter. You speak English and German.
PARTNER C: You are the foreign student. You only speak English.

11 **Write an email home for the foreign student. Mention the things he/she likes about Germany and the things he/she misses about home. Make up any details you like. (80–100 words)**

12 **Draw a mind map about Australia. Read the advice about mind maps in the 'Learning to learn' box. Review all the information about Australia in this unit (texts, photos, exercises, etc.). Use the example below as your starting point.**

LEARNING TO LEARN

Eine Mind Map erstellen

Bevor Sie einen Text schreiben, bringen Sie zunächst Ihre Ideen in eine sinnvolle Ordnung. Eine Mind Map (auf Deutsch etwa „Gedankengerüst") ist eine einfache und praktische Methode, Begriffe und Ideen übersichtlich auf einem Blatt festzuhalten.

1. Nehmen Sie ein leeres Blatt und schreiben Sie das Thema in Großbuchstaben in einen Kreis in die Mitte.
2. Finden Sie Oberbegriffe für die einzelnen Bereiche des Themas und tragen Sie diese auf starken „Ästen" ein, die von dem Thema in der Mitte abzweigen.
3. Zeichnen Sie nun für jeden Begriff, den Sie in den Texten finden oder der Ihnen zusätzlich beim Schreiben einfällt, einen „Zweig", der von dem jeweiligen Oberbegriff nach außen führt.
4. Noch anschaulicher wird das Ganze, wenn Sie verschiedene Farben für die Oberbegriffe verwenden und einzelne Begriffe durch kleine Zeichnungen illustrieren.

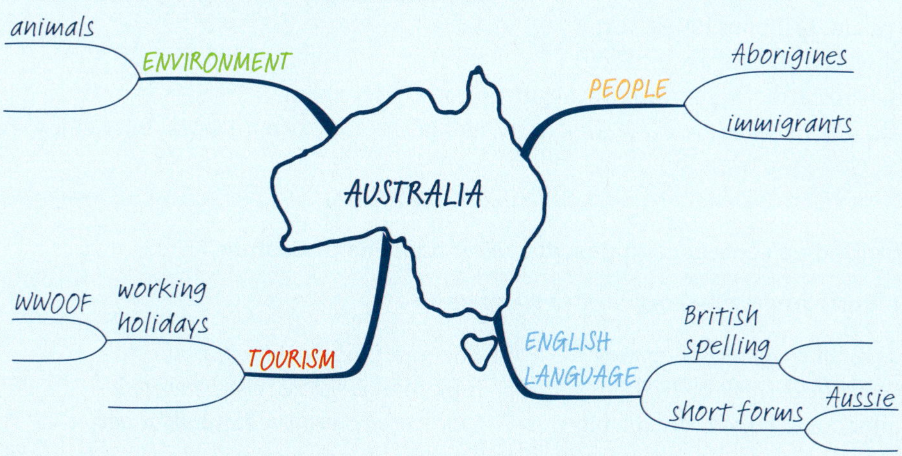

The world of work

Working in an office

1 **Read the text. Which of these advertisements is for Nicky's job?**

① Small but busy T-shirt design company needs a **graphic designer** with creative ideas ...

② Can you organize our busy office? We need a **receptionist/secretary** ...

③ Small clothing company needs a reliable **accounts clerk / bookkeeper** ...

I'm Nicky Adams. I work at Custom-T, a company which designs T-shirts. Customers order T-shirts from our website, then the T-shirts are printed here in our studio and sent to the customer by post. It's a small company – there are only five of us. Teresa and I run the office. Teresa is the bookkeeper – she updates the accounts and takes care of all the financial work, but I'm responsible for all the general office work.

When I get to work in the mornings, the first thing I do is make coffee for everyone. Then I switch on my computer and check my email inbox. If there are any urgent emails, I answer them straight away.

The post arrives about 9.30, and I have to open and sort it all. There's always a lot of junk mail, and I throw all that straight into the bin!

What I do for the rest of the day varies. On a typical day, I answer the phone, I file the paperwork and I fax or email invoices to customers. I type and print out letters for the managing director, Mrs Logan. If there are any visitors, I look after them until Mrs Logan is ready to see them.

It's always hectic, and I always go home tired at the end of the day. It's hard work, but I enjoy working here because everyone's so friendly.

2 **Sort out these mixed-up sentences to describe what happens at Custom-T.**

Example: 1 T-shirts *are printed and sent to customers.*

1 T-shirts *are faxed or emailed to customers.*
2 The accounts *are looked after by Nicky.*
3 Nicky's email inbox *is thrown straight into the bin.*
4 Urgent emails *are updated by Teresa.*
5 The post *is filed in the office.*
6 Junk mail *is checked every morning.*
7 Invoices *are answered straight away.*
8 The paperwork *is opened and sorted by Nicky.*
9 Visitors *are printed and sent to customers.*

3 **What did Nicky do today? Write her diary. Try to use your own words. Start like this:**

Today was a hectic day! At nine o'clock I made coffee for everyone.
From quarter past nine to ten o'clock I ...

4 **It's Dan's first day at work as an office clerk. Mrs Patel is explaining the filing system to him.**
35 **Listen to the recording and match the paperwork (1–5) to the destinations (a–h).**

Example: *1 d, b, g*

1 letters	a blue file	e green file
2 orders	b yellow file	f red file
3 bank statements	c bin	g Mr Jones' in-tray
4 invoices	d photocopier	h fax machine
5 junk mail		

5 **Work with a partner and do this role-play.**
Partner A: You are the office manager. Decide what happens to each type of paperwork. Explain the filing system to the new office clerk.

Example: A *Invoices are photocopied and put in the grey file ...*

bank statements
invoices
junk mail
orders
letters

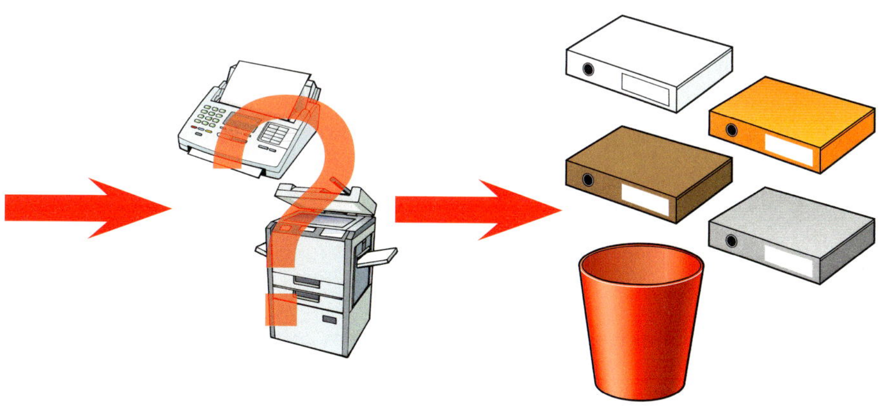

Partner B: You are the new office clerk. Listen to the office manager and make notes, then read back the instructions to the office manager.

Exam practice

International workcamps

A workcamp is a place where people of all nationalities live together for two to four weeks and work on a project which has been organized by a local sponsor. Most workcamps are held during the summer. Between 10 and 20 people usually take part. Most volunteers are between 18 and 35, but there is no upper age limit.

It's important to remember that a workcamp is not a free holiday. The work is real: it has not been set up just to bring people together. Workcamp volunteers have worked with drug addicts in Spain, helped to build an ecotourism centre in Thailand, planted trees in Iceland and organized games and activities at a children's home in Russia – to give just a few examples.

Decisions and problems are discussed by the whole group. You will not be told what to do by the camp leaders: their role is to guide and give advice. Volunteers pay for and arrange their own travel to the camp, but accommodation and food are provided by the camp sponsor. (176 words)

Source: abridged extracts from: http://camps.sciint.org/

Text comprehension

1 Finish the sentences using information from the text. Use your own words.

a Workcamp volunteers come from ...
b The camp leaders don't ...
c Travel to the workcamp ...

2 Answer the questions about the text.

a What is the aim of a workcamp?
b What happens when there is a problem?
c What don't volunteers have to pay for?

3 Do you think the people on a workcamp should be paid for their work? Give your opinion.

4 Ask three questions about international workcamps. Use three different question words or types of question.

Grammar

5 Complete the sentences with the correct form of the verbs in the brackets.

a 'I've lost my camera.' – 'Oh no! If I ... (find) it, I ... (let you know).'
b The school ... (build) by workcamp volunteers.
c I enjoy ... (find out) about foreign countries.

6 Complete the sentences with a relative pronoun.

a The people ... organize the projects are the camp sponsors.
b The workcamp ... sounds most interesting is the one in India.

7 **Find the comparative and superlative forms of these adjectives.**

a much   b important   c a few

Vocabulary

8 **Complete the sentences with the corresponding adjectives for the words in brackets.**

a The atmosphere in the workcamp was very … . (live)
b I found the advice very … . (help)

9 **Complete the sentences with words or phrases which mean the same as the words in brackets.**

a … that workcamps are a good way of practising your English. (keep in mind)
b Don't you think we should … this problem? (discuss)

10 **Complete the sentences with the opposites of the words in brackets.**

a I hate being … when I'm on holiday. (together)
b Don't … your mum's birthday! (remember)

11 **Use a dictionary to translate the underlined expressions.**

a You should stay for the whole workcamp.
b On the whole, workcamp volunteers are in their twenties or thirties.
c Du kannst umsonst bei uns wohnen, wenn du mit den Kindern aushilfst.
d Unsere ganze Arbeit war umsonst – das Erdbeben hat alles zerstört.

Writing

12 **Imagine you are taking part in an international workcamp in Africa. Write an email to an American friend. Talk about the other volunteers, the work, the weather and any good or bad experiences you have had. (80–100 words)**

Mediation

13 **Übertragen Sie den Inhalt des Textes 'International workcamps' ins Deutsche. Übersetzen Sie nicht Wort für Wort. Schreiben Sie ganze Sätze.**

14 **Complete the dialogue with your own ideas.**

TOURIST: Excuse me! Do you speak English?
YOU: …
TOURIST: Oh, good! Can you tell me how to get to the train station from here?
YOU: …
TOURIST: OK, I think I've got that. Thanks very much for your help.
YOU: …

13 Modern love

1 **Read or listen to the text. How are the people in the photographs on the opposite page (A–F) connected to Declan? (Not all of them are named in the text.)**

Example: *A his ex-girlfriend*

his daughter • his friends • his ex-girlfriend's father • ~~his ex-girlfriend~~ • his parents • his ex-girlfriend's mother

A teenage dad

36 *Declan O'Connell, 19, is an apprentice metalworker in Cork, Republic of Ireland. Two years ago he became a teenage dad. Declan had just left school and his girlfriend Paula had just started college when she realized that she was pregnant. Declan tells his story:*

We had only been together for three months when Paula found out that she was pregnant. We didn't know what to do.

Paula said that her parents would take it badly. She was right. Margaret and Patrick are strict Catholics and they made life very difficult for her. They said that she had ruined her life, and that she was a bad example to her younger sister.

My parents saw things differently. They said that Paula and I could count on them to help. They were brilliant – really helpful and loving.

I never asked Paula if she wanted to keep the baby: we just knew that abortion wasn't an option for us. I asked her if she wanted to get married, and she said, 'Don't be silly!' She's a very independent person.

Paula's pregnancy was difficult for me. Paula's parents banned me from their house because I had got their 'little girl' pregnant.

The birth went well, and we had a little girl. We called her Maeve. Margaret and I were both there at the hospital when Maeve was born. Afterwards, Margaret was much nicer to me because we had shared that incredible experience.

Patrick still didn't like me, though. After Paula and Maeve had come out of hospital, he didn't allow me to visit my girlfriend and daughter at home.

Paula and I agreed that we would share Maeve's upbringing. Maeve comes to stay with my family every weekend, and I see her during the week as well. I pick her up from the childminder, and Paula knows that I'm always there to help.

Our friends have been a great help, too. Maeve is the first baby in the gang, and everybody adores her. She gets lots of love and attention.

Sadly, Paula and I have split up now. She says that she still wants me to be a real dad to Maeve, though, and so far everything is OK. But what if Paula gets a new boyfriend? My mum says that I will always be Maeve's dad, but I'm worried about the future. (390 words)

BEFORE YOU START

What problems can single parents have? Discuss in a small group and make a list.

– not enough money
– ...

Paula

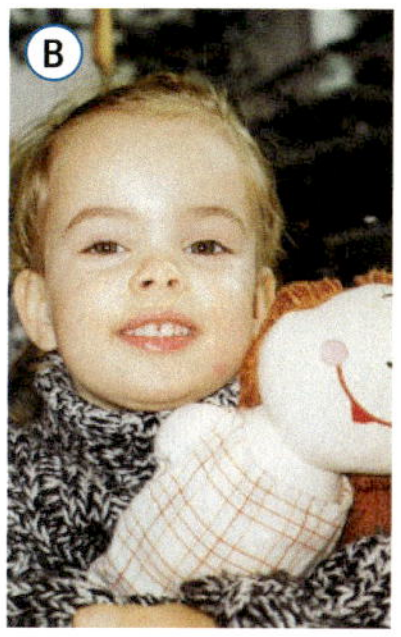

Maeve

Patrick

Margaret

Mr and Mrs O'Connell

Ian, Sue, Dave and Laura

2 Read the text again. Are these statements true or false? Correct the false statements.

Example: Declan's parents were angry with Paula.
False: Paula's parents were angry with Declan and Paula.

1 Paula wanted to marry Declan.
2 Paula wasn't allowed to visit Declan at home.
3 Paula's mother likes Declan now.
4 Declan only sees Maeve at weekends.
5 Declan and Paula's friends love Maeve.
6 Some of their friends have babies.
7 Paula is not Declan's girlfriend any more.
8 Paula has got a new boyfriend now.

LEARNING TO LEARN

Wie man mit schwierigen Texten zurechtkommt

Man stößt beim Lesen immer mal wieder auf Sätze, die man einfach nicht versteht, egal wie sehr man sich konzentriert und wie viele Vokabeln man nachschlägt. Das ist ganz normal und passiert allen, die eine Fremdsprache lernen.

- Wenn Sie auf eine unbekannte Vokabel stoßen, überlegen Sie, ob Sie den Satz nicht auch ohne sie verstehen. Wenn es z. B. im Text heißt: **She gets lots of love and attention**, kann man ahnen, dass es sich bei **attention** um etwas Positives handelt – das reicht für ein grobes Verständnis.
- Manchmal wird das Verständnis eines Satzes auch durch so genannte **False friends** erschwert – das sind Wörter, die deutschen Wörtern ähnlich sehen, aber etwas anderes bedeuten. **Pregnant** im Text oben bedeutet z. B. keineswegs „prägnant", sondern „schwanger".
- Im Englischen haben Nomen und Adjektive oft dieselbe Form – **love** bedeutet nicht nur „Liebe", sondern auch „lieben". So etwas kann auch den Sinn eines Satzes entstellen.
- Hakt es immer noch, lesen Sie einfach weiter. Vielleicht erschließt sich der Satz aus dem weiteren Textverlauf.

INTERCULTURAL CORNER

Abtreibung und Sexualmoral in Irland

Die Republik Irland ist ein zu 90 Prozent katholisches Land, daher überwiegt bei Fragen wie Verhütung und Abtreibung eine konservative Haltung. Bis 1985 durften nur verheiratete Paare legal Verhütungsmittel einsetzen. In den letzten Jahren hat sich die Einstellung etwas gelockert; eine Umfrage hat ergeben, dass mittlerweile etwa 80 Prozent der Paare in Irland verhüten, um ungewollte Schwangerschaften zu vermeiden.
Abtreibung ist in Irland nur dann legal, wenn die Gesundheit der Mutter durch die Geburt gefährdet ist. Wer auch in anderen Fällen abtreiben will, muss ins Ausland fahren – in der Regel nach Großbritannien, wo jede Frau ein Recht auf Abtreibung hat.

3 **Copy the table and complete the word families. Most of the words you need are in the text.**

	noun	verb	adjective	adverb
1	?		pregnant	
2	?	?	?	helpfully
3	?	?	?	lovingly
4	reality	?	?	?
5	goodness		?	?

4 **Discuss these questions in a group.**

1 Why do you think Paula and Declan split up? Do you think it was Declan's idea or Paula's?
2 Declan is worried because Paula might get a new boyfriend. What other problems might there be?
3 What can Declan do to stay close to his daughter?

Language

PAST PERFECT (vollendete Vergangenheit)

Das **past perfect** wird benutzt, wenn eine Handlung bereits abgeschlossen war, bevor eine zweite begann. Beide Handlungen liegen in der Vergangenheit.
Das **past perfect** wird gebildet aus **had/hadn't** und dem Partizip Perfekt (3. Form des Verbs).
*Paula **had left** school when she found out that she was pregnant.*

Man kann mit dem **past perfect** die Hintergründe für eine Handlung erklären, die im **simple past** steht:
*Paula's parents banned me from their house because **I had got** Paula pregnant.*

INDIRECT SPEECH (indirekte Rede)

In der indirekten Rede wird einem Dritten berichtet, was jemand gesagt hat.
Wenn das einleitende Verb in der Vergangenheit steht (**said**, **agreed** usw.), verschieben sich die Zeiten der Verben im berichtenden Satzteil, meistens um eine Zeitstufe in die Vergangenheit.

Direkte Rede		Indirekte Rede
Simple present *'You **are** a bad example.'*	→ →	Simple past *They said ... (that) she **was** a bad example.*
Simple past *'The birth **went** well.'*	→ →	Past perfect *She said (that) the birth **had gone** well.*
Present perfect *'You **have ruined** your life.'*	→ →	Past perfect *They said (that) she **had ruined** her life.*
will *'My parents **will take** it badly.'*	→ →	would *Paula said (that) her parents **would take** it badly.*
can *'You **can** count on us.'*	→ →	could *They said (that) we **could** count on them.*

- Die einleitende Konjunktion **that** (= dass) kann weggelassen werden.

- Wenn das einleitende Verb im **simple present** steht (**says**, **agrees** usw.), sind die Zeiten genau wie in der direkten Rede: *Declan **says** (that) he still **wants** to be Maeve's dad.*

Fragen in der indirekten Rede	
Mit Fragewort: *'Why **do** you **hate** Declan?'*	*Paula asked her dad why he **hated** Declan.*
Ohne Fragewort: *'**Do** you **want** to get married?'*	*I asked her **if/whether** she **wanted** to get married.*

Practice

5 Complete the sentences with the past perfect forms of the verbs in brackets.

Example: After Declan (leave) school, he got an apprenticeship.
After Declan had left school, he got an apprenticeship.

1 After Paula (have) the baby, she split up with Declan.
2 The exam was a disaster because I (not do) enough work.
3 After we (leave) the pub, a fight started.
4 We (start) breakfast when the phone rang.
5 Declan was sad because Paula (split up with) him.
6 I missed the party because Dan (not tell) me the right time.
7 After I (replace) the battery, my mobile phone worked fine.
8 I tried to phone her, but she (not give) me the right number.

After Phil had eaten five hotdogs, ...

6 Look at the cartoon strip and explain why these things happened.

1 Andy's boss fired him because *he had dropped the food.*
2 Katie was angry with Andy because ...
3 Andy was sad because ...
4 Andy kissed Lisa because ...
5 Katie split up with Andy because ...
6 Katie phoned Andy because ...
7 Andy was happy because ...

7 Put these sentences into indirect speech, using said.

Example: Declan: 'I need a new job.' *Declan said he needed a new job.*

1 Paula: 'Declan has given me 200 euros.'
2 Lisa: 'I don't like watching soaps.'
3 Katie: 'I'm not angry with Andy.'
4 Dan: 'I won't get married until I'm 30.'
5 You: 'I only drank two beers.'
6 They: 'We don't like cola as much as beer.'
7 Carol: 'I'll call him on Friday.'
8 Ben: 'I haven't seen my dad for ages.'

8 **Put these questions into indirect speech, using asked.**

Example: Paula: 'Why don't you like Declan, dad?'
Paula asked her dad why he didn't like Declan.

1 We: 'Do you still love Declan, Paula?'
2 Lisa: 'Is it OK to smoke here?'
3 Emma: 'Who did you see in the pub, Katie?'
4 Declan: 'Have you ever been to Ireland, Ken?'
5 Katie: 'Won't you miss Lisa, Andy?'
6 They: 'Has Andy stopped drinking, Katie?'
7 Declan: 'Why did you lose your job, Andy?'
8 Dan: 'Can I have your phone number, Lisa?'

9 **Young Irish men and women were asked about single-parent families. Here are some of the results of the survey. Describe the graph using indirect speech.**

Example: *A: More than eighty per cent said that it was OK for a woman to bring up a child by herself.*
B: Yes, but about ten per cent said that ... .

	yes	don't know	no
'It's OK for a woman to bring up a child by herself.'	85%	5%	10%
'It's OK for a man to bring up a child by himself.'	75%	5%	20%
'Children of single parents have more problems.'	25%	15%	60%

10 **Write your own opinion about the statements in exercise 9. Give reasons.**

11 **Paula phones Declan. Listen to the conversation.**

37

1 What is Paula's news?
2 Why is it bad news for Declan?

12 **Declan writes to his friend Andy about his conversation with Paula. Listen again, then put Declan's sentences in the right order.**

37

Hi Andy,
Paula phoned me last night.
a She said that she had a job interview with the Bank of Ireland.
b She said she would phone me on Monday, after the job interview.
c Then she said that she didn't have the job yet and that it was just an interview.
d I said that that was good news.
e Then she told me that the job was in London.
f I was really shocked. I said that London was too far away.
g I said that Maeve needed two parents.
I don't know what to do. I'm feeling quite down.
Declan :-(

The world of work

Manufacturing jobs

1 **Scan the text to find out what 'CNC' means.**

a computer numbered components
b central numerical computer
c computer numerically controlled

Women in Engineering

Samantha O'Hara, CNC machinist

I'm a CNC machinist at Marotta Ireland, Ltd in Dublin. We design and manufacture components for aircraft and spacecraft.

I left school at 16, after I had got my Leaving Certificate. At that time I didn't really know what I wanted to do, though. I worked in a clothes shop for six months, but it wasn't really what I wanted.

My big brother said I should try engineering – I had been quite good at maths at school. My dad said I would never get a job because I was a girl, but my mum said it was a good idea.

I wrote a lot of letters and had a few interviews, and eventually I got an apprenticeship as a machinist at Automotion, a company that made car parts.

I had just finished my apprenticeship when the chance came up to work for Marotta. I was really keen, because Marotta makes components for Boeing aircraft and for the Ariane rocket, for example.

I operate a CNC mill. A mill is a machine which makes metal components. 'CNC' stands for 'computer numerically controlled' – basically, it means that the mill is controlled by a computer. I plan the job, program the computer and set up the mill. After the component is finished, I clean the mill so that it is ready for the next job.

2 **Read the text, then copy and complete the timeline. The expressions from the box will help you.**

Samantha got her Leaving Certificate.

worked at Automotion • finished apprenticeship • left school • got Leaving Certificate • got job at Marotta Ireland • wrote a lot of letters • worked in clothes shop

3 Answer the questions.

1 What jobs did Samantha do before she got her apprenticeship?
2 Which two people encouraged Samantha to try engineering?
3 Why does Samantha like working at Marotta?
4 Name four things that Samantha does in her job.

4 Find words from the text which match these definitions.

1 A person who operates a machine in a factory or workshop. (line 1–7)
2 To use machinery to make large quantities of something. (line 1–7)
3 A vehicle which flies through the air. (line 1–7)
4 The use of science to make machines, buildings, etc. (line 8–17)
5 A machine which shapes metal, wood or plastic. (line 18–23)
6 To enter a list of instructions into a computer or computerized machine. (line 18–23)

5 Why do you think there are fewer women than men in engineering jobs? Discuss in small groups.

6 Ali, Emma and Jack have just left school and are looking for jobs. Listen to the recording, then match the industry to the person. (There is one industry too many.) 38

Example: *Ali works in the ... industry.*

brewing

papermaking

electronics

food processing

7 Listen again. What positive points did the careers advisor make about each industry? Were there any negative points? Make notes. 38

8 Which of the industries in this 'World of work' would you most like to work in? Why? If you don't want to work in any of them, say why not.

Exam practice

It's never easy

One day, Beth's dad told her that he was going to leave the family home. He said he would still see Beth at the weekends, but he couldn't live with her and her mum any longer. Beth was only eight years old. 'At the time, I was confused and angry,' says Beth, now 17. 'I thought that dad didn't love me any more.'
Beth lives with her mum in Cardiff, Wales. Nowadays, she understands why her parents got divorced, and she has a good relationship with both of them. Last year Beth's mum got married again and now Beth has a stepsister, Emma. Beth's dad moved to London and Beth stays with him and his girlfriend in her holidays from college.
Some people say that parents should stay together 'for the children'. Beth disagrees: 'It isn't good for children to be in an unhappy home where the parents are arguing all the time. If the parents aren't happy, the kids can't be happy. Anyway, growing up with one parent is normal these days. That's life!'
Forty per cent of marriages in the UK end in divorce, so perhaps Beth is right. (190 words)

Text comprehension

1 Finish the sentences using information from the text. Use your own words.

a When Beth's father said that he was leaving, ...
b Since her parents got divorced, Beth has three 'new relatives.' They are ...
c During the college breaks, Beth ...

2 Answer questions about the text.

a What happened when Beth was eight years old?
b What is Beth's relationship with her parents like now?
c Why does Beth think her parents' divorce wasn't such a bad thing after all?

3 Give your opinion on the following statement from the text.

'Growing up with one parent is normal these days.'

4 Ask Beth three questions about her family. Use three different question words or types of question.

Grammar

5 Fill in the gaps with the correct forms of the verbs in brackets.

a By 2050, China ... (be) richer than the USA.
b Liam's parents ... (not want) to get divorced even though they argued a lot.
c ... you ... (do) your homework yet?
d After I ... (read) the newspaper, I looked at some websites.

6 **Complete the sentences with some or any.**

a I want ... cheese. Is there ... in the fridge?
b Chloe can't buy a car because she hasn't got ... money.

Vocabulary

7 **Complete the sentences with the corresponding noun for the word in brackets.**

a Beth felt a lot of ... towards her parents. (angry)
b Is a traditional family more important than your own or your children's ... ? (happy)

8 **Complete the sentences with a word or phrase which means the same as the word in brackets.**

a ... we understand more about environmental problems. (nowadays)
b The concert ... at 11 o'clock, doesn't it? (ends)

9 **Complete the sentences with the opposite of the word in brackets.**

a It's ... for European couples to have large families nowadays. (usual)
b I completely ... with what you just said. (disagree)

10 **Use a dictionary to translate the underlined expressions.**

a In the end, happiness is the most important thing.
b At the end of the book he died in a car crash.
c Wen willst du heiraten?
d „Wollt ihr heiraten?" – „Niemals!"

Writing

11 **Should parents stay together 'for the children'? Write a letter to a magazine. (80–100 words). Consider both sides of the argument.**

Mediation

12 **Übertragen Sie den Inhalt des Textes 'It's never easy' ins Deutsche. Übersetzen Sie nicht Wort für Wort. Schreiben Sie ganze Sätze.**

13 **What would you say in these situations?**

14 Kicking the habit

1 **Scan the text. Which of these sentences best summarizes the standpoint of the author?**

1 The author is against smoking; she wants to persuade people not to smoke.
2 The author is in favour of smoking; she wants to persuade people to carry on smoking.
3 The author is against smoking; she wants to show why some people refuse to stop smoking.
4 The author is in favour of smoking; she wants to show why some people are against it.

39

Why do we do it?

by Sarah Couzens

(1) Smoking – we all know that it is bad for us. The health statistics are shocking: each cigarette shortens your life by 11 minutes. Cigarette packets carry health warnings in big letters. Smoking is banned in most public buildings. Yet young people carry on smoking.

(2) Why don't the anti-smoking arguments work? To find out, I spoke to Paul Sommers. Paul is 18; he smokes about 20 cigarettes a day and he started smoking when he was 15.

(3) **Argument 1: If you stopped smoking, you would be more attractive to the opposite sex.**

Smoking makes your teeth yellow. It also gives you wrinkles, so that you look older than you really are. Your breath, hair, skin and clothes all smell of cigarette smoke.

(4) *Paul's answer: My girlfriend smokes, so I wouldn't be more attractive to her! Smoking is something we do together. If my girlfriend wanted me to give up, I would stop smoking tomorrow. But she doesn't. In fact, if I hadn't been a smoker, she probably wouldn't have gone out with me.*

(5) **Argument 2: If you stopped smoking, you would be healthier.**

You would be able to do more exercise. Smoking makes your heart and your lungs work less efficiently. You might also live longer.

(6) *Paul's answer: My grandad died last year. He was 85 and he smoked all his adult life. He was fit and healthy and he had a good life. Would he have lived even longer if he hadn't been a smoker? Perhaps – but 85 isn't bad, is it?*

(7) *Besides, I'm 18 now – why should I worry about what will happen in 50 years' time? I'm young and I want to enjoy life. We're here for a good time, not a long time!*

(8) **Argument 3: If you stopped smoking, you would have more money.**

It costs a lot of money to smoke. Cigarettes are expensive because the government has put a lot of tax on them. The reason for this is to discourage people from smoking.

(9) *What is money for? To spend on things you enjoy – and I enjoy smoking! If the government really wanted to discourage people from smoking, they would make it illegal. Why don't they do that? Because they just want our money.*

(374 words)

BEFORE YOU START

1 What does this photo make you think of? Write key words. Now compare ideas with your partner.

2 More and more countries in Europe are banning smoking in pubs and restaurants. What do you think about this? With your partner, write a list of arguments for and against this.

for	against

2 **Read the text carefully. Put these arguments in the order in which Paul uses them in his answers.**

a I like smoking.
b It doesn't seem important to me because I'm young.
c You should spend your money on things you enjoy.
d The government doesn't really want to stop people smoking.
e Smoking brings my girlfriend and me together.
f I know someone who smoked and didn't have health problems.

INTERCULTURAL CORNER

Eine britische Aufklärungskampagne gegen das Rauchen

In Großbritannien garantiert der National Health Service (NHS) den Bürgern kostenlose medizinische Versorgung. Dazu gehört auch Aufklärung über Gesundheitsrisiken. Hier sehen Sie Anzeigen aus einer Fernseh- und Zeitungskampagne des NHS gegen das Rauchen. Überlegen Sie, an wen sich die einzelnen Anzeigen richten. Glauben Sie, sie haben etwas bewirkt?

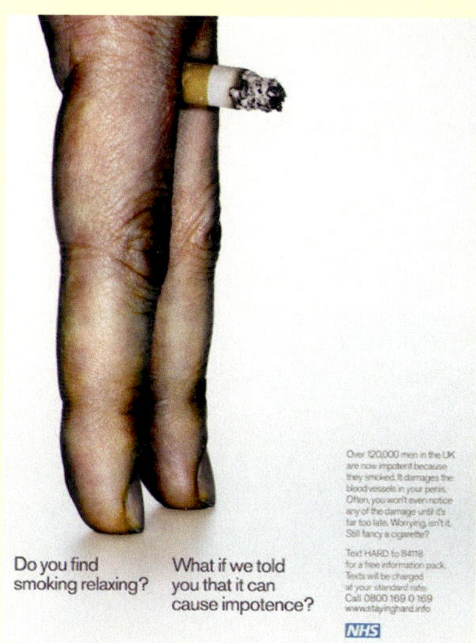

3 **Can you find the opposites of these words? (They are all in the text.)**

1 stopped (Section 2)
2 same (Section 3)
3 alone (Section 4)
4 was born (Section 6)
5 cheap (Section 8)
6 earn (Section 9)

4 **Your friend is looking for some arguments to persuade his girlfriend to stop smoking. Summarize the relevant parts of the text in German.**

5 **a** **Brainstorming: Make two lists. You can use ideas from the text, but add your own ideas.**

1 'pro-smoking': reasons why people start/continue smoking
2 'anti-smoking': arguments against smoking

b **Now use your lists to role-play this situation.**

PARTNER A: You are a smoker. Explain why you carry on smoking.
PARTNER B: You are a non-smoker. Try to persuade your partner to stop smoking.

Example: A: *I smoke because ...*
B: *You should stop smoking because ...*

Language

CONDITIONAL SENTENCES TYPE II (Bedingungssätze Typ II)

Bedingungssätze des Typs II werden benutzt, wenn man eine Situation beschreibt, die zwar theoretisch möglich, aber in der Wirklichkeit eher unwahrscheinlich ist („Was wäre, wenn ... ?"). Achtung: Im if-Satz steht zwar die Vergangenheitsform, der Satz bezieht sich aber auf die Gegenwart oder Zukunft.

DANGER!

If und would bzw. would have kommen nie im selben Teilsatz vor:

If I ~~would stop~~ smoking, ...
stopped

Bedingung	Folge
Simple past	would
If you stopped smoking,	you would be healthier.

CONDITIONAL SENTENCES TYPE III (Bedingungssätze Typ III)

Mit Bedingungssätzen des Typs III kann man ausdrücken, was in der Vergangenheit hätte geschehen können („Was wäre gewesen, wenn ... ?"). Dabei stellt man sich etwas vor, was in Wirklichkeit gar nicht geschehen ist.

Bedingung	Folge
Past perfect	would have + Partizip Perfekt
If I hadn't been a smoker,	she wouldn't have gone out with me.

Practice

6 Choose the correct alternative to complete each sentence.

1 Ben wouldn't smoke if he *knows* / *knew* the risks.
2 If smoking *would be* / *was* illegal, people would still smoke.
3 More people would take drugs if they *would be* / *were* legal.
4 If cigarettes were cheaper, smokers *would have* / *had* more money.
5 People would smoke more cigarettes if they *aren't* / *weren't* so expensive.
6 If you *drank* / *would drink* less, you would be fitter.

7 Choose the correct answer.

1 If I smoked, ...

a He/She is a smoker.
b He/She is a non-smoker.

2 If I smoked less, ...

a He/She smokes a lot.
b He/She hardly ever smokes.

3 If I was a health freak, ...

a He/She doesn't care about his/her health.
b He/She cares a lot about his/her health.

4 If I drank less beer, ...

a He/She drinks a lot of beer.
b He/She doesn't drink much beer.

5 If I worked harder, ...

a He/She does a lot of work.
b He/She doesn't do much work.

6 If I didn't go to parties, ...

a He/She goes out a lot.
b He/She hardly ever goes out.

8 Complete the sentences from exercise 7 with the ideas from the box.

Example: *If I smoked, I would have less money.*

watch more TV • not eat junk food • ~~have less money~~ •
earn more money • drink more cola • be fitter

9 Find the best ending for each sentence and put the verbs in the correct form.

1 If I had driven more slowly, *I wouldn't have hit the tree.*	... he (live) longer.
2 If he had given up smoking, ...	... I (call) her.
3 If we had left home earlier, ...	... the teacher (not be) angry.
4 If I hadn't lost her phone number, ...	~~I (not hit) the tree.~~
5 If you hadn't used your phone in class, ...	... I (not help) him.
6 If he hadn't been my best friend, ...	... we (not miss) the bus.

10 Discuss what you would do in these situations.

1 What would you do if you saw your neighbours' 10-year-old daughter smoking a cigarette?
2 What would you do if you found €1000 and some pills in an unmarked envelope in the street?

11 Find the English equivalents of these words in the webpage below. They are in the same order.

1 unberechenbar
2 abhängen von
3 Stimmung
4 angespannt
5 sich zusammenreißen
6 schläfrig
7 bewusstlos
8 Krankenwagen
9 Fähigkeit

12 Do the drugs quiz.

http://www.drugs-help.com/quiz

Google

Drugs – do you know what to do?

Drugs are unpredictable. Their effect can depend on the person's mood, how much they have taken and the situation. It's important to know what to do if someone has a bad reaction to a drug.
Would you know what to do? Do our quick drugs quiz to find out.

1 What would you do if your friend had a panic attack?
[Drugs like speed, cannabis, ecstasy and LSD can sometimes make the user feel tense and frightened.]
- a I would tell her to pull herself together.
- b I would take her to a quiet, dimly-lit place and talk to her calmly.

2 What would you do if your friend became very drowsy?
[Tranquillizers, heroin and glue can make you very drowsy.]
- a I would make sure he didn't become unconscious.
- b I would give him a cup of coffee.

3 What would you do if your friend became unconscious?
[An overdose of most drugs can make you unconscious.]
- a I would call for an ambulance.
- b I would let her sleep it off.

4 What would you do if your friend became very thirsty?
[Some drugs affect the body's ability to stay cool, so users may lose a lot of water.]
- a I would give him a cold beer.
- b I would give him some water or fruit juice.

[SUBMIT]

13 (40) A local radio show is doing a programme about drugs. Young people in a Manchester pub are asked the questions from the drugs quiz. Listen and check your answers. Did you answer all the questions correctly?

14 Pick ONE of the forum threads. Write a reply: write what you would do and what you wouldn't do, and why.

Example: *Hi bigbro. If I were you, I would ... , because ... . If that didn't work, I would ... . I wouldn't ... because ... Good luck!*

http://www.drugs-help.com/forum

forum: alcohol and drug problems

I think my little brother (12) has started sniffing glue. Sometimes he's really spaced out, and his clothes stink of glue. He denies it, of course. I don't want to tell our dad – he would probably beat us both up. We don't have a mum. I don't know what to do. bigbro
reply to this thread

My girlfriend is three months pregnant. I'm over the moon – I can't wait to be a dad :~) But what worries me, is, she won't stop smoking. She says that it won't hurt the baby. I'm worried sick. What would you do? dad2b
reply to this thread

My boyfriend is great. He's funny, kind and romantic – until he starts drinking. He's OK when he just has a couple of beers, but when he gets drunk he gets really angry and cold. He hasn't ever been violent, but he scares me a bit. I'm not sure what to do about it. chickybabe
reply to this thread

LEARNING TO LEARN

Wie man aus seinen Fehlern lernt

Jeder Fehler stellt eine Gelegenheit dar, etwas daraus zu lernen, damit man ihn beim nächsten Mal vermeidet – nutzen Sie diese Gelegenheit!

1 Schauen Sie sich Ihren Fehler genau an. Was genau ist falsch?

2 Überlegen Sie sich, warum es falsch ist. Ihr Lehrer bzw. Ihre Lehrerin kann Ihnen sicher dabei helfen.

3 Schreiben Sie den korrekten Satz auf.
Schritt 3 ist ganz wichtig! Damit prägen Sie sich die richtige Version noch einmal ein, so dass sie stärker im Gedächtnis haften bleibt als die falsche.

The world of work

Working with young people

http://www.youthwork-community.co.uk

Make a difference – be a youth worker

Ⓐ Youth workers work in youth clubs or community centres, but they also work in colleges and schools, or they meet young people in places like cafés and shopping centres and on the street.
Youth workers offer help and advice to young people, and they organize all sorts of projects to make life better for young people and the whole community. By getting young people involved in something worthwhile, they can help them to deal with problems like homelessness, unemployment and alcohol or drug abuse.

Ⓑ **Jenny Heath is a youth worker in Birmingham, England. Here are her top tips for new youth workers:**

Tip 1: Get organized
As a youth worker, I need to remember what I am doing, who with and when. I use a diary which has a whole page for each day, and I check and update it every day. If I didn't keep a work diary, my work would be complete chaos!
Tip 2: Get together
Ninety per cent of this job is knowing the 'right' people – in other words, networking. If a client wanted to know about unemployment benefits, about getting a job, about coming off drugs or dealing with sexual abuse, I could immediately put them in touch with somebody who could help.
Tip 3: Get a life!
If I didn't have any interests outside work, I'd soon go crazy! I play softball with a local team. It helps me to relax and keeps me fit.

1 **Read text A and make notes in German about youth workers. Include the following points:**

1 where they work
2 what they do
3 what kind of of problems they deal with

2 **Read text B. Why does Jenny do these things? Explain in your own words.**

Example: *1 Jenny keeps a diary so that she can …*

1 keep a diary
2 meet other youth workers
3 play softball

3 a Look at these two photos of youth projects. What do you think the projects are about?

'Fab Pad' project, Glasgow

'Get the Message' project, Lewisham, London

b Match each speech bubble to the correct project.

1. We show them how they can make it into a real home.
2. They learn to create real art.
3. We find walls the kids can spray paint on – legally.
4. It also gives them a nicer home to live in.
5. Some of them do college courses in painting and decorating.
6. The whole town gets something out of it.

4 Listen to youth workers talking about the two projects. Copy and complete the table.

41

Project	Get the Message	Fab Pad
Who is it for?	*graffiti sprayers*	...
What things are needed?	...	...
How does it help people?	...	...

5 a Think of a youth project for your local area. You can choose one of the ideas from the box or think of your own.

website • radio station • magazine • single parents' group • coffee bar • rap competition

b Discuss these aspects.

1 What is the idea and what will it be called?
2 Who will it be for?
3 What materials and equipment will be needed?
4 How will it help people?

6 Write about your youth project. Write two or three sentences for each of the three headings in exercise 4. (80–100 words)

Exam practice

Friday night, Saturday morning

It's two o'clock on Saturday morning in Wigan, a town in the northwest of England. The nightclubs are closing and crowds of young people are on their way home. Most of them are wearing light summer clothes – shirts and trousers for the boys, short skirts and tops for the girls – but it's December and -1°C.

Rachel and her friends Amy and Georgia started drinking seven hours ago. They started with wine, then they drank vodka and Bacardi rum. Now they are completely drunk. None of them is 18 yet and Rachel is the youngest at 16. It's against the law to sell alcohol to people under 18, but it's easy to get drinks when the bar is busy – nobody has time to check your ID.

This is a normal Friday night out for thousands of young people in Wigan and in other ordinary British towns: several hours of drinking and dancing in pubs and nightclubs, perhaps half an Ecstasy tablet, then a long walk home.

'What's wrong with that?' asks Rachel. 'We're young and we want to enjoy life. Don't tell us that the drink, the drugs and the late nights are bad for us, because we don't care!'

(199 words)

Text comprehension

1 Finish the sentences using information from the text. Use your own words.

a Even though it's winter ...
b This evening, Rachel and her friends ...
c If you aren't 18 yet, you ...

2 Answer the questions about the text.

a At what time do the nightclubs close in Wigan?
b Why are Rachel and her friends able to buy alcoholic drinks?
c What do young people in Wigan like to do on Friday nights? (4 things)

3 Give your opinion on the following statement from the text.

'Don't tell us that the drink, the drugs and the late nights are bad for us, because we don't care!'

4 Ask Rachel and her friends three questions about their night out. Use three different question words or types of question.

Grammar

5 Fill in the gaps with the correct forms of the verbs in brackets.

a This evening we ... (go) to a nightclub – do you want to come?
b If Ben ... (not drink) so much, he would be fitter.
c ... (you / give up) smoking yet?
d Rachel ... (go) home by taxi if she hadn't spent all her money.

6 **Find the comparative and superlative forms of these adjectives.**

a busy   b long   c bad

Vocabulary

7 **Complete the sentences with the corresponding adverb for the word in brackets.**

a Mike and Beth ... go to the cinema on Saturday evenings. (normal)
b We passed the test ... . (easy)

8 **Complete the sentences with a word or phrase which means the same as the word in brackets.**

a I ... agree with you. (completely)
b Smoking cannabis is ... in the UK. (against the law)

9 **Complete the sentences with the opposite of the word in brackets.**

a Albert Smith, 105, is the ... man in Britain. (youngest)
b When are you going to ... talking and get on with your work? (start)

10 **Use a dictionary to translate the underlined expressions.**

a That was the wrong answer.
b What's wrong? Are you feeling sick?
c Es ist nicht leicht, diese Frage zu beantworten.
d Die Jugendlichen haben leichte Sommerkleidung getragen.

Writing

11 **Which do you think is a bigger problem – alcohol or drugs? Why? Write a message for a web forum (80–100 words).**

Mediation

12 **Übertragen Sie den Inhalt des Textes 'Friday night, Saturday morning' ins Deutsche. Übersetzen Sie nicht Wort für Wort. Schreiben Sie ganze Sätze.**

13 **Complete the dialogues with your own ideas.**

Dialogue A
SHOP ASSISTANT: Can I help you?
YOU: ...
SHOP ASSISTANT: We have two kinds of headache pills – Nurofen or Panadol. Which would you like?
YOU: ...
SHOP ASSISTANT: What size packet do you want?
YOU: ...
SHOP ASSISTANT: Here you are. That'll be four pounds fifty, please.
YOU: ...

15 Drive to arrive alive

1 Cover the text on the opposite page. Look at the pictures below. They tell the story of Brad's first drive in his new car. What happened?

INTERCULTURAL CORNER

Der Führerschein in den USA

- In 19 US-Staaten darf man mit 14 Jahren ein Auto fahren, wenn ein Mitfahrer bzw. eine Mitfahrerin mit Führerschein dabei ist.
- In zwei US-Staaten (Alabama und Montana) kann man mit 15 Jahren den Führerschein machen.
- In 22 anderen Staaten bekommt man den Führerschein mit 16.
- Zwei von fünf Todesfällen unter amerikanischen Jugendlichen sind die Folge von Autounfällen.

BEFORE YOU START

1 **How often do you use these forms of transport?**

public transport • moped/scooter • bicycle • car • motorbike

2 **Give each form of transport a score (1 = best, 5 = worst) for:**

a safety
b usefulness
c 'cool factor'
d eco-friendliness

3 **Add up the scores for each form of transport. Which one has the best total score?**

42

A trip downtown

I got my license when I was 16. My first car was a beat-up old Ford, but for my 18th birthday my parents bought me a brand-new Chrysler SUV. Four-wheel drive. Bright red. It was a real beauty. It felt great driving such a big, powerful car.

To celebrate, I took my buddies Troy, Rob and Chris downtown. Troy and I were in the front, and Rob and Chris were in the back seat. We had the music up loud and we were cruising around.

We were all having a great time. My buddies were drinking beer, and Rob and Chris were hanging out of the windows and calling out to girls. I thought their behavior was kind of dumb, but I didn't want to seem lame, so I let them do it. I didn't drink any beer, though.

In the end, things got a bit out of control. I couldn't concentrate on the road because the others were making so much noise. I told Rob and Chris to calm down and quit fooling around, but they didn't take any notice.

Anyway, we came to this intersection, just next to the shopping mall. The light was on red, I guess, but I didn't see it because I was yelling at Rob and Chris.

So I didn't stop at the intersection and the next thing I knew, this other car came right across in front of me. A little blue car. I didn't have time to stop or swerve – I ran straight into the driver's door.

My buddies and I were all OK, but the woman driving the other car was hurt pretty badly. We phoned for an ambulance straight away.

Then the cops turned up. They were hard on us – they knew it was our fault. They said I would probably have to go to court.

The other driver had to spend a month in hospital. I felt bad about that. I was also mad at my buddies because they were the ones behaving like idiots, but I was the one going to court.

The judge made my parents pay a big fine. I also had to apologize to the other driver and do 20 hours' community service. I don't feel ready to get back behind the wheel yet, so the SUV stays in our garage for now. The accident really shook me up and I still get flashbacks.

(402 words)

2 Read the text, then answer the questions in full sentences.

1 How was Brad's new car different from his old one? (At least three differences.)
2 Explain in your own words what Brad and his friends were doing before the accident.
3 Why didn't Brad see the red traffic light?
4 What did Brad find unfair?

3 **Brad uses several colloquial American expressions in his story. What words or phrases does he use instead of the following?**

1 friends (lines 1-8)
2 stupid (lines 1–8)
3 to stop (doing something) (lines 9–17)
4 to behave stupidly (lines 9–17)
5 I think (lines 9–17)
6 to shout at somebody (lines 9–17)
7 police officers (lines 18–24)
8 to be angry with somebody (lines 18–24)

4 a **Who was to blame for the accident? Discuss these questions in small groups.**

- What did Brad's friends do wrong?
- What did Brad do wrong?
- Did Brad's parents do anything wrong?
- Did the other driver do anything wrong?

b **Now give your opinion on the following statement from the text.**

'I thought their behavior was kind of dumb, but I didn't want to seem lame, so I let them do it.'

LEARNING TO LEARN

Tipps für das Gruppengespräch auf Englisch

Sich zu Wort melden
Can I just say that ... ? · Well, if you ask me ...
Jemand anderen ins Gespräch einbringen
What do you think, Svenja?
Höflich widersprechen
You may be right, but ... · I don't think that's quite right.

5 **The judge told Brad to write a letter of apology to the other driver. Write the letter for Brad. Explain how and why the accident happened and say that you are sorry. (80–100 words) The start of each paragraph is given on the right.**

Dear Ms Zachary

I am writing to apologize for ... .
When the accident happened ... .
The accident happened because ... .
I'm really sorry about ... . I hope that ... .

Yours truly
Brad Lowe

Language

PAST PROGRESSIVE (Verlaufsform der Vergangenheit)

Aussagen	Verneinungen	Ja/Nein-Fragen	Kurzantworten
I **was driving** / We **were driving** when the accident happened.	When the police arrived, they **weren't fighting** / I **wasn't fighting** any more.	**Was** he / **Were** they **listening** to music when the bell rang?	Yes, he **was**. / No, she **wasn't**. Yes, they **were**. / No, they **weren't**.

- Mit dem past progressive wird eine Handlung beschrieben, die zu einem bestimmten Zeitpunkt im Gange war. Es wird vor allem dann benutzt, wenn eine Handlung im Gange war, als eine zweite Handlung (simple past) geschah.
- Das past progressive wird gebildet aus was/were und der -ing-Form des Verbs.
- Es wird oft nach while (= während) benutzt.

DANGER!

während + Substantiv = during

During breakfast I heard the phone.

während + Nebensatz = while

While we were having breakfast, I heard the phone.

RELATIVE CLAUSES (Relativsätze) 2

- Relativsätze, in denen das Verb im present progressive oder im past progressive steht, kann man oft verkürzen. Man kann das Relativpronomen und is/are bzw. was/were weglassen, wenn das Relativpronomen das Subjekt des Relativsatzes vertritt.
  The woman (who was) driving the other car was hurt. / They are the ones (who are) behaving like idiots.

Practice

6 What was everyone doing when the accident happened? Take it in turns to describe the picture.

Example: A: *A man was riding a moped.*
B: *A boy and a girl were ...*

eat an ice cream • kiss • ride a moped • go skateboarding • take a dog for a walk • talk on the phone • watch TV

7 Complete these sentences using the past progressive / simple past forms of the verbs in brackets.

Example: Brad *was driving* (drive) too fast when the accident *happened* (happen).

1 I ... (watch) TV when the phone ... (ring).
2 'Why ... (you / not hear) the doorbell?' – 'We ... (listen) to music on our iPods.'
3 Brad ... (talk) to the police when the ambulance ... (arrive).
4 Harry ... (deliver) a pizza when he ... (fall off) his moped.
5 I ... (see) your brother – he ... (smoke) a cigarette in the garden.
6 Who ... (you / talk to) on the phone when I ... (see) you?

8 Complete the sentences using while or during.

Example: I ate my dinner *while* I was watching TV.

1 You didn't pay attention ... the lesson.
2 Did you see Mike ... you were shopping in town?
3 ... we were waiting for you, we drank a cup of coffee.
4 Were you very nervous ... the interview?
5 ... he was sleeping, his girlfriend rang.
6 Her mobile rang three times ... the film.

9 a Make these sentences shorter.

Example: The woman who was driving the car was drunk.
The woman driving the car was drunk.

1 The girls who are walking along the street are sisters.
2 The dog which is running down the street belongs to my neighbour.
3 The boy who was sitting in the back seat was drinking beer.
4 The police officer who was asking the questions looked very angry.

b Rewrite these sentences with full relative clauses.

Example: The boy lying in the road was badly hurt.
The boy who was lying in the road was badly hurt.

1 Do you remember the boy riding the moped? He's my brother.
2 The passengers sitting on the bus were injured in the accident.
3 When the accident happened yesterday, the man sitting on the bench didn't see anything.
4 The boys playing in the street are twelve or thirteen.

10 Can you match the German driving expressions to their English equivalents?

1 driving instructor
2 driving lesson
3 give way
4 learner driver
5 pull away
6 roundabout
7 brake
8 horn

a anfahren, wegfahren
b Bremse
c Fahrschüler/in
d Kreisverkehr
e Hupe
f Fahrstunde
g Fahrlehrer/in
h Vorfahrt gewähren

11 Jen is learning to drive. She is telling her friend Vikki about her last driving lesson.

43 Listen to the dialogue, then look at the diagram. Which car is Jen driving?

12 Complete Jen's weblog with words from exercise 10, then listen again to the dialogue
43 to check your answers.

http://www.jensweblog.com/blog17

15 May

Death on wheels!

As regular readers of this weblog know, I'm learning to drive. I had another …[1] yesterday. It was all going fine. I was driving along, and then we came to this …[2]. So I stopped the car. Then I tried to …[3], but the engine stopped. The driver behind me was getting really cross. He started honking his …[4] at me.

I started the engine again, and started to pull away, but I was so nervous that I didn't see that a car was coming around the roundabout. The …[5] nearly had a heart attack. He yelled '…[6]!' There's a car coming!' and put his foot on the …[7].

After that I was just a nervous wreck, so the instructor had to drive me home.

I'm never going to learn to drive! I must be the worst …[8] in the world!

13 You were on holiday in England when you saw this accident. Decide what happened, then write a short statement (80–100 words) for the police.

Example: *I had just come out of the supermarket and I was walking along the street. I saw a red car which was going too fast …*

Driver had drunk 10 beers

'It was all the red car's fault,' said the driver, Derek Roberts, 45.

'It's lucky that nobody was hurt,' said the policewoman, PC Jenkins.

The world of work

Vocational training in Germany and the UK

After I finished secondary school at the age of 16 I went to a vocational college. During that time I did work experience in a courier company. I really enjoyed that. My teacher said that I should do an apprenticeship in transport and logistics.
I got an apprenticeship with Jeantex. Now I'm training to be a transport management assistant. In Germany, apprentices have a three-year training contract with an employer who gives us on-the-job training and we also go to college on day release.
Jasmin Wolters

I left school at 16 and got a job as an office management assistant in a finance company. I didn't need any vocational qualifications to get the job.
After a year I got a job as a receptionist at Pickup, a small British courier company. Again, I didn't need any vocational qualifications. My boss allowed me to go to college one day a week on day release. At college I did a computer course.
After two years, an opportunity came up at Tesco, a big supermarket chain. They wanted a transport management assistant and I was able to show them that I had the right practical experience and computer skills.
That's the job that I do now. Several times a year I go on short courses (one to five days). Next year I'm going to do evening classes and become a transport manager.
Dee Chapman

1 Find the English expressions in the texts.

Example: Berufsfachschule – *vocational college*

1 Praktikum
2 Ausbildung(sstelle)
3 Kauffrau für Transport und Logistik
4 Auszubildende/r
5 Ausbildungsvertrag
6 berufliche Qualifizierung
7 Berufserfahrung
8 Abendkurs

2 **Who is it: Jasmin, Dee or both?**

Example: She did general office work. – *Dee*

1 She did work experience at a transport company.
2 She goes on short training courses.
3 She got a job as a transport management assistant.
4 She left school at 16.
5 She attended a vocational college.
6 She applied for an apprenticeship.
7 She goes or went to college part-time.
8 She is going to do extra training in the evenings.

3 **Discuss these questions in a group.**

- How has Dee's training been different from Jasmin's?
- Are there any things about Dee's training which surprise you?
- Which system of training do you think is better? Why?

4 **A careers expert is interviewed about vocational training in England. Work with a partner. Predict what the expert will say: a, b, and/or c. (More than one answer may be correct.) Then listen to the recording to check your answers.**

44

1 It's difficult to get an apprenticeship in England because ...
   a there aren't enough people applying to do an apprenticeship.
   b there aren't enough companies offering apprenticeships.
   c there are too many apprentices already.

2 In Germany ...
   a there are six times as many apprentices as in England.
   b there are a quarter of a million apprentices.
   a there are one and a half million apprentices.

3 Young employees in England ...
   a are trained on the job.
   b go to college on day release.
   c do short courses to update their skills.

4 In England, if you want to be a transport manager ...
   a you have to go to university.
   b you can do an apprenticeship.
   c you can start as a driver and work your way up.

5 **Write an email to Dee. Tell her about your course and what you want to do when you have finished. Explain to her how the German vocational training system works.**

6 **Look again at the 'World of work' pages in Units 9–15. Discuss with a partner:**

- Which of the jobs would you most like to do? Why?
- Which would you least like to do? Why?

Exam practice

How to pass your driving test

I finally got my UK driving licence last week – on the third attempt. Here are some tips for other learner drivers:

Make sure that you are ready. A lot of learners fail because they take their test too soon. It's better to wait until your instructor says that you are ready.

Get plenty of practice. The week before my driving test I practised every day in my own car with my dad. Just before my test I had one final lesson with my instructor. She told me the mistakes I had made, so I remembered not to make the same ones during my test.

Don't panic. It's normal to feel nervous on the day of your test, and the examiners are used to this. If you make a mistake, don't give up. I made a mistake and I thought that I had failed, but the rest of my test went really well. At the end of the test the examiner said that my mistake was only a small one, so I still got my driving licence.

Don't worry if you fail. You should know that the majority of people don't pass their test the first time. Failing doesn't mean that you are stupid or slow.

Cameron Warner (205 words)

Text comprehension

1 Finish the sentences using information from the text. Use your own words.

a If you don't have enough driving lessons, ...
b It's a good idea to have extra lessons before the test, because ...
c If you make a small mistake, ...

2 Answer the questions about the text.

a How many times did Cameron take his driving test?
b Why did Cameron think that he had failed his test?
c What happens to most people the first time they take their driving test?

3 In Britain, you can practise driving before your test as long as you are with an experienced driver. Do you think that should be allowed in Germany too? Give your opinion.

4 Ask Cameron three questions about learning to drive. Use three different question words or types of question.

Grammar

5 Fill in the gaps with the correct forms of the verbs in brackets.

a Lisa ... her driving test tomorrow. (take)
b We ... on the motorway when the accident happened. (drive)
c I ... ten driving lessons so far. (have)
d If Jack ... his driving test, his parents will give him a car. (pass)

6 **Make these sentences passive.**

a Cars kill many people every year.
b The police stopped him outside the pub.

Vocabulary

7 **Complete the sentences with the corresponding noun for the word in brackets.**

a A few extra lessons can make the difference between ... and success. (fail)
b What's the ... of this word? (mean)

8 **Complete the sentences with a word or phrase which means the same as the expression in brackets.**

a Don't feel bad: ... of people fail their driving test. (plenty)
b In fact, ... people fail the first time. (the majority of)

9 **Complete the sentences with the opposite of the word in brackets.**

a He arrived too ... for the party. (early)
b Leah passed her exam without any problems – she's quite ... . (stupid)

10 **Use a dictionary to translate the underlined expressions.**

a Alice got her driving licence last year.
b Get your coat – it's time to go.
c Kannst du mich zum Bahnhof fahren?
d 'Wie kommen wir nach München?' – 'Wir fahren mit dem Zug.'

Writing

11 **What do you think about driving: Is it important to get a driving licence as soon as possible? Have you started driving yet? Are you going to buy a car? Write an email to a British or American penfriend (80–100 words).**

Mediation

12 **Übertragen Sie den Inhalt des Textes 'How to pass your driving test' ins Deutsche. Übersetzen Sie nicht Wort für Wort. Schreiben Sie ganze Sätze.**

13 **What would you say in these situations?**

a Jemand lädt Sie zu einer Party ein. Sie lehnen höflich ab.
b Sie erkundigen sich nach dem Preis für eine CD.
c Sie fragen eine neue Bekannte, was sie beruflich macht.
d Ein Bekannter plant einen Sommerurlaub. Sie fragen ihn nach seinen Plänen.
e Sie haben einen Termin beim Arzt verpasst. Sie rufen an, um sich zu entschuldigen.
f Sie lesen einen Zeitungsartikel und verstehen einen Satz nicht. Sie bitten eine britische Austauschschülerin um Hilfe.

Pairwork files

File 1

Unit 1, Exercise 14

PARTNER A

1 **Choose one card and answer your partner's questions.**

Example: *What's your name? – My name's Ronald Scott.*

Name:	Ronald Scott
From:	Manchester, England
Family:	Lives with mum, stepfather, three sisters and two stepsisters
Pet:	no. Sisters have hamsters and rabbits
Hobbies:	plays lead-guitar in a reggae band
Favourite music:	reggae

Name:	Maria Lopez
From:	New Mexico, USA
Family:	Lives with parents, three brothers and one sister
Pet:	no
Hobbies:	jazz dance, disco
Favourite music:	salsa

2 **Now ask your partner questions.**

File 2

Unit 5, Exercise 14

PARTNER B

Snacky Snacks

Drinks

Tea	£1.00
Coffee	£1.25
Energy drink	£1.50
Mineral water	£0.75

Sandwiches

Ham and tomato	£1.75
Tuna mayonnaise	£1.90
Cheese and pickle	£1.80

Pizza

Margherita	£1.00
Salami	£1.20
Ham and mushroom	£1.30

Extras

Salad	£0.75
Chips	£0.50

File 3

Unit 8, The world of work, Exercise 7

PARTNER A

You are the manager. You are interviewing two or more candidates for the job. Ask each candidate:

- why he/she wants the job
- if he/she is healthy and fit
- about his/her qualications and work experience
- one other question

Choose the best candidate for the job.

File 4

Unit 9, Exercise 5

PARTNER A

1 **You are on holiday in Scotland. You are going to phone your friend back home to tell him/her about your holiday. Before you phone, choose one option for each day. Decide what you think about the activity, eg *fun*, *exciting*, *scary*, *boring*.**

Example: PARTNER: *How's your holiday going?*
YOU: *Great!*
PARTNER: *Cool! What did you do yesterday?*
YOU: *We went bungy jumping. It was really scary!*

Yesterday	EITHER:	bungy jumping	OR:	bus tour in the mountains
Today	EITHER:	barbecue in the park	OR:	nightclub
Tomorrow	EITHER:	shopping in Glasgow	OR:	rock concert

2 **Your friend phones you from Ireland. Ask about his/her holiday. You want to know:**

- what he/she did yesterday,
- what he/she is doing today,
- what he/she is going to do tomorrow.

Is he/she enjoying the holiday?
Use some of the phrases from the Learning to Learn box on page 80.

File 5

Unit 9, The world of work, Exercise 5

PARTNER A

1 **Your name is Chris Jones and your booking reference number is 234034. You are booked on flight BA1707 on Monday 21 March from Frankfurt to Manchester. You need to stay in Frankfurt another day.**

Phone BA and ask the flight sales executive whether you can take the same flight on Tuesday instead. If not, choose another flight that he/she suggests. (You would prefer a morning flight.)

2 **Now you are a flight sales executive. Take the customer's booking reference number and name. Find out what alteration he/she wants to make. Try to find a flight which matches his/her wishes.**

Berlin Tegel–London Heathrow		Tuesday 4 May	
Flight	Depart Berlin Tegel	Arrive London Heathrow	
BA0981	07:35	08:35	
BA0991	10:40	11:35	
BA0983	12:20	13:20	full
BA0985	16:25	17:20	full
BA0987	19:15	20:10	

File 6

Unit 1, Exercise 14

PARTNER B

1 Ask your partner questions about the following things:

- his/her name
- where he/she's from
- his/her family
- his/her hobbies
- his/her favourite music

Example: *What's your name?*

2 Now choose one card and answer your partner's questions.

Name:	Sabine Pfeiffer
From:	Vienna, Austria
Family:	Lives with parents and brother
Pet:	no
Hobbies:	sport, aerobics
Favourite music:	trance/techno

Name:	Philip Hunter
From:	Chicago, USA
Family:	Lives with parents and three sisters
Pet:	two cats. Names: Tiger and Snowy
Hobbies:	in-line skating, skateboarding, climbing
Favourite music:	heavy metal

File 7

Unit 9, The world of work, Exercise 5

PARTNER B

1 You are a flight sales executive. Take the customer's booking reference number and name. Find out what alteration he/she wants to make. Try to find a flight which matches his/her wishes.

2 Your name is Alex Smith and your booking reference number is 794232. You are booked on flight BA0985 on Wednesday 5 May from Berlin Tegel to London Heathrow. You need to fly to London a day earlier.

Phone BA and ask the flight sales executive whether you can take the same flight on Tuesday instead. If not, choose another flight that he/she suggests. (You would prefer an afternoon flight.)

Frankfurt–Manchester		Tuesday 22 March	
Flight	Depart Frankfurt	Arrive Manchester	
BA1705	07:05	07:55	
BA1707	11:00	11:50	full
BA1711	18:10	19:00	
BA1711	19:30	20:20	

File 8

Unit 8, The world of work, Exercise 7

PARTNER B, C, etc.

You are the candidates. The manager will interview you for the job.

Read the advertisement again thoroughly and think about what the manager will ask you. Make some notes to help you answer their questions.
Answer the manager's questions:

- Try to show that you have the relevant personal qualities.
- Say that you have the relevant qualifications and experience.
- Say why you want the job.

File 9

Unit 9, Exercise 5

PARTNER B

1 Your friend phones you from Scotland. Ask about his/her holiday. You want to know:

- what he/she did yesterday,
- what he/she is doing today,
- what he/she is going to do tomorrow.

Is he/she enjoying the holiday?
Use some of the phrases from the Learning to Learn box on page 80.

Example:
YOU: *How's your holiday going?*
PARTNER: *Great!*
YOU: *Cool! What did you do yesterday?*
Partner: *We went … . It was … .*
YOU: *Really?*

2 You are on holiday in Ireland. You are going to phone your friend back home to tell him/her about your holiday.
Before you phone, choose one option for each day. Decide what you think about the activity, eg *fun*, *exciting*, *scary*, *boring*.

Yesterday	EITHER:	shopping in Dublin	OR:	typical Irish pub (Guinness!)
Today	EITHER:	whitewater rafting	OR:	party at the youth hostel
Tomorrow	EITHER:	boat trip	OR:	football match (Ireland v Germany)

Further reading

UNIT 1

The typical British teenager

What is the 'typical' British teenager? Some adults say that teenagers are lazy and irresponsible. They believe that most teenagers drink a lot of alcohol and spend their pocket money on cigarettes and drugs. Parents often complain that their teenage children are rude and don't care what their parents say.

A recent survey shows, however, that most British teenagers respect their parents. They work hard at school and make plans for their future. As for alcohol, smoking and drugs – most teens behave in a responsible way.

However, a lot of teenagers regularly drink alcohol or smoke cigarettes. Some of them smoke cannabis. A smaller number use Ecstasy and LSD. Nearly every teenager knows where to buy drugs.

It seems that the most important thing in British teenagers' lives is music. Some of them spend up to £50 a month on CDs. Tickets for concerts can also cost a lot, but most teenagers get pocket money from their parents. Some British teenagers have part-time jobs – delivering newspapers, washing cars or doing babysitting.

Like a lot of adults, teenagers also worry about things. Their main fear is having a serious illness. A lot of teenagers are afraid that someone will rob them. Teenagers are also interested in healthy food, animal rights and having enough money when they are older. (217 words)

Text comprehension

Choose the best ending for the statements based on the article.

1 British teenagers ...
- a don't do any work and don't think about their future.
- b drink too much alcohol and take drugs.
- c don't smoke cigarettes.

2 A lot of teenagers consume ...
- a nicotine.
- b Ecstasy.
- c cannabis.

3 Some teenagers spend a lot of money on ...
- a music.
- b cars.
- c newspapers.

4 Teenagers think a lot about ...
- a older people in the family who are ill.
- b their own health.
- c sick animals.

Vocabulary

1 Find an opposite.

a) irresponsible (line 1) b) future (line 6) c) older (line 16)

2 **Find a noun.**

a) work (line 5) b) drink (line 8) c) know (line 9)

3 **Complete the sentences with the plural forms of the words in the box.**

adult • child • parent • teenager

1 My ... don't give me any pocket money.
2 Cigarette smoke can be dangerous for small ... .
3 A lot of ... think young people are lazy.
4 British ... spend a lot of money on music.

Grammar

1 **Put the verbs in brackets into the correct form.**

1 My teenage sister ... (work) hard.
2 Troy's parents ... (not think) he is lazy.
3 Amy ... (enjoy) babysitting.
4 Jimmy ... (go) to a concert almost every weekend.
5 Flo ... (not spend) a lot of money on CDs.
6 Some teenagers ... (drink) too much alcohol.

2 **A journalist is asking teenagers some questions. Write the questions using the simple present.**

1 What time *do you get up* (you / get up)?
2 When ... (you / go to school)?
3 How often ... (you / clean your room)?
4 How much ... (you / spend on CDs)?
5 What ... (you / do at weekends)?
6 How ... (you / get on with your parents)?

Writing

Give your opinion on the following statement. Write about 50 words.

'Teenagers are lazy, irresponsible and rude!'

UNIT 2

Volunteering – working for free in our free time

Schools in the south of England are taking part in the 'Clean up our countryside' campaign. 'Clean up our countryside' is an organization which asks young volunteers to clean up woods, rivers and wild meadows in their free time.

It's the Easter holidays, but instead of going away, Alan Simms (18) is working with his sister Pat (16) and ten other pupils in the New Forest. 'Most people love nature and they like to go into the forest for walks and picnics,' Alan says. 'The countryside authorities keep telling us to take our rubbish home, and there are litter bins everywhere. Even so, some people leave their litter all over the place. That's really bad.'

Pat agrees. 'There are beautiful plants and animals here,' she says. 'It's springtime now and the forest is coming alive but a lot of visitors to the forest don't think about the animals. We found an owl with its head in a plastic bag. People just don't think.'

By giving up some of their holiday time and working as volunteers, teenagers like Alan and Pat are doing a lot of good in the English countryside. Is anything like this going on in your area? Perhaps your school could also help clean up the countryside near you. (211 words)

Text comprehension

1 Match the beginnings of sentences 1–5 with the endings a–e.

1 'Clean up our countryside'
2 Alan and Pat
3 Plants and animals
4 The countryside authorities
5 Some other teenagers

a are not taking any Easter holidays this year.
b are suffering because people behave badly in the countryside.
c is an organization where young people do voluntary work.
d are working with Alan and Pat in the New Forest.
e are asking people to use litter bins.

2 Now ask Alan three questions about his work.

Vocabulary

Find words in the text which match the following definitions. They are in the same order.

1 an area where there are no towns and cities, with fields and forests
2 a group of people who get together to coordinate some work
3 a person who does not get paid for doing a job
4 time when you don't have to go to school or work
5 groups of people who make laws about things
6 places to put waste

Grammar

1 Translate the missing parts of the sentences.

1 Diese Woche arbeiten wir im Wald.	*This week we ... in the forest.*
2 Alan macht heute den Fluss sauber.	*Alan ... the river today.*
3 Wir schlafen nie im Zelt.	*We never ... in a tent.*
4 Du arbeitest momentan zu viel.	*At the moment you ... too much.*
5 Was machst du im Wald?	*What ... in the forest?*
6 Die Leute denken nicht an die Natur.	*People ... about Nature.*

2 Make sentences using the present progressive or the simple present.

1 Alan and Pat / be / voluntary workers
2 They / work hard / at the moment.
3 you / enjoy / your work, Alan?
4 why / you / not help me?
5 They / not use / the litter bins.
6 the animals and plants / need / our help?

Writing

Your school is doing a voluntary project to clean up the environment. Write a short text for an American website (about 60 words) about the project. Include these points:

- describe the environment around your school
- say who you are working with
- say what you are doing

UNIT 3

A year in Singapore

Yasmin Frey's dad worked in Singapore for a year and the family went with him. Read about what Yasmin did when she was there.

We really loved shopping in Singapore. Although it's a small country, there are lots of places to shop. There was a street called Orchard Road which had so many fun shops. At night, the shopkeepers switched on all the lights and it looked like Christmas. It was beautiful!

There was a nice park near where we lived and my mum and I often went for a walk in the evening. There were always lots of joggers in the park. My dad told me that a lot of his colleagues went jogging to get rid of stress.

Singapore is so small that there wasn't much to do there in the holidays. Australia is a very popular place to go and we went there for three weeks. There's also Malaysia, of course. A lot of Singaporeans go there to buy cheap things but we didn't manage to fit in a trip ourselves.

The most famous place is Sentosa, an island on the southern side of Singapore. Sentosa is theme parks, beaches, restaurants, hotels, theme parks, beaches .... We went there for 10 days. It was great!

During school time I read a lot and studied for exams. Education in Singapore is very tough compared to Germany. We had so much homework and loads of tests. It was so bad! I was so happy to come back to our school. (253 words)

Text comprehension

Answer these questions on the text.

1 How long did Yasmin's father work in Singapore?
2 What did Yasmin enjoy most in Singapore?
3 Did Yasmin see joggers on the streets?
4 What did Yasmin's father say about his colleagues?
5 Where did Yasmin and her family go on holiday?
6 Was school work in Singapore easy for Yasmin?

Vocabulary

Use the opposites of the adjectives in brackets to complete the sentences.

1 Yasmin went to Singapore ... her friends. (with)
2 Singapore isn't a very ... place. (small)
3 Compared to Singapore, Germany is quite .... (cheap)
4 We lived on the ... side of Singapore. (southern)
5 After a year in Singapore, I was a bit ... to leave my new friends there. (happy)

Grammar

1 Complete the dialogue with the verbs in the simple past.

A: Where ... [1] (you/go) on your last holiday?
B: I ... [2] (go) to Greece with my friends.
A: What ... [3] (you/do) there?
B: In the daytime we ... [4] (lie) on the beach. Then we ... [5] (dance) all night in the disco. We ... [6] (not go) to bed before 5 a.m.
A: ... [7] (you/enjoy) your holiday?
B: Yes, it ... [8] (be) fantastic!

2 Complete the answers to these questions.

1 Did you go to Spain last year? – No, *I didn't.*
2 Did your parents give you money? – No, ...
3 Did Ben have a nice holiday? – Yes, ...
4 Did he go with Paul? – No, ...
5 Did Astrid do a lot of sunbathing? – Yes, ...
6 Did I tell you about my holidays? – No, ...

Writing

Write an email for Yasmin to her friends, telling them what she did last week in Singapore.

UNIT 4

The re-mix generation

It's 9 p.m. on Friday night at the Plan B in Brixton. Punjabe MC is going to boom out his music for eight hours non-stop and the kids are going to dance like crazy. Twenty years ago Plan B was a black club. Tonight the dancers are black, Asian and white.

It's the same all over Britain. Blacks and Asians are moving away from old-fashioned, colour-based ideas and white kids are moving towards traditional black lifestyles. They are coming together and making a new youth group – not black, not Asian, not white, just British kids who follow 'black' culture.

Black fashion, music and sport are more popular in Britain than ever before. In the past, any white kid who copied 'black' hairstyles or wore the same type of clothes as his or her black schoolmates was called a 'wigga' (white nigger). Today, 'wiggas' are everywhere. More than half of the Top 40 albums and singles sold last year were black acts. The music magazines say that white soul singers will collect a lot of Mobo (Music of Black Origin) awards this year.

A few years ago there was a TV documentary about black people in Britain. In the documentary a reporter said that David Beckham was the most famous 'black' man in the country. 'Blacks admire him because he is a superstar and he has money and a beautiful wife. He loves the things that lots of black men love – fast cars, fashion and jewellery; he gets on well with blacks and goes to their clubs,' the reporter said. 'He's the most popular white footballer among black kids,' he went on. 'Beckham has taken on a lot of elements of black culture.'

Other young people in Britain are doing the same as David Beckham. The barriers between black and white are down. Black urban culture will be the mainstream culture in Britain for the next few years.

(315 words)

Text comprehension

Who is *he*, *she*, *they*, *it* in the following sentences?

1 They are leaving their traditions behind.
2 They are taking on things from another culture.
3 He or she is a 'wigga'.
4 They will win prizes.
5 He is a black man in a white skin.
6 It will be the favourite lifestyle of young people in Britain soon.

Vocabulary

1 Find the English for the following phrases in the text.

1 dröhnen
2 ohne Pause
3 wie verrückt
4 nachmachen
5 sich gut verstehen mit

2 **Translate the underlined phrases.**

1 Funk und Soul sind nicht dasselbe.
2 Andere Musiker machen das gleiche wie Eminem.
3 Have you got Eminem's latest single?
4 He's thirty-three and still single.

Grammar

1 **Make sentences using be going to + one of these verbs.**

buy • come • have • spend • start • wear

1 We ... a lot of fun this evening.
2 I ... some soul CDs on Saturday.
3 What ... you ... to the disco?
4 When ... DJ ... the music?
5 John ... not ... to the club tonight.
6 They ... not ... so much money on clothes this year.

2 **Choose the correct phrase.**

1 Twenty years ago Plan B was not as loud *as/than* it is today.
2 Black music is *more popular / most popular* than ever.
3 There are more 'wiggas' around today *as/than* a few years ago.
4 *Most/More* people know David Beckham.
5 David Beckham is one of England's *famoust / most famous* footballers.
6 The new Eminem CD is *more cheap / cheaper* than his last one.

Writing

There's a writing competition in an English pop magazine this month – a short article about readers' favourite music. Write 80 words about the music or musicians you like best.

UNIT 5

Fit teens in Texas

(A) A Texas hospital runs a fitness programme for overweight teenagers. The participants follow a 10-week diet and exercise plan. They meet once a week to talk about progress and check their weight.

(B) Dr Tom Gold, the leader of the programme, explains, 'We give the teenagers a low-calorie food plan and send them to the gym for a workout twice a week. It's important to do physical activity regularly.'

(C) Teenagers who want to live in a healthy way face big challenges in today's world. There is food and drink everywhere they go. The typical teenager drinks three soft drinks per day – that's about 400 calories – and they like to eat fast food like pizza and burgers. These are really fatty foods, and in Texas the portions are usually large enough to feed three people.

(D) On top of that, most teenagers sit around too much – in front of computers, TVs and video games.

(E) 'You shouldn't lose weight too quickly and you can't change people's ideas overnight,' Dr Gold says. 'Our aim is to help these young people change their eating habits slowly, take exercise regularly and start to live in a healthy way.'

(F) The Texas programme offers teenagers a chance to lead a healthier life. 'We want to help these kids change their attitudes about eating and exercise,' Dr Gold concludes. 'That way they can lose weight in a healthy way and keep it off for a lifetime.' (236 words)

Text comprehension

1 Match these statements to paragraphs A–F.

1 A lot of young people don't take enough exercise.
2 Our programme is based on a diet and an exercise plan.
3 XXL teenagers can get help in Texas.
4 We encourage people to take it slowly.
5 We hope that the teenagers will stay slim.
6 It's difficult to lose weight nowadays.

2 Now ask Dr Tom Gold three questions about the fitness programme.

Vocabulary

1 Find a word with a similar meaning.

a) usually (Section C) b) start (Section E)

2 **Find an opposite.**

a) low-calorie (Section B) b) important (Section B)

3 **Complete the sentences with the words in the box.**

per day • once a week • twice a week • regularly

1 Try to go to the gym ... – say, on Tuesdays and Thursdays.
2 Don't check your weight more than ... .
3 Some people eat only one meal ... when they're slimming, but that's not healthy.
4 You have to keep on exercising ... if you want to lose weight.

Grammar

1 **Adjective or adverb? Choose the correct forms.**

1 Frank speaks English very *good/well.*
2 The boys are always *late/lately* for school.
3 Helen always answers *quick/quickly.*
4 Can you speak more *slow/slowly* please?
5 You have to be *quiet/quietly* in the library.
6 Karen copies everything *careful/carefully.*

2 **Complete the sentences with some or any.**

1 Are there ... good gyms near you?
2 We had ... lessons about fitness at school.
3 He never has ... time to go to the gym.
4 Rachel knows ... good exercises.
5 Would you like ... tips on keeping fit?
6 I haven't done ... sports for ages.

Writing

A friend would like to lose weight and get fit. Use information from the text to write an email giving your friend advice. Write 80 words.

UNIT 6

Earning money

Greg Johnson is a high school student in New York. He emails his German pen-friend and tells him about jobs he has done.

Lots of American students work to earn money. I've worked since I was twelve years old. I did a paper route in our neighborhood. Have you ever seen American kids delivering newspapers? They don't put the paper into a mailbox like you do in Germany, they just throw it onto the path in front of the house. My paper route really helped my pitching arm. My baseball game has gotten a lot worse since I stopped delivering newspapers ;-)

I've had a lot of different jobs since then. For a while I worked in a supermarket. I put people's groceries into bags at the checkout, then I carried the bags out to the customers' cars. It was boring, but some of the customers gave good tips. Later, I worked at a gas station washing windows and filling up the cars with gas. The money was better there. I did these jobs after school and on the weekend.

I haven't done any after-school jobs for a while as I'm working hard for my tests at the moment. I still need to earn money, of course, so I applied for a summer vacation job on a farm. I've never done farm work but I heard it can be tough. The money's good, though, and that's the main thing. I opened a savings account already. (245 words)

Text comprehension

Complete the following statements about the text.

1 In America ...
2 In the supermarket, Greg ...
3 At the gas station, Greg ...
4 At the moment, ...
5 Next summer Greg ...

Vocabulary

1 Find a noun.

a) deliver (line 4) b) help (line 6) c) different (line 8)

2 Find an adjective.

a) year (line 3) b) really (line 6) c) hard (line 12)

3 Find an adverb.

a) different (line 8) b) good (line 10) c) main (line 14)

4 **Find an opposite.**

a) worse (line 6) b) stopped (line 6) c) different (line 8)

Grammar

1 **Make questions and answers in the present perfect.**

Example: Your father often sends you money.
your father / send any money this week? – No, ...
Has your father sent you any money this week?
No, he hasn't.

1 You work in a shop.
you / work there long? – Yes, ...
2 Irene is unemployed.
she / find a job yet? – No, ...
3 You sometimes write emails in English.
you / write an email in English today? – Yes, ...
4 Tony usually makes a lot of phone calls.
he / make a lot of phone calls this week? – Yes, ...
5 The computer often crashes.
it / crash today? – No, ...
6 May does a lot of overtime.
she / do overtime this month? – Yes, ...

2 **Complete the sentences with since or for.**

1 I've worked here ... five years.
2 Have you seen Lucy ... last week?
3 Pat hasn't been at work ... a few weeks now.
4 We haven't had any payment from them ... three months.
5 She's been on the internet ... early this morning.
6 Sammy has done a lot of jobs ... last year.

Now translate the sentences into German.

Writing

Have you worked before? If not, which job would you like to do after school? Write a short text (about 80-100 words).

UNIT 7

Casting – dos and don'ts

Are you interested in a career in the pop business but don't know how to get started? Have you thought about going on a TV casting programme? Here are some tips.

First, you should do some research. You have to check out what the people in charge of the programme are looking for. If your hobby is yodelling or singing German folk songs, forget it. The pop world is looking for people who are able to sing modern songs in English. Don't worry if your English isn't perfect. You can sing a cover version of your favourite song – but you have to know all the words by heart!

Second, you have to enter for the casting. Look on the internet or in pop magazines to find out how to apply. You must check the application forms carefully to see if you are allowed to go on a casting show. The TV company of the show where you would like to apply may not allow people under the age of 18 to enter.

If you are invited to the casting studio, the TV people will look after your hair and make-up for you. What you wear is up to you but remember, your outfit has to look good.

One guy who went to a casting show last year didn't realize he had to dress smartly for the casting so he wore his everyday jeans and sweatshirt. He was allowed to sing for exactly 20 seconds. I don't have to tell you, that guy was really sick that he hadn't bought a new outfit for the show. How do I know? Well, I am that unhappy guy. But I might try again, and I promise you, I'll be allowed to sing for longer that time! (293 words)

Text comprehension

Answer the questions on the text.

1 What is the text about?
2 What do pop programmes expect if you apply?
3 What should you do before you apply?
4 What did the writer of the text do wrong when he applied?
5 What is he going to do next time?

Vocabulary

1 Find an expression with a similar meaning.

a) some (line 2) b) check out (line 3) c) realize (line 14)

2 Find an opposite.

a) forget (line 4) b) under (line 10) c) last (line 14)

3 Find the English in the text.

1 Mach dir keine Sorgen (lines 1–7)
2 auswendig (lines 1–7)
3 sich kümmern um (lines 12–18)
4 (das) ist dir überlassen (lines 12–18)

Grammar

1 Choose the correct modal verb.

1 You *must* / *can* wear the right clothes when you go to a casting.
2 You *shouldn't* / *couldn't* sing folk songs.
3 You *aren't allowed to* / *don't have to* speak perfect English.
4 You *are able to* / *might* be too young for the show.
5 For some shows you *mustn't* / *don't have to* fill in an application form.
6 *Must I* / *Do I have to* give them my email address?

2 Complete the story below using these modal verbs. Use each modal only once. The first one has been done for you.

~~can~~ • could • couldn't • might • should • shouldn't

Dean Howell (16) from Leeds, always wanted to be a singer. He sent a card to the ATV casting show, 'You *can*[1] do it!', and he was thrilled to bits when he ...[2] take part in the show. Dean thought he ...[3] win but the judges, Gerry James and Frankie Lo, told him he ...[4] sing.

After the show, Gerry James said, 'That boy from Leeds was terrible. He ...[5] only be allowed to sing in the shower behind a locked door.' Frankie Lo added, 'I told Dean to work hard at school and get a job in an office. He ...[6] dream about a career in showbusiness.'

Dean's mum said, 'I don't care what Gerry and Frankie think, my son has a beautiful voice.'

Writing

A TV company in London is looking for a German student for a soap opera. Write a letter to the TV company about yourself and ask them about the casting (date, time, accommodation, etc.). Write 80–100 words.

Dear Sir or Madam
I am ...

UNIT 8

Living and working in London

Would you like to live and work in the United Kingdom? Because Germany and the UK are both in the European Union, you can.

Of course, it isn't quite as simple as that. You need good English to get a job, and good luck to find a cheap flat.

Florian Meyer is now doing an apprenticeship in Stuttgart, but last year he worked in London for nine months. Florian tells his story:

'I wanted to improve my English, get some work experience and also have fun, so I decided to go to London.

'It wasn't easy to find a job. I looked for jobs on the internet while I was still in Germany, and the British Council website gave me some useful tips. However, the jobs which I found on the internet were all for people with experience, and I had just finished school. Finally I decided to go to London and try to find a job there.

'My uncle lives in London, so he let me stay in his flat for a month. I had to sleep on the floor, but it was better than nothing.

'When I was in London, it was a lot easier to find a job. I read the Evening Standard newspaper every day. After three weeks I got a job as a hotel porter. It was a very expensive hotel in Kensington. Unfortunately, a porter's salary was only about £6 an hour.

'At the hotel I became friends with a colleague who had a free room in his flat, so I moved in with him. There were five of us in the flat: Scottish, Australian, French, Canadian and German. It was a small flat but the rent was very high: £120 each a week!

'I love London. It's a very exciting place: there are lots of pubs, bars and nightclubs, and it's very multicultural – there are people from all over the world. My time in London was a great experience.'

(326 words)

Text comprehension

Choose the correct answer(s).

1 Florian looked for jobs ...
- a on the internet.
- b in German hotels.
- c in the newspaper.

2 The British Council ...
- a provided useful information.
- b found a job for Florian.
- c sent Florian a list of jobs.

3 When Florian got to London ...
- a he stayed with his uncle.
- b he looked for work.
- c he stayed in an expensive hotel.

4 Florian's job was ...
- a in a cheap hotel.
- b badly paid.
- c in a restaurant.

Vocabulary

1 Find an opposite.

a) cheap (line 4) b) useful (line 10) c) easier (line 15)

2 Find a noun.

a) live (line 1) b) improve (line 7) c) exciting (line 21)

3 Use a dictionary to translate the underlined expressions.

1 Our flat was on the fourth floor.
2 The countryside was very flat – there were no hills.
3 Hast du deine Ausbildung schon abgeschlossen?
4 Hast du die Wohnung abgeschlossen?

Grammar

1 Complete the sentences with the simple past or present perfect form of the verbs in brackets.

1 Florian ... (have to) find a job quickly.
2 He ... (not find) a flat for three weeks now.

2 Complete the sentences with the simple present or present progressive form of the verbs in brackets.

1 Lisa ... (work) in a restaurant today.
2 She ... (not live) in London now.

3 Translate the missing parts of the sentences.

1 Ich habe ein Mädchen kennen gelernt, das in einem Hotel arbeitet.
I met a girl ... in a hotel.
2 Florian fand eine Website, die ihm einige nützliche Hinweise gab.
Florian found a website ... him some useful advice.
3 Er bewarb sich um eine Stelle, die er im Internet fand.
He applied for a job ... on the internet.

4 Ask for the underlined words.

1 Jana worked in an office.
2 She lived in New York last year.

Writing

For young Germans, why is it a good idea to work in an English-speaking country? What problems are there? Write about 80 words.

UNIT 9

The future of travel

Have you ever thought about what travel will be like in the future? Will we still drive cars? Will there still be traffic jams? Will public transport be free?

Here are some predictions about travel in the year 2050:

- Motorways will be a thing of the past because vehicles won't travel on the ground. Even cars and buses will fly between three and five metres above the ground. There will still be streets in towns, though, for pedestrians and cyclists.
- Cars will still be popular, but they will be very different to today's cars. You won't need a driving licence, because a computer will control the car. You will just get in and tell the car where you want to go. During the journey, you will be able to sleep, watch TV or get on with your work. Car travel will be a lot safer.
- Space tourism will be available to more people, but it will still be quite expensive and not very popular. After all, it's very quiet and black out there, and there's no atmosphere! It will be fun for half an hour, then it will get boring.
- Public transport will be very fast (about 500 kilometres per hour), so people will be able to travel further to work. For example, you might live in Stuttgart and work in Berlin, Paris or even London. However, 60% of people will work at home in a personal 'cyber-office'. It will be just like working in a real office, but you will see holograms of your colleagues, not the real people.
- All vehicles will have electric motors. This means that there will be much less pollution and vehicles will also be much quieter.

Of course, these are just guesses ... (294 words)

Text comprehension

1 **Answer the questions on the text.**

1 Why won't space tourism be a success?
2 Why won't we need as many roads?
3 How will people control their cars in 2050?
4 How will faster transport change the way we work?
5 What won't 60% of people do in 2050?
6 Why will the environment be healthier?

2 **Ask three questions about the future of travel.**

Vocabulary

1 **Find a word with a similar meaning.**

a) streets (line 5) b) journey (line 9) c) boring (line 13)

2 **Find a verb.**

a) prediction (line 3) b) pollution (line 18) c) guess (line 20)

3 **Use the opposites of the words in brackets to complete the sentences.**

1 Lexi's car is ... my brother's. (different to)
2 ... people walk to work these days. (More)
3 In London, cars are a ... method of transport. (fast)
4 Older cars are a lot ... . (quieter)

Grammar

1 **Complete the sentences with the going to future or the will future of the verbs in brackets.**

1 We ... (fly) to New Zealand next year.
2 In 2050 there ... (be) twice as many cars as today.
3 'Where's the nearest bus stop?' – 'I ... (take) you there.'
4 When ... (you / learn) to drive?

2 **Copy the table and fill in the missing forms.**

	positive	comparative	superlative
1	?	quieter (line 19)	?
2	popular (line 7)	?	?
3	?	safer (line 10)	?
4	?	more (line 11)	?

3 **Ask for the underlined words.**

1 Pollution will be a thing of the past.
2 We won't need driving licences.
3 Jack will be 60 in 2050.
4 Most people will work at home.

Writing

Imagine that it's the year 2050. What are you going to do today? Write about a typical day in your life. (80–100 words)

UNIT 10

Mobile phone debt

Young mobile phone users are getting into financial trouble because they are spending too much on calls.

A recent survey in Australia suggests that around 40% of teenage mobile phone users have received monthly phone bills of $200 (€125) or more. One Sydney teenager had to go to the post office to collect his phone bill – the bill had so many pages, it was too big for his parents' letterbox. Four per cent of teenagers have spent $1500 (€940) or more on phone calls in one month.

'If you have ever wondered how young people can afford a mobile phone, the answer is that many can't,' says youth activist Lexi O'Rourke. 'Mobile phone tariffs are often very complicated, and it's easy to spend much too much on calls and text messages.'

Mobile phone companies recommend that teenagers or their parents choose a pay as you go phone. 'If teenagers have a pay as you go phone, they won't be able to get into debt,' says one mobile phone expert.

However, pay as you go phones are unpopular with teenagers because each call costs more. 'If I switch to a pay as you go phone, I'll spend more money but make fewer calls,' says Dwayne Smith, 16. 'It doesn't make sense.'

The survey also found that the average age to begin using a mobile is 13 and many children got their first mobile before the age of ten.

Lexi O'Rourke says that the phone companies could help to reduce young people's phone debts. 'Phone companies should simplify their mobile phone tariffs, so that young users know how much they are spending,' says Lexi. 'They should also offer tariffs which have a cap – a limit on the number of calls you can make.'

(288 words)

Text comprehension

Complete the sentences in your own words.

1 Forty per cent of Australian teenagers spend ...
2 As mobile phone tariffs are difficult to understand ...
3 Teenagers who have pay as you go phones ...
4 Dwayne doesn't want a pay as you go phone because ...
5 On average, children ...
6 A mobile phone tariffs with a cap can reduce phone bills because ...

Vocabulary

1 Find an opposite.

a) complicated (line 8) b) first (line 17) c) reduce (line 18)

2 Find an adverb.

a) recent (line 3) b) easy (line 8) c) help (line 18)

3 Find a word in the text which matches the definition.

1 To make a suggestion about the best thing to do. (lines 7–15)
2 An adjective to describe something which most people don't like. (lines 7–15)

4 Explain in a complete sentence.

1 phone bill (line 4) 2 pay as you go (line 10)

Grammar

1 Translate the missing parts of the sentences.

1 Wenn sie viel telefonieren, werden sie sich verschulden.
If they ... a lot of phone calls, they ... into debt.
2 Wenn du mir eine SMS schickst, treffe ich dich in der Stadt.
If you ... me a text, I ... you in town.
3 Wenn Anja weniger Geld für Anrufe ausgibt, wird sie mehr Geld fürs Ausgehen haben.
If Anja ... less on phone calls, she ... more money for going out.

2 Complete the principal parts of the verbs.

1	...	got	...
2	...	...	spent
3	choose	...	...
4	...	found	...

Writing

What tips can you think of which will help young people spend less on mobile phone calls? (80–100 words)

UNIT 11

Why do they call them newspapers?

Britain has a large number of national daily newspapers – newspapers which appear six days a week and are available everywhere in Britain.
Some, like *The Guardian*, *The Independent* and *The Times*, publish informative articles about current affairs, politics and daily life. People often call them 'quality' newspapers.
However, there is another group which is much more popular. This group includes *The Sun*, *The Star* and *The Mirror*. They are called 'tabloid' newspapers.
These tabloid newspapers don't contain much real *news*, in the sense of information about important things that are happening in the world. Instead, they are obsessed with the lives – especially the sex lives – of celebrities like film stars, footballers and the Royal Family. In addition, they contain 'human interest' stories: these are reports about strange, sad or funny things that have happened to ordinary people. At the back of every tabloid are several pages of sports reports.
So why do Britons enjoy reading the tabloids so much? Well, they are easy and quick to read – just right for a 20-minute bus ride to work or a 10-minute coffee break. They are also very entertaining. Most of us love reading gossip about celebrities – even if we don't admit it.
Some people think that all this gossip is harmless fun. In their opinion it is the price which the celebrities pay for being rich and famous. Other people argue that everyone has the right to privacy – even celebrities.

(238 words)

Text comprehension

Choose the correct answer(s).

1 In Britain ...
- a most newspapers appear once a week.
- b there are several national newspapers.
- c all newspapers contain lots of news.

2 Quality newspapers ...
- a are more popular than tabloid newspapers.
- b are only interested in politics.
- c contain lots of information.

3 Tabloid newspapers ...
- a are obsessed with politics.
- b are good for people who like sport.
- c contain lots of gossip.

4 Human interest stories ...
- a are untrue.
- b are about ordinary people.
- c are often funny.

Vocabulary

1 Find a word with a similar meaning.

a) large (line 1)　b) ordinary (line 10)　c) several (line 11)

2 Find an adjective.

a) politics (line 4)　b) enjoy (line 12)　c) privacy (line 16)

3 **Use a dictionary to translate the underlined expressions.**

1 Ben is interested in current affairs.
2 The footballer's wife was having an affair with a rock star.
3 Fußballspieler wie David Beckham sind für Boulevardzeitungen sehr interessant.
4 Sie ist fast so berühmt wie Madonna.

Grammar

1 **Complete the sentences with the correct verb forms (-ing-form or infinitive).**

1 We enjoyed ... (watch) the TV show.
2 I hate ... (hear) gossip about celebrities.
3 Many stars would like ... (have) more privacy.
4 Please stop ... (read) that newspaper!

2 **Ask for the underlined words.**

1 My bus ride to work takes half an hour.
2 Paul buys a newspaper once a week.
3 We read *The Sun* in our coffee break.
4 Jo hates reading stories about celebrities.

Writing

Do you think that newspapers should write gossip about celebrities? (80–100 words)

UNIT 12

A glass of recycled water, anyone?

In the modern world, we use a lot of recycled products. Car tyres are recycled to make shoes, athletics tracks and tennis courts. Aluminium drinks cans are crushed, melted and made into ... aluminium cans. With modern technology, old plastic bottles can be recycled to make all kinds of things, from clothes to building materials. Paper has been recycled for many years, of course.

How do you feel, though, about recycled water? Would you wash your clothes in it, shower in it or even *drink* it?

The inhabitants of the Australian city of Sydney may soon have to drink recycled water, because their water supply is running out.

There are other possibilities:

- Sea water can be turned into fresh water, but the process takes a lot of electricity – and that causes environmental problems.
- Water can be pumped to Sydney from other parts of Australia, along thousand-kilometre pipelines, but this is very expensive. Again, a lot of energy is needed to pump the water.

Waste water can be cleaned and used again. UV light is used to kill harmful bacteria. Recycled water is already widely used in agriculture, but the question is: can Australians be persuaded to drink it?

In the end, they probably won't be given a choice. Some other cities, such as Singapore and Washington DC, already treat waste water and put it back into reservoirs so that it can be used again. There is no difference in taste from normal water and it is perfectly safe to drink.

Next time you drink a glass of water, think about where it came from! (266 words)

Text comprehension

Answer the questions on the text.

1 What can be made from recycled car tyres?
2 What can recycled plastic bottles be used for?
3 What problem does Sydney face?
4 Why is recycling water the best way to solve the problem?
5 Why might this solution not work?
6 What does recycled water taste like?

Vocabulary

1 Find an opposite.

a) many (line 4) b) expensive (line 13) c) harmful (line 14)

2 Find a noun.

a) recycled (line 1) b) cause (line 10) c) safe (line 18)

3 Complete each sentence with the best word from the text.

1 The people who live in a place are its … . (lines 1–8)
2 Rubbish is an … problem. (lines 9–15)
3 Yuck! I don't like the … of this water. (lines 16–19)

Grammar

1 Put the sentences into the passive.

1 Australians use a lot of recycled products.
2 We will recycle these aluminium cans
3 Their arguments didn't persuade the residents.
4 Will they treat the waste water?

2 Translate the missing parts of these sentences into English.

1 Diese Sportschuhe werden aus alten Reifen hergestellt.
These trainers … old car tyres.
2 Das Wasser wird gereinigt werden, bevor es wiederverwendet wird.
The water … before it is reused.

3 Fill the gaps with a, an, some or any.

A: Would you like ...[1] drink?
B: Yes, please. I'll have ...[2] water.
A: I haven't got ...[3] mineral water.
B: I'll have ...[4] tap water then.
A: Are you sure? It's recycled.
B: In that case, I'll have ...[5] orange juice, please.

Writing

Do you think that recycled water is a good idea? Would you drink it? Say why (not). (80 words)

UNIT 13

The two Irelands

Did you know that Ireland is actually two countries? The south of Ireland is called the Republic of Ireland or Eire and has about 4 million inhabitants. Dublin is its capital city. In the north is Northern Ireland with its capital city in Belfast. Northern Ireland is part of the United Kingdom and has about 1.7 million inhabitants.

The most important event in modern Irish history was the Anglo-Irish Treaty of December 1921. Before that, the British had ruled the whole of Ireland for hundreds of years.

The Treaty said that Ireland would become an independent country. However, it also said that the people of Northern Ireland could choose to stay in the UK. Most people in Northern Ireland wanted to stay British, so Ireland became two countries.

Unfortunately the arguments didn't end with the Anglo-Irish Treaty. In Northern Ireland there is still disagreement between Unionists and Nationalists. Unionists want to stay in the United Kingdom, but Nationalists want to join the Republic of Ireland. Unionists are mostly Protestant and Nationalists are mostly Roman Catholic, but the argument isn't really about religion: it is about politics and different cultures.

The conflict between Unionists and Nationalists has created many extremist groups. The best known is the IRA (Irish Republican Army). The IRA carried out many bomb attacks and shootings in Ireland and Britain from the 1960s until the late 1990s. The IRA said that they were fighting for Irish freedom; the British government said that it would never let terrorists win. It sent many soldiers to Northern Ireland to fight the IRA.

People said that the violence would go on for ever. However, in the late 1990s the two sides began to talk and in 1998 came the Good Friday Agreement. This was an agreement between the British government, Unionists and Nationalists. Under the agreement, Nationalists and Unionists agreed to work together peacefully to govern Northern Ireland.

There have been many problems since then, and the two sides are still suspicious of each other, but there is less terrorism and people in Northern Ireland can start to hope for a better future. (351 words)

Text comprehension

Complete the sentences in your own words.

1 Ireland has been two countries ...
2 Until 1921, Ireland ...
3 Unionists say that ...
4 Nationalists say that ...
5 The IRA tried to ...
6 In 1998, ...

Vocabulary

1 Use the noun forms of the words in brackets to complete the sentences.

1 The Republicans demanded ... for Northern Ireland. (independent)
2 In the end, we have no ... but to work together. (choose)

2 Use the verb forms of the words in brackets to complete the sentences.

1 I ... with everything you say. (disagreement)
2 It's okay for Unionists and Republicans to ... as long as they don't fight. (argument)

3 Complete the sentences with a word or phrase with a similar meaning.

1 ... people were killed in the bomb attack. (many)
2 Unionists are ... Protestant. (mostly)

Grammar

1 Put these sentences into reported speech, using 'Declan/Paula said that ... .'

1 Declan: 'Arguments about politics are stupid.'
2 Paula: 'There will be less violence in the future.'
3 Declan: 'The violence has ended.'

2 Put put these sentences into direct speech.

1 The IRA said that they had carried out the attack.
2 Unionists and Nationalists said that they would work together.
3 Nationalists said that they still wanted an independent Ireland.

Writing

What problems does terrorism cause for ordinary people? (80–100 words)

UNIT 14

Disposable children

If you walk through any British town centre, you will see homeless people. They lie in doorways and beg for money. When one of them asks you for 'any spare change', it's easy to look away and walk on. But would you still look away if the person was a child?

In Britain around 15,000 children are forced to leave home every year. They are society's disposable children. Reasons why parents throw out their kids include new partners, drug or alcohol addiction and money problems. Young people on the streets often have to commit crimes to pay for food and shelter.

Simon is now 17. He was 13 when his mother threw him out. These days he lives with a foster family, but he remembers life on the streets as if it was yesterday:

'I lived alone with my mum. She went out drinking all the time. Every weekend she brought home a different man. When they saw me, mostly they didn't want to stay. She blamed me, so she threw me out.

'I remember crying myself to sleep on the first night. I slept under a bridge. It was cold and wet and I could hear people walking by.

'When I was living rough I lost track of time: I didn't know what day it was. I spent Christmas on the streets, but I didn't even realize. Most people just ignored me, but there were some kind-hearted people who gave me a few coins. It was enough for food and drink.

'Eventually I was picked up by the police. I didn't know it at the time, but it was the best thing that ever happened to me.

'Social services found a foster home for me. I have changed my name now. If I told you my real name, people from my past might try to contact me, and I don't want that. I want to start a new life: I'm going to college and want to become a police officer.'

Simon is one of the lucky ones. (338 words)

Text comprehension

Choose the correct answer(s).

1 In Britain ...
- a there are about fifteen thousand homeless people.
- b about fifteen thousand children don't have a home.
- c about fifteen thousand children are thrown out by their parents every year.

2 When Simon was thirteen ...
- a he lived with a foster family.
- b he left home.
- c he lived on the streets.

3 When Simon was living rough ...
- a some people gave him money.
- b some people gave him food and drink.
- c some people gave him drugs.

4 These days, Simon ...
- a lives with a family.
- b is studying at college.
- c is a police officer.

Vocabulary

1 Find a word with a similar meaning.

a) These days (line 8) c) kind-hearted (line 16) c) start (line 21)

2 Find an adjective.

a) alcohol (line 5) b) crimes (line 6) c) past (line 21)

3 Use a dictionary to translate the underlined expressions.

1 I spent two months on the streets.
2 He spent all his money on drugs.
3 Simon hatte Glück.
4 Er war glücklich in seiner neuen Familie.

Grammar

1 Complete these sentences with the correct verb forms.

1 If you ... (see) a homeless person, would you walk on?
2 If Simon ... (stay) at home, his life would have been different.
3 Social services ... (find) Lexi a home if she wanted one.
4 If Tim ... (go) to college, he could have become a police officer.

2 Translate the missing parts of these sentences into English.

1 Was würden Sie machen, wenn Sie obdachlos wären?
What ... if you were homeless?
2 Wenn er kein Geld hätte, würde er um Kleingeld betteln.
... any money, he would beg for spare change.

Writing

Who should help these young people, and how? (80–100 words)

UNIT 15

Want to see the USA? Go Greyhound!

If you have more time than money, Greyhound buses are a great way to see the United States. You can cross the continent from New York to Los Angeles (LA) for under $100 one-way – you couldn't drive for that price. I wouldn't recommend doing the journey non-stop, though. That's a 64-hour trip!

I did it once because I had to get home quickly for Christmas – my folks live in LA, but I'm studying in New York. By the time I got to Chicago (a third of the way) I was beginning to regret it. When the bus stopped at Kansas City (about half way), my back was hurting. When the bus arrived at Denver (two thirds of the way), my whole body was aching. When I got to Las Vegas (nearly there, just nine more hours to go) I was feeling sick and when I finally arrived at LA, I could hardly walk!

If you have the time, it's best to do the trip in about ten days each way. That way, you can travel every second day and you can spend time sightseeing. Most US cities have cheap backpackers' hostels where you can sleep for a few dollars.

Some people always travel overnight so that they can sleep on the bus, but I don't recommend doing that: the seats are narrow and you won't get much sleep – particularly if you sit next to someone fat!

I have met some great people on Greyhound buses. There are some real 'characters' and some really nice people. One of my best friends is a girl I met on a bus to Miami.

You need to be careful, however, because there are weirdos as well as nice people on buses. Girls travelling alone shouldn't wear 'sexy' clothes, shouldn't walk alone outside the bus stations and shouldn't tell personal information to strangers. Take a music player – listening to music on headphones is a good way to avoid an unwanted conversation.

Bon voyage!

Kelly Jaeger (328 words)

Text comprehension

Answer the questions on the text.

1 Why are Greyhound buses a good way to travel around the USA?
2 What did Kelly Jaeger do once and why?
3 Why wasn't it a good idea?
4 How much time should you allow, ideally, to make a return trip from New York to Los Angeles and back?
5 Why isn't it a good idea to travel overnight on a Greyhound bus?
6 What four precautions should girls take when they are travelling by themselves?

Vocabulary

1 Find an opposite.

a) quickly (line 4) b) always (line 12) c) careful (line 16)

2 Find an adverb.

a) cheap (line 10) b) personal (line 18) c) good (line 19)

3 Explain in a whole sentence.

a) continent (line 2) b) sightseeing (line 10) c) backpackers' hostel (line 10)

Grammar

1 Complete these sentences with the correct forms of the verbs.

1 I didn't hear what he said because I ... (listen) to music.
2 Sheryl was reading a magazine when the weirdo ... (sit down) next to her.
3 Before he got to Las Vegas, Ray ... (meet) lots of nice people.

2 Ask for the underlined information.

1 I was sleeping when the bus crashed.
2 Ben was studying in Chicago.
3 I was feeling tired by the time I got to New York.

3 Copy the table and fill in the missing forms.

	positive	comparative	superlative
1	fat	?	?
2	careful	?	?
3	sexy	?	?

Writing

Write about an interesting or annoying journey you have made. (80–100 words)

Grammar summary

SIMPLE PRESENT (S. 17)

Das simple present wird verwendet für gleich bleibende Zustände und regelmäßige, wiederholte Handlungen.

Aussagen	Verneinungen	Fragen
I like sport. Lucy plays the guitar.	I don't have any brothers or sisters. Jerry doesn't see his father often.	Do you like it? Does Ronnie like school?
· *I/we/you/they*: Grundform · *he/she/it*: Grundform + *-(e)s* · Verben auf *-y* → *-ies*, z. B. *I carry / he carries*	· *I/we/you/they don't* · *he/she/it doesn't*	· *Do I/we/you/they ...?* · *Does he/she ...?*
Signalwörter: *always, never, often, sometimes, usually, every day/week, hardly ever*		

PRESENT PROGRESSIVE (S. 24)

Das present progressive steht für vorübergehende oder im Moment des Sprechens ablaufende Handlungen und Situationen.

Aussagen	Verneinungen	Fragen
I'm waiting for my friends. He's making the tea.	You're not / You aren't listening. She's not / She isn't talking.	Is anyone sitting here? Are you working?
· *am/is/are* + *-ing*-Form des Verbs · Verben auf -e: das *-e* fällt weg · Bei einsilbigen Verben, die auf einen einfachen Konsonanten enden, wird dieser verdoppelt, z. B. *sit* → *sitting*	· *'m not/isn't/aren't* + *-ing*-Form des Verbs	· *am/is/are* werden mit dem Subjekt getauscht
Signalwörter: *at the moment, (just) now, today, this week/month*		

SIMPLE PAST (S. 32)

Die simple past beschreibt abgeschlossene Handlungen, Ereignisse und Zustände.

Aussagen	Verneinungen	Fragen
I watched TV last night. She sold her bicycle last week. He was happy. Things were great.	My mum and dad didn't come with me. He wasn't worried. They weren't happy.	Did you find your book? Why didn't you tell me? Was it easy to get here? Were you in the museum?
· regelmäßige Verben: Grundform + *-ed* · unregelmäßige Verben: siehe Seite 242	· *didn't* + Infinitiv · *to be*: *wasn't/weren't*	· *did* + Infinitiv · *to be*: *was/were*
Signalwörter: *yesterday, last week/month/year, three days / two years ago, When ...?*		

PRESENT PERFECT (S. 57)

Das present perfect wird für abgeschlossene Vorgänge und Handlungen verwendet, wenn nicht der Zeitpunkt, sondern das Ergebnis wichtig ist. Mit dem present perfect drückt man auch aus, seit wann oder wie lange ein Zustand schon andauert.

Aussagen	Verneinungen	Fragen
I've / I have done that already. She's / She has lived in Dublin for six years now.	Paul hasn't started work yet. They haven't had any problems. I haven't seen my cousin since Christmas.	Have you done your homework? How long has she lived with Paul?
· *have/has* + Partizip Perfekt (3. Form des Verbs) · unregelmäßige Verben: siehe Seite 242	· *haven't/hasn't* + Partizip Perfekt	· *have/has* werden mit dem Subjekt getauscht
Signalwörter: *already*, *always*, *before*, *ever*, *How long ...?*, *just*, *lately*, *never*, *recently*, *up till now*, (*not*) *yet*, *since* (+ Zeitpunkt), *for* (+ Zeitdauer)		

THE FUTURE (S. 40, 80)

Die Zukunft kann im Englischen durch vier verschiedene Möglichkeiten ausgedrückt werden.

going to future	I'm going to buy a moped. What are you going to do now?	· Pläne, Absichten, Abmachungen
will future	He will be 18 next month. It won't rain at the weekend. I'll phone you later. I'll help you, I promise.	· feststehende Ereignisse · Vorhersagen · spontane Entscheidungen · Versprechen
present progressive	I'm staying at home tomorrow.	· Pläne, Absichten, Abmachungen (mit Zeitangabe)
simple present	The bus leaves at 10 a.m.	· Fahrpläne, Stundenpläne usw.

PAST PROGRESSIVE (S. 140)

Das past progressive beschreibt eine Handlung, die andauerte, während sich eine zweite Handlung (simple past) ereignete.

Aussagen	Verneinungen	Fragen
While I was working, the phone rang.	I wasn't working when the boss came in.	What were you doing when the phone rang?
· *was/were* + *ing*-Form	· *wasn't/weren't* + *ing*-Form	· *was/were* wird mit dem Subjekt getauscht
Signalwörter: *while*, *when*		

PAST PERFECT (S. 120)

Das past perfect beschreibt eine Handlung, die bereits abgeschlossen war, als eine zweite (simple past) begann.

Aussagen	Verneinungen	Fragen
After/When I had finished my homework, I read a book.	I failed my driving test because I hadn't taken enough lessons.	Had you ever been to England before your trip last year?
· *had* + Partizip Perfekt (3. Form des Verbs)	· *hadn't* + Partizip Perfekt	· *had* wird mit dem Subjekt getauscht
Signalwörter: *after, when*		

CONDITIONAL SENTENCES (S. 91, 130)

Conditional sentences (*if*-Sätze) drücken Bedingungen aus.

Conditional Type I (S. 91) für reale Bedingungen	If you use your phone in class, *if*-Satz: *simple present*	the teacher will be angry. Hauptsatz: *will future*
Conditional Type II (S. 130) für unwahrscheinliche Bedingungen	If I had a thousand euros, *if*-Satz: *simple past*	I would buy a moped. Hauptsatz: *would* + Infinitiv
Conditional Type III (S. 130) beschreibt Situationen, die in der Vergangenheit geschehen sein könnten, aber nicht geschehen sind	If you had done your homework, *if*-Satz: *past perfect*	the teacher would have been happy. Hauptsatz: *would have* + Partizip Perfekt

PASSIVE (S. 110)

Das Passiv wird verwendet, wenn man nicht den Verursacher, sondern den Vorgang hervorheben will.

simple present	Phones are stolen every day.	*am/is/are* + Partizip Perfekt
present perfect	My phone has been stolen.	*has/have been* + Partizip Perfekt
simple past	My phone was stolen yesterday.	*was/were* + Partizip Perfekt
will future	Perhaps your phone will be stolen too.	*will* + *be* + Partizip Perfekt

MODAL VERBS (S. 64)

Can / be able to (können)	He **can** speak English very well. We **won't be able to** get tickets for the concert. I **couldn't** hear what he said.	· *Can* drückt eine Fähigkeit oder eine Möglichkeit aus. · *Can* wird nur in der Gegenwart benutzt. Das *simple past* lautet *could*. Andere Zeiten werden mit dem Ersatzverb *to be able to* gebildet.
must / have to (müssen)	You **must** do your homework before you watch TV. He always **had to** get home in time. **Do** I **have to** wait till your soap opera is finished? We **didn't have to** pay for the tickets. You **mustn't smoke** in the garage.	· *Must* und *have to* drücken eine Verpflichtung oder Notwendigkeit aus. · *Must* wird nur in der Gegenwart benutzt, in anderen Zeiten steht *have to*. · Achtung: *mustn't* = nicht dürfen, *not have to* = nicht müssen
be allowed to (dürfen)	We **won't be allowed to** watch that film. It's too late.	Erlaubnis und Verbot in zusammengesetzten Zeitformen wie *present perfect* oder *will future* werden mit dem Ersatzverb *to be allowed to* ausgedrückt.
Could, may und might (könnte)	That film **could** be interesting. Phil **may** have a chance today. He **might** even win the whole competition.	· *Could*, *may* und *might* drücken eine Möglichkeit aus.
should/shouldn't (sollen / nicht sollen, sollte/n)	What **should** I do now? You **shouldn't** watch too much TV.	· *Should/shouldn't* werden für Ratschläge verwendet.

COMPARATIVES AND SUPERLATIVES OF ADJECTIVES (S.41)

Im Englischen gibt es zwei Arten der Steigerung: eine mit -er/-est und eine mit more/most.
Auf welche Art ein Adjektiv gesteigert wird, hängt vor allem von seiner Länge ab.

	Adjektiv	Komparativ	Superlativ
einsilbige Adjektive	long big	longer bigger	(the) longest (the) biggest
zweisilbige Adjektive, die auf -y enden	lucky	luckier	(the) luckiest
mehrsilbige Adjektive	famous horrible	more famous more horrible	(the) most famous (the) most horrible
unregelmäßige Adjektive	good bad	better worse	(the) best (the) worst

ADVERBS OF MANNER (S. 49)

In der Regel werden Adverbien durch Anhängen von -ly an das Adjektiv gebildet.

	Adjektiv	Adverb
Adjektiv + -ly	different quick	differently quickly
Adjektiv auf y → -ily	easy happy	easily happily
unregelmäßige Adverbien	good hard fast early late	well hard fast early late

SOME/ANY (S. 49)

Some and any werden mit Pluralformen und nicht zählbaren Begriffen gebraucht. Some wird in Aussagen, Angeboten und Bitten verwendet, any in Verneinungen und Fragen (in denen es nicht um ein Angebot geht).

Aussagen	Verneinungen	Fragen	Angebote/Bitten
You may have some problems. Somebody decided to change the menus. They bought something at the market.	I don't have any time. I don't know anybody who eats fish. He never eats anything for breakfast.	Have you eaten any of these things? Has anybody seen my pen? Have you got anything to drink?	Would you like some sugar? Would you like somebody to help you? Would you like something to drink?

QUANTIFIERS (S. 11, 48)

Much und many stehen in Fragen und verneinten Sätzen. A lot of steht in Aussagesätzen.
(A) few wird mit zählbaren, (a) little mit nicht zählbaren Substantiven verwendet.

many	viele	much	viel	more	mehr	most	die/am meisten
a few	einige	few	wenige	fewer	weniger (zählbar)	fewest	die/am wenigsten (zählbar)
a little	ein wenig	little	wenig	less	weniger (nicht zählbar)	least	die/am wenigsten (nicht zählbar)

INDIRECT SPEECH (S. 121)

In der indirekten Rede wird einem Dritten berichtet, was jemand gesagt hat. Wenn das einleitende Verb in der Vergangenheit steht (said, asked usw.) verschieben sich die Zeiten der Verben im berichtenden Teil um eine Stufe in die Vergangenheit.

Direkte Rede	Indirekte Rede
'I like sport.' 'Did you play football yesterday?'	She said (that) she liked sport. He asked whether I had played football yesterday.
simple present → present continuous → simple past → present perfect → will → can →	simple past past continuous past perfect past perfect would could

-*ING*-FORM AND INFINITIVE (S. 101)

Auf bestimmte Verben folgt eine -ing-Form, während auf andere ein Infinitiv folgt.

-ing-Form	-ing -Form oder Infinitiv	Infinitiv
I enjoy reading magazines.	I like playing football. I like to play football.	When did you learn to drive?
admit, avoid, dislike, don't mind, enjoy, involve, stop, suggest	*begin, continue, hate, like, love, start*	*agree, choose, decide, expect, hope, learn, manage, prefer, want, would like*
Achtung: Auf eine Präposition folgt immer eine *ing*-form: I'm not interested in being famous.		

RELATIVE CLAUSES (S. 73, S. 141)

Relativsätze sind Nebensätze, die ein Substantiv näher definieren.
Das Relativpronomen kann weggelassen werden, wenn es das Objekt des Relativsatzes vertritt.

Personen: who/that	People who/that eat meat are not vegetarians. That's the girl (who/that) I saw on the bus.
Dinge: which/that	That's the car which/that costs a million euros. This is the house (which/that) Jack lives in.
verkürzte Relativsätze: wenn das Relativpronomen das Subjekt des Relativsatzes vertritt und das Verb in einer Verlaufsform steht	The girl (who is) riding the motorbike is only 18 years old. Was the man (who was) talking to you when I phoned you your father?

Chronologisches Wörterverzeichnis

Dieses Wörterverzeichnis enthält alle Wörter, die nicht in der Liste des Grundwortschatzes enthalten sind, d. h. die nicht als bekannt vorausgesetzt werden. t = das Wort befindet sich in den *Transcripts* (Hörverständnistexten). p = das Wort befindet sich in den *Pairwork Files*.
Die Wörter der *World of work*-Teile der Units 9–15 werden bei den darauffolgenden Units nicht vorausgesetzt.

Let's work with English!

6		
grammar ['græmə]	*We sometimes learn grammar at school.*	Grammatik
category ['kætəgəri]	*Each book is from a different category.*	Kategorie
add [æd]	*Add the names to the list.*	hinzufügen
correct(ly) [kə'rektli]	*She writes all the names correctly.*	richtig
near [nɪə]	*↔ far*	nahe
sentence ['sentəns]	*The first sentence of the story was too long.*	Satz
example [ɪg'zɑ:mpl]	*For ~*	Beispiel
doctor ['dɒktər]		Arzt/Ärztin
assistant [ə'sɪstənt]	*shop ~*	Verkäufer/in
nurse [nɜ:s]		Krankenschwester, -pfleger
7		
road [rəʊd]		Straße
dentist ['dentɪst]		Zahnarzt, Zahnärztin
surgery ['sɜ:dʒəri]	*The surgery is open from 8am until 2pm.*	(Arzt-)Praxis
at the moment [ət ðə 'məʊmənt]	*There is nobody at home at the moment.*	im Augenblick
8		
column ['kɒləm]	*The text is in three columns.*	Spalte
join [dʒɔɪn]	*Join the beginnings of the sentences to the endings.*	verbinden
form [fɔ:m]	*Use the correct form of the verb.*	Form
cousin ['kʌzn]	⚠ *Aussprache*	Cousin/e
country ['kʌntri]	*America is a big country.*	Land, Staat
interesting ['ɪntrəstɪŋ]	*Our English lessons are always interesting!*	interessant
prefer [prɪ'fɜ:]	*I prefer football to golf.*	lieber mögen, bevorzugen
tired ['taɪəd]	*I danced until 3am last night. Today I'm very tired.*	müde
translate [træns'leɪt]	*Can you translate this letter into German, please?*	übersetzen
bathroom ['bɑ:θru:m]		Bad(ezimmer)
9		
decide [dɪ'saɪd]	*I don't know what to do. I can't decide.*	entscheiden
odd one out [ɒd wʌn 'aʊt]		Außenseiter, hier: überzähliges Wort
complete [kəm'pli:t]	*Laura completed her training last year.*	vervollständigen
gap [gæp]	*"Mind the gap between the train and the platform!"*	Lücke
wait [weɪt]	*You always have to wait so long for the bus here.*	warten
ago [ə'gəʊ]	*Two years / five months / fifteen minutes ago ...*	vor
complain [kəm'pleɪn]	*She complained because the food was cold.*	sich beschweren, sich beklagen
care about ['keər əbaʊt]	*Here really cares about his children.*	sich Sorgen machen um, sich kümmern um, sich interessieren für
frozen ['frəʊzn]	*At the supermarket you can buy frozen foods.*	(tief)gefroren
thick [θɪk]	*↔ thin*	dick
sock [sɒk]	*a pair of ~s*	Socke
glove [glʌv]	*a pair of ~s*	Handschuh
complaint [kəm'pleɪnt]	*We had a complaint about the food.*	Beschwerde

any longer [eni 'lɒŋgə]	*I can't listen to this any longer.*	länger
pet [pet]	*Our family has three pets: two dogs and a cat.*	Haustier
snake [sneɪk]	*Some snakes come from Australia.*	Schlange
be called [bi 'kɔ:ld]	*My pet cat is called Sophia.*	heißen
favourite ['feɪvərɪt]	*Tim's favourite food is pasta.*	Lieblings-
group [gru:p]	*here: ≈ band*	Gruppe
collect [kə'lekt]	*Sarah collects Rolling Stones albums.*	sammeln
plate [pleɪt]		Teller
empty ['empti]	*↔ full*	leer
cupboard ['kʌbəd]	*All the food is in the cupboard.*	Schrank
kitchen ['kɪtʃɪn]		Küche
10		
put [pʊt]	*Please put these words into the plural.*	setzen
bracket ['brækɪt]	*Translate the words in brackets.*	Klammer
list [lɪst]	*Here's a list of England's best football players.*	Liste
own [əʊn]	*Mr Jefferson owns the football club.*	besitzen
game [geɪm]	*The game is good fun.*	Spiel
dictionary ['dɪkʃənri]	⚠ *Aussprache*	Wörterbuch
speech bubble ['spi:tʃ bʌbl]		Sprechblase
mobile (phone) [ˌməʊbaɪl 'fəʊn]	*Call me on my mobile phone.*	Mobiltelefon, Handy
11		
be afraid of [bi ə'freɪd əv]	*Lots of children are afraid of the dark.*	sich fürchten vor
spend time (on/doing sth) [spend taɪm ɒŋ]	*Michael doesn't spend enough time on his homework.*	damit zubringen
pocket money ['pɒkɪt mʌni]	*How much pocket money do you have?*	Taschengeld
chance [tʃɑ:ns]	⚠ *Aussprache*	Chance
player ['pleɪə]	*Some top football players are very rich.*	Spieler/in
ill [ɪl]	*Andrea isn't at school today because she is ill.*	krank
hungry ['hʌŋgri]	*After school my brother is always hungry.*	hungrig
lunchtime ['lʌntʃtaɪm]	*At work our lunchtime is at 12.30.*	Mittagszeit
ride [raɪd]	*You drive a car. You ride a bike.*	fahren (mit)
drive [draɪv]	*Shall we drive to Rostock this summer?*	(mit dem Auto) fahren
speak [spi:k]	*How many languages can you speak?*	sprechen
12		
in full [ɪn fʊl]	*Please write your name in full.*	vollständig
match [mætʃ]	*Match the nouns with the verbs.*	zuordnen
above [ə'bʌv]	*↔ below*	oben (stehend)
special ['speʃl]	*A birthday is a special day.*	besondere/r/s
New Year's Eve [ˌnju: jɪəz 'i:v]		Silvester
Valentine's Day ['væləntaɪnz deɪ]		Valentinstag
final ['faɪnl]		Endspiel
World Cup [ˌwɜ:ld 'kʌp]		Weltmeisterschaft
Christmas Eve [ˌkrɪsməs 'i:v]		Heiligabend
Fall of the Berlin Wall [fɔ:l əv ðə bɜ:ˌlɪn 'wɔ:l]		Fall der Berliner Mauer
Christmas Day [ˌkrɪsməs 'deɪ]		1. Weihnachtsfeiertag
Independence Day [ɪndɪ'pendəns deɪ]		Unabhängigkeitstag
following ['fɒləʊɪŋ]	*Do the exercise on the following page.*	folgend
date of birth [ˌdeɪt əv 'bɜ:θ]		Geburtsdatum
be born [bi 'bɔ:n]	*Marina was born in 1978.*	geboren werden/sein
last [lɑ:st]	*↔ first*	letzte/r/s

iː	ɪ	e	æ	ɑː	ɒ	ɔː	ʊ	uː	ʌ	ɜː	ə
see	sit	ten	bad	arm	got	saw	put	too	cut	bird	about

13

nationality [ˌnæʃəˈnæləti]	*I have German nationality.*	Staatsangehörigkeit
finish [ˈfɪnɪʃ]	↔ *start*	fertig sein
combine [kəmˈbaɪn]	*When you combine the two parts you have a full sentence.*	zusammenfügen, kombinieren
chocolate bar [ˈtʃɒklət bɑː]	*Jessica eats chocolate bars very quickly!*	Schoko(laden)riegel
dance [dɑːns]	*The dance at the end of the film was fantastic!*	Tanz, Tanzveranstaltung, tanzen
swap [swɒp]	*After the meeting they swapped telephone numbers.*	tauschen
role [rəʊl]	*Leonardo DiCaprio has a big role in the film.*	Rolle

UNIT 1 Saying hello

14

workcamp [ˈwɜːkkæmp]	*There are lots of workcamps in Europe and America.*	Workcamp, Freiwilligenprojekt
seat [siːt]		Stuhl, Sitz
it's her turn [ɪts ˈhɜː tɜːn]	*It's your turn now!*	sie ist dran
exercise [ˈeksəsaɪz]	*First read the text, then do the exercise below.*	Übung
hear [hɪə]	*Can you hear me?*	hören
divorced [dɪˈvɔːst]	*These days, lots of parents are divorced.*	geschieden
stepfather [ˈstepfɑːðə]	*My stepfather is my mother's new partner.*	Stiefvater
patchwork family [ˌpætʃwɜːk ˈfæməli]	⚠ *Aussprache*	Patchworkfamilie
understand [ˌʌndəˈstænd]	*Do you understand what to do?*	verstehen
together [təˈgeðə]		zusammen
stepbrother [ˈstepbrʌðə]	*My stepbrother Christopher is the son of my father's new girlfriend.*	Stiefbruder
stepsister [ˈstepsɪstə]	*My stepsister Hannah is the daughter of my mother's new boyfriend.*	Stiefschwester
married [ˈmærid]	*My brother is married to a German woman.*	verheiratet
half-brother [ˈhɑːf brʌðə]	*My half-brother, James, is the son of my mother and my stepfather.*	Halbbruder
horrible [ˈhɒrəbl]	*I don't like pop music at all. It's horrible.*	schrecklich, furchtbar

15

vocational college [vəʊˌkeɪʃənl ˈkɒlɪdʒ]	*We learn a lot at our vocational college.*	Berufs(fach)schule
office administration [ˌɒfɪs ədmɪnɪˈstreɪʃn]	*Office administration is important for most companies.*	Büroorganisation
computer studies [kəmˈpjuːtə stʌdiz]	*Lots of people do computer studies at school.*	Informatik
interested in [ˈɪntrəstɪd ɪn]	*I'm interested in reggae music.*	interessiert an
what kind of …? [wɒt ˈkaɪnd əv]	*~ music do you prefer, heavy metal or reggae?*	welche Art von …?
(lead) guitar [ˌliːd gɪˈtɑː]	*Ronnie plays lead guitar in a band.*	(Solo-)Gitarre
gig [gɪg]	*My band plays lots of gigs.*	Konzert, Auftritt
all over the place [ɔːl ˌəʊvə ðə ˈpleɪs]	*In her bedroom she leaves her things ~.*	überall
usual(ly) [ˈjuːʒuəl, ˈjuːʒuəli]	*We usually like school.*	gewöhnlich
well [wel]	*Well, do you have everything with you? Let's go to the park then!*	also, nun
step- [step]	*Anna is my stepmother.*	Stief-

16

description [dɪˈskrɪpʃn]	*There are lots of details in the description.*	Beschreibung
visit [ˈvɪzɪt]	*My first visit to Berlin was great.*	Besuch
typical [ˈtɪpɪkl]	*On a typical day, I go to school at 8.00.*	typisch
boss around [ˌbɒs əˈraʊnd]	*My mum always bosses me around.*	herumkommandieren

poor [pʊə]	*Do you feel sad today? You poor thing.*	arm
conversation [ˌkɒnvə'seɪʃn]	*Sometimes it is good to have a good conversation with your family.*	Gespräch, Unterhaltung
never ['nevə]	*↔ always*	nie(mals)
17		
practice ['præktɪs]	*Practice makes Perfect!*	Übung, Training
office ['ɒfɪs]	*Angela finds her office too small.*	Büro
careful(ly) ['keəfəli]	*Mike always does his homework carefully.*	sorgfältig
talk [tɔːk]	*How often do you talk to Susan?*	sprechen, reden
pay attention [peɪ ə'tenʃn]	*Rachel always pays attention in class.*	aufpassen
wear [weə]	*In Great Britain lots of pupils wear a uniform at school.*	tragen, anhaben
flat [flæt]	*Do you like your new flat?*	Wohnung
18		
canteen [kæn'tiːn]	*At lunchtime we often eat in the canteen.*	Kantine
busy ['bɪzi]	*I'm very busy at the moment because I have four tests next week.*	(viel)beschäftigt
necessary ['nesəsəri]	*When you are ill it is sometimes necessary to go to the doctor's.*	notwendig, erforderlich
drums [drʌmz]	*I play drums in two different bands.*	Schlagzeug
trainee [treɪ'niː]	*He is a trainee nurse.*	Auszubildende/r, Praktikant/in
mechanic [mɪ'kænɪk]		Mechaniker/in
19		
through [θruː]	*The road through the town centre is always busy.*	durch
still [stɪl]	*Do you still fly to America every summer?*	(immer) noch
application form [ˌæplɪ'keɪʃn fɔːm]	*The application form was quite difficult.*	Antrag
19 t		
passport ['pɑːspɔːt]	*Don't forget your passport!*	Pass
driver's license (AE) ['draɪvəz laɪsns]	*BE = driving licence*	Führerschein
wish [wɪʃ]	*Ronnie wishes he had a driver's license.*	wünschen
health insurance ['helθ ɪnʃʊərəns]	*Health insurance is important for everyone.*	Krankenversicherung
19		
file [faɪl]	*You can practise speaking English with the Pairwork Files at the end of the book.*	Akte
instruction [ɪn'strʌkʃn]	*Read the instructions carefully.*	Anweisung

The world of work

20		
world of work [wɜːld əv 'wɜːk]	*The world of work can be exciting.*	Arbeitswelt
statement ['steɪtmənt]	*Each statement on the page is quite short.*	Aussage
nervous ['nɜːvəs]	*I am nervous about the job interview.*	nervös
firm [fɜːm]	*I work in a firm from Monday to Thursday, and I go to college on Friday.*	Firma
produce [prə'djuːs]	*The company produces very good cars.*	produzieren, herstellen
personnel manager [ˌpɜːsə'nel mænɪdʒə]	*The personnel manager in our office helps us a lot.*	Personalleiter/in
plant [plɑːnt]	*Andy loves plants; he has 'green fingers'!*	Pflanze
go back [ˌgəʊ 'bæk]	*After the summer holiday, pupils and teachers go back to school.*	zurückgehen, -kehren
get started [get 'stɑːtɪd]	*Today I want to get started on my new project.*	anfangen
21		
phrase [freɪz]	*Find the correct phrase.*	(Rede-)Wendung
21 t		
fine [faɪn]	*Everything's fine here, thanks.*	gut, alles klar
introduce [ˌɪntrə'djuːs]	*Good morning, I would like to introduce you to my friend Anna.*	vorstellen
colleague ['kɒliːg]	*Our new colleague is called Julian.*	Kollege/Kollegin
21		
dialogue ['daɪəlɒg]	*The dialogue was interesting.*	Dialog

iː	ɪ	e	æ	ɑː	ɒ	ɔː	ʊ	uː	ʌ	ɜː	ə
see	sit	ten	bad	arm	got	saw	put	too	cut	bird	about

note [nəʊt]	*It is easier to do your homework if you have good notes from class.*	Notiz
rest [rest]	*The rest of my friends don't like techno music.*	Rest

UNIT 2 Free time

22		
opposite ['ɒpəzɪt]	*Paul's new house is opposite our flat.*	gegenüber liegend
wrong [rɒŋ]	*Sorry, that is the wrong answer.*	falsch
by the way [baɪ ðə 'weɪ]	*My name's Anne, by the way. I'm from Germany.*	übrigens
bright [braɪt]	*I'm tired today. I don't feel very bright.*	heiter
hardly ever [ˌhɑːdli 'evə]	*We hardly ever do sport after school.*	fast nie
dance class ['dɑːns klɑːs]	*Paul always enjoys his dance class.*	Tanzstunde
pick up [ˌpɪk 'ʌp]	*Normally I pick up my brother from school.*	abholen
instead [ɪn'sted]	*I don't really want to go swimming tomorrow. Let's play golf instead.*	stattdessen
anything else ['eniθɪŋ els]	*Can I do anything else to help you?*	nichts anderes
a few [ə 'fjuː]	*Before I can go to the party, I have a few more things to do.*	ein paar
mate [meɪt]	*I like Sharon very much. She's a really good mate.*	Kumpel, Freund/in
come round [ˌkʌm 'raʊnd]	*Come round tomorrow for lunch with us.*	vorbeischauen, -kommen
my place [maɪ 'pleɪs]	*On Friday come to my place and have dinner if you like.*	mein Zuhause
definitely ['defɪnətli]	*Sarah and John definitely don't want to play tennis at the weekend.*	bestimmt, sicher(lich)
do wrong [du 'rɒŋ]	*If you do something wrong, tell me.*	falsch machen
annoy [ə'nɔɪ]	*This horrible weather is really annoying me!*	belästigen
somewhere else [ˌsʌmweər 'els]	*I can't find my passport here. It must be somewhere else.*	irgendwo anders
23		
take photos [teɪk 'fəʊtəʊz]	*When I'm on holiday I always take lots of nice photos.*	fotografieren
leisure activity ['leʒə æktɪvəti]	*My favourite leisure activity is dance. I do jazz and salsa every week.*	Freizeitbeschäftigung
come in [ˌkʌm 'ɪn]	*Come in, please!*	hereinkommen
24		
go clubbing [gəʊ 'klʌbɪŋ]	*On Saturday night we're going clubbing.*	auf Partys gehen
seldom ['seldəm]	*I seldom go to the shops after work.*	selten
loud [laʊd]	*This music is too loud.*	laut
25		
fight [faɪt]	*The two brothers are always fighting with each other.*	streiten
study ['stʌdi]	*We are studying for our English test.*	lernen, studieren
sound [saʊnd]	*"Cinema tomorrow night? Sounds good. I'll be there!"*	klingen
rude [ruːd]	*Michael is always rude to his parents.*	unhöflich
simply ['sɪmpli]	*Your new flat is simply perfect.*	einfach
polite [pə'laɪt]	*Be polite please!*	höflich
classmate ['klɑːsmeɪt]	*Do you like your new classmates?*	Klassenkamerad/in
exam [ɪg'zæm]	*I'm a bit nervous because our exam is tomorrow.*	Prüfung
rain [reɪn]	*Does it rain a lot in Stuttgart?*	regnen
concentrate ['kɒnsntreɪt]	*I'm so tired. I can't concentrate on my homework at the moment.*	(sich) konzentrieren
gymnastics [dʒɪm'næstɪks]	*I do gymnastics every Tuesday evening.*	Gymnastik
regular(ly) ['regjələli]	*I play football regularly.*	regelmäßig
stay [steɪ]	*Natalie is staying at her brother's house this week.*	übernachten, bleiben
expensive [ɪk'spensɪv]	*New cars are usually expensive.*	teuer
26		
leave alone [ˌliːv ə'ləʊn]	*Please leave me alone! I'm studying for the exam.*	in Ruhe lassen
chat up [ˌtʃæt 'ʌp]	*Paul never concentrates at school. He's always chatting up the girls.*	anquatschen, anmachen
invitation [ˌɪnvɪ'teɪʃn]	*I have an invitation to Jenny's party too.*	Einladung
sure [ʃʊə]	*Sure! I really like to go dancing at the weekend!*	sicherlich, natürlich

tʃ	dʒ	ʃ	ʒ	θ	ð	ŋ	s	z	v	w
chips	**j**et	**sh**ip	gara**g**e	**th**ing	**th**e	ri**ng**	i**c**e	a**s**	**v**ery	**w**et

27		
situation [ˌsɪtʃu'eɪʃn]	*This is a difficult situation.*	Situation, Lage
invite [ɪn'vaɪt]	*Jemma always invites lots of people to her parties.*	einladen
pass [pɑːs]	*When I pass somebody I know in the street, I always say hello.*	vorbeigehen an
excuse me [ɪk'skjuːz mi]	*Excuse me, can you tell me which bus goes to the town centre?*	Entschuldigung
refuse [rɪ'fjuːz]	*What a fantastic invitation! How can I refuse?!*	ablehnen
record ['rekɔːd]	*The museum has some very good records of life in Britain in the 1950s.*	Dokumentation
mankind [mæn'kaɪnd]		Menschheit
greatest ['greɪtɪst]	*here: ≈ best*	größte/r/s
invention [ɪn'venʃn]	*Sophie's new invention is very good.*	Erfindung
achievement [ə'tʃiːvmənt]	*Wow! That is a great achievement!*	Leistung
machinery [mə'ʃiːnəri]	*The machinery was quite old.*	Maschinenbau
steam locomotive [ˌstiːm ˌləʊkə'məʊtɪv]	*Today you only really see steam locomotives in museums.*	Dampflok

The world of work

28		
programmer ['prəʊgræmə]	*When I finish school, I want to work as a programmer in a big company.*	Programmierer/in
department store [dɪ'pɑːtmənt stɔː]	*In department stores, you can buy almost everything!*	Kauf-, Warenhaus
28 t		
normally ['nɔːməli]	*≈ usually*	normalerweise
break [breɪk]	*When you are studying for school tests, you should take regular short breaks.*	Pause
until [ən'tɪl]	*Football training is on Monday mornings, from 8am until 11am.*	bis
mind [maɪnd]	*Which shoes do you prefer, the black or the brown ones? I don't mind.*	etw dagegen haben
electrical goods [ɪˌlektrɪkl 'gʊdz]	*Do you know a good shop for electrical goods?*	Elektrowaren
customer ['kʌstəmə]	*The customer is always the boss!*	Verbraucherberatung
give advice [gɪv əd'vaɪs]	*My friend gives me good advice.*	Rat geben
satisfaction [ˌsætɪs'fækʃn]	*It is important to get satisfaction from your work.*	Befriedigung
reason ['riːzn]	*There are many reasons why I like my job.*	Grund
clerk [klɑːk]	*I'm a trainee clerk.*	Büroangestellte/r
better ['betə]	*↔ worse*	besser
electrician [ɪˌlek'trɪʃn]		Elektriker/in
28		
dental ['dentl]		Zahn-, zahnärztlich
29		
manners ['mænəz]	*Naomi always has good manners.*	Umgangsformen, Manieren
important [ɪm'pɔːtnt]	*Small talk is often important in Great Britain and America.*	wichtig
behave [bɪ'heɪv]	*Sarah always behaves well at school.*	sich verhalten, sich benehmen
shake hands [ʃeɪk 'hændz]	*In business situations it is usual to shake hands when you meet someone for the first time.*	sich die Hand geben
unusual [ʌn'juːʒuəl]	*↔ usual*	unüblich, ungewöhnlich
informal [ɪn'fɔːml]	*At our house, dinner is always quite informal.*	informell, locker
unfriendly [ʌn'frendli]	*↔ friendly*	unfreundlich
reply [rɪ'plaɪ]	*Thanks for your friendly reply.*	Antwort, Reaktion
unless [ən'les]	*Unless she calls me this afternoon, we're going to the cinema tonight.*	es sei denn
while [waɪl]	*While you like sport, I prefer dance.*	während
tend [tend]	*They tend to go to France on holiday these days. It's not as far as Spain.*	(dazu) neigen

iː	ɪ	e	æ	ɑː	ɒ	ɔː	ʊ	uː	ʌ	ɜː	ə
see	sit	ten	bad	arm	got	saw	put	too	cut	bird	about

during ['djʊərɪŋ]	*During the afternoon I like to phone my friends.*	während
integrate ['ɪntɪgreɪt]	*In Great Britain small talk is integrated into normal office life.*	eingliedern, integrieren
probably ['prɒbəbli]	*Mr Jones is probably in a meeting at the moment.*	wahrscheinlich

UNIT 3 Other cultures

30		
weblog ['weblɒg]	*Jenny is writing a weblog about her travels.*	Online-Tagebuch
couple (of) ['kʌpl əv]	*Go and buy a couple of drinks from the bar.*	ein paar
month [mʌnθ]		Monat
brilliant ['brɪliənt]	*≈ fantastic, great*	großartig, fabelhaft
faraway ['fɑːrəweɪ]	*Next year, my friend Jenny wants to travel to some faraway places.*	weit entfernt
insist (on) [ɪn'sɪst]	*My dad insists that I come home from the disco at midnight.*	(darauf) bestehen
be (not) allowed [bi nɒt ə'laʊd]	*You are not allowed to talk on your mobile phone in class.*	(nicht) dürfen
backpackers' hostel [ˌbækpækəz 'hɒstl]	*The backpackers' hostel is in the town centre.*	Jugendherberge für Rucksack-touristen
loads of ['ləʊdz əv]	*≈ lots of*	jede Menge
end up [ˌend 'ʌp]	*We ended up on the wrong side of town!*	landen
though [ðəʊ]	*I would like to go clubbing tonight. I'm quite tired though.*	allerdings, jedoch
tower ['taʊə]	*Lots of tourists like to visit the Tower of London.*	Turm
juggler ['dʒʌglə]		Jongleur/in
fire-eater ['faɪə iːtə]		Feuerschlucker
wicked ['wɪkɪd]	*My favourite band have a wicked new song.*	großartig, toll
line-up ['laɪn ʌp]	*There are some famous groups on the line-up.*	Aufstellung, Programm
31		
imagine [ɪ'mædʒɪn]	*I like to imagine long holidays in the sun.*	sich vorstellen, sich einbilden
round the world [raʊnd ðə 'wɜːld]	*One day I want to travel round the world.*	um die ganze Welt
route [ruːt]	*Which is the best route?*	Route, Strecke, (Reise-)Weg
colloquialism [kə'ləʊkwiəlɪzəm]	*In internet chatrooms you see lots of colloquialisms.*	umgangssprachlicher Ausdruck
neighbour ['neɪbə]	*We have friendly neighbours.*	Nachbar/in
summary ['sʌməri]	*The summary was nice and short.*	Zusammenfassung
famous ['feɪməs]	*Some very famous people live in Hollywood.*	berühmt
cheap [tʃiːp]	*The backpackers' hostel was quite cheap.*	billig, preisgünstig
32		
compare [kəm'peə]	*It is interesting to compare the two pictures.*	vergleichen
map [mæp]	*Can I buy a map of London here?*	(Stadt-)Plan
worry ['wʌri]	*I sometimes worry about my homework.*	sich Sorgen machen
room [ruːm]	*Was the hotel room expensive?*	Zimmer
whole [həʊl]	*We were in London for a whole week.*	ganz
33		
faithful ['feɪθfl]	*Alice is always a faithful best friend.*	treu
geyser ['giːzə]	*Have you ever seen a geyser?*	Geysir
shoot [ʃuːt]	*The geyser shoots water into the air.*	hochschleudern
steam [stiːm]	*The water is too hot! There is even lots of steam!*	Dampf
foot [fʊt]	*My dad is about 6 feet tall.*	Fuß (1 Fuß = 30,48 cm)
guide [gaɪd]	*When you visit somewhere new, it is a good idea to read the guide first.*	(Reise-)Führer/in
expect [ɪk'spekt]	*I expect Australia to be beautiful!*	erwarten
terrible ['terəbl]	*How terrible!*	furchtbar
fright [fraɪt]	*What a fright that was!*	Angst
hostel ['hɒstl]	*I liked the hostel.*	(Wohn-)Heim, Pension

excited [ɪk'saɪtɪd]	*I can't wait for my holiday. I'm so excited!*	aufgeregt, gespannt
musician [mjuː'zɪʃn]		Musiker/in
hire ['haɪə]	*We hired a car in Spain.*	mieten, leihen
34		
cable car ['keɪblkɑː]	*From the cable car you can see the whole city!*	Seilbahn, (in San Francisco) Straßenbahn
freezing ['friːzɪŋ]	*Canada is absolutely freezing in winter.*	eiskalt
explore [ɪk'splɔː]	*I wanted to explore Montreal, but we didn't have enough time.*	erforschen, erkunden
countryside ['kʌntrisaɪd]	*I prefer the countryside to the cities.*	Landschaft
outside of [ˌaut'saɪd əv]	↔ *inside of*	außerhalb
amazing [ə'meɪzɪŋ]	≈ *fantastic, wonderful*	erstaunlich, unglaublich
describe [dɪ'skraɪb]	*Describe the photo.*	beschreiben
activity [æk'tɪvəti]	*On holiday there were lots of fun activities.*	Aktivität, Tätigkeit
get back [ˌget 'bæk]	*I got back to Munich last Tuesday.*	zurückkommen
34 t		
mention ['menʃn]	*Sorry, I forgot to mention my new telephone number.*	erwähnen
be based in [bi 'beɪst ɪn]	*Volkswagen is based in Wolfsburg.*	seinen Sitz haben in
brewery ['bruːəri]	*The old Guinness brewery in Dublin is now a museum.*	Brauerei
pint [paɪnt]	*A pint is a little more than half a litre.*	Pint
suppose [sə'pəʊz]	*I suppose I should go to bed now.*	glauben, schätzen
incredible [ɪn'kredəbl]	*The dancers were really amazing. The show was incredible.*	unglaublich

The world of work

36		
volunteer [ˌvɒlən'tɪə]	*Would you like to volunteer to help at a youth hostel?*	freiwillig arbeiten
notice ['nəʊtɪs]	*Please read the notice.*	Notiz, Anschlag
youth [juːθ]	*My grandad always talks about his youth.*	Jugend
youth hostel ['juːθ hɒstl]	*There are youth hostels all over the world.*	Jugendherberge
aim [eɪm]	*The aim of school is to help you learn.*	Ziel
possible ['pɒsəbl]	*Please call me as quickly as possible.*	möglich
just in case [dʒʌst ɪn 'keɪs]	*Just in case you can't find me, here's my mobile number.*	nur für den Fall
toothache ['tuːθeɪk]	*My toothache is so bad now!*	Zahnschmerzen
fire brigade [b'faɪə brɪgeɪd]	*Is your sister in the fire brigade?*	Feuerwehr
caretaker ['keəteɪkə]	*The caretaker lives in the house next to the youth hostel.*	Hausmeister/in
receptionist [rɪ'sepʃənɪst]	*Our receptionist, Mark, is very friendly.*	Empfangsmitarbeiter/in
37		
guest [gest]	*Tonight fifty guests are staying in the hostel.*	Gast
notice board ['nəʊtɪs bɔːd]	*There are some great photos on the notice board.*	Schwarzes Brett
37 t		
apply for [ə'plaɪ fə]	*I applied for the job last week.*	sich bewerben um
certain(ly) ['sɜːtnli]	*I would certainly like to go to Australia.*	gewiss, bestimmt
be the case [bi ðə 'keɪs]	*You're right, that is the case.*	der Fall sein
practise ['præktɪs]	*Joanne wants to practise her English this summer.*	(ein)üben
accommodation [əˌkɒmə'deɪʃn]	*Our accommodation in England was fine.*	Unterkunft
partly ['pɑːtli]	*The free travel was partly why she applied.*	teilweise, zum Teil
37		
teach [tiːtʃ]	*Ms Williams teaches us English.*	unterrichten, beibringen
foreign ['fɒrən]	*One day I want to live in a foreign country.*	fremd
voluntary ['vɒləntri]	*Voluntary work can teach you a lot.*	freiwillig
include [ɪn'kluːd]	*Don't forget to include your address on the application.*	enthalten, hier: einbeziehen
appropriate [ə'prəʊpriət]	*In job interviews, it is good to talk about appropriate experience that you have.*	geeignet, passend
skill [skɪl]	*At vocational college we learn lots of different skills.*	Fertigkeit, Fähigkeit

iː	ɪ	e	æ	ɑː	ɒ	ɔː	ʊ	uː	ʌ	ɜː	ə
see	sit	ten	bad	arm	got	saw	put	too	cut	bird	about

UNIT 4 Keeping up to date

38

keep up to date [kiːp ʌp tə 'deɪt]	*The internet makes it easy to keep up to date with the modern world.*	aktuell bleiben
(body) decoration [ˌbɒdi ˌdekə'reɪʃn]	*Tattoos and piercings are body decorations.*	Körperschmuck
agree [ə'griː]	*I agree with Simon.*	übereinstimmen, zustimmen
disagree [ˌdɪsə'griː]	*↔ agree*	nicht zustimmen
cover in ['kʌvə r ɪn]	*Katie always covers her face in make-up.*	bedecken mit
weird [wɪəd]	*I think my new hairstyle is a bit weird!*	merkwürdig, seltsam
drawing ['drɔːɪŋ]	*Sam's drawings are always very good.*	Zeichnung
belly button ['beli bʌtn]	*Emily wanted a silver belly button ring.*	Bauchnabel
jewellery ['dʒuːəlri]	*Jewellery is sometimes expensive.*	Schmuck
be a turn-off [bi ə 'tɜːnɒf]	*I think that lots of tattoos are a real turn-off.*	abstoßend wirken
pale [peɪl]	*My favourite colour is pale blue.*	hell
pink [pɪŋk]	*red + white = pink*	pink(farben), rosa
black [blæk]	*↔ white*	schwarz
eyelashes ['aɪlæɪz]	*That girl has nice eyes, with long eyelashes.*	Wimpern
pierce [pɪəs]	*She has a pierced belly button.*	piercen
point out [ˌpɔɪnt 'aʊt]	*He pointed out the problems.*	hinweisen auf, erklären
shoulder ['ʃəʊldə]	*The baby sat on her father's shoulders.*	Schulter
scream [skriːm]	*People often scream in horror films.*	schreien
embarrassing [ɪm'bærəsɪŋ]	*It is embarrassing when you forget somebody's name.*	peinlich
sudden(ly) ['sʌdnli]	*The car suddenly stopped.*	plötzlich
stall [stɔːl]	*The market stall sells fruit.*	Marktstand
cross [krɒs]	*The Scottish flag has a cross.*	Kreuz
forehead ['fɔːhed]	⚠ *Aussprache*	Stirn
laugh [lɑːf]	*Don't laugh! This isn't funny!*	lachen

39

beginning [bɪ'gɪnɪŋ]	*The beginning of the story is on page 1.*	Anfang
believe [bɪ'liːv]	*I don't believe what she says. It isn't true.*	glauben
area ['eəriə]	*This is a nice area of town, with quiet streets.*	Gegend
pleased [pliːzd]	*I'm pleased with my new job. It's great.*	froh, zufrieden
tough [tʌf]	⚠ *Aussprache*	hart
decorate ['dekəreɪt]	*Let's decorate the Christmas tree.*	schmücken
upset [ˌʌp'set]	*Don't be upset. It's OK really.*	entsetzt
mostly ['məʊstli]	*We have mostly German tourists at this hotel.*	hauptsächlich, meistens
permanent(ly) ['pɜːmənənt]	*This is a permanent job, not just for the summer.*	dauerhaft, fest
wash off [ˌwɒʃ 'ɒf]	*The tattoo will wash off in the shower.*	abwaschen
such [sʌtʃ]	*This is such a silly book.*	solche/r/s, so
in my opinion [ɪn maɪ ə'pɪniən]	*In my opinion, boy bands are terrible.*	meiner Meinung nach

40

brainstorm ['breɪnstɔːm]	*Think of some good ideas. Let's brainstorm.*	(Ideen) sammeln
topic ['tɒpɪk]	*"Problems with money" is an interesting topic.*	Thema
below [bɪ'ləʊ]	*Please do not write below this line.*	unten (stehend), unter
most [məʊst]	*Most people like ice cream.*	die meisten
piece of paper [piːs əf 'peɪpə]	*Write your name on a piece of paper.*	Zettel, Stück/Blatt Papier
guess [ges]	*Can you guess my job?*	(er)raten
earring ['ɪərɪŋ]	*I like your earrings. They're beautiful.*	Ohrring
scarf [skɑːf]	*Wear a scarf in the winter.*	Schal
in my view [ɪn 'maɪ vjuː]	*In my view, English is an easy subject.*	meiner Ansicht nach
in addition [ɪn ə'dɪʃn]	*In addition, English is very useful.*	darüber hinaus
on the one hand [ɒn ðə 'wʌn hænd]	*On the one hand I like chocolate, ...*	einerseits

tʃ	dʒ	ʃ	ʒ	θ	ð	ŋ	s	z	v	w
chips	jet	ship	garage	thing	the	ring	ice	as	very	wet

on the other hand [ɒn ði 'ʌðə hænd]	*... on the other hand I know it isn't good for me.*	andererseits
conclude [kən'klu:d]	*To conclude, chocolate is a problem for me.*	(ab)schließen
role-play ['rəʊl pleɪ]	*Let's role-play. Which role do you want to play?*	als Rollenspiel durchführen
41		
down the road [daʊn ðə 'rəʊd]	*She walked down the road to her car.*	die Straße entlang
travel agency ['trævl eɪdʒənsi]	*You can book a holiday at a travel agency or on the internet.*	Reisebüro
42		
happen ['hæpən]	*What's happening?*	geschehen
pair of jeans [peər əv 'dʒi:nz]	*I bought two pairs of jeans yesterday.*	(eine) Jeans
thin [θɪn]	*You're too thin – eat more!*	dünn
lose weight [lu:z 'weɪt]	*I want to lose weight before my holiday.*	abnehmen
healthy ['helθi]	*Eating lots of fruit is very healthy.*	gesund
stamp [stæmp]	*Here's a stamp from Germany.*	Briefmarke
43 t		
jacket ['dʒækɪt]	*Bring a jacket. It's cold here.*	Jacke, Jackett
suit [su:t]	*That pullover suits you.*	(jdm) stehen
mood [mu:d]	*I'm in a good mood today.*	Stimmung, Laune
grey [greɪ]	*I've got a grey cat.*	grau
tight [taɪt]	*These jeans are too tight.*	eng (anliegend)
glad [glæd]	*I'm glad you're here.*	froh

The world of work

44		
extract ['ekstrækt]	*Read this extract from a newspaper.*	Auszug
headline ['hedlaɪn]	*What's the headline in the newspaper today?*	Schlagzeile, Überschrift
impression [ɪm'preʃn]	*First impressions are important.*	Eindruck
count [kaʊnt]	*First impressions count.*	zählen (wichtig sein)
even though ['i:vn ðəʊ]	*Even though he's young, he's very good at the job.*	obwohl
hairstyle ['heəstaɪl]	*Do you like my new hairstyle?*	Frisur
insurance agent [ɪn'ʃʊərəns eɪdʒənt]	*I'm an insurance agent.*	Versicherungsmakler/in
dress code ['dres kəʊd]	*Most schools in England have a dress code.*	Kleiderordnung
employee [ɪm'plɔɪi:]	*The company has lots of employees.*	Angestellte/r, Beschäftigte/r
must [mʌst]	*I must go now. It's late.*	müssen
follow ['fɒləʊ]	*Follow me. I know the way.*	(be)folgen
similar ['sɪmələ]	*All the women had similar hairstyles.*	ähnlich
realize ['rɪəlaɪz]	*She realized she was different from the others.*	feststellen
look alike [lʊk ə'laɪk]	*All the other people looked alike.*	gleich aussehen
bright [braɪt]	*I like bright colours.*	leuchtend, hell
hand in [ˌhænd 'ɪn]	*I handed in my project yesterday.*	einreichen, abgeben
notice ['nəʊtɪs]	*John is leaving us. He handed in his notice last week.*	Kündigung
discount price ['dɪskaʊnt praɪs]	*These prices are great. They're real discount prices.*	herabgesetzte Preise
be worth it [bi 'wɜ:θ ɪt]	*Waiting for you isn't a problem. You're worth it.*	sich lohnen
pass [pɑ:s]	*The test was difficult. Do you think you passed it?*	(Prüfung) bestehen
45		
workplace ['wɜ:kpleɪs]	*The people at my workplace are friendly.*	Arbeitsplatz
employment [ɪm'plɔɪmənt]	*What kind of employment would you like?*	Beschäftigung, Beruf
lose [lu:z]	*I don't want to lose my job.*	verlieren
discuss [dɪ'skʌs]	*Let's discuss the problem.*	besprechen, diskutieren (über)
kind [kaɪnd]	*What kind of holiday do you like best?*	Art
ideal [aɪ'di:əl]	*This isn't my ideal job.*	ideal
sort of ['sɔ:t əv]	*What sort of job would you like?*	Art von
feel [fi:l]	*How do you feel today?*	(sich) fühlen
casual ['kæʒuəl]	*Is it OK to wear casual clothes?*	leger, sportlich, Freizeit-

i:	ɪ	e	æ	ɑ:	ɒ	ɔ:	ʊ	u:	ʌ	ɜ:	ə
see	sit	ten	bad	arm	got	saw	put	too	cut	bird	about

neat [ni:t]	*His clothes are always neat.*	ordentlich, sauber
tidy ['taɪdi]	*My room is tidy today.*	ordentlich
on foot [ɒn 'fʊt]	*I go to work on foot.*	zu Fuß
by bike [baɪ 'baɪk]	*My friend goes by bike.*	mit dem Rad
45 t		
salary ['sæləri]	*I get a good salary.*	Gehalt
responsibility [rɪˌspɒnsə'bɪləti]	*As a manager, she has lots of responsibility.*	Verantwortung
flexi-time ['fleksi taɪm]	*We have flexi-time at work.*	Gleitzeit
job satisfaction ['dʒɒb sætɪsfækʃn]	*Job satisfaction is very important to me.*	Zufriedenheit im Beruf
main [meɪn]	*It's the main thing for me.*	wichtigste
abroad [ə'brɔ:d]	*I'd like to work abroad.*	im Ausland
earn [ɜ:n]	*How much do you earn?*	verdienen
mechanical [mɪ'kænɪkl]	*I don't like mechanical work. I work in an office.*	mechanisch, technisch

UNIT 5 Eating and drinking

46		
skim [skɪm]	*I only have time to skim the newspaper.*	überfliegen
refer to [rɪ'fɜ: tə]	*I'm referring to the last unit.*	sich beziehen auf
collapse [kə'læps]	*He was so ill, he collapsed at work.*	zusammenbrechen
heart failure ['hɑ:t feɪljə]	*He died of heart failure.*	Herzversagen
teammate ['ti:mmeɪt]	*I'm going out with my teammates after the match.*	Mannschaftskamerad/in
sweat [swet]	*Aussprache*	schwitzen
breathe [bri:ð]	*She breathed deeply when she heard the news.*	atmen
half-time [ˌhɑ:f 'taɪm]	*The players went inside at half-time.*	Halbzeit(pause)
can [kæn]	*I bought two cans of fanta for us.*	Dose
report [rɪ'pɔ:t]	*There's a report about the accident in the newspaper.*	Bericht
health [helθ]	*Do something for your health – go jogging!*	Gesundheit
contain [kən'teɪn]	*This bag contains my sports clothes.*	enthalten
caffeine ['kæfi:n]	*Caffeine can make you nervous.*	Koffein
equivalent [ɪ'kwɪvələnt]	*One mile is the equivalent of 1.6 kilometres.*	Entsprechung
space of time [ˌspeɪs əv 'taɪm]	*Amy finished the work in a very short space of time.*	Zeitspanne
might [maɪt]	*I might watch TV later, I'm not really sure.*	könnte(n) (vielleicht)
beat [bi:t]	*My heart beats faster when I'm with you!*	schlagen
dizzy ['dɪzi]	*All the caffeine made me a little dizzy.*	schwindlig
circulation [ˌsɜ:kjə'leɪʃn]	*My mother often has circulation problems.*	Kreislauf
notice ['nəʊtɪs]	*I noticed that my bag wasn't there.*	(be)merken
consume [kən'sju:m]	*He consumed three cans of cola in ten minutes!*	verzehren, konsumieren
sweet [swi:t]	*I don't like sweets very much.*	Bonbon
Institute for Heart Studies [ˌɪnstɪtju:t fə 'hɑ:t stʌdɪz]	*She's a doctor at the Institute for Heart Studies in London.*	Herzzentrum
cut down [ˌkʌt 'daʊn]	*I have to cut down on sweets.*	reduzieren
habit ['hæbɪt]	*I want to change my eating habits.*	Gewohnheit
kick a habit [kɪk ə 'hæbɪt]	*He has to give up sweets, but he can't kick the habit.*	eine Gewohnheit aufgeben
advertising ['ædvətaɪzɪŋ]	*I like the advertising for the new car.*	Werbung, Reklame
purpose ['pɜ:pəs]	*The purpose of a newspaper is to inform people.*	Zweck, Ziel
persuade [pə'sweɪd]	*Can I persuade you to stay longer?*	überzeugen
entertain [ˌentə'teɪn]	*Pop stars want to entertain their fans.*	unterhalten
47		
take a shower [teɪk ə 'ʃaʊə]	*I take a shower every morning.*	duschen
cup [kʌp]	*I like a cup of tea with my breakfast.*	Tasse
have a rest [həv ə 'rest]	*She always has a rest after work.*	sich ausruhen
deal with [di:l wiθ]	*He has to deal with many problems in his job.*	umgehen, zu tun zu haben mit

heart trouble ['hɑ:t trʌbl]	*He's unfit and has heart trouble.*	Herzprobleme
smoking ['sməʊkɪŋ]	*This year I'm going to stop smoking.*	Rauchen
opposite ['ɒpəzɪt]	*'Big' is the opposite of 'small'.*	Gegensatz
alive [ə'laɪv]	*Is your grandmother still alive?*	lebendig
hurry up [ˌhʌri 'ʌp]	*Hurry up, we're waiting for you!*	sich beeilen
awake [ə'weɪk]	*I was still awake when he came home.*	wach
helmet ['helmɪt]	*You have to wear a helmet on a motorbike.*	Schutzhelm
safe [seɪf]	*It isn't safe to drive too fast.*	sicher
increase [ɪn'kri:s]	*The price of cigarettes increased this year.*	erhöhen, zunehmen, steigen
nicotine patch ['nɪkəti:n pætʃ]	*If you want to give up smoking, try nicotine patches.*	Nikotinpflaster
several ['sevrəl]	*Several letters arrived this morning.*	einige
48		
heading ['hedɪŋ]	*Each group of words has a heading.*	Überschrift
meal [mi:l]	*We had a nice meal yesterday.*	Essen, Mahlzeit
homemade [ˌhəʊm'meɪd]	*Try my homemade cake.*	selbst zubereitet, hausgemacht
part [pɑ:t]	*The film has two parts.*	Teil
nutrition [nju'trɪʃn]	*Good nutrition is important for your health!*	Ernährung
including [ɪn'klu:dɪŋ]	*There are eight in our group, including three children.*	einschließlich
fountain ['faʊntən]	*Do you have water fountains at your school?*	Trinkbrunnen
thirsty ['θɜ:sti]	*Sport makes you thirsty.*	durstig
sugary ['ʃʊgəri]	*I don't like sugary snacks.*	sehr süß, zuckerhaltig
freshness ['freʃnəs]	*The freshness of fruit is very important.*	Frische
variety [və'raɪəti]	*The shop has a good variety of snacks.*	Abwechslung, Auswahl
healthiness ['helθɪnəs]	*I eat oranges because of their healthiness.*	Gesundheit
49		
transform [træns'fɔ:m]	*here:* ≈ *change*	umwandeln
replace [rɪ'pleɪs]	*Computers will replace TVs one day.*	ersetzen
driver ['draɪvə]	*I can't drink. I'm the driver tonight.*	Fahrer/in
talker ['tɔ:kə]	= *somebody who talks*	Redner/in
50		
solve [sɒlv]	*Can you solve the problem?*	lösen
season ['si:zn]	*The football season is starting soon.*	Spielzeit
knife [naɪf]	*Can you give me the bread knife please?*	Messer
behave [bɪ'heɪv]	*The rock star didn't behave very well.*	sich benehmen
smoke [sməʊk]	*I never smoked when I was a teenager.*	rauchen
fewer ['fju:ə]	*There are fewer children at school now.*	weniger
piece [pi:s]	*Would you like another piece of cake?*	Stück
fridge [frɪdʒ]	*The milk is in the fridge.*	Kühlschrank
town [taʊn]	*I live in a small town.*	Stadt
cupboard ['kʌbəd]	⚠ *Aussprache*	Schrank
cook [kʊk]	*Let's cook a nice meal on Sunday.*	zubereiten, kochen
smell [smel]	*I can smell cigarette smoke.*	riechen, duften
51		
crisps [krɪsps]	*Let's buy four big bags of crisps for the party.*	Kartoffelchips
takeaway ['teɪkəweɪ]	*Let's get a takeaway – I don't want to cook.*	(Essen) zum Mitnehmen
starve [stɑ:v]	*I'm starving! Are you hungry too?*	vor Hunger sterben
fancy ['fænsi]	*Do you fancy a beer?*	mögen
sit-down meal ['sɪt daʊn mi:l]	*Let's go for a sit-down meal at the weekend.*	Essen im Restaurant
51 t		
tell you what ['tel ju wɒt]	*Tell you what, let's get pizzas tonight.*	hör mal
take sb's order [teɪk 'ɔ:də]	*Can I take your order now?*	jds Bestellung aufnehmen
51 p		
ham [hæm]		(gekochter) Schinken
cheese [tʃi:z]		Käse
pickle ['pɪkl]		eingelegtes Gemüse
mushroom ['mʌʃrʊm]		Pilz

i:	ɪ	e	æ	ɑ:	ɒ	ɔ:	ʊ	u:	ʌ	ɜ:	ə
see	sit	ten	bad	arm	got	saw	put	too	cut	bird	about

The world of work

52

face to face [ˌfeɪs tə 'feɪs]	*I want to talk to him face to face.*	von Angesicht zu Angesicht, persönlich
greet [gri:t]	*He greeted all the people at the party.*	(be)grüßen
immediate(ly) [ɪ'mi:diətli]	*You have to phone the police immediately.*	sofort
take notes [teɪk 'nəʊts]	*I always take notes when he phones me.*	(sich) Notizen machen

53

I'm afraid [aɪm ə'freɪd]	*Can I talk to Sue, please? – I'm afraid she isn't here.*	leider

UNIT 6 Jobs and training

54

match [mætʃ]	*Let's match the names to the photos.*	zuordnen
foreign language [ˌfɒrən 'læŋgwɪdʒ]	*German is a foreign language for British people.*	Fremdsprache
foreign language correspondent [ˌfɒrən ˌlæŋgwɪdʒ ˌkɒrə'spɒndənt]	*She works as a foreign language correspondent.*	Fremdsprachenkorrespondent/-in
commercial correspondence [kəˌmɜ:ʃl ˌkɒrə'spɒndəns]	= *business letters*	Geschäftskorrespondenz
bookkeeping ['bʊk ki:pɪŋ]	*The bookkeeping department pays the bills.*	Buchhaltung
disappointed [ˌdɪsə'pɔɪntɪd]	*I didn't win. I'm very disappointed.*	enttäuscht
qualification [ˌkwɒlɪfɪ'keɪʃn]	*You need a good qualification for this job.*	(Abschluss einer) Ausbildung
primary school ['praɪməri sku:l]	*The first school you go to is primary school.*	Grundschule
secondary school ['sekəndri sku:l]	*After primary school pupils go to secondary school.*	weiterführende Schule
bully ['bʊli]	*Tom isn't nice. He bullies other pupils.*	tyrannisieren, mobben
drop out [ˌdrɒp 'aʊt]	*Tom dropped out of school when he was 16.*	ausscheiden
final exam [ˌfaɪnl ɪg'zæm]	*Before you leave school you take a final exam.*	Abschlussprüfung
dusty ['dʌsti]	*This room needs cleaning. Everything is dusty.*	staubig
stick sth out [ˌstɪk 'aʊt]	*Frank is sticking the job out. He needs the money.*	etw durchstehen, aushalten
day release class [ˌdeɪ rɪ'li:s klɑ:s]	*I go to day release classes one day a week.*	freier Tag (zur Fortbildung)
frustrated [frʌ'streɪtɪd]	*Greg was frustrated because he didn't win the prize.*	frustriert
learning difficulty ['lɜ:nɪŋ dɪfɪkəlti]	*My teachers found out that I have a learning difficulty.*	Lernschwäche
take sb on [ˌteɪk 'ɒn]	*The firm took me on after my training.*	jdn einstellen

55

force [fɔ:s]	*Unfortunately the bad weather forced me to stay at home.*	zwingen
troublemaker ['trʌblmeɪkə]	*He always starts fights. He's a troublemaker.*	Unruhestifter/in
confident ['kɒnfɪdənt]	*I'm very confident that I can do it.*	selbstsicher
definition [ˌdefɪ'nɪʃn]	*What's the definition of 'confident'? What does it mean?*	Definition
examination [ɪgˌzæmɪ'neɪʃn]	*An examination is an important test.*	(Abschluss-)Prüfung, Examen
business letter ['bɪznəs letə]	*A business letter is a letter from one company to another.*	Geschäftsbrief
factory ['fæktəri]	*This factory makes TVs.*	Fabrik
counting ['kaʊntɪŋ]	*I find counting very difficult!*	Rechnen
Italian [ɪ'tæljən]		Italienisch
French [frentʃ]		Französisch

56

take turns [teɪk 'tɜ:nz]	*Let's take turns. First you, then me.*	(sich) abwechseln
awful ['ɔ:fl]	*This isn't nice. It's awful!*	furchtbar, schrecklich

57

recent(ly) ['ri:sntli] — *I saw John recently – about two weeks ago I think.* — in letzter Zeit, jüngst, jünger

58

exam result [ɪg,zæm rɪ'zʌlts] — *My exam result was great – 95%!* — Prüfungsergebnisse
lately ['leɪtli] — *Have you seen Paul lately? – Yes. Yesterday.* — in letzter Zeit
text message ['tekst mesɪdʒ] — *Each week I send about ten text messages.* — SMS(-Nachricht)
plan [plæn] — *What are you planning for the summer?* — planen
crash [kræʃ] — *Cars often crash here.* — verunglücken (mit)
split up [,splɪt 'ʌp] — *My boyfriend and I split up last week.* — sich (voneinander) trennen

59 t

pretty ['prɪti] — *I think this is a pretty good CD.* — ziemlich, recht
hard [hɑ:d] — *Learning can be hard sometimes.* — hart, anstrengend, schwer
up till now [,ʌp tɪl 'naʊ] — *Up till now I've done four exercises.* — bis jetzt
working hours [,wɜ:kɪŋ 'aʊəz] — *My working hours are 9 am to 5 pm.* — Arbeitszeit
shiftwork ['ʃɪftwɜ:k] — *Shiftwork means sometimes working at night too.* — Schichtarbeit
season ['si:zn] — *Summer is my favourite season.* — Saison

59

full time [,fʊl 'taɪm] — *I work full time, from 9 till 5 every weekday.* — ganztags
once [wʌns] — einmal
social worker ['səʊʃl wɜ:kə] — *A social worker often deals with young people's problems.* — Sozialarbeiter/in
baker ['beɪkə] — *A baker makes bread and cakes.* — Bäcker/in
rank [ræŋk] — anordnen
according to [ə'kɔ:dɪŋ tə] — nach, entsprechend
provide [prə'vaɪd] — *Can you provide your name and address, please?* — liefern, vorgeben

The world of work

60

satisfied ['sætɪsfaɪd] — *I'm not satisfied with your work. It's simply not good enough.* — zufrieden
dissatisfied [dɪs'sætɪsfaɪd] — *I'm dissatisfied with my job. I want to do something different.* — unzufrieden
workmate ['wɜ:kmeɪt] — *My workmates are very friendly.* — Kollege
survey ['sɜ:veɪ] — *The survey said that Germans work very hard.* — (Meinungs-)Umfrage, Untersuchung
benefit ['benɪfɪt] — *You get lots of benefits as a worker in Germany.* — zusätzliche Leistung, Vergünstigung
paid sick leave [peɪd 'sɪk li:v] — *If you are ill, you get paid sick leave.* — Lohnfortzahlung im Krankheitsfall
rise [raɪz] — *Last year the number of complaints rose to sixty-five.* — (an)steigen, klettern
wage [weɪdʒ] — *Five euros an hour! That isn't a good wage!* — Lohn, Gehalt
identify [aɪ'dentɪfaɪ] — *Can you identify the man in the photo?* — (sich) identifizieren
dissatisfaction [,dɪs,sætɪs'fækʃn] — *My dissatisfaction is very high.* — Unzufriedenheit
percentage [pə'sentɪdʒ] — *What percentage of your wages do you spend on entertainment?* — Prozentsatz

61

co-worker ['kəʊwɜ:kə] — *Kate is my favourite co-worker. We work well together.* — Arbeitskollege, -kollegin
waste of time [,weɪst əf 'taɪm] — *I think watching TV is a waste of time.* — Zeitverschwendung

61 t

goods [gʊdz] — *Our firm produces high-quality goods.* — Ware(n)
never mind [,nevə 'maɪnd] — *Never mind. We can go home soon.* — macht nichts
get the hang of sth [get ðə 'hæŋ əv] — *I can't get the hang of this new computer.* — dahinter kommen
handbook ['hændbʊk] — *I need a handbook to understand how this program works.* — Bedienungsanleitung, Handbuch
feed in [,fi:d 'ɪn] — *Please feed the paper into the machine.* — eingeben, einschieben
metal ['metl] — *Cars are made of metal.* — Metall
sheet [ʃi:t] — *The metal sheet was huge.* — Platte, Scheibe
button ['bʌtn] — *Press the red button for "Stop".* — Taste, Knopf

scary ['skeəri]	*"Horror house" is a scary film.*	schrecklich, furchtbar, unheimlich, beängstigend
give sb a lift [gɪv ə 'lɪft]	*Can you give me a lift to town, please?*	jdn mitnehmen
61		
continuation [kən,tɪnju'eɪʃn]	*The continuation of the story is in next week's magazine.*	Fortsetzung

UNIT 7 That's life (or is it?)

62		
run [rʌn]	*The BBC is running a series on the world of work.*	(Geschichte) bringen
article ['ɑːtɪkl]	*I wrote an article for the newspaper.*	Artikel
destroy [dɪ'strɔɪ]	*The fire destroyed the house.*	zerstören
brain cell ['breɪn sel]	*We need a lot of our brain cells to think.*	Hirnzelle
soap opera ['səʊp ɒprə]	*Which soap (opera) do you watch?*	Seifenoper, TV-Serie
popular ['pɒpjələ]	*"Gute Zeiten, Schlechte Zeiten" is a popular soap opera in Germany.*	beliebt, populär
share [ʃeə]	*We don't need two cars. We can share one.*	gemeinsam haben, teilen
at least [ət 'liːst]	*The film is at least 120 minutes long.*	mindestens
disagreement [,dɪsə'griːmənt]	*Sue isn't talking to me. We had a disagreement.*	Meinungsverschiedenheit
adopt [ə'dɒpt]	*We liked his ideas, so we adopted them.*	adoptieren, hier: annehmen
attitude ['ætɪtjuːd]	*What's your attitude to soap operas?*	Einstellung
spend [spend]	*I can't spend much money on holidays.*	ausgeben
clothes [kləʊðz]	*Let's go shopping, I need some new clothes.*	Kleidung
long for ['lɒŋ fə]	*I really long for my own flat.*	sich sehnen nach
plot [plɒt]	*I don't like that book. The plot is boring.*	Handlung(sverlauf)
unbelievable [,ʌnbɪ'liːvəbl]	*Mike's story is unbelievable. Is it true?*	unglaublich
remember [rɪ'membə]	*Do you remember my party last year?*	sich erinnern (an)
one-night stand [,wʌn naɪt 'stænd]	*I want a partner for life, not just a one-night stand.*	Affäre für eine Nacht
wedding ['wedɪŋ]	*It was a small wedding, just friends and family.*	Hochzeit, Trauung
appear [ə'pɪə]	*↔ disappear*	erscheinen
bridegroom ['braɪdgruːm]	*the bride and the bridegroom*	Bräutigam
unrealistic [,ʌnriːə'lɪstɪk]	*Your ideas about life are very unrealistic.*	unrealistisch
63		
rank ['ræŋkɪŋ]	*The new soap ranks high on my list.*	der Rangfolge nach anordnen
reflect [rɪ'flekt]	*The film reflects the problems of young people.*	wiedergeben
left [left]	*Have you got some money left?*	übrig
investigate [ɪn'vestɪgeɪt]	*They will investigate how the woman died.*	ermitteln
review [rɪ'vjuː]	*I always watch the sports review on Saturday evening.*	Überblick
game show ['geɪmʃəʊ]	*"Who wants to be a millionaire?" is a game show.*	Spielshow
documentary [,dɒkju'mentri]	*A documentary is a film about real life.*	Dokumentarsendung
news broadcast [,njuːz 'brɔːdkɑːst]	*"Tagesschau" is a news broadcast.*	Nachrichtensendung
detective story [dɪ'tektɪv stɔːri]	*Agatha Christie wrote detective stories.*	Krimi
64		
be able to [bi 'eɪbl tə]	*Will you be able to come on holiday with me next year?*	können
65		
driving licence (BE) ['draɪvɪŋlaɪsns]	*In England you have to be 17 to get a car driving licence.*	Führerschein
stuck [stʌk]	*The driver was stuck in his car.*	festgeklemmt
suitable ['suːtəbl]	*I'm looking for a suitable job.*	geeignet, passend
flea powder ['fliː paʊdə]	*You use flea powder for a dogs' fleas.*	Flohpulver
police [pə'liːs]	*They called the police and the fire brigade.*	Polizei
66		
clean [kliːn]	*I clean my room every Saturday.*	sauber machen

ID card [ˌaɪ 'di: kɑ:d]	*The police wanted to see my ID card.*	Personalausweis
light [laɪt]	*She must be at home. The lights are on.*	Licht, Lampe
67 t		
leave [li:v]	*I'm leaving my job next month.*	verlassen
car crash ['kɑ: kræʃ]	*The police investigated the car crash.*	Autounfall
look after o.s. [ˌlʊk 'ɑ:ftə]	*Paula is very ill. She can't look after herself anymore.*	sich kümmern um sich selbst
wheelchair ['wi:ltʃeə]	*She has to use a wheelchair because she can't walk.*	Rollstuhl
67		
enemy ['enəmi]	↔ *friend*	Feind
accident ['æksɪdənt]	*They had a bad car accident.*	Zufall

The world of work

68		
rewarding [rɪ'wɔ:dɪŋ]	*Working with children can be very rewarding.*	lohnend
tiring ['taɪərɪŋ]	*This is such a tiring job. I'm always tired after work.*	anstrengend
depressing [dɪ'presɪŋ]	*That soap opera is depressing – all those problems!*	deprimierend
home for the elderly [həʊm fə ði 'eldəli]	*I work in a home for the elderly.*	Seniorenresidenz
apart from [ə'pɑ:t frəm]	*Apart from watching soaps, I also watch documentaries.*	abgesehen von, darüber hinaus
forgetful [fə'getfl]	*My brother is very forgetful.*	vergesslich
patience ['peɪʃns]	*I don't have the patience to work with children.*	Geduld
import [ɪm'pɔ:t]	*England imports coffee from other countries.*	importieren
order ['ɔ:də]	*How many orders have arrived this week?*	Auftrag
parcel ['pɑ:sl]	*I sent you a parcel of books.*	Paket, Päckchen
get bored [get 'bɔ:d]	*There's nothing to do here, I'm getting really bored.*	sich langweilen
demanding [dɪ'mɑ:ndɪŋ]	*My new job is very demanding, but I like that.*	anspruchsvoll
police force [pə'li:s fɔ:s]	*My sister is looking for a job in the police force.*	Polizei
alcoholic [ˌælkə'hɒlɪk]	*An alcoholic can't stop drinking.*	Alkoholiker/in
look forward to [ˌlʊk 'fɔ:wəd tə]	*I'm looking forward to your party on Saturday.*	sich freuen auf
69 t		
announcer [ə'naʊnsə]	*He's a TV announcer.*	Sprecher/in
waste [weɪst]	*Don't waste your money on that old car.*	verschwenden
youngster ['jʌŋstə]	*Lots of youngsters are looking for jobs.*	Jugendliche/r
pleasant ['pleznt]	*John is a very pleasant young man. He's very friendly.*	angenehm, nett
troublesome ['trʌblsəm]	*Teachers often have to deal with troublesome students.*	schwierig
patient ['peɪʃnt]	*Mr Hall is a very patient teacher. He never gets angry.*	geduldig
hard-working [ˌhɑ:d 'wɜ:kɪŋ]	*Sally is a hard-working student.*	fleißig
previous ['pri:viəs]	*My previous job was better than this job.*	vorherig
personality [ˌpɜ:sə'næləti]	*Paula is nice. She has a great personality.*	Persönlichkeit
unpleasant [ʌn'pleznt]	↔ *pleasant*	unangenehm
without a fuss [wɪˌðaʊt ə 'fʌs]	*He wasn't troublesome. He did the job without a fuss.*	ohne viel Aufhebens

UNIT 8 The right job

70		
research [rɪ'sɜ:tʃ]	*I use the Internet to do research.*	Nachforschung(en)
smart(ly) ['smɑ:tli]	*You have to look smart for a job at the bank.*	elegant, schick
suitable ['su:təbl]	*The dress is very nice, but it isn't suitable for a job interview.*	geeignet, passend
untidy [ʌn'taɪdi]	↔ *tidy*	unordentlich
appearance [ə'pɪərəns]	*At a job interview, your appearance is very important.*	Aussehen
careless ['keələs]	*Don't be careless about your appearance.*	nachlässig
suit [su:t]	*I need a grey suit for my job interview.*	Anzug, Kostüm
dirty ['dɜ:ti]	↔ *clean*	schmutzig
strength [streŋθ]	*My biggest strength is that I'm good at talking to people.*	Kraft, Stärke

weakness ['wiːknəs]	*My biggest weakness is that I'm not good at listening.*	Schwäche
preparation [ˌprepə'reɪʃn]	*You need a lot of preparation for the interview.*	Vorbereitung
excuse [ɪk'skjuːs]	*You need a very good excuse if you're late for an interview.*	Entschuldigung
unexpected [ˌʌnɪk'spektɪd]	*I didn't expect to get the job. It was totally unexpected.*	unerwartet
respectful [rɪ'spektfl]	*Some young people aren't respectful to their parents.*	respektvoll
tell jokes [tel 'dʒəʊks]	*I often tell jokes when I'm nervous.*	Witze erzählen
lie [laɪ]	*Don't lie to me.*	lügen
work experience ['wɜːk ɪkspɪəriəns]	*It's useful to get work experience before you leave school.*	Berufserfahrung
take a risk [ˌteɪk ə 'rɪsk]	*Never drink and drive. Don't take the risk.*	ein Risiko eingehen
71		
apprenticeship [ə'prentɪʃɪp]	*You have to do an apprenticeship before you can do the job.*	Lehre, Ausbildung
prepare [prɪ'peə]	*I have to prepare myself for the job interview.*	vorbereiten
qualified ['kwɒlɪfaɪd]	*After an apprenticeship you are qualified for the job.*	qualifiziert
72		
recording [rɪ'kɔːdɪŋ]	*You can listen to the recording of the text on CD.*	Aufnahme
72 t		
trousers ['traʊzəz]	*I bought a pair of trousers yesterday.*	Hose(n)
newspaper ['njuːzpeɪpə]	*You can look for jobs in the newspaper and on the Internet.*	Zeitung
job vacancy ['dʒɒb veɪkənsi]	*Our firm doesn't have any job vacancies at the moment.*	offene Stelle, Stellenangebot
career [kə'rɪə]	*There are lots of different careers at big companies.*	Beruf
74		
pick [pɪk]	*= choose*	auswählen
grid [grɪd]	*Put the words in the right place on the grid.*	Schema, Tabelle
supervise ['suːpəvaɪz]	*You always have to supervise young children.*	beaufsichtigen
clerk [klɑːk]	*Most clerks work in offices.*	(Büro-)Angestellte/r
meaning ['miːnɪŋ]	*Do you know the meaning of the word 'supervise'?*	Bedeutung
expression [ɪk'spreʃn]	*What's the German expression for 'job interview'?*	Ausdruck
letter of application [ˌletər əv æplɪ'keɪʃn]	*When you apply for a job, you write a letter of application.*	Bewerbungsschreiben
operative ['ɒpərətɪv]	*My brother works as a call centre operative.*	Mitarbeiter/in (Call-Center)
fluent ['fluːənt]	*My English is almost fluent.*	fließend
75		
summer camp ['sʌmə kæmp]	*My younger sister is going to a summer camp for her holiday*	Ferienlager
childcare ['tʃaɪldkeə]	*Childcare is looking after children.*	(Kinder-)Erziehung
energetic [ˌenə'dʒetɪk]	*She's a very energetic child – never tired.*	energisch, tatkräftig
responsible [rɪ'spɒnsəbl]	*You have to be a responsible person to work with children.*	verantwortungsvoll
Dear ... [dɪə]	*Dear Jane, I'm writing to you today because ...*	Sehr geehrte(r) ...,
enclosed [ɪn'kləʊzd]	*Please find your travel documents enclosed.*	beigefügt
Yours sincerely/faithfully [jɔːz sɪn'sɪəli, 'feɪθfəli]		Mit freundlichen Grüßen
submit [səb'mɪt]	*≈ send*	einreichen, abschicken
basic ['beɪsɪk]	*My French skills are basic.*	elementar
native speaker [ˌneɪtɪv 'spiːkə]	*I was born in Germany, but I'm a native speaker of Turkish.*	Muttersprachler/in

The world of work

76		
care for ['keə fə]	*My sister wants to care for the elderly.*	pflegen
repair [rɪ'peə]	*My friend repaired my car.*	reparieren
carpenter ['kɑːpəntə]	*A carpenter often works in houses.*	Zimmermann, Tischler/in
estate agent [ɪ'steɪt eɪdʒənt]	*An estate agent sells houses.*	Immobilienmakler/in
travel agent ['trævl eɪdʒənt]	*A travel agent sells holidays and trips.*	Reiseverkehrskaufmann/frau
enthusiastic [ɪnˌθjuːzi'æstɪk]	*She's very enthusiastic about singing.*	begeistert
communicate [kə'mjuːnɪkeɪt]	*As a travel agent you have to be good at communicating.*	kommunizieren
self-confident [ˌself 'kɒnfɪdənt]	*As an estate agent you have to be self-confident.*	selbstsicher

technically-minded ['teknɪkli maɪndɪd]	*I can't be an electrician because I'm not technically-minded.*	technisch interessiert
well-organized [ˌwel 'ɔːgənaɪzd]	*I'm usually tidy and well-organized.*	gut organisiert
requirement [rɪ'kwaɪəmənt]	*One of the job requirements is a tidy appearance.*	Bedingung, Anforderung
apprentice [ə'prentɪs]	*I started my job as an apprentice nurse last week.*	Lehrling, Auszubildende/r
construction [kən'strʌkʃn]	*A construction firm builds houses.*	Bau(firma)
opportunity [ˌɒpə'tjuːnəti]	*The youth camp is a great opportunity to make new friends.*	Gelegenheit, Chance
practical ['præktɪkl]	*I've got practical skills, so I want to be a carpenter.*	praktisch (veranlagt)
essential [ɪ'senʃl]	*In this job, it's essential to speak French.*	(absolut) notwendig
accurate ['ækjərət]	*Don't guess. We need accurate information.*	genau
measurement ['meʒəmənt]	*What's the measurement? – Five metres.*	Messung
77 t		
carpentry ['kɑːpəntri]	*A carpenter does carpentry.*	Tischlerei
involve [ɪn'vɒlv]	*This job involves lots of maths.*	umfassen
that sort of thing [ˌðæt sɔːt əv 'θɪŋ]	*Practical work? Yes, I'm very good at that sort of thing.*	in diesen Dingen
trade [treɪd]	*Carpentry is a practical trade.*	Handwerk, Beruf
local ['ləʊkl]	*I work for a local firm.*	örtlich, lokal, hiesig
mend [mend]	*Can you mend a car?*	reparieren, ausbessern
fence [fens]	*There's a fence around our garden.*	Zaun
paint [peɪnt]	*I'm painting the fence today.*	(an)streichen
favourite subject [ˌfeɪvərɪt 'sʌbdʒɪkt]	*English is my favourite subject.*	Lieblingsfach

UNIT 9 Destination NZ

78		
caption ['kæpʃn]	*Captions tell you about a photo or picture.*	Bildunterschrift
whale watching ['weɪl wɒtʃɪŋ]		Whale-Watching, Walbeobachtung
hang-gliding ['hæŋ glaɪdɪŋ]		Drachenfliegen
bungy jumping ['bʌndʒi dʒʌmpɪŋ]		Bungee-Springen
white-water rafting [ˌwaɪt wɔːtə 'rɑːftɪŋ]		Wildwasserfahren
welcome party ['welkəm pɑːti]	*There was a welcome party on the first evening.*	Willkommensfeier, -party
wildlife ['waɪldlaɪf]	*The wildlife in New Zealand is different from in Germany.*	Tierwelt
plane [pleɪn]	*Airbus planes are made in Europe.*	Flugzeug
take off [ˌteɪk 'ɒf]	*The plane took off from Hamburg at 6 pm.*	abheben, abfliegen, starten
land [lænd]	*It landed in Munich at 7.30 pm.*	landen
79		
spring [sprɪŋ]	*Spring is my favourite season.*	Frühling, Frühjahr
autumn ['ɔːtəm]	*Autumn starts in September.*	Herbst
winter ['wɪntə]	*I love the snow in winter.*	Winter
inhabitant [ɪn'hæbɪtənt]	*The Maori people are the oldest inhabitants of New Zealand.*	Bewohner/in, Einwohner/in
Aborigine [ˌæbə'rɪdʒəni]	*The original inhabitants of Australia are called Aborigines.*	Ureinwohner Australiens
adventure [əd'ventʃə]	*If you want adventure, have a holiday in New Zealand.*	Abenteuer
island ['aɪlənd]	*Several islands are part of Great Britain.*	Insel
contrast ['kɒntrɑːst]	*Contrasts: black and white, city and countryside, summer and winter.*	Kontrast
mountain ['maʊntən]	*Mont Blanc is the highest mountain in Europe.*	Berg
forest ['fɒrɪst]	*The New Forest in Southern England is huge.*	Wald
river ['rɪvə]	*There are no fish in this river.*	Fluss
lake [leɪk]	*We can swim in the lake in summer.*	(Binnen-)See

iː	ɪ	e	æ	ɑː	ɒ	ɔː	ʊ	uː	ʌ	ɜː	ə
see	sit	ten	bad	arm	got	saw	put	too	cut	bird	about

penguin ['peŋgwɪn]	*My little brother really liked the penguins at the zoo.*	Pinguin
Southern Hemisphere [ˌsʌðən 'hemɪsfɪə]	*New Zealand is in the Southern Hemisphere.*	Südhalbkugel
jump [dʒʌmp]	*That was a very high jump!*	Sprung
bridge [brɪdʒ]	*There's a bridge over the river in the next town.*	Brücke
be scared of heights [bi ˌskeəd əv 'haɪts]	*I can't come up there with you. I'm scared of heights.*	nicht schwindelfrei sein
chill out [ˌtʃɪl 'aʊt]	*Let's chill out with some good music after work today.*	sich entspannen, abhängen
require [rɪ'kwaɪə]	*≈ need*	benötigen, erfordern, verlangen
instructor [ɪn'strʌktə]	*The instructor told us what to do.*	Lehrer/in, Ausbilder/in
boat trip ['bəʊt trɪp]	*I went on a boat trip on the lake yesterday.*	Bootsausflug, Bootsfahrt
dolphin ['dɒlfɪn]	⚠ *Aussprache! (Betonung)*	Delphin
seal [siːl]	*There were lots of seals in the water.*	Seehund
traditional [trə'dɪʃənl]	*Some Germans sometimes wear traditional clothes.*	traditionell
barbecue ['bɑːbɪkjuː]	*It's warm this evening. Let's have a barbecue.*	Grillparty
client ['klaɪənt]	*The company has many German clients.*	Kunde/Kundin
80		
You're kidding! [ˌjɔː 'kɪdɪŋ]	*You're kidding! I don't believe it!*	Das ist doch nicht dein Ernst!
81		
promise ['prɒmɪs]	*I promise I won't be late.*	versprechen
paragliding ['pærəglaɪdɪŋ]	*Is paragliding the same as hang-gliding?*	Gleitschirmfliegen
airline pilot ['eəlaɪn paɪlət]	⚠ *Aussprache (Betonung von "pilot")*	Pilot/in (für zivile Luftfahrt)
82 t		
organize ['ɔːgənaɪz]	*Let's organize a party for our guests.*	organisieren, arrangieren
get sth straight [ˌget 'streɪt]	*Let me get this straight. Our plane leaves at 4 p.m, right? – Yes, that's right.*	etw deutlich machen
83		
exchange [ɪks'tʃeɪndʒ]	*We have an exchange with a vocational college in England.*	Austausch
boarding pass ['bɔːdɪŋ pɑːs]	*Your boarding pass is an important document.*	Bordkarte
sir / madam [sɜː, 'mædəm]	*Good morning, sir. Hello, madam.*	mein Herr / meine Dame
flight [flaɪt]	*Flight BA 956 goes to Düsseldorf.*	Flug
gate [geɪt]	*The flight leaves from gate 5.*	Gate, Ausgang, Flugsteig
pocket ['pɒkɪt]	⚠ *pocket = (Hosen-)Tasche; bag = (Trage-)Tasche*	Tasche
baggage reclaim [ˌbægɪdʒ 'riː kleɪm]	*Your bags are at baggage reclaim.*	Gepäckausgabe

The world of work

84		
salesperson ['seɪlz pɜːsn]	*Paul is a travel agency salesperson.*	Verkäufer/in
passenger ['pæsɪndʒə]	*There are 123 passengers on the flight.*	Passagier/in
luggage ['lʌgɪdʒ]	*These two bags are my luggage.*	Gepäck
departure [dɪ'pɑːtʃə]	*The next departure to London is in two hours.*	Abflug
journey ['dʒɜːni]	*The journey takes one hour.*	Reise
air [eə]	*Can I buy the air and rail tickets here?*	Luft
rail [reɪl]	*You can also go to London by rail, on the Eurostar train.*	(Eisen-)Bahn
ferry ['feri]	*There are ferries to England too.*	Fähre
stay calm [ˌstaɪ 'kɑːm]	*If there's a problem during the journey, you must stay calm.*	ruhig bleiben
fault: be sb's ~ [fɔːlt]	*I haven't done anything wrong! It's not my fault!*	Schuld
pressure: be under ~ ['preʃə]	*This week we have a lot to at work. We're under pressure.*	Druck: unter ~ sein
off duty ['ɒf 'duːti]	*When I'm off duty I can use the hotel swimming pool. It's great.*	nicht im Dienst
facility [fə'sɪləti]	*Our hotel has some of the best relaxation facilities in the city.*	Einrichtung, Anlage
aircraft ['eəkrɑːft]	⚠ *One aircraft, two aircraft.*	Flugzeug
distant ['dɪstənt]	*New Zealand is a distant place for people in Germany.*	weit entfernt, fern

85

sales executive ['seɪlz ɪgzekjətɪv]	*Emma is a sales executive for a big German company.*	Vertriebsmitarbeiter/in
receive [rɪ'si:v]	*She receives lots of emails from clients every week.*	erhalten, empfangen, bekommen

85 t

arrive [ə'raɪv]	*When does your flight arrive in London?*	ankommen, eintreffen
date [deɪt]	*What's the date today?*	Datum, Termin
availability [əˌveɪlə'bɪləti]	*What's the availability of flights on Monday?*	Verfügbarkeit
alteration [ˌɔ:ltə'reɪʃn]	*I'm sorry. I can't make any alterations to this ticket.*	Änderung
go ahead [ˌgəʊ ə'hed]	*Go ahead and book the hotel.*	anfangen, Schießen Sie los!
prior to ['praɪə tə]	*prior to = before*	vor

85

flight reservation ['flaɪt rezəveɪʃn]	*It's best to have a flight reservation long before the flight date.*	Flugreservierung

86

go on holiday [gəʊ ɒn 'hɒlədeɪ]	*I often go on holiday to Germany.*	in Urlaub fahren
experience [ɪk'spɪəriəns]	*White-water rafting was an exciting experience.*	Erfahrung, Erlebnis
quarter ['kwɔ:tə]	*Twenty-five per cent is a quarter.*	Viertel
romance [rəʊ'mæns]	*Lots of people want romance.*	Romanze, Liebesaffäre
on holiday [ɒn 'hɒlədeɪ]	*When I'm on holiday I like to sleep a lot.*	im Urlaub
look for ['lʊk fə]	*Lots of people look for romance on holiday.*	suchen nach
location [ləʊ'keɪʃn]	*What's the location of the hotel? = Where's the hotel?*	(Stand-)Ort
by the sea [baɪ ðə 'si:]	*The hotel is by the sea.*	am Meer
good value for money [gʊd ˌvælju: fə 'mʌni]	*It isn't cheap, but it's good value for money.*	ein gutes Preis-Leistungs-Verhältnis
local people [ˌləʊkl 'pi:pl]	*Local people often know the best restaurants.*	Ortsansässige
activity holiday [æk'tɪvəti hɒlədeɪ]	*I want an activity holiday this year.*	Aktivurlaub
close(ly) ['kləʊsli]	*The beach is very close to the hotel.*	dicht
beach holiday ['bi:tʃ hɒlədeɪ]	*Beach holidays can be boring.*	Strandurlaub
amongst [ə'mʌŋst]	*Amongst many older people, watching TV is the most popular activity.*	unter
young adult [jʌŋ 'ædʌlt]	*Older teenagers are young adults.*	junge/r Erwachsene/r
get to ['get tə]	*How did you get to Berlin?*	erreichen, gelangen
by train [baɪ 'treɪn]	*– By train. It was an ICE from Hamburg.*	mit der Bahn
define [dɪ'faɪn]	*How do you define a good holiday?*	beschreiben, definieren
holiday destination [ˌhɒlədeɪ ˌdestɪ'neɪʃn]	*Spain is my favourite holiday destination.*	Urlaubsziel
scenery ['si:nəri]	*Southern Germany has some beautiful scenery.*	Landschaft
unpopular [ʌn'pɒpjələ]	*↔ popular*	unbeliebt, unpopulär
give an opinion [gɪv ən ə'pɪnjən]	*Let me give you my opinion: awful!*	seine Meinung äußern
twice [twaɪs]	*I saw him twice – on Saturday and on Sunday.*	zweimal, zwei Mal
so far [ˌsəʊ 'fɑ:]	*So far I've learned 600 words.*	bis jetzt

87

on the beach [ˌɒn ðə 'bi:tʃ]	*She's on the beach again.*	Strand
be careful [bi 'keəfl]	*Be careful not to forget your ticket.*	vorsichtig sein
underline [ˌʌndə'laɪn]	*This word is underlined.*	unterstreichen
relaxation [ˌri:læk'seɪʃn]	*I don't want an activity holiday. I want relaxation.*	Entspannung
look at ['lʊk ət]	*Oh no! Look at that car! It's going to crash!*	ansehen, anschauen
penfriend ['penfrend]	*I must write to my penfriend.*	Brieffreund/in

i:	ɪ	e	æ	ɑ:	ɒ	ɔ:	ʊ	u:	ʌ	ɜ:	ə
see	sit	ten	bad	arm	got	saw	put	too	cut	bird	about

UNIT 10 Keep in touch

88		
keep in touch [ki:p in tʌtʃ]	*Let's keep in touch. Send me an email when you can.*	in Kontakt bleiben
angry ['æŋgri]	*He was so angry, he couldn't speak.*	wütend
89		
phone rage ['fəʊn reɪdʒ]	*Phone rage is when you get angry about phones.*	Telefon-Wutanfall
turn [tɜ:n]	*I turned to the girl and we started talking.*	sich drehen, sich umdrehen
user ['ju:zə]	*Some mobile phone users really annoy me!*	Benutzer/in
drive sb crazy [draɪv 'kreɪzi]	*Your loud music drives me crazy!*	jdn zur Verzweiflung treiben, jdn verrückt machen
stranger ['streɪndʒə]	*Children should always say "no" to strangers.*	Fremde/r
public place [ˌpʌblɪk 'pleɪs]	*In Ireland, you're not allowed to smoke in any public places.*	öffentlicher Ort
serves you right [ˌsɜ:vz ju 'raɪt]	*Tim lost his phone. That serves him right. He didn't look after it.*	geschieht dir recht
kill [kɪl]	*He was in a car accident that killed two people.*	töten, umbringen
shout [ʃaʊt]	*I shouted, but you didn't hear me.*	schreien
for goodness' sake [fə 'gʊdnəs seɪk]	*Stop shouting now, for goodness' sake!*	um Himmels willen
switch [swɪtʃ]	*In meetings, switch your phone to "silent" mode.*	schalten, umschalten
vibrate ['vaɪbreɪt]	*I could feel my mobile vibrating in my jacket pocket.*	vibrieren
ringtone ['rɪŋtəʊn]	*I found a cool ringtone for my mobile.*	Klingelton
incredibly [ɪn'kredəbli]	*The music was incredibly loud.*	unglaublich
constant(ly) ['kɒnstənt]	*That wasn't very polite – you were constantly talking on your mobile.*	ständig
interrupt [ˌɪntə'rʌpt]	*Can I interrupt your conversation for a second?*	unterbrechen
turn off [ˌtɜ:n 'ɒf]	*Turn off the TV, please. I'm tired.*	ausschalten, abstellen
spoil [spɔɪl]	*Please don't spoil my party – be nice to the others.*	verderben
avoid [ə'vɔɪd]	*It's better to avoid problems with strangers.*	vermeiden, aus dem Wege gehen
step [step]	*The first step to health for many people is to stop smoking.*	Schritt
90		
overhear [ˌəʊvə'hɪə]	*They were talking loudly, so I overheard their conversation.*	zufällig mithören
whisper ['wɪspə]	*She whispered something to me.*	flüstern
keep sth to o.s. ['ki:p tə]	*Don't tell anyone about that, it's private. Keep it to yourself.*	etw für sich behalten
honest ['ɒnɪst]	*Be honest. Could you live without a mobile phone?*	ehrlich
91		
wet [wet]	*↔ dry*	nass, feucht
get in trouble [ˌget ɪn 'trʌbl]	*Be good! Don't get into trouble at school!*	in Schwierigkeiten kommen
return a call [rɪ'tɜ:n ə kɔ:l]	*Hi, Sue. I'm just returning your call. How are you?*	zurückrufen
delete [dɪ'li:t]	*Oh no! I've deleted the document!*	löschen
shut down	*I'm tired. I think I'll shut down my computer now.*	herunterfahren
92		
pay as you go ['peɪ əs ju ˌgəʊ]	*I have a pay as you go mobile.*	prepaid, mit Karte
contract ['kɒntrækt]	*My mobile contract is great – I have 500 free minutes per month!*	Vertrag
unlimited [ʌn'lɪmɪtɪd]	*I can send unlimited text messages – yes, as many as I want!*	unbegrenzt
92 t		
saleswoman ['seɪlzwʊmən]	*I found a job as a saleswoman in a small shop.*	Verkäuferin
as much as you like [əz ˌmʌtʃ əz ju 'laɪk]	*There's enough food. Take as much as you like.*	so viel Sie möchten
browse [braʊz]	*I don't often browse the Internet. It's too expensive.*	durchsehen, surfen
webpage ['webpeɪdʒ]	*A website has many webpages.*	Internetseite
tariff ['tærɪf]	*Which tariff do you have at the moment?*	Tarif
suits you best [ˌsu:ts ju 'best]	*Of all the shirts, the red one suits you best.*	am geeignetsten für jdn sein
access ['ækses]	*Most people have access to the internet now.*	Zugang, Zugriff
suit sb's needs [su:t ˌsʌmbədiz 'ni:dz]	*We have tariffs to suit everyone's needs.*	jds Bedürfnissen entsprechen

sound like ['saʊnd laɪk]	*That sounds like a great idea!*	sich anhören wie, klingen wie
budget ['bʌdʒɪt]	*Our monthly budget is $750.*	Etat, Kostenplan, Budget
fee [fi:]	*The monthly fee is 25 euros.*	Gebühr

The world of work

94		
profession [prə'feʃn]	*What's your profession? – I'm a nurse.*	Beruf
technician [tek'nɪʃn]	*Technicians have to be technically-minded.*	Techniker/in
future ['fju:tʃə]	*We need to plan for the future.*	Zukunft
depend on [dɪ'pend ɒn]	*Lots of people depend on computers now.*	abhängig sein von, angewiesen sein auf
fix [fɪks]	*My bike is broken. Can you fix it?*	in Ordnung bringen, lösen, reparieren
communicator [kə'mju:nɪkeɪtə]	*Teachers should be good communicators.*	Kommunikator/in
install [ɪn'stɔ:l]	*The technician installed our new TV.*	installieren, einrichten, anschließen
site [saɪt]	*I work at lots of different sites all over Germany.*	Baustelle, Anlage
upgrade ['ʌpgreɪd]	*I have to upgrade my browser.*	aufrüsten, upgraden
peripheral [pə'rɪfərəl]	⚠ *Aussprache*	Peripherie(gerät)
printer ['prɪntə]	*I need a different printer for my new computer.*	Drucker/in
be part of sth [bi pa:t o]	*In our company, I'm part of the sales team.*	beteiligt sein an etw
after-sales ['a:ftə seɪlz]	*Our after-sales team helps customers who work with our computers.*	Kundenbetreuung
store [stɔ:]	*We live near a huge electrical goods store.*	Geschäft, Laden, Warenhaus
I.T. department [ˌaɪ 'ti: dɪ'pa:tmənt]	*When our computers don't work we depend on our I.T. department!*	EDV-Abteilung
organization [ˌɔ:gənaɪ'zeɪʃn]	*I work for an international organization.*	Organisation
95		
telephone line ['telɪfəʊn laɪn]	*Our telephone line didn't work, so we called the technician.*	Telefonleitung
fault [fɔ:lt]	*If I can't find the fault, I can't repair it.*	Fehler, Defekt
95 t		
screen [skri:n]	*I only need a small computer screen.*	Bildschirm
cable ['keɪbl]	*You need a special TV cable for that.*	Kabel
plug [plʌg]	*You need different plugs in the USA.*	Stecker
memory ['meməri]	*My computer has got one gigabyte of memory.*	Speicher
paper ['peɪpə]	*The printer hasn't got any paper.*	Papier
eject [i'dʒekt]	*Push 'eject' to get the CD out.*	auswerfen
95		
blank [blæŋk]	*I can copy it for you if you give me a blank CD.*	leer, ohne Anzeige
run [rʌn]	*The new computer game runs well on my PC.*	laufen
solution [sə'lu:ʃn]	*I found the solution to our problem!*	Lösung
desk [desk]	*Phone the help-desk if you can't solve the problem.*	Pult, Schalter
96		
generation [ˌdʒenə'reɪʃn]	⚠ *Aussprache*	Generation
grow up [ˌgrəʊ 'ʌp]	*I grew up in Hamburg.*	aufwachsen, groß werden
place [pleɪs]	*Look! This is a good place for a party.*	Stelle, Platz, Ort
teenager ['ti:neɪdʒə]	*Teenagers are between 13 and 19 years old.*	Teenager
each other [i:tʃ 'ʌðə]	*They looked at each other and laughed.*	einander, sich
on average [ɒn 'ævərɪdʒ]	*On average, I watch about 2 hours of TV a day.*	im Durchschnitt, durchschnittlich
forum ['fɔ:rəm]	*I know a good internet forum for young people.*	Forum
by email [baɪ 'i:meɪl]	*Let's keep in touch by email.*	per E-Mail
keep up with sth [ˌki:p 'ʌp wɪð]	*I try to keep up with all the new software, but that's expensive.*	mit etw Schritt halten
news [nju:z]	*My parents watch the news every evening.*	Neuigkeiten, Nachrichten

set up [ˌset 'ʌp]	*I'd like to set up my own blog. Can you help me?*	einrichten
personal space [ˌpɜ:sənl 'speɪs]	*My room is my personal space at home.*	persönlicher Freiraum
comment ['kɒment]	*I'd like to read your comments on my blog.*	Bemerkung, Kommentar
all over the world [ɔ:l ˌəʊvə ðə 'wɜ:ld]	*People use the internet all over the world now.*	in der ganzen Welt
last night [lɑ:st 'naɪt]	*We went to the cinema last night.*	gestern Abend
in what ways [ɪn ˌwɒt 'weɪz]	*In what ways can the internet help you in daily life?*	auf welche Art, wie
paragraph ['pærəgrɑ:f]	*Read the last paragraph.*	Absatz

UNIT 11 Fame and fortune

98		
fame [feɪm]	*Leonardo diCaprio found fame as a film star.*	Ruhm
fortune ['fɔ:tʃu:n]	*"Fortune" most often means lots of money.*	Glück, Vermögen, Schicksal
iron mask ['aɪən mɑ:sk]	*An iron mask covered his face.*	eiserne Maske
movie theater ['mu:vi θɪətə]	*Americans say "movie theater" for "cinema."*	Kino
movie ['mu:vi]	*Americans say "movie" for "film."*	(Spiel-)Film
director [də'rektə]	*Steven Spielberg is a film director.*	Direktor/in, Regisseur/in
box office hit ['bɒks ɒfɪs hɪt]	*"Titanic" was a box office hit.*	Kassenschlager
flop [flɒp]	*Nobody liked my new film. It was a flop.*	Reinfall, Flop
extra ['ekstrə]	*I was an extra in "Lindenstraße" for a day.*	Statist/in
Tinsel Town ['tɪnsl taʊn]	*I'd really like to visit Tinsel Town one day.*	Hollywood
arthouse cinema ['ɑ:thaʊs sɪnəmə]	*Our local arthouse cinema often shows German films.*	Programmkino
subtitle ['sʌbtaɪtl]	*I saw a French film – in French, with English subtitles.*	Untertitel
snapshot ['snæpʃɒt]	*He took a snapshot as the film star drove past.*	Schnappschuss, Kurzdarstellung
celebrity [sə'lebrəti]	*= star*	Prominente/r
99		
admire [əd'maɪə]	*I don't admire her. She isn't a good director.*	bewundern
script [skrɪpt]	*Who wrote the script for "Titanic"?*	Drehbuch
admit [əd'mɪt]	*OK, OK. I admit that I took the money.*	zugeben, gestehen
obsessed [əb'sest]	*Katie's obsessed with celebrities. She wants to know all about them.*	besessen
serious side ['sɪəriəs saɪd]	*John makes me laugh, but he has got a serious side too.*	ernsthafte Seite
environmental [ɪnˌvaɪrən'mentl]	*Cars are a big environmental problem.*	Umwelt-, umweltbezogen
campaign [kæm'peɪn]	*Have you heard about the campaign to save the whales?*	Kampagne, Aktion
Natural Resources Defense Council [nætʃrəl rɪˌsɔ:sɪz dɪ'fens kaunsl]	*Water is a natural resource.*	Umweltschutzorganisation in den USA
involve [ɪn'vɒlv]	*This job involves meeting lots of people.*	mit sich bringen, beinhalten
audition (for) [ɔ:'dɪʃn]	*My friend auditioned for a role in a film last week.*	vorsprechen (für)
unsuccessful(ly) [ˌʌnsək'sesfəli]	*He was unsuccessful. Another man got the role.*	erfolglos
actor ['æktə]	*Leonardo diCaprio and Kate Winslet are actors.*	Schauspieler
big-screen [ˌbɪg 'skri:n]	*There are DVDs of lots of big-screen films.*	Kinoleinwand, hier: Spielfilm-
nomination [ˌnɒmɪ'neɪʃn]	*He got an Oscar nomination, but he didn't win an Oscar.*	Nominierung
romantic [rəʊ'mæntɪk]	*Is "Titanic" just a romantic film? Or is there action too?*	romantisch
blockbuster ['blɒkbʌstə]	*"Titanic" was a blockbuster. It made millions of dollars.*	Kinohit
teen idol ['ti:n aɪdl]	*Teenagers loved James Dean. He was a real teen idol.*	Teenageridol
businessman ['bɪznəsmən]	*Mr Kent is a businessman. His company makes clothes.*	Geschäftsmann
critics' choice ['krɪtɪks tʃɔɪs]	*Which film will be the critics' choice this year?*	Bestenliste

produce a film [prəˌdjuːs ə 'fɪlm]	*She wants to produce another film.*	einen Film produzieren
risk sth [rɪsk]	*I risked my job to meet you yesterday.*	etw riskieren
go mad [gəʊ 'mæd]	*My grandfather went mad when he was very old.*	verrückt werden, durchdrehen
discover [dɪ'skʌvə]	*I've discovered a great new café in town.*	entdecken
community [kə'mjuːnəti]	*I live in a very friendly community.*	Gemeinde, Gemeinschaft
hidden ['hɪdn]	*This car looks OK, but I'm sure there are hidden problems.*	verborgen, versteckt
con man ['kɒn mæn]	*In "Catch me if you can" Leonardo DiCaprio plays a con man.*	Betrüger
lawyer ['lɔːjə]	*I didn't do it! I want to phone my lawyer. Now!*	(Rechts-)Anwalt/Anwältin
100		
confusing [kən'fjuːzɪŋ]	*"Der, die, das"! – German is confusing.*	verwirrend
good-looking [ˌgʊd 'lʊkɪŋ]	*Leonardo diCaprio is good-looking.*	gut aussehend
unfortunately [ʌn'fɔːtʃənətli]	*Unfortunately you're too old for the job.*	leider
thrilling ['θrɪlɪŋ]	*"Tatort" is sometimes exciting, but it's never really thrilling.*	packend, spannend
disaster [dɪ'zɑːstə]	*I've crashed mum's car. This is a disaster!*	Katastrophe
drama ['drɑːmə]	*"Das Boot" is a drama.*	Drama
fool [fuːl]	*You can't fool me. I know what you're planning.*	täuschen, an der Nase herumführen
selfish ['selfɪʃ]	*Don't be selfish. Give him some of your chocolate.*	egoistisch, selbstsüchtig
some kind of [sʌm 'kaɪnd əv]	*He thinks he's some kind of British DiCaprio.*	eine Art
all-American [ˌɔːl ə'merɪkən]	*I'm an all-American boy. I love soccer and hamburgers!*	typisch amerikanisch
101		
dislike [dɪs'laɪk]	*I really dislike most Hollywood films.*	nicht mögen
date sb [deɪt]	*Meg is dating Paul at the moment.*	mit jdm ausgehen
performance [pə'fɔːməns]	*His performance in "The Aviator" was very good.*	Vorstellung, Auftritt, Leistung
sitcom ['sɪtkɒm]	*= situation comedy*	Situationskomödie
gossip ['gɒsɪp]	*Some German magazines have lots of gossip about stars.*	Klatsch
102		
guitar [gɪ'tɑː]	*I can't play the guitar.*	Gitarre
temper ['tempə]	*She has got a terrible temper.*	Temperament
I don't mind [aɪ dəʊnt 'maɪnd]	*I don't mind staying here. It's OK.*	ich habe nichts (da)gegen
sit down [ˌsɪt 'daʊn]	*You can sit down here.*	sich (hin)setzen
102 t		
talent competition [ˌtælənt ˌkɒmpə'tɪʃn]	*How many of today's stars started their careers in a talent competition?*	Talentwettbewerb
professional [prə'feʃənl]	*I'm a professional musician. It's a great job.*	Berufs-, Profi-, professionell
keep on (doing sth) [ˌkiːp 'ɒn duːɪŋ]	*I want to keep on playing music for a long time.*	etw weiter tun
103		
well-known [ˌwel 'nəʊn]	*Is she famous, or just well-known?*	sehr bekannt, berühmt
it's been a pleasure [ɪts ˌbiːn ə 'pleʒə]	*I've enjoyed this interview. It's been a pleasure.*	war mir ein Vergnügen

The world of work

104		
Caring ['keərɪŋ]	*Caring for other people can be difficult.*	Pflege
caring ['keərɪŋ]	*He's a caring father.*	sozial (eingestellt)
hospital ['hɒspɪtl]	*He works in a hospital.*	Krankenhaus
temperature ['temprətʃə]	*You feel hot. Let me check your temperature.*	Temperatur, Fieber
blood pressure ['blʌd preʃə]	*Old people often have high blood pressure.*	Blutdruck
give an injection [ˌgɪv ən ɪn'dʒekʃn]	*I must give you an injection.*	eine Spritze geben
injury ['ɪndʒəri]	*That's a bad injury.*	Verletzung
dress a wound [ˌdres ə 'wuːnd]	*You poor thing! Don't worry, I'll dress the wound for you.*	eine Wunde verbinden

iː	ɪ	e	æ	ɑː	ɒ	ɔː	ʊ	uː	ʌ	ɜː	ə
see	sit	ten	bad	arm	got	saw	put	too	cut	bird	about

blood transfusion [ˌblʌd trænsˈfjuːʒn]	*You've lost a lot of blood. You need a blood transfusion.*	Bluttransfusion
surgeon [ˈsɜːdʒən]	*The surgeon is talking to the patient at the moment.*	Chirurg/in
doctor's surgery [ˌdɒktəz ˈsɜːdʒəri]	*The doctor's surgery isn't open at the weekend.*	Arztpraxis
treat [triːt]	*Doctors treat patients.*	behandeln
blood sample [ˈblʌd sɑːmpl]	*Nurses sometimes take blood samples.*	Blutprobe
infant school [ˈɪnfənt skuːl]	*My son is 5. He goes to an infant school.*	Grundschule (für Kinder von 4 bis 7 Jahren)
bathe [beɪð]	*Have you bathed the baby?*	baden
change (a baby's nappy) [tʃeɪndʒ kləʊðz]	*Oh no. I must change the baby again before we leave.*	wickeln, Windeln wechseln
feed [fiːd]	*Can you feed the baby now, please?*	füttern
care assistant for the elderly [ˌkeər əsɪstənt fə ði ˈeldəli]	*He's a care assistant for the elderly.*	Altenpfleger/in
daily life [ˌdeɪli ˈlaɪf]	*My daily life is so boring.*	Alltag
day centre [ˈdeɪ sentə]	*My grandmother goes to a day centre every day.*	Tagesstätte
nursing home [ˈnɜːsɪŋ həʊm]	*Mr Jones lives in a nursing home now.*	Pflegeheim
social activity [ˌsəʊʃl ækˈtɪvəti]	*Playing cards is a popular social activity in nursing homes.*	gesellige Unternehmungen
less able [ˌles ˈeɪbl]	*Our less able clients need extra help of course.*	hier: hilfsbedürftig
intimate [ˈɪntɪmət]	*Don't ask such intimate questions!*	intim
wash [wɒʃ]	*Cats often wash themselves.*	(sich) waschen
household chore [ˈhaʊshəʊld tʃɔː]	*chore = task*	Haushaltsarbeit
laundry [ˈlɔːndri]	*= washing clothes*	Wäsche
105		
join together [ˌdʒɔɪn təˈgeðə]	*I can't join the parts of this table together.*	zusammenfügen
minor [ˌmaɪnər]	*It's only a minor injury.*	geringfügig
look after sb [ˌlʊk ˈɑːftə]	*Can you look after Tim this evening, please?*	sich kümmern um, betreuen
105 t		
sort of thing [ˌsɔːt əv ˈθɪŋ]	*I enjoy walking, running, that sort of thing.*	Sache, Sachen
specific [spəˈsɪfɪk]	*I'm sorry, I can't be more specific.*	genau, präzise
spare time [ˌspeə ˈtaɪm]	*What do you do in your spare time?*	Freizeit
105		
careers adviser [kəˈrɪəz ədvaɪzə]	*A careers adviser helps people to find jobs.*	Berufsberater/in
jobseeker profile [ˌdʒɒbsiːkə ˈprəʊfaɪl]	*And a jobseeker profile helps the careers adviser to do this.*	Bewerberprofil
be good at sth [bi ˈgʊd ət]	*What are you good at?*	gut in etw sein, etw gut können
106		
talent [ˈtælənt]	*What talents do pop stars need?*	Talent, Begabung
succeed [səkˈsiːd]	*You won't succeed in this business if you aren't tough.*	Erfolg haben
perform [pəˈfɔːm]	*The band performed all their big hits.*	auftreten (mit)
audience [ˈɔːdiəns]	*The audience loved the music.*	Publikum
improvement [ɪmˈpruːvmənt]	*The company has made lots of improvements to the product.*	Verbesserung
recording studio [rɪˈkɔːdɪŋ stjuːdiəʊ]	*Are there any recording studios near where you live?*	Aufnahmestudio
track [træk]	*How many tracks are there on the new CD?*	Spur, Stück, Song
107		
piano [piˈænəʊ]	*I can't play the piano.*	Klavier
music industry [ˌmjuːzɪk ˈɪndəstri]	*She works in the music industry.*	Musikbranche

UNIT 12 How others live

108		
au pair [ˌəʊ 'peə]	*She's working as a German au pair for an English family.*	Au-pair-Mädchen
holiday resort ['hɒlədeɪ rɪzɔ:t]	*I'd like to work for a big hotel in a holiday resort.*	Urlaubsort
farm [fɑ:m]	*They have a small farm in Louisiana.*	Bauernhof, Farm
conservation [ˌkɒnsə'veɪʃn]	*Conservation of the world's wildlife is important.*	Naturschutz
volunteer [ˌvɒlən'tɪə]	*As a volunteer, I don't get any money from the organization.*	Freiwillige/r
place to stay [ˌpleɪs tə 'steɪ]	*If you need a place to stay in London, come to me.*	Unterkunft, Logis
surprised [sə'praɪzd]	*He just phoned me – I was really surprised.*	überrascht, erstaunt
lonely ['ləʊnli]	*All my friends are on holiday, so I feel lonely.*	einsam
nickname ['nɪkneɪm]	*My nickname for internet chatrooms is "Byteboy."*	Spitzname
109		
willing ['wɪlɪŋ]	*The hospital needs willing helpers for the summer party.*	bereit(willig), arbeitswillig
working visa ['wɜ:kiŋ vi:zə]	*If you're going to work in Australia, you need a working visa.*	Arbeitserlaubnis
organic farm [ɔ:ˌgænɪk 'fɑ:m]	*Food from organic farms is very healthy.*	Bio-Bauernhof, Öko-Farm
board [bɔ:d]	*You don't need to pay for food, you're given free board.*	Kost, Verpflegung
lodging ['lɒdʒɪŋ]	*You don't need a hotel, you're given free lodging.*	Logis, Unterkunft
host family [həʊst 'fæməli]	*You're going to live with a host family.*	Gastfamilie
exotic [ɪg'zɒtɪk]	*Aussprache*	exotisch
Outback ['aʊtbæk]	*The Australian Outback is big and empty countryside.*	australischer Busch
kangaroo [ˌkæŋgə'ru:]	*Aussprache*	Känguru
outsider [ˌaut'saɪdə]	*You can feel like an outsider in exotic countries.*	Außenseiter/in
immigrant ['ɪmɪgrənt]	*I was 9 years old when I came to England as an immigrant from Somalia.*	Einwanderer, Einwanderin
powered by ['paʊəd baɪ]	*My mobile is powered by two batteries.*	versorgt mit
solar energy [ˌsəʊlə 'enədʒi]	*If the sun shines enough, solar energy is a good idea.*	Sonnenenergie
rainwater tank ['reɪnwɔ:tə tæŋk]	*We collect rainwater in special tanks.*	Regenwassertank, Regentonne
chemical ['kemɪkl]	*Organic farms don't use chemicals.*	Chemikalie
vegetable ['vedʒtəbl]	*I eat mostly vegetables.*	Gemüse
plant [plɑ:nt]	*Let's plant a tree in the garden.*	pflanzen
chicken ['tʃɪkɪn]		Huhn
sheep [ʃi:p]	*Plural: sheep*	Schaf
goat [gəʊt]		Ziege
downside ['daʊnsaɪd]	*The downside of the holiday resort is that there are too many people.*	Nachteil, Haken
isolated ['aɪsəleɪtɪd]	*The hotel is quite isolated, so you need a car.*	isoliert
gorgeous ['gɔ:dʒəs]	*The countryside here is just gorgeous!*	prachtvoll, wunderschön
unspoilt [ʌn'spɔɪlt]	*Not many people come here, so it's all quite unspoilt.*	unberührt, unzerstört
nature ['neɪtʃə]	*I want to do voluntary work for nature conservation.*	Natur
wonder ['wʌndə]	*You love nature – no wonder you like animals too!*	Wunder
laid-back [ˌleɪd 'bæk]	*He doesn't have much stress, no wonder he's laid-back.*	entspannt
protect [prə'tekt]	*If we don't protect the animals here, they will all die.*	schützen, beschützen
environment [ɪn'vaɪrənmənt]	*We have to protect the environment before it's too late.*	Umwelt
continent ['kɒntɪnənt]	*Australia is a continent, like Africa or Europe.*	Erdteil, Kontinent
amount [ə'maʊnt]	*A small amount of money from everybody will help a lot.*	Menge
agriculture ['ægrɪkʌltʃə]	*There aren't many jobs in agriculture.*	Landwirtschaft
make sth worse [meɪk 'wɜ:s]	*The film wasn't good, and the small TV screen made it worse.*	verschlimmern
global warming [ˌgləʊbl 'wɔ:mɪŋ]	*Global warming is a very serious problem.*	Erderwärmung
110		
dangerous ['deɪndʒərəs]	*I wouldn't go out at night here. It's dangerous!*	gefährlich
in some ways [ɪn sʌm 'weɪz]	*In some ways, I prefer activity holidays to beach holidays.*	in mancher Hinsicht
farmwork ['fɑ:mwɜ:k]	*Farmwork is hard work.*	Landarbeit

i:	ɪ	e	æ	ɑ:	ɒ	ɔ:	ʊ	u:	ʌ	ɜ:	ə
see	sit	ten	bad	arm	got	saw	put	too	cut	bird	about

look forward to [ˌlʊk 'fɔ:wəd tə]	*I'm looking forward to seeing you soon.*	sich freuen auf
111		
equal(ly) ['i:kwəli]	*There's an equal number of boys and girls in the class.*	
FAQs (= frequently asked questions) [ˌef eɪ 'kju:z ˌfri:kwəntli ɑ:skt 'kwestʃənz]	*Lots of companies answer FAQs on their website.*	häufig gestellte Fragen
pronounce [prə'naʊns]	*It's difficult to pronounce my name correctly.*	aussprechen
method ['meθəd]	*What method of farming is used on this farm?*	Methode, Verfahren
make a booking [meɪk ə 'bʊkɪŋ]	*Do you want to make a booking for this hotel?*	eine Reservierung vornehmen
invent [ɪn'vent]	*Who invented the computer?*	erfinden
oil [ɔɪl]	*One day there won't be enough oil for all the cars in the world.*	Öl
cricket ['krɪkɪt]	*There are lots of cricket fans in England.*	Kricket
member ['membə]	*I'm a member of the cricket club here.*	Mitglied
112		
traffic ['træfɪk]	*There's always a lot of traffic in town centres.*	(Straßen-)Verkehr
soccer ['sɒkə]	*'Soccer' is another word for 'football.'*	Fußball
formal ['fɔ:ml]	*People who work in banks have to be quite formal.*	formell, förmlich
castle ['kɑ:sl]	*If you want to see castles, go to Germany or France.*	Burg, Schloss
meat [mi:t]	*I don't like meat.*	Fleisch
112 t		
historic building [hɪˌstɒrɪk 'bɪldɪŋ]	*The historic buildings here are about 800 to 1200 years old.*	historisches Gebäude
back home [bæk 'həʊm]	*Back home in Germany, Daniela's family is waiting for news.*	daheim
traffic jam ['træfɪk dʒæm]	*After the accident there was a terrible traffic jam.*	Stau
surprise [sə'praɪz]	*They surprised me – I didn't think they would come.*	überraschen
surname ['sɜ:neɪm]	*My surname is Fox.*	Nach-, Familienname
match [mætʃ]	*Let's watch the football match on TV later.*	Spiel
112		
official [ə'fɪʃl]	*'Soccer' is the official name for football in Great Britain.*	offiziell
general term ['dʒenrəl tɜ:m]	*General terms are useful, but often you need to be exact.*	Oberbegriff
113		
interpreter [ɪn'tɜ:prɪtə]	*They didn't speak the same language, so they needed an interpreter.*	Dolmetscher/in
draw [drɔ:]	*Here's a pencil and paper – can you draw a horse for me?*	zeichnen
mind map ['maɪnd mæp]	*A mind map is useful when you're brainstorming.*	Gedankengerüst
advice [əd'vaɪs]	*I can give you some advice about travelling to Australia.*	Ratschlag, Ratschläge
starting point ['stɑ:tɪŋ pɔɪnt]	*Frankfurt airport was the starting point for our journey to Australia.*	Ausgangspunkt

The world of work

114		
office ['ɒfɪs]	*Clerks often work in offices.*	Büro
busy ['bɪzi]	*In the holidays, the shops here are very busy.*	beschäftigt, hier: umtriebig
graphic designer [ˌgræfɪk dɪ'zaɪnə]	*Graphic designers need lots of good ideas.*	Grafiker/in
creative [kri'eɪtɪv]	*She's very creative – she writes her own songs.*	kreativ
reliable [rɪ'laɪəbl]	*My car isn't very reliable; it's too old.*	zuverlässig
accounts clerk [ə'kaʊnts klɑ:k]	*= bookkeeper*	Buchhalter/in
secretary ['sekrətri]	*My secretary organizes my office – and me!*	Sekretär/in
update [ˌʌp'deɪt]	*I think I have to update my software soon.*	aktualisieren
financial [faɪ'nænʃl]	*I'm not very good at financial things – I hate numbers.*	finanziell, Finanz-
be responsible for [bi rɪ'spɒnsəbl fə]	*As a teacher, I'm responsible for the pupils.*	verantwortlich sein
switch on [ˌswɪtʃ 'ɒn]	*Can you switch on the TV please?*	anschalten, einschalten

urgent ['ɜːdʒənt]	*Mark, come quickly. There's an urgent phone call for you!*	dringend
straight away [streɪt ə'weɪ]	*This is urgent. Please do it straight away.*	sofort, gleich, auf der Stelle, umgehend
vary ['veəri]	*What time do you start work? – It varies.*	unterschiedlich sein, variieren
paperwork ['peɪpəwɜːk]	*We use computers, of course, but there's still a lot of paperwork to do.*	Papierkram
invoice ['ɪnvɔɪs]	*If you order something on the internet, you usually get an invoice.*	Rechnung
managing director [ˌmænɪdʒɪŋ də'rektə]	*Ms Lee is the big boss, I mean, the managing director.*	Geschäftsführer/in
visitor ['vɪzɪtə]	*We're popular, we always have lots of visitors.*	Besucher/in, Gast
hectic ['hektɪk]	*Work can get quite hectic in the office.*	hektisch
mixed-up [ˌmɪkst 'ʌp]	*I feel so mixed-up today. I can't work well.*	durcheinander gewürfelt
115		
diary ['daɪəri]	*(Taschen-)Kalender = diary, (Wand-)Kalender = calendar*	Terminkalender, Terminplan
filing system ['faɪlɪŋ sɪstəm]	*A filing system helps you to find papers.*	Ablagesystem
destination [ˌdestɪ'neɪʃn]	*Mallorca is a popular holiday destination.*	Ziel, Bestimmungsort
bank statement ['bæŋk steɪtmənt]	*I look at my bank statements online.*	Kontoauszug
115 t		
in-tray ['ɪn treɪ]	*The in-tray is for all the post that came in today.*	(Post-)Eingangskorb
116		
sponsor ['spɒnsə]	*Our company is one of the sponsors for the local football team.*	Geldgeber/in, Sponsor/in
hold [həʊld]	*We hold all our meetings in this room.*	veranstalten
take part [teɪk 'pɑːt]	*I'm going to take part in the new project.*	teilnehmen, mitmachen
age limit ['eɪdʒ lɪmɪt]	*The age limit for driving a car in Britain is 17.*	Altersgrenze
keep in mind [ˌkiːp ɪn 'maɪnd]	*Please keep me in mind for that summer job.*	daran denken, beachten
drug addict ['drʌg ædɪkt]	*Andy is a drug addict. He takes hard drugs.*	Drogenabhängige/r
ecotourism [ˌiːkəʊ 'tʊərɪzəm]	*Ecotourism is better for the environment.*	Ökotourismus
arrange [ə'reɪndʒ]	*Please arrange the hotel for our meeting.*	arrangieren, organisieren
guide [gaɪd]	*Lights guided the ship into the port.*	anleiten
provide [prə'vaɪd]	*We will provide breakfast every morning.*	zur Verfügung stellen
117		
atmosphere ['ætməsfɪə]	*There was a great atmosphere at the party.*	Stimmung, Atmosphäre

UNIT 13 Modern love

118		
teenage dad ['tiːneɪdʒ dæd]	*I was a father before I was 20, a teenage dad.*	Vater im Teenager-Alter
metalworker ['metlwɜːkə]	*Declan works with metal. He's a metalworker.*	Metallarbeiter/in
pregnant ['pregnənt]	*Sally is pregnant. She's in the third month.*	schwanger
take sth badly [teɪk 'bædli]	*Her parents took the news badly.*	etw schlecht aufnehmen, dagegen sein
strict [strɪkt]	*My dad is so strict. I can't do anything!*	streng
Catholic ['kæθəlɪk]	*Most Irish people are Catholics.*	Katholik/in; katholisch
ruin ['ruːɪn]	*Alcohol ruins many lives.*	ruinieren
abortion [ə'bɔːʃn]	*Abortion is a difficult topic.*	Abtreibung, Schwangerschaftsabbruch
get married [get 'mærid]	*I don't want to get married too young.*	heiraten
independent [ˌɪndɪ'pendənt]	*I want to look after myself and be independent.*	unabhängig
ban (from sth) [bæn]	*Kings School pupils are banned from this shop.*	verbannen (aus)
get a woman pregnant [get ə ˌwʊmən 'pregnənt]	*Declan got his girlfriend pregnant.*	eine Frau schwängern
afterwards ['ɑːftəwədz]	*Two more hours! Afterwards, we can have fun.*	nachher, danach, hinterher
upbringing ['ʌpbrɪŋɪŋ]	*Some children don't have a good upbringing.*	Erziehung
childminder ['tʃaɪldmaɪndə]	*I'm a childminder. I look after other people's children.*	Tagesmutter

iː	ɪ	e	æ	ɑː	ɒ	ɔː	ʊ	uː	ʌ	ɜː	ə
see	sit	ten	bad	arm	got	saw	put	too	cut	bird	about

gang [gæŋ]	*I meet all my friends on Friday. We're a great gang.*	Clique
adore [ə'dɔː]	*I adore her new CD. It's so good.*	anhimmeln, nach jdm verrückt sein
attention [ə'tenʃn]	*Listen. This is important. I need all your attention.*	Aufmerksamkeit
be worried about sth [bi 'wʌrid əbaʊt]	*I'm worried about the exam next week.*	sich um etw Sorgen machen
119		
single parent [ˌsɪŋgl 'peərənt]	*My son's mother has left me. I'm a single parent now.*	Alleinerziehende/r
121		
battery ['bætəri]	*Mobile phones need batteries.*	Batterie
122		
fire sb ['faɪə]	*The manager said, "You're fired!"*	jdn feuern, entlassen
drop sth [drɒp]	*I dropped my mobile and now it's broken.*	etw fallen lassen
kiss [kɪs]	*I'm worried. My boyfriend didn't kiss me yesterday.*	küssen
123		
result [rɪ'zʌlt]	*My exam results were very good.*	Ergebnis
123 t		
definite ['defɪnət]	*The doctor says it's definite. I'm pregnant.*	fest, definitiv

The world of work

124		
manufacturing [ˌmænju'fæktʃərɪŋ]	*Manufacturing companies make things.*	Fertigung, Herstellung, Produktion
numerical(ly) [njuː'merɪkli]	*"One thousand" is "1,000" numerically.*	numerisch
controlled [kən'trəʊld]	*A plane is controlled by the pilot.*	gesteuert
engineering [ˌendʒɪ'nɪərɪŋ]	*You have to be good at maths for engineering.*	Ingenieurwesen, Maschinenbau
manufacture [ˌmænju'fæktʃə]	*= make*	herstellen, produzieren
component [kəm'pəʊnənt]	*= part*	Bauteil
spacecraft ['speɪskrɑːft]	⚠ *one spacecraft, two spacecraft*	Raumfahrzeug, -schiff
Leaving Certificate ['liːvɪŋ səˌtɪfɪkət]	*Successful pupils get a Leaving Certificate.*	Abgangs-, Abschlusszeugnis
machinist [mə'ʃiːnɪst]	*A machinist works at a machine.*	Maschinenschlosser/in, Maschinist
keen [kiːn]	*I'm really keen to get the job. I want it so much!*	(sehr) interessiert
come up [ˌkʌm 'ʌp]	*Don't worry. Another job will come up soon.*	sich ergeben
rocket ['rɒkɪt]	*A rocket sends spacecraft into space.*	Rakete
operate ['ɒpəreɪt]	*I can't operate this DVD player.*	bedienen, arbeiten an
mill [mɪl]	*Put the metal in the mill, please.*	Fräse
basically ['beɪsɪkli]	*The basic idea is very simple.*	grundsätzlich, eigentlich
timeline ['taɪmlaɪn]	*A timeline tells you when things happened.*	Zeitachse
125		
quantity ['kwɒntəti]	*We need a few boxes, please – just a small quantity.*	Menge
vehicle ['viːəkl]	*There are too many vehicles on the roads.*	Fahrzeug
science ['saɪəns]	*Science was my favourite subject at school.*	Wissenschaft
shape [ʃeɪp]	*The carpenter shaped the wood for the doors.*	formen
plastic ['plæstɪk]	*I don't like plastic chairs.*	Plastik, Kunststoff
enter ['entə]	*Please enter your email address.*	eingeben
computerized [kəm'pjuːtəraɪzd]	*Most cars are computerized now.*	computergesteuert
encourage [ɪn'kʌrɪdʒ]	*My dad encouraged me to get an apprenticeship.*	ermutigen, fördern, unterstützen
brewing ['bruːɪŋ]	*Machines do a lot of the work in brewing.*	Brauereigewerbe
papermaking ['peɪpə meɪkɪŋ]	*Papermaking is a noisy job.*	Papierherstellung
food processing ['fʊd prəʊsesɪŋ]	*Food processing saves time later for customers.*	Lebensmittelherstellung

125 t

overtime ['əʊvətaɪm]	*I do a lot of overtime every week.*	Überstunden
(vocational) qualification [vəʊˌkeɪʃənl ˌkwɒlɪfɪ'keɪʃn]	*I can get a vocational qualification here too.*	Berufsausbildung
touch [tʌtʃ]	*Don't touch the food!*	berühren, anfassen
starting salary ['stɑ:tɪŋ sæləri]	*The starting salary isn't great, but I want the job.*	Anfangsgehalt

125

make a point [meɪk ə 'pɔɪnt]	*I want to make a positive point about my work.*	ein Argument anbringen

126

nowadays ['naʊədeɪz]	*Nowadays it is not so unusual when parents get divorced.*	heutzutage
confused [kən'fju:zd]	*I was confused by all the bad things I read about my favourite band.*	verwirrt
get divorced [get dɪ'vɔ:st]	*Have you heard? Sue and Frank are getting divorced!*	sich scheiden lassen
relationship [rɪ'leɪʃnʃɪp]	*I have a very good relationship with my girlfriend.*	Beziehung, Verhältnis
get married [get 'mærid]	*We're going to get married one day.*	heiraten
argue ['ɑ:gju:]	*Don't argue. We have to go – now!*	(sich) streiten
after all [ˌɑ:ftər 'ɔ:l]	*Why don't you come with us? It was your idea after all!*	schließlich (doch)

127

consider [kən'sɪdə]	*You have to consider the effects of planes on the environment.*	bedenken, berücksichtigen

UNIT 14 Kicking the habit

128

standpoint ['stændpɔɪnt]	*≈ view*	Standpunkt
be in favour of sth [bi ɪn 'feɪvər əv]	*We're all in favour of solar power.*	für etw sein, etw befürworten
carry on [ˌkæri 'ɒn]	*The music stopped, but she carried on dancing.*	weitermachen
refuse [rɪ'fju:z]	*I was so angry, I refused to answer.*	sich weigern
shocking ['ʃɒkɪŋ]	*Even my father danced – that was really shocking.*	schrecklich, schockierend
shorten ['ʃɔ:tn]	*The film was too long, so they shortened it by 30 minutes.*	kürzen
packet ['pækɪt]	*Throw away your cigarette packet and stop smoking now!*	Packung, Schachtel
health warning ['helθ wɔ:nɪŋ]	*"Smoking kills" is one of the health warnings on cigarette packets.*	Hinweis auf Gesundheitsgefahren
ban [bæn]	*Smoking will be banned in all restaurants soon.*	verbieten
public building [ˌpʌblɪk 'bɪldɪŋ]	*Everybody can walk into a public building.*	öffentliches Gebäude
anti-smoking [ˌænti 'sməʊkɪŋ]	*The class made anti-smoking posters for their school.*	Nichtraucher-
argument ['ɑ:gjumənt]	*We collected lots of anti-smoking arguments in class.*	Argument
attractive [ə'træktɪv]	⚠ *Aussprache*	attraktiv, anziehend
opposite sex ['ɒpəzɪt seks]	*For men, women are the opposite sex.*	das andere Geschlecht
tooth [tu:θ]	*My teeth are very good, but I lost one tooth when I was a teenager.*	Zahn
wrinkle ['rɪŋkl]	*My grandfather's face is full of wrinkles.*	Falte
breath [breθ]	*Smoking gives you bad breath.*	Atem
skin [skɪn]	*She's old but she still has nice skin.*	Haut
smell [smel]	*The room smells of food.*	riechen, stinken
in fact [ɪn 'fækt]	*She looks good. In fact, I think she's very attractive.*	tatsächlich, eigentlich
smoker ['sməʊkə]	*We left the restaurant because there were too many smokers.*	Raucher/in
go out with sb [ˌgəʊ 'aʊt wɪð]	*I saw you two last night. Are you going out together?*	mit jdm ausgehen
heart [hɑ:t]	*My heart is beating really fast.*	Herz
lung [lʌŋ]	*Smoking can give you lung problems.*	Lunge
efficient(ly) [ɪ'fɪʃntli]	*He's a fast and efficient worker.*	leistungsfähig
besides [bɪ'saɪdz]	*I'm too old for sport now. Besides, I'm ill.*	außerdem, abgesehen (da)von
government ['gʌvənmənt]	*The government of this country isn't very efficient.*	Regierung
discourage [dɪs'kʌrɪdʒ]	*My parents tried to discourage me from smoking.*	abbringen von
illegal [ɪ'li:gl]	*It's illegal to smoke if you're under 16.*	illegal, verboten, gesetzwidrig

iː	ɪ	e	æ	ɑː	ɒ	ɔː	ʊ	uː	ʌ	ɜː	ə
see	sit	ten	bad	arm	got	saw	put	too	cut	bird	about

129		
impotence ['ɪmpətəns]	*Smoking can cause impotence.*	Impotenz
130		
pro- [ˌprəʊ]	↔ *anti*	pro-, für
non-smoker [ˌnɒn 'sməʊkə]	↔ *smoker*	Nichtraucher/in
131		
health freak ['helθ friːk]	*I'm no health freak, but I don't smoke and I do a lot of sport.*	Gesundheitsapostel
junk food ['dʒʌŋk fuːd]	*I try to eat as little junk food as possible.*	minderwertiges Essen
hit [hɪt]	*The bus hit the parked car.*	gegen etw fahren
132		
pill [pɪl]	*My mother is ill and has to take lots of pills.*	Pille
unmarked [ʌn'mɑːkt]	*They didn't know what to do when they found the unmarked bag.*	unbezeichnet, ohne Adresse
envelope ['envələʊp]	*I opened the envelope and took out a letter.*	Briefumschlag
unpredictable [ˌʌnprɪ'dɪktəbl]	*The weather in April is unpredictable.*	unvorhersagbar
effect [ɪ'fekt]	*Global warming will have a terrible effect one day.*	Wirkung
reaction [ri'ækʃn]	*What was his reaction to the news?*	Reaktion
panic attack [ˌpænɪk ə'tæk]	*In a panic attack, your heart beats very fast.*	Panikanfall
cannabis ['kænəbɪs]	*Buying or selling cannabis is illegal in many countries.*	Haschisch
tense [tens]	*I feel so tense. It must be all the stress.*	angespannt, nervös
frightened ['fraɪtnd]	*I felt really frightened after the film.*	verängstigt, erschreckt
pull o.s. together [ˌpʊl tə'geðə]	*I felt terrible, but I had to pull myself together for the interview.*	sich zusammenreißen, -nehmen
dimly-lit [ˌdɪmli 'lɪt]	*They went into a dimly-lit bar.*	schwach beleuchtet, schummerig
calm(ly) ['kɑːmli]	↔ *nervous(ly)*	ruhig
become [bɪ'kʌm]	*Suddenly I became very tired.*	werden
drowsy ['draʊzi]	*I feel a bit drowsy after all that food.*	schläfrig, müde
tranquillizer ['træŋkwəlaɪzə]	*The doctor gave me tranquillizers for the panic attacks.*	Beruhigungsmittel
glue [gluː]	*I needed glue to close the envelope.*	Klebstoff
unconscious [ʌn'kɒnʃəs]	*I was unconscious after the accident.*	bewusstlos
overdose ['əʊvədəʊs]	*Don't take too many of these pills – an overdose can kill you.*	Überdosis
ambulance ['æmbjələns]	*Quick, call an ambulance and the police!*	Krankenwagen
affect [ə'fekt]	*The weather doesn't affect our dog.*	beeinträchtigen, betreffen
body ['bɒdi]	*Hands and feet are parts of the body.*	Körper
ability [ə'bɪləti]	*Drinking beer affects your ability to drive a car.*	Fähigkeit
sleep sth off [ˌsliːp 'ɒf]	*He's had too much beer. I think he has to sleep it off.*	etw ausschlafen
fruit juice ['fruːt dʒuːs]	*I don't like fruit juice – it's too sweet for me.*	Fruchtsaft
133 t		
reckon ['rekən]	*I reckon that the weather will be fine tomorrow.*	glauben, der Meinung sein, denken
smack [smæk]	*It's illegal to smack a child.*	einen Klaps geben
brightly lit [ˌbraɪtli 'lɪt]	↔ *dimly lit*	hell erleuchtet
sleepy ['sliːpi]	≈ *tired, drowsy*	schläfrig
keep an eye on sb [kiːp ən 'aɪ ɒn]	*Can you keep an eye on my dog for a minute?*	auf jdn aufpassen
pass out [ˌpɑːs 'aʊt]	≈ *become unconscious*	ohnmächtig werden
133		
forum thread ['fɔːrəm θred]	*If you have a question about a topic, start a thread in a forum.*	Thread in einem Internet-Forum
sniff [snɪf]	*The dog sniffed everywhere and found the drugs.*	schnüffeln
spaced out [ˌspeɪst 'aʊt]	*Taking drugs can make you feel spaced out.*	breit, auf Droge
stink [stɪŋk]	*Their house stinks of cats.*	stinken
deny [dɪ'naɪ]	*I know that Kim did it, but she denies it.*	abstreiten
beat sb up [ˌbiːt 'ʌp]	*They didn't just smack him, they really beat him up.*	jdn zusammenschlagen
be over the moon [bi ˌəʊvə ðə 'muːn]	*I'm over the moon about her letter. It's great!*	überglücklich sein

couple ['kʌpl]	*You can't even have a couple of beers when you're driving.*	Paar, paar
drunk [drʌŋk]	*He was so drunk, he was ill for a couple of days.*	betrunken
cold [kəʊld]	*↔ warm*	kalt
violent ['vaɪələnt]	*Violent people beat other people up.*	gewalttätig
scare sb [skeə]	*The man really scared me. I was so frightened!*	jdm Angst einjagen

The world of work

134		
make a difference [meɪk ə 'dɪfrəns]	*I want to make a difference, because I really care about people.*	etw bewegen, etw verändern
youth worker ['ju:θ wɜ:kə]	*Youth workers help young people.*	Sozialarbeiter/in für Jugendliche
community centre [kə'mju:nəti sentə]	*Every month there's a disco night at the community centre.*	Bürgerzentrum
college ['kɒlɪdʒ]	*After school you can go to college.*	Fachschule, Hochschule
get sb involved [get ɪn'vɒlvd]	*My new friend got me involved in the youth club.*	jdn dazu bringen, sich zu engagieren
worthwhile [ˌwɜ:θ'waɪl]	*Looking after old people is very worthwhile.*	lohnend, der Mühe wert (sein)
unemployment [ˌʌnɪm'plɔɪmənt]	*After a year of unemployment, she found a great job.*	Arbeitslosigkeit
drug abuse [ˌdrʌg ə'bju:s]	*Alcohol or drug abuse can kill people.*	Drogenmissbrauch
remember [rɪ'membə]	*Do you remember that great party last year?*	daran denken, sich merken
get together [ˌget tə'geðə]	*People get together to talk about work or just to have fun.*	sich treffen, zusammenkommen
sexual abuse [ˌsekʃuəl ə'bju:s]	*In some families there is sexual abuse of children.*	sexueller Missbrauch
put sb in touch with sb [ˌpʊt ɪn 'tʌtʃ wɪð]	*If you need advice, I can put you in touch with a youth worker.*	jdn an jdn verweisen, jdn mit jdn in Verbindung setzen
get a life [get ə 'laɪf]	*Work isn't the most important thing. You have to get a life too.*	was Interessanteres machen
135		
create [kri'eɪt]	*The government has to create more jobs for young people.*	(er)schaffen, machen
decorate ['dekəreɪt]	*I love painting and decorating houses.*	tapezieren, streichen, renovieren
135 t		
aimed at ['eɪmd ət]	*The book is aimed at young children.*	an ... gerichtet
homeless ['həʊmləs]	*Homeless people have lots of problems.*	obdachlos
move into a house / flat [ˌmu:v ɪntu ə 'haʊs, 'flæt]	*We moved from a flat into a house.*	in ein Haus/eine Wohnung ziehen
135		
competition [ˌkɒmpə'tɪʃn]	*Who won the competition?*	Wettbewerb
aspect ['æspekt]	⚠ *Aussprache*	Aspekt
equipment [ɪ'kwɪpmənt]	*I've got all my sports equipment in this bag.*	Ausrüstung, Geräte
136		
on the way home [ɒn ðə ˌweɪ 'həʊm]	*Tim was on his way home when his mobile rang.*	auf dem Nachhauseweg
night club ['naɪt klʌb]	*After the film we went to a nightclub.*	Nachtklub
close [kləʊz]	*Close the window, please.*	zumachen, schließen
crowd [kraʊd]	*There was a crowd outside the studios.*	(Menschen-)Menge
light [laɪt]	*Wear light clothes tomorrow. It will be hot!*	leicht
shirt [ʃɜ:t]		Hemd
skirt [skɜ:t]		Rock
against the law [əˌgenst ðə 'lɔ:]	*Selling drugs is against the law.*	illegal
walk [wɔ:k]	*It was a long walk home*	Weg, Gang, Wanderung
care [keə]	*How much do you care about where you live?*	sich kümmern (um)
I/We don't care [ˌaɪ dəʊnt 'keə]	*I don't care what my parents say.*	das ist mir/uns egal
feel sick [fi:l 'sɪk]	*I'm feeling sick this morning.*	sich krank/unwohl fühlen
headache pill ['hedeɪk pɪl]	*Can I have a headache pill, please, Mum?*	Kopfschmerztablette

i:	ɪ	e	æ	ɑ:	ɒ	ɔ:	ʊ	u:	ʌ	ɜ:	ə
see	sit	ten	bad	arm	got	saw	put	too	cut	bird	about

UNIT 15 Drive to arrive alive

138		
cover ['kʌvə]	*The road was covered in ice.*	zu-, abdecken
139		
public transport [ˌpʌblɪk 'trænspɔ:t]	*Public transport in cities is usually cheap.*	öffentliche Verkehrsmittel, öffentlicher Nahverkehr
usefulness ['ju:sfəlnəs]	*What's the usefulness of cars in cities?*	Nützlichkeit
eco-friendliness [ˌi:kəʊ 'frendlinəs]	*The eco-friendliness of electric trains is important.*	Umweltfreundlichkeit
beat-up [ˌbi:t 'ʌp]	*My car isn't new, it's really beat-up.*	kaputt
brand new [ˌbrænd 'nju:]	*Sue's car is brand new. She bought it last week.*	nagelneu
four-wheel drive [ˌfɔ:wi:l 'draɪv]	*You don't need a four-wheel drive car in towns.*	Vierradantrieb
beauty ['bju:ti]	*My new bike looks great. It's a real beauty.*	Schönheit
powerful ['paʊəfl]	*The President is very powerful.*	leistungsstark
celebrate ['selɪbreɪt]	*How are you going to celebrate your birthday?*	feiern
buddy ['bʌdi]	*= friend*	Kumpel, Freund
downtown ['daʊntaʊn]	*The shops and restaurants are downtown.*	(im/ins) Stadtzentrum
back seat [ˌbæk 'si:t]	*Children must sit in the back seat.*	Rücksitz
cruise around [ˌkru:z ə'raʊnd]	*We aren't going anywhere, we're just cruising around.*	herumfahren
hang out [ˌhæŋ 'aʊt]	*Oh no! That little boy is hanging out of the window.*	rumhängen
call out [ˌkɔ:l 'aʊt]	*Don't call out to him. He'll fall.*	rufen
behavior (AE) [bɪ'heɪvjə]	*BE: behaviour.*	Verhalten, Benehmen
dumb (AE) [dʌm]	*It's very dumb to drink and drive.*	blöd, doof
lame [leɪm]	*People who are very interested in computers can seem lame.*	lahm, hier: blöd
out of control [ˌaʊt əv kən'trəʊl]	*The spacecraft was out of control.*	außer Kontrolle
calm down [ˌkɑ:m 'daʊn]	*Calm down. We aren't going to miss the plane.*	(sich) beruhigen
quit [kwɪt]	*I want to quit smoking.*	aufhören mit
fool around [ˌfu:l ə'raʊnd]	*You shouldn't fool around with drugs.*	herumalbern
intersection [ˌɪntə'sekʃn]	*Turn right at the intersection.*	Kreuzung
yell at sb ['jel ət]	*Don't yell at your dog.*	jdn anschreien, anbrüllen
across [ə'krɒs]	*I walked across the road.*	(her)über
swerve [swɜ:v]	*The bus swerved to the right to miss the car.*	das Steuer/Auto herumreißen, einen Schlenker machen
run into ['rʌn ɪntə]	*= crash into*	gegen ... fahren
driver's door ['draɪvəz dɔ:]	*The driver's door is still open.*	Fahrertür
cop [kɒp]	*She's a cop, I mean, a police officer.*	Polizist, Bulle
turn up [ˌtɜ:n 'ʌp]	*He turned up late for the interview.*	auftauchen
be hard on sb [ˌbi 'hɑ:d ɒn]	*My dad was hard on me when I got home late.*	mit jdm hart ins Gericht gehen
fault [fɔ:lt]	*The crash was your fault.*	Schuld
court [kɔ:t]	*I have to go to court because of the crash.*	Gericht
judge [dʒʌdʒ]	*There was a really tough judge in court.*	Richter/in
fine [faɪn]	*The fine for my bad driving was $500.*	Geldstrafe, Bußgeld
apologize [ə'pɒlədʒaɪz]	*Say sorry to her. You must apologize.*	sich entschuldigen
community service [kə'mju:nəti sɜ:vɪs]	*I did my community service at an old people's home.*	gemeinnützige Tätigkeit
garage ['gærɑ:ʒ]	*The car is in the garage.*	Garage
accident ['æksɪdənt]	*There was a terrible accident in Hill Street yesterday.*	Unfall
shake sb up [ˌʃeɪk 'ʌp]	*What Sally said really shook me up.*	aufschütteln, aufrütteln
still [stɪl]	*But I still want to be with her.*	noch immer
flashback ['flæʃbæk]	*I saw the accident again – in a flashback.*	Rückblende
unfair [ˌʌn'feə]	*It's unfair that women often earn less money than men.*	unfair, ungerecht

140		
colloquial [kə'ləʊkwiəl]	*"Cop" is a colloquial word for "police officer".*	umgangssprachlich
shout at sb ['ʃaʊt ət]	*Don't shout at me. It isn't my fault.*	jdn anschreien
be angry with sb [bi 'æŋgri wɪð]	*Tim was late and his girlfriend was very angry with him.*	auf jdn böse sein
to blame [bleɪm]	*It's your fault. = You are to blame.*	verantwortlich machen
kind of dumb [ˌkaɪnd əv 'dʌm]	*"That was a kind of dumb thing to do, Brad," said his dad.*	ziemlich blöd
letter of apology [ˌletər əv ə'pɒlədʒi]	*He said sorry in a letter of apology.*	Entschuldigungsbrief
141		
bench [bentʃ]	*Let's sit on a park bench.*	Bank
go skateboarding [gəʊ 'skeɪtbɔːdɪŋ]	*I'm going skateboarding this afternoon.*	Skateboard fahren
take a dog for a walk [teɪk ə ˌdɒg fər ə 'wɔːk]	*We take our dog for a walk three times a day.*	einen/den Hund ausführen
doorbell ['dɔːbel]	*That was the doorbell. There's somebody at the door.*	Türklingel
fall off [ˌfɔːl 'ɒf]	*Jill fell off her bike yesterday.*	herunterfallen (von)
142		
passenger ['pæsɪndʒə]	*The passengers were in the back seat.*	Fahrgast
be injured [bi 'ɪndʒəd]	*She was injured in the car crash.*	verletzt werden
driving instructor ['draɪvɪŋ instrʌktə]	*Driving instructors don't usually get nervous.*	Fahrlehrer/in
learner driver [ˌlɜːnə 'draɪvə]	*I'm a learner driver. I'm still learning to drive.*	(Fahr)Anfänger
pull away [ˌpʊl ə'weɪ]	*The bus pulled away from the bus stop.*	anfahren, wegfahren
roundabout ['raʊndəbaʊt]	*There are more roundabouts in Britain than in Germany.*	Kreisverkehr
brake [breɪk]	*Bikes have two brakes.*	Bremse
horn [hɔːn]	*Don't use your horn near the hospital.*	Hupe
142 t		
nightmare ['naɪtmeə]	*Dracula was in my bedroom. What a terrible nightmare!*	Albtraum
stall [stɔːl]	*Stalling the engine at a busy roundabout can be dangerous.*	abwürgen
cross [krɒs]	*= angry*	böse, ärgerlich
honk (a horn) [ˌhɒŋk ə 'hɔːn]	*I've told you before. Don't honk your horn near a hospital.*	hupen
heart attack ['hɑːt ətæk]	*John smoked too much and had a heart attack.*	Herzinfarkt, Herzanfall
slam on (the brakes) ['slæm ɒn ðə ˌbreɪks]	*The bus driver slammed on the brakes, but it was too late.*	auf die Bremse treten, eine Vollbremsung machen
nervous wreck [ˌnɜːvəs 'rek]	*It's the test tomorrow. I'm a nervous wreck.*	Nervenbündel
hopeless ['həʊpləs]	*I'm hopeless at cooking.*	hoffnungslos
make a mistake [ˌmeɪk ə mɪ'steɪk]	*I made a big mistake when I kissed Emma.*	einen Fehler machen

The world of work

144		
at the age of [ət ði 'eɪdʒ əv]	*I left home at the age of 18.*	im Alter von
courier company ['kʊriə kʌmpəni]	*Courier companies deliver parcels.*	Kurierdienst, Logistikunternehmen
logistics [lə'dʒɪstɪks]	*Logistics is all about moving goods.*	Logistik
supermarket chain ['suːpəmɑːkɪt tʃeɪn]	*Tesco is a chain. There's a Tesco supermarket in every town.*	Supermarktkette
practical ['præktɪkl]	*What practical experience do you have?*	praktisch
evening class ['iːvnɪŋ klɑːs]	*You can get more qualifications if you do evening classes.*	Abendschule, Abendschulkurs
145		
attend [ə'tend]	*What school did you attend before college?*	besuchen
part-time ['pɑːt taɪm]	*I work part-time, from 9 a.m. to 1 p.m.*	Teilzeit
predict [prɪ'dɪkt]	*Football experts can't predict who will win the match tomorrow.*	vorhersagen
offer ['ɒfə]	*He offered me a lot of money for my old car.*	anbieten

iː	ɪ	e	æ	ɑː	ɒ	ɔː	ʊ	uː	ʌ	ɜː	ə
see	sit	ten	bad	arm	got	saw	put	too	cut	bird	about

university [ˌjuːnɪ'vɜːsəti]	*This university has 10,000 students.*	Universität
145 t		
unusual [ʌn'juːʒuəl]	*It's unusual to earn a lot of money in your first job.*	ungewöhnlich
in theory [ɪn 'θɪəri]	*In theory men can stay at home and look after the children.*	theoretisch
proper ['prɒpə]	*You can't get a proper meal at "Joe's Café", just a snack.*	ordentlich, angemessen
lower-skilled ['ləʊə skɪld]	*Students often do lower-skilled jobs.*	mit geringeren Anforderungen
degree [dɪ'griː]	*You can get a degree at university.*	Abschluss
146		
attempt [ə'tempt]	*She passed on the first attempt.*	Versuch
learner ['lɜːnə]	*She isn't a learner driver any more.*	Fahrschüler /in
fail [feɪl]	*fail ↔ pass*	keinen Erfolg haben, scheitern (bei), durchfallen
plenty ['plenti]	*= lots*	genügend, viel, genug, reichlich
normal ['nɔːml]	*It's normal to be unhappy if you fail a test.*	normal
go well [ˌgəʊ 'wel]	*The test went well. I passed!*	gut gehen
examiner [ɪg'zæmɪnə]	*The examiner was very strict.*	Prüfer/in
majority [mə'dʒɒrəti]	*The majority of dogs don't like cats.*	Mehrheit
take a test [ˌteɪk ə 'test]	*You can always take the test again.*	eine Prüfung ablegen
motorway ['məʊtəweɪ]	*The A4 motorway passes Cologne.*	Autobahn
147		
success [sək'ses]	*success ↔ failure*	Erfolg
coat [kəʊt]	*Wear a coat. It's very cold.*	Mantel, Jacke

Further reading

Dieser Teil des Wörterverzeichnisses enthält alle neuen Wörter aus den *Further reading*-Texten im Anhang. Vorausgesetzt wird jeweils der Wortschatz aus dem Hauptteil des Buches einschließlich der entsprechenden Unit. D. h. der *Further reading*-Text zu Unit 7 setzt die Vokabeln der Units 1–7 sowie der *Further reading*-Texte 1-6 voraus.

UNIT 1

152	
adult ['ædʌlt]	Erwachsene/r
lazy ['leɪzi]	faul, träge
irresponsible [ˌɪrɪ'spɒnsəbl]	unverantwortlich
pocket money ['pɒkɪt mʌni]	Taschengeld
rude [ruːd]	unhöflich
care [keə]	sich kümmern um
recent ['riːsnt]	jünger
survey ['sɜːveɪ]	Studie, Untersuchung
make plans [meɪk 'plænz]	Pläne machen
concert ['kɑːnsərt]	Konzert
part-time [ˌpɑːt'taɪm]	Teilzeit-, Halbtags-
deliver [dɪ'lɪvə]	austragen, zustellen
wash [wɒʃ]	waschen
worry about sth ['wʌri əbaʊt]	sich um etw Sorgen machen
fear [fɪə]	Angst, Furcht
serious ['sɪəriəs]	schwer, ernst
illness ['ɪlnəs]	Krankheit
rob sb [rɒb]	jdn (be)rauben, jdn ausrauben
healthy ['helθi]	gesund
animal rights [ˌænɪml 'raɪts]	Tierrechte
consume [kən'sjuːm]	einnehmen, konsumieren
sick [sɪk]	krank
153	
dangerous ['deɪndʒərəs]	gefährlich
get on with sb [ˌget 'ɒn wɪð]	sich mit jdm verstehen

UNIT 2

154	
volunteer [ˌvɒlən'tɪə]	freiwillig (arbeiten)
for free [fər ˌfriː]	umsonst
free time [ˌfriː 'taɪm]	Freizeit
clean up [ˌkliːn 'ʌp]	sauber machen, aufräumen

countryside ['kʌntrisaɪd] Landschaft
campaign [kæm'peɪn] Kampagne, Aktion
volunteer [ˌvɒlən'tɪə] Freiwillige/r
wood [wʊd] (kleinerer) Wald
river ['rɪvə] Fluss
wild meadow [waɪld 'medəʊ] Wiese
Easter ['i:stə] Ostern
go away [ˌgəʊ ə'weɪ] verreisen
pupil ['pju:pl] Schüler/in
nature ['neɪtʃə] Natur
walk [wɔ:k] Spaziergang, Wanderung
authority [ɔ:'θɒrəti] Behörde, Amt, Verwaltung
take sth home [teɪk 'həʊm] mit nach Hause nehmen
rubbish ['rʌbɪʃ] Abfall, Müll
litter ['lɪtə] Müll, Abfall
bin [bɪn] Mülleimer, (Müll-)Tonne
all over the place [ɔ:l ˌəʊvə ðə 'pleɪs] überall in der Gegend
plant [plɑ:nt] Pflanze
animal ['ænɪml] Tier
springtime ['sprɪŋtaɪm] Frühling(szeit)
come alive [kʌm ə'laɪv] zum Leben erwachen
forest ['fɒrɪst] Wald
owl [aʊl] Eule
give up [ˌgɪv 'ʌp] opfern, verzichten auf
do a lot of good [du ə lɒt əv 'gʊd] viel Gutes tun
go on [ˌgəʊ 'ɒn] geschehen, vor sich gehen, dauern
suffer ['sʌfə] leiden
behave [bɪ'heɪv] sich verhalten, sich benehmen
voluntary ['vɒləntri] freiwillig
field [fi:ld] Feld, Wiese
coordinate [kəʊ'ɔ:dɪneɪt] aufeinander abstimmen, koordinieren
get paid [get 'peɪd] bezahlt werden
make laws [meɪk lɔ:z] Gesetze erlassen
waste [weɪst] Abfall, Müll

155

environment [ɪn'vaɪrənmənt] Umwelt

UNIT 3

fun ['fʌn] witzig
shopkeeper ['ʃɒp ki:pə] Ladeninhaber/in, -besitzer/in
switch on [ˌswɪtʃ 'ɒn] an-, einschalten
Christmas ['krɪsməs] Weihnachten
go for a walk [gəʊ fər ə 'wɔ:k] spazieren gehen
get rid of [get 'rɪd əv] loswerden
Singaporean [ˌsɪŋə'pɔ:riən] Einwohner/in Singapurs
manage ['mænɪdʒ] (es) schaffen
fit in [ˌfɪt 'ɪn] einschieben
island ['aɪlənd] Insel
southern ['sʌðən] Süd-, südlich
theme park ['θi:m pɑ:k] Freizeitpark
study for exams [ˌstʌdi fər ɪg'zæmz] für Prüfungen lernen
tough [tʌf] hart, streng
compared to [kəm'peəd tə] verglichen mit

156

in the daytime [ɪn ðə 'deɪtaɪm] tagsüber
sunbathing ['sʌnbeɪðɪŋ] Sonnenbaden

UNIT 4

157

boom out [ˌbu:m 'aʊt] hinauswummern
non-stop [ˌnɒn'stɒp] ununterbrochen, pausenlos
dance like crazy [dɑns laɪk 'kreɪzi] wie verrückt tanzen
Asian ['eɪʃn] asiatisch
old-fashioned [ˌəʊld'fæʃənd] altmodisch, veraltet
colour-based ['kʌlə beɪst] auf der Hautfarbe basierend
move towards [mu:v tə'wɔ:dz] sich bewegen in Richtung auf
traditional [trə'dɪʃənl] traditionell
lifestyle ['laɪfstaɪl] Lebensstil
in the past [ɪn ðə 'pɑ:st] in der Vergangenheit
copy ['kɒpi] nachahmen
hairstyle ['heəstaɪl] Frisur
schoolmate ['sku:lmeɪt] Schulkamerad
origin ['ɒrɪdʒɪn] Ursprung, Herkunft
award [ə'wɔ:d] Auszeichnung, Preis
documentary [ˌdɒkju'mentri] Dokumentarbericht, -film, -sendung
admire [əd'maɪə] bewundern
wife [waɪf] (Ehe-)Frau
fashion ['fæʃn] Mode
jewellery ['dʒu:əlri] Schmuck(stücke)
element ['elɪmənt] Element
barrier ['bæriə] Schranke
down [daʊn] aufgehoben
urban ['ɜ:bən] städtisch, Stadt-
mainstream culture ['meɪnstri:m kʌltʃə] tonangebende Kultur
leave behind [li:v bɪ'haɪnd] hinter sich lassen
take on sth [ˌteɪk 'ɒn] an-, übernehmen
prize [praɪz] Preis

158

competition [ˌkɒmpə'tɪʃn] Wettbewerb

UNIT 5

159

run [rʌn] durchführen
overweight [ˌəʊvə'weɪt] übergewichtig
participant [pɑ:'tɪsɪpənt] Teilnehmer/in

i:	ɪ	e	æ	ɑ:	ɒ	ɔ:	ʊ	u:	ʌ	ɜ:	ə
see	sit	ten	bad	arm	got	saw	put	too	cut	bird	about

diet ['daɪət]	Diät(kost)
progress ['prəʊgres]	Fortschritt/e
low-calorie [ˌləʊ'kæləri]	mit wenig Kalorien
gym [dʒɪm]	Sportstudio
twice [twaɪs]	zweimal
physical ['fɪzɪkl]	körperlich
face a challenge [feɪs ə 'tʃælɪndʒ]	sich einer Herausforderung gegenübersehen
fatty ['fæti]	fetthaltig, -reich
in front of [ɪn 'frʌnt əv]	vor
lose weight [lu:z 'weɪt]	abnehmen
overnight [ˌəʊvə'naɪt]	über Nacht
lead (your) life [li:d jɔ: 'laɪf]	(dein) Leben führen
kid [kɪd]	Kind
attitude ['ætɪtju:d]	Einstellung
conclude [kən'klu:d]	(ab)schließend bemerken
keep (the weight) off [ˌki:p ðə weɪt 'ɒf]	(das Gewicht) fernhalten
lifetime ['laɪftaɪm]	(auf) Lebenszeit
take exercise [teɪk 'eksəsaɪz]	sich bewegen
be based on [bi 'beɪst ɒn]	basieren auf
encourage [ɪn'kʌrɪdʒ]	auffordern
slim [slɪm]	schlank
nowadays ['naʊədeɪz]	heutzutage
160	
lesson ['lesn]	Unterricht(sstunde), Kurs
keep fit	fit bleiben
for ages [fər 'eɪdʒɪz]	eine Ewigkeit

UNIT 6

161	
high school ['haɪ sku:l]	Oberschule, Gymnasium
paper route (AE) ['peɪpə ru:t]	Zeitungsaustragen
neighborhood ['neɪbəhʊd]	Nachbarschaft
mailbox (AE) ['meɪlbɒks]	Briefkasten
throw [θrəʊ]	werfen
path [pɑ:θ]	(Fuß-)Weg
pitching arm ['pɪtʃɪŋ ɑ:m]	Wurfarm
for a while [fər ə 'waɪl]	eine Zeit lang
groceries ['grəʊsəri:z]	Lebensmittel, Einkäufe
checkout ['tʃekaʊt]	Kasse
carry ['kæri]	tragen
tip [gʊd 'tɪp]	Trinkgeld
gas station (AE) ['gæs steɪʃn]	Tankstelle
window ['wɪndəʊ]	Fenster
fill up [ˌfɪl 'ʌp]	(voll-, auf)tanken
gas (AE) [gæs]	Benzin
apply for [ə'plaɪ fə]	sich bewerben um
vacation job [və'keɪʃn dʒɒb]	Ferienjob
main thing [meɪn 'θɪŋ]	Hauptsache
savings account ['seɪvɪŋz əkaʊnt]	Sparkonto
162	
unemployed [ˌʌnɪm'plɔɪd]	arbeitslos, ohne Beschäftigung
crash *(computer)* [kræʃ]	abstürzen
overtime ['əʊvətaɪm]	Überstunden
payment ['peɪmənt]	Zahlung

UNIT 7

163	
interested in ['ɪntrəstɪd ɪn]	interessiert an
career [kə'rɪə]	Karriere, Laufbahn
pop business ['pɒp bɪznəs]	Showgeschäft
get started [get 'stɑ:tɪd]	anfangen
casting programme [ˌkɑ:stɪŋ 'prəʊgræm]	Casting-Sendung
do research [du rɪ'sɜ:tʃ]	Nachforschungen anstellen
check out [ˌtʃek 'aʊt]	herausfinden
in charge of [ɪn 'tʃɑ:dʒ əv]	verantwortlich für
look for ['lʊk fə]	suchen nach
yodel ['jəʊdl]	jodeln
folksong ['fəʊksɒŋ]	Volkslied
cover version ['kʌvə vɜ:ʃn]	Cover-Version
by heart [baɪ 'hɑ:t]	auswendig
enter for ['entə fə]	sich bewerben um
on the internet [ɒn ði 'ɪntənet]	im Internet
application form [ˌæplɪ'keɪʃn fɔ:m]	Antragsformular
look after [lʊk 'ɑ:ftə]	sich kümmern um
wear [weə]	tragen, anhaben
up to you [ʌp tə 'ju:]	(das ist) deine Sache
outfit ['aʊtfɪt]	Kleidung
realize ['rɪəlaɪz]	sich klar werden/sein
everyday ['evrideɪ]	Alltags-
exact(ly) [ɪg'zæktli]	genau
promise ['prɒmɪs]	versprechen
writer ['raɪtə]	Autor/in, Verfasser/in
164	
be thrilled to bits [bi θrɪld tə 'bɪts]	völlig begeistert sein
take part in [teɪk 'pɑ:t ɪn]	teilnehmen an, mitmachen bei
judge [dʒʌdʒ]	Preisrichter/in
shower ['ʃaʊə]	Dusche
behind [bɪ'haɪnd]	hinter
locked [lɒkt]	verschlossen
son [sʌn]	Sohn
voice [vɔɪs]	Stimme

UNIT 8

165	
simple ['sɪmpl]	einfach
good luck [ˌgʊd 'lʌk]	(viel) Glück
flat [flæt]	Wohnung
improve [ɪm'pru:v]	verbessern

work experience ['wɜ:k ɪkspɪəriəns] Berufserfahrung
have fun [həv 'fʌn] Spaß haben
decide to [dɪ'saɪd tə] sich entscheiden für, sich entschließen zu
final(ly) ['faɪnl, 'faɪnəli] schließlich, zum Schluss
uncle ['ʌŋkl] Onkel
floor [flɔ:] (Fuß-)Boden
hotel porter [həʊ'tel pɔ:tə] Hotelportier
unfortunately [ʌn'fɔ:tʃənətli] unglücklicherweise, leider
move in [ˌmu:v 'ɪn] einziehen
Canadian [kə'neɪdiən] Kanadier/in
multicultural [ˌmʌlti'kʌltʃərəl] multikulturell
from all over the world [frəm ɔ:l ˌəʊvə ðə 'wɜ:ld] aus der ganzen Welt
166
hill [hɪl] Hügel

UNIT 9

167
traffic jam ['træfɪk dʒæm] Verkehrsstau, Stau
public transport [ˌpʌblɪk 'trænspɔ:t] öffentlicher Nahverkehr
prediction [prɪ'dɪkʃn] Vorhersage
motorway ['məʊtəweɪ] Autobahn
vehicle ['vi:əkl] Fahrzeug
on the ground [ɒn ðə graʊnd] auf der Erde
pedestrian [pɪ'destriən] Fußgänger/in
cyclist ['saɪklɪst] Radfahrer/in
driving licence ['draɪvɪŋlaɪsns] Führerschein
control [kən'trəʊl] steuern
get in [ˌget 'ɪn] einsteigen
get on with sth [ˌget 'ɒn wɪð] etw erledigen
space tourism ['speɪs tʊərɪzəm] Weltraumtourismus
after all [ˌɑ:ftər 'ɔ:l] schließlich (doch)
further ['fɜ:ðə] weiter
cyber office ['saɪbə ɒfɪs] Cyber-Büro
hologram ['hɒləgræm] Hologramm
electric motor [ɪˌlektrɪk 'məʊtə] Elektromotor
pollution [pə'lu:ʃn] (Umwelt-)Verschmutzung
guess [ges] Vermutung
success [sək'ses] Erfolg
meaning ['mi:nɪŋ] Bedeutung
168
these days [ði:z 'deɪz] in diesen Tagen
method of transport [ˌmeθəd əv 'trænspɔ:t] Verkehrsmittel

UNIT 10

169
debt [det] Schuld(en)
financial trouble [faɪˌnænʃl 'trʌbl] finanzielle Probleme
bill [bɪl] Rechnung
post office ['pəʊst ɒfɪs] Postamt
letterbox ['letəbɒks] Briefkasten
afford sth [ə'fɔ:d] (es) sich leisten (können)
complicated ['kɒmplɪkeɪtɪd] kompliziert
recommend [ˌrekə'mend] empfehlen
account [ə'kaʊnt] Konto
get into debt [get ɪntə 'det] Schulden machen
unpopular [ʌn'pɒpjələ] unbeliebt, unpopulär
switch to ['swɪtʃ tə] sich umstellen auf
make sense [meɪk 'sens] sinnvoll sein
phone company ['fəʊn kʌmpəni] Telefongesellschaft
reduce [rɪ'dju:s] reduzieren
simplify ['sɪmplɪfaɪ] vereinfachen
cap [kæp] Obergrenze
limit ['lɪmɪt] Grenze, Begrenzung
on average [ɒn 'ævərɪdʒ] im Durchschnitt, durchschnittlich
170
suggestion [sə'dʒestʃən] Vorschlag

UNIT 11

171
publish ['pʌblɪʃ] veröffentlichen
informative [ɪn'fɔ:mətɪv] informativ
include [ɪn'klu:d] umfassen, einschließen
tabloid ['tæblɔɪd] Boulevardblatt
be obsessed with [bi ə b'sest wɪð] sich vorwiegend beschäftigen mit
celebrity [sə'lebrəti] Promi(nente/r)
footballer ['fʊtbɔ:lə] Fußballspieler/in
in addition [ɪn ə'dɪʃn] darüber hinaus
human ['hju:mən] menschlich
ordinary ['ɔ:dnri] gewöhnlich, normal
read [ri:d] lesen
gossip ['gɒsɪp] Klatsch, Tratsch
harmless ['hɑ:mləs] harmlos
argue ['ɑ:gju:] der Meinung sein
privacy ['prɪvəsi] Privatsphäre
untrue [ʌn'tru:] unwahr
politics ['pɒlətɪks] (die) Politik
172
current affairs [ˌkʌrənt ə'feəz] Tagespolitik, Zeitgeschehen
affair [əˌfeə] Affäre

UNIT 12

recycle [ˌri:'saɪkl] recyceln, (wieder) aufbereiten
recycled product [ˌri:ˌsaɪkld 'prɒdʌkt] wieder verwertetes Produkt
tyre ['taɪə] Reifen

i:	ɪ	e	æ	ɑ:	ɒ	ɔ:	ʊ	u:	ʌ	ɜ:	ə
see	sit	ten	bad	arm	got	saw	put	too	cut	bird	about

shoe [ʃu:]	Schuh
athletics track [æθ'letɪks træk]	Laufbahn
tennis court ['tenɪs kɔ:t]	Tennisplatz
aluminium [ˌæljə'mɪniəm]	Aluminium
drinks can ['drɪŋks kæn]	Getränkedose
crush [krʌʃ]	zusammenpressen
melt [melt]	schmelzen
make sth into [meɪk 'ɪntə]	etw verarbeiten zu
bottle ['bɒtl]	Flasche
all kinds of things [ɔ:l kaɪndz əv 'θɪŋz]	alles Mögliche
building materials [ˌbɪldɪŋ mə'tɪəriəlz]	Baustoffe
inhabitant [ɪn'hæbɪtənt]	Bewohner/in, Einwohner/in
supply [sə'plaɪ]	Vorrat, Vorräte
run out [ˌrʌn 'aʊt]	zu Ende gehen
possibility [ˌpɒsə'bɪləti]	Möglichkeit
sea water ['si: wɔ:tə]	Meerwasser
turn sth into [tɜ:n 'ɪntə]	etw umwandeln in
fresh water [freʃ 'wɔ:tə]	Süßwasser
process ['prəʊses]	Verfahren, Prozess
electricity [ɪˌlek'trɪsəti]	Elektrizität, Strom
pump [pʌmp]	pumpen
along [ə'lɒŋ]	entlang
pipeline ['paɪplaɪn]	Rohrleitung
UV light [ˌju: 'vi: laɪt]	ultraviolettes Licht
harmful ['hɑ:mfl]	schädlich
bacteria [bæk'tɪəriə]	Bakterien
widely ['waɪdli]	in großem Umfang
persuade [pə'sweɪd]	überreden, verleiten
choice [tʃɔɪs]	Wahl
waste water [ˌweɪst 'wɔ:tə]	Abwasser
put back [ˌpʊt 'bæk]	zurückleiten
reservoir ['rezəvwɑ:]	Staubecken
taste [teɪst]	Geschmack
173	
resident ['rezɪdənt]	Einwohner/in
trainer ['treɪnə]	Turn-, Tennisschuh
reuse [ˌri:'ju:z]	wieder verwenden
174	
mineral water ['mɪnərəl wɔ:tə]	Mineralwasser
tap water ['tæp wɔ:tə]	Leitungswasser

UNIT 13

capital city [ˌkæpɪtl 'sɪti]	Hauptstadt
event [ɪ'vent]	Ereignis
rule [ru:l]	(be)herrschen, regieren
treaty ['tri:ti]	Vertrag
argument ['ɑ:gjumənt]	Streit, Auseinandersetzung
Unionist ['ju:niənɪst]	Unionist
Nationalist ['næʃnəlɪst]	Nationalist
join [dʒɔɪn]	sich anschließen, beitreten
Protestant ['prɒtɪstənt]	protestantisch
Roman Catholic [ˌrəʊmən 'kæθəlɪk]	römisch-katholisch
religion [rɪ'lɪdʒən]	Religion, Konfession
conflict ['kɒnflɪkt]	Konflikt
create [kri'eɪt]	schaffen
extremist [ɪk'stri:mɪst]	Extremist/in
Irish Republican Army [ˌaɪrɪʃ rɪˌpʌblɪkən 'ɑ:mi]	Irisch-Republikanische Armee
bomb [bɒm]	Bombe
attack [ə'tæk]	Angriff, Überfall
shooting ['ʃu:tɪŋ]	Schießerei
fight [faɪt]	kämpfen
terrorist ['terərɪst]	Terrorist/in
soldier ['səʊldʒə]	Soldat/in
violence ['vaɪələns]	Gewalt
Good Friday [gʊd 'fraɪdeɪ]	Karfreitag
agreement [ə'gri:mənt]	Abkommen
peaceful(ly) ['pi:sfəli]	friedlich
govern ['gʌvn]	regieren
suspicious [sə'spɪʃəs]	misstrauisch
terrorism ['terərɪzəm]	Terrorismus
175	
demand [dɪ'mɑ:nd]	fordern
Republican [rɪ'pʌblɪkən]	Republikaner/in
prisoner ['prɪznə]	Häftling, Gefangene/r
carry out [ˌkæri 'aʊt]	aus-, durchführen

UNIT 14

176	
disposable [dɪ'spəʊzəbl]	Wegwerf-
homeless ['həʊmləs]	obdachlos
doorway ['dɔ:weɪ]	(Haus-)Eingang
beg for sth ['beg fə]	um etw betteln
spare change ['speə tʃeɪndʒ]	(übriges) Kleingeld
look away [lʊk ə'weɪ]	wegschauen
walk on [ˌwɔ:k 'ɒn]	weitergehen, -laufen
force [fɔ:s]	zwingen
leave home [li:v 'həʊm]	von zu Hause weggehen
society [sə'saɪəti]	(die) Gesellschaft
addiction [ə'dɪkʃn]	Sucht, Abhängigkeit
commit (a) crime [kə'mɪt ə kraɪm]	(ein) Verbrechen begehen
shelter ['ʃeltə]	Unterkunft
throw s.o. out [ˌθrəʊ 'aʊt]	jdn hinauswerfen
foster family [ˌfɒstə 'fæməli]	Pflegefamilie
blame [bleɪm]	die Schuld geben
cry o.s. to sleep [kraɪ tə 'sli:p]	weinen bis zum Einschlafen
live rough [lɪv 'rʌf]	als Obdachlose/r leben
lose track of sth [lu:z 'træk əv]	das Gefühl für etw verlieren

spend [spend]	verbringen
ignore [ɪg'nɔː]	ignorieren, nicht beachten
kind-hearted [ˌkaɪnd 'hɑːtɪd]	gütig, gutherzig
coin [kɔɪn]	Münze
pick up [ˌpɪk 'ʌp]	mitnehmen, aufgreifen
social services [ˌsəʊʃl 'sɜːvɪsɪz]	Sozialamt, -dienste,
foster home ['fɒstə həʊm]	Pflegeheim, -familie
contact ['kɒntækt]	Kontakt aufnehmen zu
police officer [pə'liːs ɒfɪsə]	Polizeibeamter/ beamtin

UNIT 15

178

cross [krɒs]	durchqueren
continent ['kɒntɪnənt]	Kontinent
folks [fəʊks]	Leute, Familie
regret [rɪ'gret]	bedauern, bereuen
back [bæk]	Rücken
hurt [hɜːt]	wehtun, schmerzen
ache [eɪk]	schmerzen, wehtun
sightseeing ['saɪtsiːɪŋ]	Besichtigungen (von Sehenswürdigkeiten)
seat [siːt]	Sitz(platz)
narrow ['nærəʊ]	eng, schmal
particular(ly) [pə'tɪkjələli]	besonders
weirdo ['wɪədəʊ]	schräger Typ, komischer Kauz
stranger ['streɪndʒə]	Fremde/r
headphone ['hedfəʊn]	Kopfhörer
unwanted [ˌʌn'wɒntɪd]	unerwünscht
ideal(ly) [aɪ'diːəli]	ideal, im Idealfall
precaution [prɪ'kɔːʃn]	Vorsichtsmaßnahme

Alphabetisches Wörterverzeichnis

Dieses Wörterverzeichnis enthält alle Wörter aus **Work with English** in alphabetischer Reihenfolge. Nicht aufgeführt sind die Wörter aus der Liste des Grundwortschatzes. t = das Wort befindet sich in den *Transcripts* (Hörverständnisübungen). p = das Wort befindet sich in den *Pairwork Files*.

(body) decoration 38 Körperschmuck
(vocational) qualification 125 t Berufsausbildung
a few 22 t ein paar
ability 132 Fähigkeit
be able to 64 können
Aborigine 79 Ureinwohner Australiens
abortion 118 Abtreibung, Schwangerschaftsabbruch
above 12 oben (stehend)
abroad 45 t im Ausland
access 92 t Zugang, Zugriff
accident 67, 139 Unfall, Zufall
accommodation 37 t Unterkunft
according to 59 nach, entsprechend
account 169 Konto
accounts clerk 114 Buchhalter/in
accurate 76 genau
ache 178 schmerzen, wehtun
achievement 27 Leistung
across 139 (her)über
activity 34 Aktivität, Tätigkeit
activity holiday 86 Aktivurlaub
actor 99 Schauspieler
add 6 hinzufügen
addiction 176 Sucht, Abhängigkeit
admire 99 bewundern
admit 99 zugeben, gestehen
adopt 62 adoptieren, hier: annehmen
adore 118 anhimmeln, nach jdm verrückt sein
adult 152 Erwachsene/r
adventure 79 Abenteuer
advertising 46 Werbung, Reklame
(give) advice 28 t Rat(schläge) (geben/erteilen)
affair 172 Affäre
affect 132 beeinträchtigen
afford sth 169 sich etw leisten (können)
be afraid of 11 sich fürchten vor
after all 126 schließlich (doch)
after sales 94 Kundenbetreuung
afterwards 118 nachher, danach, hinterher
against the law 136 illegal
age limit 116 Altersgrenze
ago 9 vor
agree 38 übereinstimmen, zustimmen
agreement 174 Abkommen
agriculture 109 Landwirtschaft
aim 36 Ziel
be aimed at 135 t an ... gerichtet
air 84 Luft
aircraft 84 Flugzeug
airline pilot 81 Pilot/in (für zivile Luftfahrt)
alcoholic 68 Alkoholiker/in
alive 47 lebendig, lebend
all kinds of things 172 alles Mögliche
all over the place 15 überall in der Gegend
all over the world 96 in der ganzen Welt
all-American 100 typisch amerikanisch
be (not) allowed to 30 (nicht) dürfen
along 172 entlang
alteration 85 p Änderung
aluminium 172 Aluminium
amazing 34 erstaunlich, unglaublich
ambulance 132 Krankenwagen
among(st) 86 unter
amount 109 Menge
angry 88 wütend
be angry with sb 140 auf jdn böse sein
animal 154 Tier
animal rights 152 Tierrechte
announcer 69 t Sprecher/in
annoy 22 t belästigen
anti-smoking 128 Nichtraucher-
any longer 9 länger
anything else 22 t nichts anderes
apart from 68 abgesehen von, darüber hinaus
apologize 139 sich entschuldigen
appear 62 erscheinen
appearance 70 Aussehen, (äußere) Erscheinung
application form 19 Antrag(sformular)
apply for 37 t sich bewerben um
apprentice 76 Lehrling, Auszubildende/r
apprenticeship 71 Lehre, Ausbildung
appropriate 37 geeignet, passend
area 39 Gegend
argue 126 (sich) streiten, der Meinung sein
argument 128 Argument, Streit, Auseinandersetzung
arrange 116 arrangieren, organisieren
arrive 85 p ankommen, eintreffen
arthouse cinema 98 Programmkino
article 62 Artikel
as much as you like 92 t so viel Sie möchten
Asian 157 asiatisch
aspect 135 Aspekt
assembly 125 Montage
assistant 6 Verkäufer/in
at least 62 mindestens
at the age of 144 im Alter von
at the moment 7 im Augenblick
athletics track 172 Laufbahn
atmosphere 116 Stimmung, Atmosphäre
attack 174 Angriff, Überfall
attempt 146 Versuch
attend 145 besuchen
attention 118 Aufmerksamkeit
attitude 62 Einstellung
attractive 128 attraktiv, anziehend
au pair 108 Au-pair-Mädchen
audience 106 Publikum
audition (for) 99 vorsprechen (für)
authority 154 Behörde, Amt, Verwaltung
availability 85 p Verfügbarkeit
on average 96 im Durchschnitt, durchschnittlich
avoid 89 vermeiden, aus dem Wege gehen
awake 47 wach
award 157 Auszeichnung, Preis
awful 56 furchtbar, schrecklich
back 178 Rücken; zurück
back home 112 t daheim
back seat 139 Rücksitz
backpackers' hostel 30 Jugendherberge für Rucksacktouristen
bacteria 172 Bakterien
baggage reclaim 83 Gepäckausgabe
baker 59 Bäcker/in

ban (from) 118 verbannen (aus); verbieten
bank statement 115 Kontoauszug
banned 128 verboten
barbecue 79 Grillparty
barrier 157 Schranke
be based in 34 t seinen Sitz haben in
be based on 159 basieren auf
basic 75 elementar, grund-
basically 124 grundsätzlich, eigentlich
bathe 104 baden
bathroom 8 Bad(ezimmer)
battery 121 Batterie
on the beach 87 am Strand
beach holiday 86 Strandurlaub
beat 46 schlagen
beat sb up 133 jdn zusammenschlagen
beat-up 139 kaputt
beauty 139 Schönheit
become 132 werden
beg for sth 176 um etw betteln
beginning 39 Anfang
behave 29 sich verhalten, sich benehmen
behaviour (BE), behavior (AE) 139 Verhalten, Benehmen
behind 164 hinter
believe 39 glauben
belly button 38 Bauchnabel
below 40 unten (stehend)
bench 141 Bank
benefit 60 zusätzliche Leistung, Vergünstigung
besides 128 außerdem, abgesehen (da)von
big-screen 99 Kinoleinwand, hier: Spielfilm-
bill 169 Rechnung
bin 154 Mülleimer, (Müll-)Tonne
black 38 schwarz
blame 140 verantwortlich machen, die Schuld geben
blank 95 leer, ohne Anzeige
blockbuster 99 Kinohit
blood pressure 104 Blutdruck
blood sample 104 Blutprobe
blood transfusion 104 Bluttransfusion
board 109 Kost, Verpflegung
boarding pass 83 Bordkarte
boat trip 79 Bootsausflug, Bootsfahrt
body 132 Körper
bomb 174 Bombe
make a booking 111 eine Reservierung vornehmen
bookkeeping 54 Buchhaltung
boom out 157 hinauswummern
be born 12 geboren werden/sein
boss around 16 herumkommandieren
bottle 172 Flasche
box office hit 98 Kassenschlager
bracket 10 Klammer
brain cell 62 Hirnzelle
brainstorm 40 (Ideen) sammeln
brake 142 Bremse
brand new 139 nagelneu
break 28 t Pause
breath 128 Atem
breathe 46 atmen
brewery 34 t Brauerei
brewing 125 Brauereigewerbe
bridegroom 62 Bräutigam
bridge 79 Brücke
bright 22 t heiter, leuchtend, hell
brightly lit 133 t hell erleuchtet
brilliant 30 großartig, fabelhaft
browse 92 t durchsehen, surfen
buddy 139 Kumpel, Freund
budget 92 t Etat, Kostenplan, Budget
building materials 172 Baustoffe
bully 54 tyrannisieren, mobben
bungy jumping 78 Bungee-Springen
business letter 55 Geschäftsbrief
businessman 99 Geschäftsmann
busy 18 (viel)beschäftigt, umtriebig
button 61 t Taste, Knopf
by bike 45 mit dem Rad
by email 96 per E-Mail
by heart 163 auswendig
by the sea 86 am Meer
by the way 22 t übrigens
by train 86 mit der Bahn
cable 95 t Kabel
cable car 34 Seilbahn, (in San Francisco) Straßenbahn
caffeine 46 Koffein
call out 139 rufen
calm(ly) 132 ruhig
calm down 139 (sich) beruhigen
campaign 99 Kampagne, Aktion
can 46 Dose
Canadian 165 Kanadier/in
cannabis 132 Haschisch
canteen 18 Kantine, Cafeteria
cap 169 Obergrenze
capital city 174 Hauptstadt
caption 78 Bildunterschrift
car crash 67 t Autounfall
care about 9 sich Sorgen machen um, sich kümmern um, sich interessieren für
care assistant for the elderly 104 Altenpfleger/in
care for 76 pflegen
career 72 t Karriere, Laufbahn, Beruf
careers adviser 105 Berufsberater/in
careful(ly) 17 sorgfältig, vorsichtig
careless 70 nachlässig
caretaker 36 Hausmeister/in
caring 104 sozial (eingestellt)
Caring 104 Pflege
carpenter 76 Zimmermann, Tischler/-in
carpentry 77 t Tischlerei
carry 161 tragen
carry on 128 weitermachen
carry out 175 aus-, durchführen
be the case 37 t der Fall sein
casting programme 163 Casting-Sendung
castle 112 Burg, Schloss
casual 45 leger, sportlich, Freizeit-
category 6 Kategorie
Catholic 118 Katholik/in; katholisch
celebrate 139 feiern
celebrity 98 Prominente/r
certain(ly) 37 t gewiss, bestimmt
chance 11 Chance
change (a baby's nappy) 104 wickeln, Windeln wechseln
chat up 26 anquatschen, anmachen
cheap 31 billig, preisgünstig
check out 163 herausfinden
checkout 161 Kasse
cheese 51 p Käse
chemical 109 Chemikalie
chicken 109 Huhn
childcare 75 (Kinder-)Erziehung
childminder 118 Tagesmutter
chill out 79 sich entspannen, abhängen
chocolate bar 13 Schoko(laden)riegel
choice 172 Wahl
Christmas 155 Weihnachten
Christmas Day 12 Weihnachtsfeiertag
Christmas Eve 12 Heiligabend
circulation 46 Kreislauf
classmate 25 Klassenkamerad/in
clean up 154 sauber machen, aufräumen
clean 66 sauber machen
clerk 28 t Verkäufer/in, (Büro-) Angestellte/r

client 79 Kunde/Kundin
close 136 zumachen, schließen
close(ly) 86 dicht
clothes 62 Kleidung
coat 146 Mantel, Jacke
coin 176 Münze
collapse 46 zusammenbrechen
colleague 21 t Kollege/Kollegin
collect 9 sammeln
college 134 Fachschule, Hochschule
colloquial 140 umgangssprachlich
colloquialism 31 umgangssprachlicher Ausdruck
colour-based 157 auf der Hautfarbe basierend
column 8 Spalte
combine 13 zusammenfügen, kombinieren
come alive 154 zum Leben erwachen
come in 23 hereinkommen
come round 22 t vorbeischauen, -kommen
come up 124 sich ergeben
comment 96 Bemerkung, Kommentar
commercial correspondence 54 Geschäftskorrespondenz
commit (a) crime 176 (ein) Verbrechen begehen
communicate 76 kommunizieren
communicator 94 Kommunikator/in
community 99 Gemeinde, Gemeinschaft
community centre 134 Bürgerzentrum
community service 139 gemeinnützige Tätigkeit
compare 32 vergleichen
compared to 155 verglichen mit
competition 135 Wettbewerb
complain 9 (sich) beschweren, sich beklagen
complaint 9 Beschwerde
complete 9 vervollständigen
complicated 169 kompliziert
component 124 Bauteil
computer studies 15 Informatik
computerized 125 computergesteuert
con man 99 Betrüger
concentrate 25 (sich) konzentrieren
concert 152 Konzert
conclude 40 (ab)schließen
confident 55 selbstsicher
conflict 174 Konflikt
confused 126 verwirrt
confusing 100 verwirrend
conservation 108 Naturschutz
consider 126 bedenken, berücksichtigen
constant(ly) 89 ständig
construction 76 Bau(firma)
consume 46 verzehren, einnehmen, konsumieren
contact 176 Kontakt aufnehmen zu
contain 46 enthalten
continuation 61 Fortsetzung
contract 92 t Vertrag
contrast 79 Kontrast
control 167 steuern
controlled (by) 124 gesteuert (von)
conversation 16 Gespräch, Unterhaltung
cook 50 zubereiten, kochen
coordinate 154 aufeinander abstimmen, koordinieren
cop 139 Polizist, Bulle
copy 157 nachahmen
correct(ly) 6 richtig
count 44 zählen (wichtig sein)
counting 55 Rechnen
country 8 Land, Staat
countryside 34 Land(schaft)
a couple (of) 30 ein paar
couple 133 Paar, Ehepaar
courier company 144 Kurierdienst, Logistikunternehmen
court 139 Gericht
cousin 8 Cousin/e
cover 138 zu-, abdecken
cover in 38 bedecken mit
cover version 163 Cover-Version
co-worker 61 Arbeitskollege, -kollegin
crash 58 verunglücken (mit)
crash (computer) 162 abstürzen
create 135 (er)schaffen, machen
creative 114 kreativ
cricket 111 Kricket
crisps 51 Kartoffelchips
critics' choice 99 Bestenliste
cross 178 durchqueren
cross 38 Kreuz; böse, ärgerlich
crowd 136 (Menschen-)Menge
cruise around 139 herumfahren
crush 172 zusammenpressen
cry o.s. to sleep 176 weinen bis zum Einschlafen
cup 47 Tasse
cupboard 9 Schrank
current affairs 172 Tagespolitik, Zeitgeschehen
customer 28 t Verbraucherberatung
cut down on 46 reduzieren
cyber office 167 Cyber-Büro
cyclist 167 Radfahrer/in
daily life 104 Alltag
dance class 22 t Tanzstunde
dangerous 110 gefährlich
date of birth 12 Geburtsdatum
date 85 p Datum, Termin
date sb 101 mit jdm ausgehen
day centre 104 Tagesstätte
day-release class 54 freier Tag (zur Fortbildung)
deal with 47 umgehen, zu tun zu haben mit
Dear ... 75 Sehr geehrte(r) ...,
debt 169 Schuld(en)
decide 9 entscheiden
decide to 165 sich entscheiden für, sich entschließen zu
decorate 39 tapezieren, streichen, renovieren, schmücken
define 86 beschreiben, definieren
definite 123 t fest, definitiv
definitely 22 t bestimmt, sicher(lich)
definition 55 Definition
degree 145 t Abschluss
delete 91 löschen
deliver 152 austragen, zustellen
demand 175 fordern
demanding 68 anspruchsvoll
dental 28 Zahn-, zahnärztlich
dentist 7 Zahnarzt, Zahnärztin
deny 133 abstreiten
department store 28 Kauf-, Warenhaus
departure 84 Abflug
depend on 94 abhängig sein von, angewiesen sein auf
depressing 68 deprimierend
describe 34 beschreiben
description 16 Beschreibung
desk 95 Pult, Schalter
destination 115 Ziel, Bestimmungsort
destroy 62 zerstören
detective story 63 Krimi
dialogue 21 Dialog
diary 115 Terminkalender, Terminplan
dictionary 10 Wörterbuch
diet 159 Diät(kost)
make a difference 134 etw bewegen, etw verändern
dimly-lit 132 schwach beleuchtet, schummerig
director 98 Direktor/in, Regisseur/in
dirty 70 schmutzig
disagree 38 nicht zustimmen

disagreement 62 Meinungsverschiedenheit
disappointed 54 enttäuscht
disaster 100 Katastrophe
discount price 44 herabgesetzte Preise
discourage 128 abbringen von
discover 99 entdecken
discuss 45 besprechen, diskutieren (über), erörtern
dislike 101 nicht mögen
disposable 176 Wegwerf-
dissatisfaction 60 Unzufriedenheit
dissatisfied 60 unzufrieden
distant 84 weit entfernt, fern
divorced 14 geschieden
dizzy 46 schwindlig
do a lot of good 154 viel Gutes tun
do research 163 Nachforschungen anstellen
do wrong 22t falsch machen
doctor 6 Arzt/Ärztin
doctor's surgery 104 Arztpraxis
documentary 63 Dokumentarsendung
dolphin 79 Delphin
doorbell 141 Türklingel
doorway 176 (Haus-)Eingang
down the road 41 die Straße entlang
down 157 aufgehoben
downside 109 Nachteil, Haken
downtown 139 (im/ins) Stadtzentrum
drama 100 Drama
draw 113 zeichnen
drawing 38 Zeichnung
dress a wound 104 eine Wunde verbinden
dress code 44 Kleiderordnung
drinks can 172 Getränkedose
drive sb crazy 89 jdn zur Verzweiflung treiben, jdn verrückt machen
drive 11 (mit dem Auto) fahren
driver 49 Fahrer/in
driver's door 139 Fahrertür
driver's license (AE) / driving licence (BE) 19t Führerschein
driving instructor 142 Fahrlehrer/in
drop out 54 ausscheiden
drop sth 122 etw fallen lassen
drowsy 132 schläfrig, müde
drug abuse 134 Drogenmissbrauch
drug addict 116 Drogenabhängige/r
drums 18 Schlagzeug
drunk 133 betrunken
dumb (AE) 139 dumm
during 29 während
dusty 54 staubig
each other 96 einander, sich
earn 45t verdienen
earring 40 Ohrring
Easter 154 Ostern
eco-friendliness 139 Umweltfreundlichkeit
ecotourism 116 Ökotourismus
effect 132 Wirkung
efficient(ly) 128 leistungsfähig
eject 95t auswerfen
electric motor 167 Elektromotor
electrical goods 28t Elektrowaren
electrician 28t Elektriker/in, Elektrotechniker/in
electricity 172 Elektrizität, Strom
element 157 Element
embarrassing 38 peinlich
employee 44 Angestellte/r, Beschäftigte/r
employment 45 Beschäftigung, Beruf
empty 9 leer
enclosed 75 beigefügt
encourage 125 ermutigen, fördern, unterstützen, auffordern
end up 30 „landen"
enemy 67 Feind
energetic 75 energisch, tatkräftig
engineering 124 Ingenieurwesen, Maschinenbau
enough 43t genug
enter 125 eingeben
enter for 163 sich bewerben um
entertain 46 unterhalten
enthusiastic 76 begeistert
envelope 132 Briefumschlag
environment 109 Umwelt
environmental 99 Umwelt-, umweltbezogen
equal(ly) 111 gleich
equipment 135 Ausrüstung, Geräte
equivalent 46 Entsprechung
essential 76 (absolut) notwendig
estate agent 76 Immobilienmakler/in
even though 44 obwohl
evening class 144 Abendschule, Abendschulkurs
event 174 Ereignis
everyday 163 Alltags-
exact(ly) 163 genau
exam 25 Prüfung
exam result 58 Prüfungsergebnisse
examination 55 (Abschluss-)Prüfung, Examen
examiner 146 Prüfer/in
example 6 Beispiel
exchange 83 Austausch
excited 33 aufgeregt, gespannt
excuse (me) 27 Entschuldigung
exercise (take ~) 14, 159 Übung, Training, Bewegung (sich bewegen)
exotic 109 exotisch
expect 33 erwarten, annehmen
expensive 25 teuer
experience 86 Erfahrung, Erlebnis
explore 34 erforschen, erkunden
expression 74 Ausdruck
extra 98 Statist/in
extract 44 Auszug
extremist 174 Extremist/in
eyelashes 38 Wimpern
face a challenge 159 sich einer Herausforderung gegenübersehen
face to face 52 von Angesicht zu Angesicht, persönlich
facility 84 Einrichtung, Anlage
factory 55 Fabrik
fail 146 keinen Erfolg haben, scheitern (bei), durchfallen
faithful 33 treu
Fall of the Berlin Wall 12 Fall der Berliner Mauer
fall off 141 herunterfallen (von)
fame 98 Ruhm
famous 31 berühmt
fancy 51 mögen
FAQs (= frequently asked questions) 111 (= häufig gestellte Fragen)
faraway 30 weit entfernt
farm 108 Bauernhof, Farm
farmwork 110 Landarbeit
fashion 157 Mode
fatty 159 fetthaltig, -reich
fault 95 Fehler, Defekt, Schuld
be sb's fault 84 Schuld
be in favour of sth 128 für etw sein, etw befürworten
favourite 9 Lieblings-
fear 152 Angst, Furcht
fee 92t Gebühr
feed 104 füttern
feed in 61t eingeben, einschieben
feel sick 136 sich krank/unwohl fühlen
fence 77t Zaun
ferry 84 Fähre
fewer 50 weniger
field 154 Feld, Wiese
fight 25 streiten, kämpfen
file 19 Akte
filing system 115 Ablagesystem

fill up 161 (voll-, auf)tanken
final 12 Endspiel
final(ly) 165 schließlich, zum Schluss
final exam 54 Abschlussprüfung
financial trouble 169 finanzielle Probleme
financial 114 finanziell, Finanz-
fine 21 t, 139 Geldstrafe, Bußgeld; gut, schön, alles klar
finish 13 fertig sein
fire sb 122 jdn feuern, entlassen
fire brigade 36 Feuerwehr
fire-eater 30 Feuerschlucker
firm 20 Firma
fit in 155 einschieben
fix 94 in Ordnung bringen, lösen, reparieren
flashback 139 Rückblende
flat 17 Wohnung
flea powder 65 Flohpulver
flexi-time 45 t Gleitzeit
flight 83 Flug
flight reservation 85 Flugreservierung
floor 165 (Fuß-)Boden
flop 98 Reinfall, Flop
fluent 74 fließend
folks 178 Leute, Familie
folksong 163 Volkslied
follow 44 befolgen
following 12 folgend
food processing 125 Lebensmittelherstellung
fool 100 täuschen, an der Nase herumführen
fool around 139 herumalbern
foot 33 Fuß (1 Fuß = 30,48 cm)
footballer 171 Fußballspieler/in
for a while 161 eine Zeit lang
for ages 160 eine Ewigkeit
for free 154 umsonst
for goodness' sake 89 um Himmels willen
force 55 zwingen
forehead 38 Stirn
foreign 37 fremd
foreign language 54 Fremdsprache
foreign-language correspondent 54 Fremdsprachenkorrespondent/in
forest 79 Wald
forgetful 68 vergesslich
form 8 Form
formal 112 formell, förmlich
fortune 98 Glück, Vermögen, Schicksal
foster family 176 Pflegefamilie
foster home 176 Pflegeheim, -familie
fountain 48 Trinkbrunnen
four-wheel drive 139 Vierradantrieb
free time 154 Freizeit
freezing 34 eiskalt
French 55 Französisch
fresh water 172 Süßwasser
freshness 48 Frische
fridge 50 Kühlschrank
fright 33 Angst
frightened 132 verängstigt, erschreckt
from all over the world 165 aus der ganzen Welt
frozen 9 (tief)gefroren
fruit juice 132 Fruchtsaft
frustrated 54 frustriert
full time 59 ganztags
fun 155 witzig
further 167 weiter
future 94 Zukunft
game 10 Spiel
game show 63 Spielshow
gang 118 Clique
gap 9 Lücke
garage 139 Garage
gas (AE) 161 Benzin
gas station (AE) 161 Tankstelle
gate 83 Gate, Ausgang, Flugsteig
general term 112 Oberbegriff
generation 96 Generation
get a life 134 was Interessanteres machen
get a woman pregnant 118 eine Frau schwängern
get back 34 zurückkommen
get bored 68 sich langweilen
get divorced 126 sich scheiden lassen
get in 167 einsteigen
get in trouble 91 in Schwierigkeiten kommen
get into debt 169 Schulden machen
get married 118 heiraten
get on with sb 153 sich mit jdm verstehen
get on with sth 167 etw erledigen
get paid 154 bezahlt werden
get rid of 155 loswerden
get sb involved 134 jdn dazu bringen, sich zu engagieren
get started 20 anfangen
get sth straight 82 t etw deutlich machen
get the hang of sth 61 t dahinter kommen
get to 86 erreichen, gelangen
get together 134 sich treffen, zusammenkommen
geyser 33 Geysir
gig 15 Konzert, Auftritt
give sb a lift 61 t jdn mitnehmen
give up 154 opfern, verzichten auf
glad 43 t (ich bin) froh
global warming 109 Erderwärmung
glove 9 Handschuh
glue 132
go ahead 85 p anfangen, Schießen Sie los!
go away 154 verreisen
go back 20 zurückgehen, -kehren
go clubbing 24 auf Partys gehen
go for a walk 155 spazieren gehen
go mad 99 verrückt werden, durchdrehen
go on holiday 86 In Urlaub fahren
go on 154 weitergehen, geschehen, vor sich gehen, dauern
go out with sb 128 mit jdm ausgehen
go skateboarding 141 Skateboard fahren
go well 146 gut gehen
goat 109 Ziege
be good at sth 105 gut in etw sein, etw gut können
Good Friday 174 Karfreitag
good luck 165 (viel) Glück
good value for money 86 ein gutes Preis-Leistungs-Verhältnis
good-looking 100 gut aussehend
goods 61 t Ware(n)
gorgeous 109 prachtvoll, wunderschön
gossip 101 Klatsch, Tratsch
govern 174 regieren
government 128 Regierung
grammar 6 Grammatik
graphic designer 114 Grafiker/in
greet 52 (be)grüßen
grey 43 t grau
grid 74 Schema, Tabelle
groceries 161 Lebensmittel, Einkäufe
on the ground 167 auf der Erde
grow up 96 aufwachsen, groß werden
guess 40, 167 (er)raten; Vermutung
guest 37 Gast
guide 33 (Reise-)Führer/in, anleiten
guitar 102 Gitarre
gym 159 Sportstudio
gymnastics 25 Gymnastik
habit 46 Gewohnheit
hairstyle 44 Frisur
half time 46 Halbzeit(pause)

half-brother 14 Halbbruder
ham 51 p (gekochter) Schinken
hand in 44 einreichen, abgeben
handbook 61 t Bedienungsanleitung, Handbuch
hang out 139 rumhängen
hang-gliding 78 Drachenfliegen
happen 42 geschehen, passieren
hard 59 t hart, anstrengend, schwer
be hard on sb 139 mit jdm hart ins Gericht gehen
hardly ever 22 t fast nie
hard-working 69 t fleißig
harmful 172 schädlich
harmless 171 harmlos
have fun 165 Spaß haben
headache pill 136 Kopfschmerztablette
heading 48 Überschrift
headline 44 Schlagzeile, Überschrift
headphone 178 Kopfhörer
health freak 131 Gesundheitsapostel
health insurance 19 t Krankenversicherung
health warning 128 Hinweis auf Gesundheitsgefahren
health 46 Gesundheit
healthiness 48 Gesundheit
healthy 42 gesund
hear 14 hören
heart 128 Herz
heart attack 142 t Herzinfarkt, Herzanfall
heart failure 46 Herzversagen
heart trouble 47 Herzprobleme
hectic 114 hektisch
helmet 47 Schutzhelm
hidden 99 verborgen, versteckt
high school 161 Oberschule, Gymnasium
hill 166 Hügel
hire 33 mieten, leihen
historic building 112 t historisches Gebäude
hit 131 gegen etw fahren
hold 116 veranstalten
on holiday 86 im Urlaub
holiday destination 86 Urlaubsziel
holiday resort 108 Urlaubsort
hologram 167 Hologramm
home for the elderly 68 Seniorenresidenz
homeless 135 t obdachlos
homemade 48 selbst zubereitet, hausgemacht
honest 90 ehrlich
honk (the horn) 142 t hupen
hopeless 142 t hoffnungslos
horn 142 Hupe
horrible 14 schrecklich, furchtbar
hospital 104 Krankenhaus
host family 109 Gastfamilie
hostel 33 (Wohn-)Heim, Pension
hotel porter 165 Hotelportier
household chore 104 Haushaltsarbeit
human 171 menschlich
hungry 11 hungrig
hurry up 47 sich beeilen
hurt 178 wehtun, schmerzen
I don't care 136 das ist mir egal
I don't mind 102 ich habe nichts (da)gegen
I.T. department 94 EDV-Abteilung
I'm afraid 53 leider
ID card 66 Personalausweis
ideal(ly) 45 ideal, im Idealfall
identify 60 (sich) identifizieren
ignore 176 ignorieren, nicht beachten
ill 11 krank
illegal 128 illegal, verboten, gesetzwidrig
illness 152 Krankheit
imagine 31 sich vorstellen, sich einbilden
immediate(ly) 52 sofort
immigrant 109 Einwanderer, Einwanderin
import 68 importieren
important 29 wichtig
impotence 129 Impotenz
impression 44 Eindruck
improve 165 verbessern
improvement 106 Verbesserung
in addition 40 darüber hinaus
in charge of 163 verantwortlich für
in fact 128 tatsächlich, eigentlich
in front of 159 vor
in full 12 vollständig
in my opinion 39 meiner Meinung nach
in my view 40 meiner Ansicht nach
in some ways 110 in mancher Hinsicht
in the daytime 156 tagsüber
in the past 157 in der Vergangenheit
in theory 145 t theoretisch
in what ways 96 auf welche Art, wie
include 37 enthalten, umfassen, hier: einbeziehen
including 48 einschließlich
increase 47 erhöhen, zunehmen, steigen
incredible/-ly 34 t unglaublich
Independence Day 12 Unabhängigkeitstag
independent 118 unabhängig
infant school 104 Grundschule (für Kinder von 4 bis 7 Jahren)
informal 29 informell
informative 171 informativ
inhabitant 79 Bewohner/in, Einwohner/in
give an injection 104 eine Spritze geben
be injured 142 verletzt werden
injury 104 Verletzung
insist 30 (darauf) bestehen
install 94 installieren, einrichten, anschließen
instead 22 t stattdessen
Institute for Heart Studies 46 Herzzentrum
instruction 19 Anweisung, Anleitung
instructor 79 Lehrer/in, Ausbilder/in
insurance agent 44 Versicherungsmakler/in
integrate 29 eingliedern, integrieren
be interested in 15 interessiert an
interesting 8 interessant
on the internet 163 im Internet
interpreter 113 Dolmetscher/in
interrupt 89 unterbrechen
intersection 139 Kreuzung
intimate 104 intim
in-tray 115 t (Post-)Eingangskorb
introduce 21 t vorstellen
invent 111 erfinden
invention 27 Erfindung
investigate 63 ermitteln
invitation 26 Einladung
invite 27 einladen
invoice 114 Rechnung
involve 77 t umfassen, mit sich bringen, beinhalten
Irish Republican Army (IRA) 174 Irisch-Republikanische Armee
iron mask 98 eiserne Maske
irresponsible 152 unverantwortlich
island 79 Insel
isolated 109 isoliert
It's been a pleasure. 103 War mir ein Vergnügen.
it's her turn 14 sie ist dran
Italian 55 Italienisch
jacket 43 t Jacke, Jackett
jewellery 38 Schmuck(stücke)

job satisfaction 45 t Zufriedenheit im Beruf
job vacancy 72 t offene Stelle, Stellenangebot
jobseeker profile 105 Bewerberprofil
join 8 verbinden, sich anschließen, beitreten
join together 105 zusammenfügen
journey 84 Reise
judge 139 Richter/in, Preisrichter/in
juggler 30 Jongleur/in
jump 79 Sprung
junk food 131 minderwertiges Essen
just in case 36 nur für den Fall
kangaroo 109 Känguru
keen 124 (sehr) interessiert
keep (the weight) off 159 (das Gewicht) fernhalten
keep an eye on sb 133 t auf jdn aufpassen
keep fit 160 Fit bleiben
keep in mind 116 daran denken, beachten
keep in touch 88 in Kontakt bleiben
keep on (doing sth) 102 t etw weiter tun
keep sth to o.s. 90 etw für sich behalten
keep up to date 38 aktuell bleiben
keep up with sth 96 mit etw Schritt halten
kick a habit 46 eine Gewohnheit aufgeben
kid 159 Kind
kill 89 töten, umbringen
kind 45 Art
kind of *(umgs.)* 140 ziemlich, irgendwie
kind-hearted 176 gütig, gutherzig
kiss 122 küssen
kitchen 9 Küche
knife 50 Messer
laid-back 109 entspannt
lake 79 (Binnen-)See
lame 139 lahm, hier: blöd
land 78 landen
last night 96 gestern Abend
lately 58 in letzter Zeit
laugh 38 lachen
laundry 104 Wäsche
make laws 154 Gesetze erlassen
lawyer 99 (Rechts-)Anwalt/Anwältin
lazy 152 faul, träge
lead (your) life 159 (dein) Leben führen
learner 146 Fahrschüler
learner driver 142 (Fahr)Anfänger
learning difficulty 54 Lernschwäche
leave 67 t verlassen
leave alone 26 in Ruhe lassen
leave behind 157 hinter sich lassen
leave home 176 von zu Hause weggehen
Leaving Certificate 124 Abgangs-, Abschlusszeugnis
left 63 übrig
leisure activity 23 Freizeitbeschäftigung
less able 104 hier: hilfsbedürftig
lesson 160 Unterricht(sstunde), Kurs
letter of apology 140 Entschuldigungsbrief
letter of application 74 Bewerbungsschreiben
letterbox 169 Briefkasten
lie 70 lügen
lifestyle 157 Lebensstil
lifetime 159 (auf) Lebenszeit
light 66 Licht, Lampe; leicht
limit 169 Grenze, Begrenzung
line-up 30 Aufstellung, Programm
list 10 Liste
litter 154 Müll, Abfall
live rough 176 als Obdachlose/r leben
loads of 30 jede Menge
local 77 t örtlich, lokal. hiesig
local people 86 Ortsansässige
location 86 (Stand-)Ort
locked 164 verschlossen
lodging 109 Logis, Unterkunft
logistics 144 Logistik
lonely 108 einsam
long for 62 sich sehnen nach
look after o.s. 67 t sich kümmern um sich selbst
look after (sb) 105 sich kümmern um (jdn), betreuen
look alike 44 gleich aussehen
look at 87 ansehen, anschauen
look away 176 wegschauen
look for 86 suchen nach
look forward to 68 sich freuen auf
lose track of sth 176 das Gefühl für etw verlieren
lose weight 42 abnehmen
lose 45 verlieren
loud 24 laut
low-calorie 159 mit wenig Kalorien
lower-skilled 145 t mit geringeren Anforderungen
luggage 84 Gepäck
lunchtime 11 Mittagszeit
lung 128 Lunge
machinery 27 Maschinenbau
machinist 124 Maschinenschlosser/in, Maschinist
mailbox (AE) 161 Briefkasten
main thing 161 Hauptsache
main 45 t wichtigste
mainstream culture 157 tonangebende Kultur
majority 146 Mehrheit
make a point 125 ein Argument anbringen
make sense 169 sinnvoll sein
make sth into 172 etw verarbeiten zu
make sth worse 109 verschlimmern
manage 155 (es) schaffen
managing director 114 Geschäftsführer/in
mankind 27 Menschheit
manners 29 Umgangsformen, Manieren
manufacture 124 herstellen, produzieren
manufacturing 124 Fertigung, Herstellung, Produktion
map 32 (Stadt-)Plan
married 14 verheiratet
match 12 zuordnen, Spiel
mate 22 t Kumpel, Freund/in
meal 48 Essen, Mahlzeit
meaning 74 Bedeutung
measurement 76 Messung
meat 112 Fleisch
mechanic 18 Mechaniker/in
mechanical 45 t mechanisch, technisch
melt 172 schmelzen
member 111 Mitglied
memory 95 t Speicher
mend 77 t reparieren, ausbessern
mention 34 t erwähnen
metal 61 t Metall
metalworker 118 Metallarbeiter/in
method 111 Methode, Verfahren
method of transport 168 Verkehrsmittel
might 46 könnte(n) (vielleicht)
mill 124 Fräse
mind map 113 Gedankengerüst
mind 28 t etw dagegen haben
mineral water 174 Mineralwasser
minor 105 klein, geringfügig
make a mistake 142 t einen Fehler machen
mixed-up 114 durcheinander gewürfelt

mobile (phone) 10 Mobiltelefon, Handy
month 30 Monat
mood 43 t Stimmung
be over the moon 133 überglücklich sein
most 40 die meisten
mostly 39 hauptsächlich, meistens
motorway 146 Autobahn
mountain 79 Berg
move in 165 einziehen
move into a house/flat 135 t in ein Haus/eine Wohnung ziehen
move towards 157 sich bewegen in Richtung auf
movie (AE) 98 (Spiel-)Film
movie theater (AE) 98 Kino
multicultural 165 multikulturell
mushroom 51 p Pilz
music industry 106 Musikbranche
musician 33 Musiker/in
must 44 müssen
my place 22 t mein Zuhause
narrow 178 eng, schmal
Nationalist 174 Nationalist
nationality 13 Staatsangehörigkeit
native speaker 75 Muttersprachler/in
Natural Resources Defence Council 99 Umweltschutzorganisation in den USA
nature 109 Natur
near 6 nahe
neat 45 ordentlich, sauber
necessary 18 notwendig, erforderlich
neighborhood 161 Nachbarschaft
neighbour 31 Nachbar/in
nervous 20 nervös
nervous wreck 142 t Nervenbündel
never mind 61 t macht nichts
never 16 nie(mals)
New Year's Eve 12 Silvester
news 96 Neuigkeiten, Nachrichten
news broadcast 63 Nachrichtensendung
newspaper 72 t Zeitung
nickname 108 Spitzname
nicotine patch 47 Nikotinpflaster
night club 136 Nachtklub
nightmare 142 t Albtraum
nomination 99 Nominierung
non-smoker 130 Nichtraucher/in
non-stop 157 ununterbrochen, pausenlos
normal 146 normal
normally 28 t normalerweise
note (take ~s) 21, 52 Notiz (sich Notizen machen)
notice board 37 Schwarzes Brett
notice 36 Notiz, Anschlag; Kündigung, (be)merken
nowadays 126 heutzutage
numerical(ly) 124 numerisch
nurse 6 Krankenschwester, -pfleger
nursing home 104 Pflegeheim
nutrition 48 Ernährung
obsessed (with) 99 besessen (von)
odd one out 9 Außenseiter, hier: überzähliges Wort
off duty 84 nicht im Dienst
offer 145 anbieten
office 17 Büro
office administration 15 Büroorganisation
official 112 offiziell
oil 111 Öl
old-fashioned 157 altmodisch, veraltet
on foot 45 zu Fuß
on the one hand 40 einerseits
on the other hand 40 andererseits
on the way home 136 auf dem Nachhauseweg
once 59 einmal
one-night stand 62 Affäre für eine Nacht
operate 124 bedienen, arbeiten an
operative 74 Mitarbeiter/in (Call-Center)
opportunity 76 Gelegenheit, Chance
opposite 22 t gegenüber liegend; Gegensatz
opposite sex 128 das andere Geschlecht
order 68 Auftrag
ordinary 171 gewöhnlich, normal
organic farm 109 Bio-Bauernhof, Öko-Farm
organization 94 Organisation
organize 82 t organisieren, arrangieren
origin 157 Ursprung, Herkunft
out of control 139 außer Kontrolle
Outback 109 australischer Busch
outfit 163 Kleidung
outside of 34 außerhalb
outsider 109 Außenseiter/in
overdose 132 Überdosis
overhear 90 zufällig mithören
overnight 159 über Nacht
overtime 125 t Überstunden
overweight 159 übergewichtig
owl 154 Eule
own 10 besitzen
packet 128 Packung, Schachtel
paid sick leave 60 Lohnfortzahlung im Krankheitsfall
paint 77 t (an)streichen
pair of jeans 42 (eine) Jeans
pale 38 hell
panic attack 132 Panikanfall
paper making 125 Papierherstellung
paper route 161 Zeitungsaustragen
paper 95 t Papier
paperwork 114 Papierkram
paragliding 81 Gleitschirmfliegen
paragraph 96 Absatz
parcel 68 Paket, Päckchen
part 48 Teil
be part of sth 94 beteiligt sein an etw
part time 145 Teilzeit
participant 159 Teilnehmer/in
particular(ly) 178 besonders
partly 37 t teilweise, zum Teil
part-time 152 Teilzeit-, Halbtags-
pass a test/exam 44 eine Prüfung bestehen
pass out 133 t ohnmächtig werden
pass 27 vorbeigehen, -fahren (an)
passenger 84 Passagier/in, Fahrgast
passport 19 t Pass
patchwork family 14 Patchworkfamilie
path 161 (Fuß-)Weg
patience 68 Geduld
patient 69 t geduldig
pay as you go 92 t prepaid, mit Karte
pay attention 17 aufpassen
payment 162 Zahlung
peaceful(ly) 174 friedlich
pedestrian 167 Fußgänger/in
penfriend 87 Brieffreund/in
penguin 79 Pinguin
percentage 60 Prozentsatz
perform 106 auftreten (mit)
performance 101 Vorstellung, Auftritt, Leistung
peripheral 94 Peripherie(gerät)
permanent(ly) 39 dauerhaft, fest
personal space 96 persönlicher Freiraum
personality 69 t Persönlichkeit
personnel manager 20 Personalleiter/-in
persuade 46 überzeugen, überreden, verleiten
pet 9 Haustier

phone company 169 Telefongesellschaft
phone rage 89 Telefon-Wutanfall
take photos 23 fotografieren
phrase 21 (Rede-)Wendung
physical 159 körperlich
piano 106 Klavier
pick up 22 t abholen, mitnehmen, aufgreifen
pick 74 auswählen
pickle 51 p eingelegtes Gemüse
piece of paper 40 Zettel, Stück/Blatt Papier
pierce 38 piercen
pill 132 Pille
pink 38 pink(farben), rosa
pint 34 t Pint
pipeline 172 Rohrleitung
pitching arm 161 Wurfarm
place to stay 108 Unterkunft
plane 78 Flugzeug
plant 20, 154 Pflanze; pflanzen
plastic 125 Plastik, Kunststoff
plate 9 Teller
player 11 Spieler/in
pleasant 69 t angenehm, nett
pleased 39 froh, zufrieden
plenty 146 genügend, viel, genug, reichlich
plot 62 Handlung(sverlauf)
plug 95 t Stecker
pocket 83 Tasche
pocket money 11 Taschengeld
point out 38 hinweisen auf, erklären
police 65 Polizei
police force 68 Polizei
police officer 176 Polizeibeamter/-beamtin
polite 25 höflich
politics 171 politische Tätigkeit, (die) Politik
pollution 167 (Umwelt-)Verschmutzung
poor 16 arm
pop business 163 Showgeschäft
popular 62 beliebt, populär
possibility 172 Möglichkeit
possible 36 möglich
post office 169 Postamt
powered by 109 versorgt mit
powerful 139 leistungsstark
practical 76 praktisch (veranlagt)
practice 17 Übung, Training
practise 37 t (ein)üben
precaution 178 Vorsichtsmaßnahme
predict 145 vorhersagen
prediction 167 Vorhersage
prefer 8 lieber mögen, bevorzugen
pregnant 118 schwanger
preparation 70 Vorbereitung
prepare 71 vorbereiten
pressure (be under ~) 84 Druck (unter ~ sein)
pretty 59 t ziemlich, recht
previous 69 t vorherig
primary school 54 Grundschule
printer 94 Drucker/in
prior to 85 p vor
prisoner 175 Häftling, Gefangene/r
privacy 171 Privatsphäre
prize 157 Preis
pro- 130 pro-, für
probably 29 wahrscheinlich
process 172 Verfahren, Prozess
produce 20 produzieren, herstellen
profession 94 Beruf
professional 102 t Berufs-, Profi-, professionell
programmer 28 Programmierer/in
progress 159 Fortschritt/e
promise 81 versprechen
pronounce 111 aussprechen
proper 145 t ordentlich, angemessen
protect 109 schützen, beschützen
Protestant 174 protestantisch
provide 59 liefern, vorgeben, zur Verfügung stellen
public building 128 öffentliches Gebäude
public place 89 öffentlicher Ort
public transport 139 öffentliche Verkehrsmittel
publish 171 veröffentlichen
pull away 142 anfahren, wegfahren
pull o.s. together 132 sich zusammenreißen, -nehmen
pump 172 pumpen
pupil 154 Schüler/in
purpose 46 Zweck, Ziel
put back 172 zurückleiten
put sb in touch with sb 134 jdn an jdn verweisen, jdn mit jdn in Verbindung setzen
qualification 54 (Abschluss einer) Ausbildung, Qualifikation, Fähigkeit
qualified 71 qualifiziert
quantity 125 Menge
quarter 86 Viertel
quit 139 aufhören mit
rail 84 (Eisen-)Bahn
rain 25 regnen
rainwater tank 109 Regenwassertank, Regentonne
rank 59 anordnen, der Rangfolge nach anordnen
reaction 132 Reaktion
read 171 lesen
realize 44, 163 feststellen, sich klar werden/sein
reason 28 t Grund
receive 85 erhalten, empfangen, bekommen
recent(ly) 57 in letzter Zeit, jüngst, jünger
receptionist 36 Empfangsmitarbeiter/-in
reckon 133 t glauben, der Meinung sein, denken
recommend 169 empfehlen
record 27 Dokumentation
recording 72 Aufnahme
recording studio 106 Aufnahmestudio
recycle 172 recyceln, (wieder) aufbereiten
recycled product 172 Recyclingprodukt
reduce 169 reduzieren
refer to 46 sich beziehen auf
reflect 63 wiedergeben
refuse 27 ablehnen; sich weigern
regret 178 bedauern, bereuen
regular(ly) 25 regelmäßig (wiederkehrend), Stamm-
relationship 126 Beziehung, Verhältnis
relaxation 87 Entspannung
reliable 114 zuverlässig
religion 174 Religion, Konfession
remember 62 sich erinnern (an), daran denken, sich merken
repair 76 reparieren
replace 49 ersetzen, austauschen
reply 29 Antwort, Reaktion
report 46 Bericht
Republican 175 Republikaner/in
require 79 benötigen, erfordern, verlangen
requirement 76 Bedingung, Anforderung
research 70 Nachforschung(en)
reservoir 172 Staubecken
resident 173 Einwohner/in
respectful 70 respektvoll
responsible 75 verantwortungsvoll
be responsible for 114 verantwortlich sein für

responsibility 45 t Verantwortung
rest 21 Rest
have a rest 47 sich ausruhen
result 123 Ergebnis
return 91 erwidern
reuse 173 wieder verwenden
review 63 Überblick
rewarding 68 lohnend
ride 11 fahren (mit)
ringtone 89 Klingelton
rise 60 (an)steigen, klettern
risk sth 99 etw riskieren
take a risk 70 ein Risiko eingehen
river 79 Fluss
road 7 Straße
rob sb 152 jdn be-/ausrauben
rocket 124 Rakete
role 13 Rolle
role-play 40 als Rollenspiel durchführen
Roman Catholic 174 römisch-katholisch
romance 86 Romanze, Liebesaffäre
romantic 99 romantisch
room 32 Zimmer
round the world 31 um die ganze Welt
roundabout 142 Kreisverkehr
route 31 Route, Strecke, (Reise-)Weg; umleiten
rubbish 154 Abfall, Müll
rude 25 unhöflich
ruin 118 ruinieren
rule 174 (be)herrschen, regieren
run into 139 gegen ... fahren
run out 172 zu Ende gehen
run 62, 159 durchführen; (Geschichte) bringen; laufen
safe 47 sicher
salary 45 t Gehalt, Lohn
sales executive 85 Vertriebsmitarbeiter/in
salesperson 84 Verkäufer/in
saleswoman 92 t Verkäuferin
satisfaction 28 t Befriedigung
satisfied 60 zufrieden
savings account 161 Sparkonto
scare sb 133 jdm Angst einjagen
be scared of heights 79 nicht schwindelfrei sein
scarf 40 Schal
scary 61 t schrecklich, furchtbar, unheimlich, beängstigend
scenery 86 Landschaft
schoolmate 157 Schulkamerad
science 125 Wissenschaft
scream 38 schreien
screen 95 t Bildschirm
script 99 Drehbuch
sea water 172 Meerwasser
seal 79 Seehund
season 50 Spielzeit; Saison
seat 178 Sitz(platz)
secondary school 54 weiterführende Schule
secretary 114 Sekretär/in
seldom 24 selten
self-confident 76 selbstsicher
selfish 100 egoistisch, selbstsüchtig
sentence 6 Satz
serious 152 schwer, ernst
serious side 99 ernsthafte Seite
serves you right 89 geschieht dir recht
set up 96 einrichten
several 47 einige, etliche, mehrere
sexual abuse 134 sexueller Missbrauch
shake hands 29 sich die Hand geben
shake sb up 139 jdn aufschütteln, aufrütteln
shape 125 formen
share 62 gemeinsam haben, teilen
sheep 109 Schaf, Schafe
sheet 61 t Platte, Scheibe
shelter 176 Unterkunft
shiftwork 59 t Schichtarbeit
shirt 136 Hemd
shocking 128 schrecklich, schockierend
shoe 172 Schuh
shoot 33 hochschleudern
shooting 174 Schießerei
shopkeeper 155 Ladeninhaber/in, -besitzer/in
space of time 46 Zeitspanne
shorten 128 kürzen
shoulder 38 Schulter
shout (~ at sb) 89, 140 schreien (jdn anschreien)
shower (take a ~) 47, 164 Dusche (duschen)
shut down 91 herunterfahren
sick 152 krank
sightseeing 178 Besichtigungen (von Sehenswürdigkeiten)
similar 44 ähnlich
simple 165 einfach
simplify 169 vereinfachen
simply 25 einfach
Singaporean 155 Einwohner/in Singapurs
single parent 119 Alleinerziehende/r
sir / madam 83 mein Herr / meine Dame
sit down 102 sich (hin)setzen
sitcom 101 Situationskomödie
sit-down meal 51 Essen im Restaurant
site 94 Baustelle, Anlage
situation 27 Situation, Lage
skill 37 Fertigkeit, Fähigkeit
skim 46 überfliegen
skin 128 Haut
skirt 136 Rock
slam on (the brakes) 142 t auf die Bremse treten, eine Vollbremsung machen
sleep sth off 132 etw ausschlafen
sleepy 133 t schläfrig
slim 159 schlank
smack 133 t einen Klaps geben
smart(ly) 70 elegant, schick
smell 50 riechen, duften, stinken
smoke 50 rauchen
smoker 128 Raucher/in
smoking 47 Rauchen
snake 9 Schlange
snapshot 98 Schnappschuss, Kurzdarstellung
sniff 133 schnüffeln
so far 86 bis jetzt
soap opera 62 Seifenoper, TV-Serie
soccer 112 Fußball
social activity 104 gesellige Unternehmungen
social services 176 Sozialamt, -dienste
social worker 59 Sozialarbeiter/in
society 176 (die) Gesellschaft
sock 9 Socke
solar energy 109 Sonnenenergie
soldier 174 Soldat/in
solution 95 Lösung
solve 50 lösen
some kind of 100 eine Art
somewhere else 22 t irgendwo anders
son 164 Sohn
sort of 45 Art von
sort of thing 105 t Sache, Sachen
sound 25 klingen
sound like 92 t sich anhören wie, klingen wie
Southern Hemisphere 79 Südhalbkugel
southern 155 Süd-, südlich
space tourism 167 Weltraumtourismus

spacecraft 124 Raumfahrzeug, -schiff
spaced out 133 breit, auf Droge
spare change 176 (übriges) Kleingeld
spare time 105 t Freizeit
speak 11 sprechen
special 12 besondere/r/s
specific 105 t genau, präzise
speech bubble 10 Sprechblase
spend (on) 86 ausgeben (für)
spend time (on) 11 damit zubringen
spend 62, 176 verbringen, ausgeben
split up 58 sich (voneinander) trennen
spoil 89 verderben
sponsor 116 Geldgeber/in, Sponsor/in
spring 79 Frühling, Frühjahr
springtime 154 Frühling(szeit)
stall 38, 142 t abwürgen; Marktstand
stamp 42 Briefmarke
standpoint 128 Standpunkt
starting point 113 Ausgangspunkt
starting salary 125 t Anfangsgehalt
starve 51 vor Hunger sterben
statement 20 Aussage
stay 25 übernachten, bleiben
stay calm 84 ruhig bleiben
steam 33 Dampf
steam locomotive 27 Dampflok
step 15 Stief-; Schritt
stepbrother 14 Stiefbruder
stepfather 14 Stiefvater
stepsister 14 Stiefschwester
stick sth out 54 etw durchstehen, aushalten
still 19 (immer) noch; noch immer
stink 133 stinken
store 94 Geschäft, Laden, Warenhaus
straight away 114 sofort, gleich, auf der Stelle, umgehend
stranger 89 Fremde/r
strength 70 Kraft, Stärke
strict 118 streng
stuck 65 festgeklemmt
study 25 lernen, studieren
study for exams 155 für Prüfungen lernen
submit 75 einreichen
subtitle 98 Untertitel
succeed 106 Erfolg haben
success 167 Erfolg
such 39 solche/r/s
sudden(ly) 38 plötzlich
suffer 154 leiden
sugary 48 sehr süß, zuckerhaltig
suggestion 170 Vorschlag
suit 43 t (jdm) stehen; Anzug, Kostüm
suit sb's needs 92 t jds Bedürfnissen entsprechen
suit sb best 92 t am geeignetsten für jdn sein
suitable 65 geeignet, passend
summary 31 Zusammenfassung
summer camp 75 Ferienlager
sunbathing 156 Sonnenbaden
supermarket chain 144 Supermarkt-kette
supervise 74 beaufsichtigen
supply 172 Vorrat, Vorräte
suppose 34 t glauben, annehmen, vermuten
sure 26 sicherlich, natürlich
surgeon 104 Chirurg/in
surgery 7 (Arzt-)Praxis
surname 112 t Nach-, Familienname
surprise 112 t überraschen
surprised 108 überrascht, erstaunt
survey 60 (Meinungs-)Umfrage, Untersuchung
suspicious 174 misstrauisch
swap 13 tauschen
sweat 46 schwitzen
sweet 46 Bonbon
swerve 139 das Steuer/Auto herumreißen, einen Schlenker machen
switch on 114 anschalten, einschalten
switch to 169 sich umstellen auf
switch 89 schalten, umschalten
tabloid 171 Boulevardblatt
take the dog for a walk 141 den Hund ausführen
take off 78 abheben, abfliegen, starten
take on sth 157 an-, übernehmen
take part in 164 teilnehmen an, mitmachen bei
take part 116 teilnehmen, mitmachen
take sb on 54 jdn einstellen
take sb's order 51 t jds Bestellung aufnehmen
take sth badly 118 etw schlecht aufnehmen, dagegen sein
take sth home 154 mit nach Hause nehmen
take turns 56 (sich) abwechseln
takeaway 51 (Essen) zum Mitnehmen
talent competition 102 t Talentwettbewerb
talent 106 Talent, Begabung
talker 49 Redner/in
tap water 174 Leitungswasser
tariff 92 t Tarif
taste 172 Geschmack
teach 37 unterrichten, beibringen
teammate 46 Mannschaftskamerad/in
technically-minded 76 technisch interessiert
technician 94 Techniker/in
teen idol 99 Teenageridol
teenage dad 118 Vater im Teenager-Alter
teenager 96 Teenager
telephone line 95 Telefonleitung
tell jokes 70 Witze erzählen
tell you what 51 t hör mal, pass auf
temper 102 Temperament
temperature 104 Temperatur, Fieber
tend 29 (dazu) neigen
tennis court 172 Tennisplatz
tense 132 angespannt, nervös
terrible 33 furchtbar
terrorism 174 Terrorismus
terrorist 174 Terrorist/in
take a test 146 eine Prüfung ablegen
text (message) 58 SMS
that sort of thing 77 t in diesen Dingen
theme park 155 Freizeitpark
these days 168 in diesen Tagen
thick 9 dick
thin 42 dünn
thirsty 48 durstig
though 30 allerdings, jedoch
thread 133 Thread in einem Internet-Forum
be thrilled to bits 164 völlig begeistert sein
thrilling 100 packend, spannend
throw 161 werfen
throw sb out 176 jdn hinauswerfen
tidy 45 ordentlich
tight 43 t eng (anliegend)
timeline 124 Zeitachse
Tinsel Town 98 Hollywood
tip 161 Trinkgeld
tired 8 müde
tiring 68 anstrengend
tooth 128 Zahn
toothache 36 Zahnschmerzen
topic 40 Thema
touch 125 t berühren, anfassen
tough 39 hart, streng
tower 30 Turm
track 106 Stück, Song, Spur
trade 77 t Handwerk, Beruf
traditional 79 traditionell
traffic 112 (Straßen-)Verkehr
traffic jam 112 t Stau
trainee 18 Auszubildende/r, Praktikant/in

trainer 173 Turn-, Tennisschuh
tranquillizer 132 Beruhigungsmittel
transform 49 umwandeln
translate 8 übersetzen
travel agency 41 Reisebüro
travel agent 76 Reiseverkehrs-kaufmann/frau
treat 104 behandeln
treaty 174 Vertrag
troublemaker 55 Unruhestifter/in
troublesome 69t schwierig
trousers 72t Hose(n)
turn 89 sich drehen, sich umdrehen
turn into 172 umwandeln in
turn off 89 ausschalten, abstellen
be a turn-off 38 abstoßend wirken
turn up 139 auftauchen
twice 159 zweimal
typical 16 typisch
tyre 172 Reifen
unbelievable 62 unglaublich
uncle 165 Onkel
unconscious 132 bewusstlos
underline 87 unterstreichen
unemployed 162 arbeitslos, ohne Beschäftigung
unemployment 134 Arbeitslosigkeit
unexpected 70 unerwartet
unfair 139 unfair, ungerecht
unfortunately 100 unglücklicherweise, leider
unfriendly 29 unfreundlich
Unionist 174 Unionist
university 145 Universität
unless 29 es sei denn
unlimited 92t unbegrenzt
unmarked 132 unbezeichnet, ohne Adresse
unpleasant 69t unangenehm
unpopular 86 unbeliebt, unpopulär
unpredictable 132 unvorhersagbar
unrealistic 62 unrealistisch
unspoilt 109 unberührt, unzerstört
unsuccessful(ly) 99 erfolglos
untidy 70 unordentlich
until 28t bis
untrue 171 unwahr
unusual 29 unüblich, ungewöhnlich
unwanted 178 unerwünscht
up till now 59t bis jetzt
up to you 163 (das ist) deine Sache
upbringing 118 Erziehung
update 114 aktualisieren
upgrade 94 aufrüsten, upgraden
upset 39 entsetzt
urban 157 städtisch, Stadt-
urgent 114 dringend
usefulness 139 Nützlichkeit
user 89 Benutzer/in
usual(ly) 15 gewöhnlich
UV light 172 ultraviolettes Licht
vacation job 161 Ferienjob
Valentine's Day 12 Valentinstag
variety 48 Abwechslung, Auswahl
vary 114 unterschiedlich sein, variieren
vegetable 109 Gemüse
vehicle 125 Fahrzeug
vibrate 89 vibrieren
violence 174 Gewalt
violent 133 gewalttätig
visit 16 Besuch
visitor 114 Besucher/in, Gast
vocational college 15 Berufs(fach)schule
voice 164 Stimme
voluntary 37 freiwillig
volunteer 36 freiwillig arbeiten; Freiwillige/r
wage 60 Lohn, Gehalt
wait 9 warten
walk 136 Weg, Spaziergang, Wanderung
walk on 176 weitergehen, -laufen
wash off 39 abwaschen
wash 104 (sich) waschen
waste of time 61 Zeitverschwendung
waste water 172 Abwasser
waste 69t, 154 verschwenden; Abfall, Müll
weakness 70 Schwäche
wear 17 tragen, anhaben
weblog 30 Internet-Tagebuch
webpage 92t Internetseite
wedding 62 Hochzeit, Trauung
weird 38 merkwürdig, seltsam
weirdo 178 schräger Typ, komischer Kauz
welcome party 78 Willkommensfeier, -party
well 15 also, nun
well-known 103 sehr bekannt, berühmt
well-organized 76 gut organisiert
wet 91 nass, feucht
whale watching 78 Whale-Watching, Walbeobachtung
what kind of ... ? 15 welche Art von ...?
wheelchair 67t Rollstuhl
while 29 während
whisper 90 flüstern
white-water rafting 78 Wildwasserfahren
whole 32 ganz
wicked 30 großartig, toll
widely 172 in großem Umfang
wife 157 (Ehe-)Frau
wild meadow 154 Wiese
wildlife 78 Tierwelt
willing 109 bereit(willig), arbeitswillig
window 161 Fenster
winter 79 Winter
wish 19t wünschen
without a fuss 69t ohne viel Aufhebens
wonder 109 Wunder
wood 154 (kleinerer) Wald
work experience 70 Berufserfahrung
workcamp 14 Workcamp, Freiwilligenprojekt
working hours 59t Arbeitszeit
working visa 109 Arbeitserlaubnis
workmate 60 Kollege
workplace 45 Arbeitsplatz
World Cup 12 Weltmeisterschaft
world of work 20 Arbeitswelt
be worried about sth 118 sich um etw Sorgen machen
worry (about sth) 32 sich (um etw) Sorgen machen
be worth it 44 sich lohnen
worthwhile 134 lohnend, der Mühe wert (sein)
wrinkle 128 Falte
writer 163 Autor/in, Verfasser/in
wrong 22t falsch
yell at sb 139 jdn anschreien, jdn anbrüllen
yodel 163 jodeln
You're kidding! 80 Das ist doch nicht dein Ernst!
young adult 86 junge/r Erwachsene/r
youngster 69t Jugendliche/r
Yours sincerely/faithfully 75 Mit freundlichen Grüßen
youth 36 Jugend
youth hostel 36 Jugendherberge
youth worker 134 Sozialarbeiter/in für Jugendliche

Grundwortschatz

Diese Liste enthält ca. 600 Grundwörter, die in **Work with English** als bekannt vorausgesetzt werden. Nicht aufgeführt, jedoch vorausgesetzt sind internationale Wörter (*taxi, email* usw.) und einige sehr elementare Wörter wie Pronomen, Zahlen und Tage.

a lot (of) viel, sehr
above über, oben
actual(ly) tatsächlich
afternoon Nachmittag
afterwards danach
again wieder
against gegen
age Zeitalter, Alter
air Luft
airport Flughafen
almost fast, beinahe
already schon, bereits
always immer
American amerikanisch
angry wütend, verärgert
animal Tier
another noch eine
answer Antwort, Lösung; (be)antworten
anybody jemand, jede/r
anyone jemand, jede/r
anything etwas, alles
around herum
arrive ankommen
ask fragen, bitten
at home zu Hause, daheim
Australian australisch
autumn Herbst
available verfügbar
away weg, entfernt
back zurück
bad schlecht, schlimm
bag Tasche, Beutel
baker Bäcker/in
bakery Bäckerei
be sein
beautiful schön
because weil
bed Bett
bedroom Schlafzimmer
before vor(her)
begin anfangen, beginnen
beginning Anfang
believe glauben
belong gehören
below unter, unten
best beste/r/s, am besten
better besser
between zwischen
big groß
bike Rad
biker (Motor-)Radfahrer/in
biography Biographie
birthday Geburtstag
bit (ein) bisschen
blue blau
body Körper
book Buch; buchen, bestellen
bored gelangweilt
boring langweilig
both beide
bottle Flasche
box Kasten, Kästchen, Schachtel
boyfriend Freund
break Pause; brechen
breakfast Frühstück
bring bringen, holen
brother Bruder
brown braun
building Gebäude
bus (Linien-)Bus
business Geschäft, Firma
busy beschäftigt, besetzt
buy kaufen
by durch, mit, bei
cake Kuchen, Torte
be called heißen
caller Anrufer/in
can dürfen, können
car Auto
card Karte
careful vorsichtig, sorgfältig
cat Katze
centre Zentrum
change (Ver-)Änderung; (aus)wechseln, (sich) ändern
character Charakter
chat Unterhaltung; sich unterhalten
chatroom Chatroom, Gesprächsrunde
cheese Käse
child Kind
children Kinder
choose (aus)wählen
Christmas Weihnachten
church Kirche
cigarette Zigarette
city (Groß-)Stadt
class Klasse
classmate Klassenkamerad/-in
clean reinigen, säubern; sauber
climb klettern, (ein)steigen
clock Uhr
close schließen
close (to) nahe
clothes Kleidung, Kleider
coffee Kaffee
cold kalt
collect sammeln
college Fachhochschule
colour Farbe
come kommen
comedy Komödie
complain sich beklagen, (sich) beschweren, reklamieren
complete vollständig; vervollständigen
continent Erdteil, Kontinent
continue fortfahren, fortsetzen
cook kochen; Koch, Köchin
copy Kopie; kopieren
cost Kosten; kosten
country Land, Staat
course Kurs, Lehrgang, Gang
crazy verrückt
cup Tasse
cut schneiden
dance tanzen; Tanz
danger Gefahr
dangerous gefährlich
dark Dunkelheit; dunkel
daughter Tochter
day Tag
dead tot
death Tod
decide (sich) entscheiden, beschließen
describe beschreiben
description Beschreibung, Schilderung
desk (Schreib-)Tisch
diagram Diagramm, Abbildung
die sterben
diet Diät
difference Unterschied
different anders, verschieden
difficult schwer, schwierig
dinner (Abend-)Essen
dislike nicht mögen
do tun, machen
document Dokument, Papier
dog Hund
door Tür
double doppelt
down unten, hinunter
drawing Zeichnung
dream Traum; träumen
drink Getränk; trinken
drive (Auto) fahren
drug Droge
dry trocken; trocknen
each jede/r/s
ear Ohr
early früh
east Osten
Easter Ostern
easy leicht, einfach
eat essen
either entweder
end Ende, Schluss; (be)enden
ending Ende
English-speaking englischsprachig
enjoy genießen, gefallen
enough ausreichend, genug
even sogar (noch)
evening Abend
ever je(mals)
every jede/r/s
everybody jede/r
everyone jede/r/s, alle
everything alles

everywhere überall
exam Examen
exercise Übung
expensive teuer
explain erklären
expression Ausdruck
eye Auge
factory Fabrik
fall fallen
false falsch
family Familie
famous berühmt
fan Fan, Anhänger/in
far weit (entfernt)
farm Bauernhof
farmer Bauer, Bäuerin
fast schnell
fast food Schnellimbiss
fat fett
favourite Lieblings-
feel (sich) fühlen
female weiblich, Frauen-
few ein paar, wenig/e
fight (be)kämpfen: Kampf, Streit
file Ordner, Datei
find finden, suchen
fine gut, schön, fein
finish Ende; (be)enden
fire Feuer
firm Firma
first erste/r/s, zuerst
first name Vorname
fly fliegen
follow (be)folgen
following folgende
food Essen, Nahrung
foot Fuß
forever für immer
forget vergessen
form Form, Formular
free kostenlos, frei
freedom Freiheit
French französisch
friend Freund/in
friendly freund(schaft)lich
from von
fruit Obst, Frucht
full voll
fun Spaß
funny komisch, merkwürdig
future Zukunft; (zu)künftig
game Spiel
German deutsch
gift Geschenk
girl Mädchen
girlfriend Freundin
give geben
glass Glas
go gehen, fahren
go away weggehen
go to work arbeiten gehen
good gut
grade Note
granddad Großvater
grandma Großmutter
great groß(artig), toll
green grün
grey grau
group Gruppe
guess Annahme; raten, schätzen
guitar Gitarre
hair Haar(e)
half Hälfte; halb
ham Schinken
hand Hand
happiness Glück
happy glücklich, froh, zufrieden
hard schwer, hart
hate hassen, nicht mögen
hear hören
help Hilfe; helfen
here hier
hero Held
high hoch, groß; äußerst
holiday Ferien, Urlaub
home Zuhause, Heim; nach Hause
homework Hausaufgaben
hope hoffen; Hoffnung
hospital Krankenhaus
hot heiß, warm
hour Stunde
house Haus
how wie
huge riesig
hungry hungrig
husband (Ehe-)Mann
idea Idee, Gedanke
ill krank
important wichtig
include enthalten, umfassen
including einschließlich
indoors innen
information Auskunft, Information(en)
inside innerhalb, drinnen
interview Interview, Vorstellungsgespräch; interviewen
into in ... hinein
invite einladen
Irish irisch
Italian italienisch
job Arbeit, Stelle
joke Witz
just einfach, nur, genau
key Schlüssel, Taste
kiss küssen; Kuss
kitchen Küche
know kennen, wissen
language Sprache
large groß, umfangreich
last letzte/r/s, zuletzt
late spät
latest neueste
laugh lachen
leader Leiter/in, Anführer
learn lernen, erfahren
least wenigstens
leave (ver)lassen
left linke/r/s, links; übrig
lesson Lektion, Unterrichtsstunde
letter Brief, Buchstabe
life Leben
lift Fahrstuhl, Aufzug
like (ähnlich) wie; mögen, gern tun
line Leitung
lipstick Lippenstift
list Liste; auflisten, notieren
listen zuhören
little klein, wenig
live wohnen, leben
long lang
longer länger
look Blick; (aus)sehen, blicken
lost verloren
loud laut
love Liebe; lieben, sehr gern mögen
lovely schön, hübsch, reizend
low niedrig
luck Glück
lucky glücklich
lunchtime Mittagspause
machine Maschine
mad verrückt, toll
magazine Zeitschrift
main reason Hauptgrund
make machen
male männlich
man Mann, Mensch
mark markieren
market Markt
maybe vielleicht
meal Essen, Mahlzeit
meat Fleisch
meet (zusammen)treffen, begegnen
message Mitteilung, Nachricht
milk Milch
miss verpassen, vermissen
month Monat
more mehr
morning Morgen
most meist
motorbike Motorrad
mountain bike Mountainbike
move (sich) bewegen, umziehen
much viel
mushroom Pilz
nationality Staatsangehörigkeit
nearly beinahe, fast
need Bedarf; brauchen, benötigen
nervous nervös
nice(ly) schön, nett
night Nacht
nightlife Nachtleben
nobody niemand
noise Geräusch, Lärm
noisy laut, geräuschvoll
north Nord(en)
note Notiz; beachten, notieren
nothing nichts
now nun, jetzt
number Nummer, Zahl
nursery nurse Kindergärtnerin
of course natürlich, selbstverständlich
office Büro, Amt
old alt
older älter
only nur, einzig
open öffnen, beginnen; offen
opinion Meinung, Einschätzung
other andere/r/s

outdoors draußen
outside außer(halb)
over (vor)über
pairwork Partnerarbeit
paper Papier, Zeitung
parents Eltern
part Teil, Rolle
past vorbei, nach; Vergangenheit
pay (be)zahlen
people Personen, Menschen
per day pro Tag
perhaps vielleicht, eventuell
phone Telefon; anrufen
phone call (Telefon-)Anruf
phone number Telefonnummer
piano Klavier
pickle eingelegtes Gemüse
picture Bild
piece Stück
place Stelle, Platz; setzen, stellen
plan Plan; planen
plant Pflanze
play spielen
please bitte
pleased zufrieden
point Punkt; Komma
policeman Polizist
poor arm, schlecht, mangelhaft
portion Portion, Menge, Anteil
postcard Postkarte
practice Übung
prefer vorziehen, bevorzugen
pretty hübsch; ziemlich
prince Prinz
probably wahrscheinlich
problem Problem
program (Computer-) Programm
pub Kneipe, Gaststätte
pull ziehen
pupil Schüler/in
push schieben, drücken
put setzen, stellen, legen
question Frage
quiet still, ruhig
quite ziemlich, ganz
rain Regen; regnen
read lesen
real echt, wirklich
reality Realität, Wirklichkit
really wirklich, eigentlich, tatsächlich
recognize erkennen
red rot
relax (sich) erholen
remember sich erinnern, daran denken
repeat wiederholen
rice Reis
rich reich
right rechts, rechte/r/s, richtig; Recht
road (Land-)Straße
role Rollen
room Zimmer, Raum
round Runde; rund
sad traurig
sale (Schluss-)Verkauf
salt Salz
same gleiche/r/s, der-, die-, dasselbe
scan (ein)scannen
school Schule
sea See
seat Sitz(platz), Stuhl
second zweite/r/s; Sekunde
secret Geheimnis
secretary Sekretär/in
section Abschnitt
see sehen
sell (sich) verkaufen
send senden, schicken
set setzen
several etliche, einige, mehrere
shock Schock
shoe Schuh
shop Laden, Geschäft; einkaufen
shopping mall Einkaufsstraße, Kaufhauspassage
short kurz, klein
should solle/n, sollte/n
shout schreien, rufen
show zeigen
showbiz party Party mit Promis aus der Showbranche
sick krank
side Seite
silent still, Stumm-
silly dumm, doof, albern, lächerlich
sing singen
singer Sänger/in
sister Schwester
sit sitzen
ski Ski (fahren)
sleep Schlaf; schlafen
slow(ly) langsam
small klein
smile lächeln; Lächeln
snow Schnee; schneien
some einige, etwas
someone jemand
something etwas
sometimes manchmal
son Sohn
soon bald
sort Sorte, Art
soup Suppe
south Süden
Spain Spanien
Spanish spanisch
speak sprechen, reden
speaker Redner/in
special besondere
spell buchstabieren, schreiben
start Beginn; anfangen, starten, beginnen
stay Aufenthalt; bleiben
stop Halt; (an) halten, aufhören (mit)
store Laden, Geschäft
story Erzählung, Geschichte
strange fremd, seltsam
street Straße
strong stark, kräftig
student Student/in, Lernende/r
stupid dumm
subject (Schul-)Fach, Thema
suggest vorschlagen, andeuten
summer Sommer
sun Sonne
supermarket Supermarkt
sure freilich, sicher(lich)
surname Nach-, Familienname
surprise Überraschung; überraschen
swim schwimmen
table Tisch, Tabelle
take nehmen, bringen, dauern
talk Gespräch, Unterhaltung; sprechen, reden
tea Tee
teach unterrichten, lehren
teacher Lehrer/in
teen(age) Teen(age), Jugendliche/r
tell sagen, erzählen
than als
these diese
thing Sache, Ding, Gegenstand
think denken, meinen, finden, glauben
though obwohl, doch
ticket Karte, Fahrschein
time Zeit, Mal
today heute
together zusammen
tomorrow morgen
tonight heute Abend/Nacht
top Spitze, Gipfel; Spitzen-
topic Thema
total(ly) völlig, (ins)gesamt
tourism Tourismus
town Stadt
toy Spielzeug
train Zug
trainee Auszubildende/r, Praktikant/in
training Training, Übung
translate übersetzen, -tragen
transport Transport, Verkehr
travel Reisen; reisen, fahren
tree Baum
true richtig, wahr
truth Wahrheit
try versuchen, probieren
turn into einbiegen in
type erfassen, tippen; Art
typical typisch
understand verstehen, begreifen
unhappy unglücklich
until bis
use benutzen, verwenden; Verwendung
useful nützlich
usual(ly) normalerweise, gewöhnlich, meistens
visit Besuch; besuchen, besichtigen
walk Spaziergang; (zu Fuß) gehen
want wollen
wash waschen
watch sehen, beobachten

watch TV fernsehen
water Wasser
way Weg, Methode, Art (und Weise)
weather Wetter
webpage Internetseite
week Woche
weekend Wochenende
west West(en)
what was, welche/r/s
where wo(hin)
will Wille; werde(n), wollen
win gewinnen, siegen
window Fenster
without ohne
woman Frau
wonder sich fragen, wundern
wood Holz, Wald
word Wort
work Arbeit, Werk; funktionieren, arbeiten
worker Arbeiter/in
workout Training
workshop Werkstatt
world Welt
written geschrieben, schriftlich
wrong falsch
year Jahr
yellow gelb
yesterday gestern
young jung

Geographische Namen

Africa ['æfrɪkə]	Afrika
Australia [ɒ'streɪliə]	Australien
Austria ['ɒstriə]	Österreich
Canada ['kænədə]	Kanada
China ['tʃaɪnə]	China
Europe ['jʊərəp]	Europa
European Union [ˌjʊərəpiːən 'juːniən]	Europäische Union
France [frɑːns]	Frankreich
Germany ['dʒɜːməni]	Deutschland
Great Britain [ˌgreɪt 'brɪtn]	Großbritannien
Iceland ['aɪslənd]	Island
India ['ɪndiə]	Indien
Ireland ['aɪələnd]	Irland
Italy ['ɪtəli]	Italien
Japan [dʒə'pæn]	Japan
Lake Constance [leɪk 'kɒnstəns]	Bodensee
Mexico ['meksɪkəʊ]	Mexiko
New Zealand [ˌnjuː 'ziːlənd]	Neuseeland
Russia ['rʌʃə]	Russland
Scotland ['skɒtlənd]	Schottland
Singapore [ˌsɪŋə'pɔː]	Singapur
Switzerland ['swɪtsələnd]	(die) Schweiz
the Netherlands [ðə 'neðələndz]	die Niederlande
United Kingdom (UK) [juˌnaɪtɪd 'kɪŋdəm]	Vereinigtes Königreich
United States (US) [juˌnaɪtɪd 'steɪts]	Vereinigte Staaten

Unregelmäßige Verben

be – was/were – been	sein
beat – beat – beaten	schlagen, besiegen
become – became – become	werden
begin – began – begun	anfangen, beginnen
break – broke – broken	brechen
build – built – built	bauen
burn – burnt/burned – burnt/burned	(ver)brennen
buy – bought – bought	kaufen
come – came – come	kommen
cut – cut – cut	schneiden
do – did – done	tun, machen
draw – drew – drawn	zeichnen
dream – dreamt – dreamt	träumen
drink – drank – drunk	trinken
drive – drove – driven	fahren
eat – ate – eaten	essen
fall – fell – fallen	fallen
feed – fed – fed	füttern, ernähren
feel – felt – felt	(sich) fühlen, empfinden
fight – fought – fought	kämpfen
find – found – found	finden
fit – fit/fitted – fitted	fit
fly – flew – flown	fliegen
forget – forgot – forgotten	vergessen
get – got – got (AE gotten)	bekommen
give – gave – given	geben
go – went – gone	gehen, fahren
grow – grew – grown	wachsen
hang – hung – hung	hängen
have – had – had	haben
hear – heard – heard	hören
hide – hid – hidden	(sich) verstecken
hit – hit – hit	schlagen
hold – held – held	halten, festhalten
keep – kept – kept	behalten
know – knew – known	kennen, wissen
lay – laid – laid	legen
learn – learnt/learned – learnt/learned	lernen
leave – left – left	abfahren, verlassen, weggehen
let – let – let	lassen
lie – lay – lain	liegen
light – lit – lit	anzünden, beleuchten, anmachen
lose – lost – lost	verlieren
make – made – made	machen
mean – meant – meant	meinen, bedeuten
meet – met – met	treffen
pay – paid – paid	bezahlen
put – put – put	setzen, stellen, legen
quit – quit/quitted – quit/quitted	verlassen, aufhören
read – read – read	lesen
ride – rode – ridden	reiten, fahren
rise – rose – risen	(an)steigen
run – ran – run	laufen, rennen
say – said – said	sagen
see – saw – seen	sehen
sell – sold – sold	verkaufen
send – sent – sent	senden, schicken
set – set – set	setzen, stellen
show – showed – shown	zeigen
sit – sat – sat	sitzen
sleep – slept – slept	schlafen
smell – smelt/smelled – smelt/smelled	riechen
speak – spoke – spoken	sprechen
spell – spelt/spelled – spelt/spelled	buchstabieren
spend – spent – spent	ausgeben, verbringen
shut – shut – shut	schließen
sing – sang – sung	singen
stand – stood – stood	stehen
steal – stole – stolen	stehen
swim – swam – swum	schwimmen
take – took – taken	nehmen
teach – taught – taught	unterrichten, beibringen
tell – told – told	sagen, erzählen
think – thought – thought	denken
throw – threw – thrown	werfen
understand – understood – understood	verstehen
wear – wore – worn	tragen
win – won – won	gewinnen
write – wrote – written	schreiben

Quellenverzeichnis

FOTOS

Titel: Corbis/G.Steiner; Visum/G. Schönharting; Caro/Oberhäuser
Alamy: S. 143/J.Davis;
Buckstegen: S. 21/RF, S. 118/RF; S. 119/2RF; S. 119/7RF; S. 123/1/2RF;
Comstock: S. 6/1/3/RF; S. 144/RF;
Corel Lib: S. 119/4; S. 119/5; S. 144
Corbis: S. 6/2/4RF; S. 32/E. Neville; S. 34/3RF; S. 44/A. Snyder; S. 47/4/Emely; S. 53/RF; S. 52/WV/A. Hornak; S. 71/Stock4B; S. 78/3/K. Fleming; S. 79/T. Graham; S. 82/1/W. Morgan; S. 82/6/Grace; S. 84/1/R. Nowitz; S. 93/R. Faris; S. 95/1/RF; S. 95/2/B. Wilson; S. 99/4/S. Sands; S. 109/2/O. Franken; S. 119/6; S. 125/3/R. Faris; S. 132/H. Benser; S. 135/C. Devan; S. 135/B.S. P.I.
Defd: S. 98/1/2/3/4
Fotofinder: S. 34/1/F1 Online/J.Images; S. 34/2/Das Fotoarchiv/Y. Arslan; S. 34/5/VISUM/F. Rothe; S. 34/3/Argus/Schröder; S. 54/1/N. Schäfer; S. 54/3/Argus/Raupach; S. 62/vario-press/DesignPics; S. 77/1/photothek/U. Grabowsky; S. 78/1/Online/Chromorange; S. 78/2/blickwinkel/P. Schaub; S. 82/3/BA-Geduldig; S. 82/4/Arco/W. Dietrich; S. 82/5/Blickwinkel/P. Royer; S. 84/2/Keystone/V. Schulz; S. 85/M. Luedecke; S. 94/2/Sorge; S. 94/3/J. Eckel; S. 104/1/Joker/D. Ausserhofer; S. 104/2/vario-press/R. Unkel; S. 104/3/Stock4B/K. Blaschke; S. 119/1/image.de/Fejer; S. 124/Caro/Oberhäuser; S. 125/2/BIOS Breton Josy; S. 125/4/Argus/W. Weber; S. 125/5/vario-press/Ulrich; S. 129/Le Brun/mediacolors; S. 144/Avenue Images/Fresh;
Getty Images: S. 14/RF; S. 15/RF; S. 19/N. Russell; S. 84/3RF; S. 95/3RF; S. 103/RF; S. 112/RF; S. 114/RF;
Picture Alliance: S. 33/W. Wisniewski; S. 34/R. Großkopf/OKAPIA; S. 39/2/F. Wartenberg; S. 63/N. Bachmann; S. 99/1/Imagno; S. 99/2/Photoshot; S. 99/3/S. Matzke; S. 109/1/van Eick; S. 125/1/F. Mächler,
Gabriel: S. 47/2; S. 50; S. 128; S. 133;
Goebel: S. 47/1; S. 53/1, S. 94/1; S. 119/3;
Gräter: S. 78/4; S. 82/2
Maly: S. 54/2; S. 77/2/3
Spratling: S. 7; S. 39/1; S. 92

KARTEN

Karten: S. 244, Innenumschläge/Carlos Borrell

TEXTE

Textrechte: S. 129/http://www.stayinghard.info/inhale.htm;http://www.uglysmoking.info/reverse_pg5.htm; http://www.givingupsmoking.co.uk/shsmoke/shs_TV_ads

Australia & New Zealand

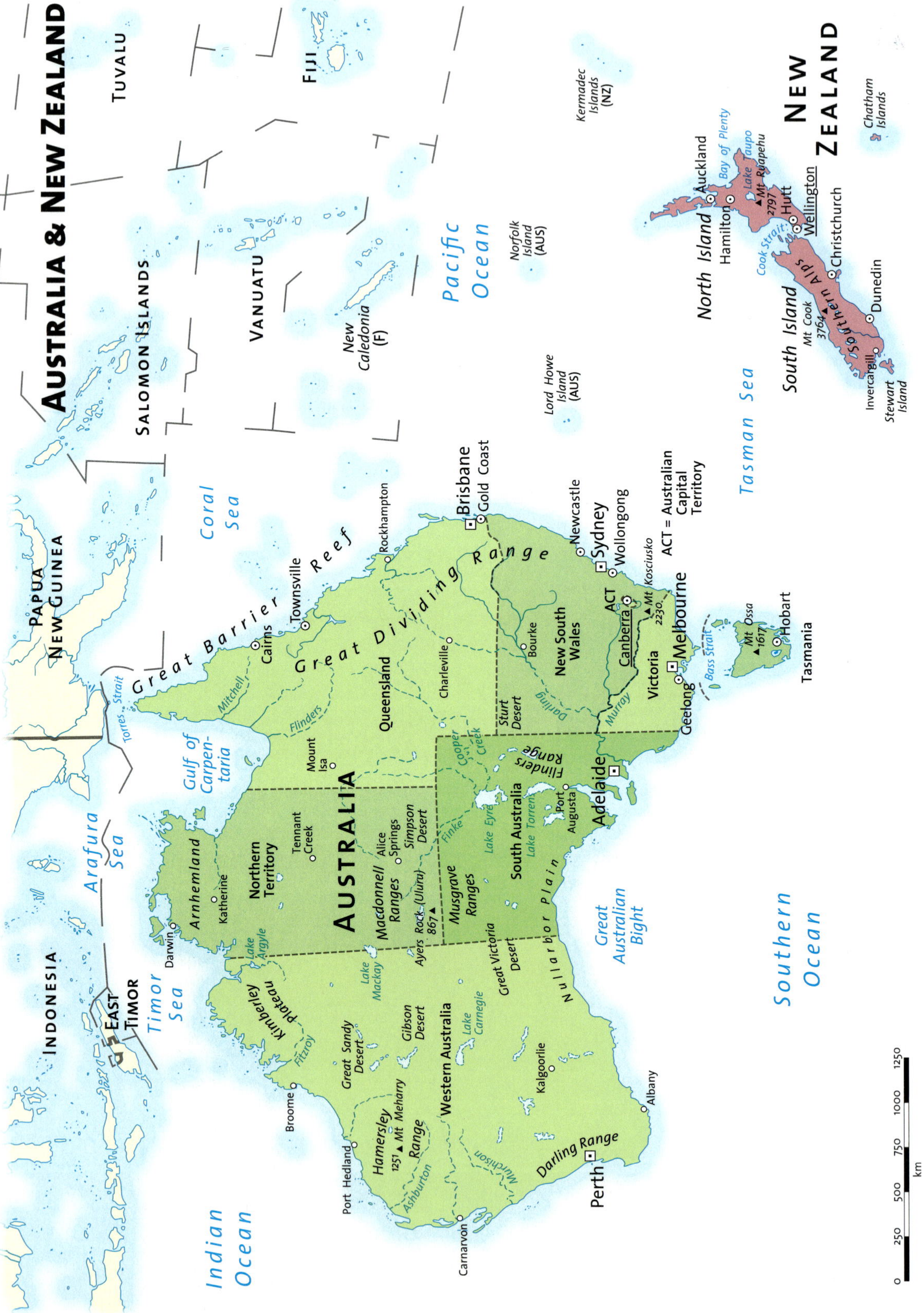